Palgrave Studies in European Union Politics

Edited by: **Michelle Egan**, American University, USA, **Neill Nugent**, Visiting Professor, College of Europe, Bruges and Honorary Professor, University of Salford, UK and **William Paterson OBE**, University of Aston, UK.

Editorial Board: **Christopher Hill**, Cambridge, UK, **Simon Hix**, London School of Economics, UK, **Mark Pollack**, Temple University, USA, **Kalypso Nicolaïdis**, Oxford, UK, **Morten Egeberg**, University of Oslo, Norway, **Amy Verdun**, University of Victoria, Canada, **Claudio M. Radaelli**, University of Exeter, UK, **Frank Schimmelfennig**, Swiss Federal Institute of Technology, Switzerland

Following on the sustained success of the acclaimed *European Union Series*, which essentially publishes research-based textbooks, *Palgrave Studies in European Union Politics* publishes cutting-edge research-driven monographs.

The remit of the series is broadly defined, both in terms of subject and academic discipline. All topics of significance concerning the nature and operation of the European Union potentially fall within the scope of the series. The series is multidisciplinary to reflect the growing importance of the EU as a political, economic and social phenomenon.

Titles include:

Jens Blom-Hansen
THE EU COMITOLOGY SYSTEM IN THEORY AND PRACTICE
Keeping an Eye on the Commission?

Oriol Costa and Knud Erik Jørgensen (*editors*)
THE INFLUENCE OF INTERNATIONAL INSTITUTIONS ON THE EU
When Multilateralism Hits Brussels

Falk Daviter
POLICY FRAMING IN THE EUROPEAN UNION

Michelle Egan, Neill Nugent, and William E. Paterson (*editors*)
RESEARCH AGENDAS IN EU STUDIES
Stalking the Elephant

Theofanis Exadaktylos and Claudio M. Radaelli (*editors*)
RESEARCH DESIGN IN EUROPEAN STUDIES
Establishing Causality in Europeanization

David J. Galbreath and Joanne McEvoy
THE EUROPEAN MINORITY RIGHTS REGIME
Towards a Theory of Regime Effectiveness

Jack Hayward and Rüdiger Wurzel (*editors*)
EUROPEAN DISUNION
Between Sovereignty and Solidarity

Wolfram Kaiser, Brigitte Leucht, and Michael Gehler
TRANSNATIONAL NETWORKS IN REGIONAL INTEGRATION
Governing Europe 1945–83

Robert Kissack
PURSUING EFFECTIVE MULTILATERALISM
The European Union, International Organizations and the Politics of Decision Making

Karl-Oskar Lindgren and Thomas Persson
PARTICIPATORY GOVERNANCE IN THE EU
Enhancing or Endangering Democracy and Efficiency?

Daniel Naurin and Helen Wallace (*editors*)
UNVEILING THE COUNCIL OF THE EUROPEAN UNION
Games Governments Play in Brussels

Dimitris Papadimitriou and Paul Copeland (*editors*)
THE EU's LISBON STRATEGY
Evaluating Success, Understanding Failure

Emmanuelle Schon-Quinlivan
REFORMING THE EUROPEAN COMMISSION

Liubomir K. Topaloff
POLITICAL PARTIES AND EUROSCEPTICISM

Richard G. Whitman and Stefan Wolff (*editors*)
THE EUROPEAN NEIGHBOURHOOD POLICY IN PERSPECTIVE
Context, Implementation and Impact

Richard G. Whitman (*editor*)
NORMATIVE POWER EUROPE
Empirical and Theoretical Perspectives

Sarah Wolff
THE MEDITERRANEAN DIMENSION OF THE EUROPEAN UNION'S
INTERNAL SECURITY

Jan Wouters, Hans Bruyninckx, Sudeshna Basu and Simon Schunz (*editors*)
THE EUROPEAN UNION AND MULTILATERAL GOVERNANCE
Assessing EU Participation in United Nations Human Rights and
Environmental Fora

Also by Yves Tiberghien

ENTREPRENEURIAL STATES: Reforming Corporate Governance in France, Japan,
and Korea. *Cornell Studies in Political Economy* (edited by Peter J. Katzenstein)

L'ASIE ET LE FUTUR DU MONDE

Palgrave Studies in European Union Politics
Series Standing Order ISBN 978–1–4039–9511–7 (hardback) and
ISBN 978 1–4039–9512–4 (paperback)

You can receive future titles in this series as they are published by placing a standing order.
Please contact your bookseller or, in case of difficulty, write to us at the address below with
your name and address, the title of the series and one of the ISBNs quoted above.

Customer Services Department, Macmillan Distribution Ltd, Houndmills, Basingstoke,
Hampshire RG21 6XS, UK.

Leadership in Global Institution Building

Minerva's Rule

Edited by

Yves Tiberghien
Associate Professor, Department of Political Science and Director of the Institute of Asian Research,
University of British Columbia, Canada

First published 2013 by
PALGRAVE MACMILLAN

Palgrave Macmillan in the UK is an imprint of Macmillan Publishers Limited,
registered in England, company number 785998, of Houndmills, Basingstoke,
Hampshire RG21 6XS.

Palgrave Macmillan in the US is a division of St Martin's Press LLC,
175 Fifth Avenue, New York, NY 10010.

Palgrave Macmillan is the global academic imprint of the above companies
and has companies and representatives throughout the world.

Palgrave® and Macmillan® are registered trademarks in the United States,
the United Kingdom, Europe and other countries

ISBN: 978–1–137–02372–8

This book is printed on paper suitable for recycling and made from fully
managed and sustained forest sources. Logging, pulping and manufacturing
processes are expected to conform to the environmental regulations of the
country of origin.

A catalogue record for this book is available from the British Library.

A catalog record for this book is available from the Library of Congress.

Transferred to Digital Printing in 2013

To my wife, Yvonne

Contents

Part IV   The Political Leadership Mode

Part V   Conclusion

List of Tables

List of Figures

Preface

Since 1945, nations have acknowledged the need for building global institutions and norms that could deliver global public goods and help coordinate their actions. The first phase of such global institution building resulted in the creation of the United Nations, as well as the International Monetary Fund (IMF), the World Bank, and the General Agreement on Trade and Tariffs (GATT) in lieu of the planned International Trade Organization (ITO). This first phase of global governance clearly followed a hegemonic pathway under the undisputed leadership of the United States. Yet, in the wake of the end of the Cold War and in the face of a gradually uncontrollable United Nations, the US interest in such global governance waned after the 1994 Congressional elections and more completely after the 2000 presidential election. The US was contented with the global economic order it had developed, particularly after the creation of the World Trade Organization (WTO) in 1995, and saw no need to expand the process of global institution building to the arenas of environment, culture, or human security.

This book focuses on the puzzling second phase of global institution building that developed during the years 1995 to 2005, at the height of US global dominance and yet at a time when the US leaned toward unilateralism. During these years, and despite US opposition, the world saw major advances in global environmental governance (the Kyoto Protocol in 1997, the Cartagena Biosafety Protocol in 2000, several international chemical treaties, and even the Nagoya treaty on biodiversity in 2010), in institutions upholding human security (the Ottawa Anti-Personnel Mine Ban Convention in 1997 and the adoption of the Responsibility to Protect Norm at the UN in 2005), in international law (the Rome Statute of the International Criminal Court in 1998), and in the protection of cultural diversity (the Convention on the Protection and Promotion of the Diversity of Cultural Expressions in 2005). To be sure, these advances were achieved in a less unanimous manner than those of earlier times; many countries, including the US, refused to participate. There were also areas of failure, such as in international migration governance and on issues such as international whaling protection. Yet, this second phase was significant and has left an important legacy.

The book argues that this second phase was a non-hegemonic period, one led by a loose coalition of actors devoted to pushing the frontier in global institution building. At the core of this coalition were three main actors: the European Union or key European states, Canada, and Japan. This book builds on the literature about the rise of the EU as a global power, and analyzes more precisely the varied motivations behind the EU's behavior and the international partners that the EU could rely on in pushing this agenda.

The book advances the concept of "Minervian actors," effective players dedicated to finding global mechanisms and tools that can stabilize the global system and advance the public good. It presents three causal pathways to explain Minervian actions: a competitive mode, a normative mode, and a domestic leadership mode. Through this analysis, this project provides the missing link between pure realist accounts and normative accounts rooted in the study of global civil society. The book also bridges relevant literatures from international relations, European external actions, Japanese foreign policy, and Canadian politics.

While emphasizing the interesting and unrecognized Minervian pattern that drove global institution building in key arenas for over a decade, the book also acknowledges that this period may have peaked. We have clearly entered a third phase of global governance, in which the functional need for global institutions is greater than ever but also in which the diffusion of power has made the task more elusive. Today, with a rising China, followed by surging India and Brazil, global governance may require minimal cooperation between the US, Europe, and China, as well as creativity in developing new pathways to make that cooperation possible. Such cooperation may require new innovative players and catalysts with the capacity to craft mutually beneficial roadmaps. One example of a new institutional emblematic of this third, post-Minervian phase of global governance is the G20. But the G20 is not yet able to deal with a large range of global issues beyond global economics.

Yet, despite its limits, the Minervian process that drove the constitutions of many novel and important international institutions holds great insights for the understanding of international relations and of the EU as a global actor.

Acknowledgements

This project about patterns of global institution building started with casual conversations in 2003 about EU–Japan concordance with Dr. Sima Godfrey, then the director of the Institute for European Studies (IES), and Dr. Julian Dierkes, the current director of the Center for Japanese Research (CJR), both at the University of British Columbia (UBC). We were struck by an unusual pattern that brought together the increasingly global European Union, a fast evolving Japan, and the traditionally multilateral Canada. We were also struck by the lack of dialogue between policy and academic communities working on Europe, Japan, and Canada. We found that UBC was an ideal host for such a dialogue, thanks to its equidistant position between Japan and Europe and its joint European and Asian identity. All three of us saw that such transcontinental dialogue toward a global common good was essential. These conversations grew into a large project, including two workshops and other meetings at UBC and around the world. For their incredible enthusiasm, creativity, and joint leadership in this project, I would like to acknowledge my two colleagues Sima and Julian. Without them, this project would not have seen the light of the day. In particular, Julian spent many working sessions hammering concepts with me. The three Minervian causal pathways emerged from this joint work with Julian.

We jointly applied for a grant from the European Commission through the IES, and the success of this grant in 2004 made the project possible. I also would like to acknowledge generous support from the Japan Foundation, the IES, the Center for International Relations (CIR), the Institute of Asian Research (IAR), and the CJR at UBC, the Peter Wall Institute for Advanced Studies (PWIAS), the International Canadian Studies Centre (ICSC), the Swedish Embassy in Canada, as well the Social Science and Humanities Research Council of Canada (SSHRC) for grants given separately to myself and Julian Dierkes.

The first workshop in the project took place in May 2004 with the title "Toward an Alternative Tricontinental Partnership: Responses to Global Issues in EU, Japanese, and Canadian Policy-Making." The scholars at this initial workshop played a tremendous role in shaping this quest. In particular, I would like to acknowledge the tremendous roles played by Julian Dierkes, Miranda Schreurs, Kyoko Sato, Kathryn Harrison, Peter

Dauvergne, Peter Gourevitch, Alan Jacobs, Mark Zacher, Mark Manger, Danielle Juteau, Hyung Gu Lynn, Jennifer Chan, Eric Remacle, Paul Evans, and Richard Price. A second workshop led by Julian and me, which focused on Japan's role in this unusual lineup, took place in May 2005. Titled "Between Realism and Institutionalism: Japan's Growing Concordance with the EU and Canada on Multilateralism," the workshop broke new ground by bringing together experts from Japan, Europe, and Canada who shared similar international concerns, and yet had never worked together. For their sharing in this path-breaking experiment, I would like to thank Eric Remacle, Miranda Schreurs, Yasuhiro Kitagawa, the founder and coordinator of Japan Campaign to Ban Landmines (JCBL), and Jennifer Chan.

The third and most important workshop organized with Julian took place in August 2006 and brought together most of the contributors of this book, in addition to David Edgington, T.J. Pempel, Atsuko Hatano (Tamura), Kurt Huebner, Miranda Schreurs, Stefan Gaenzle, Midori Okabe (in absentia), Hideaki Uemura, Hyung-Gu Lynn, Eric Remacle, Christian Hansen, Brian Job, and Sima Godfrey. It is during this workshop that Eric Remacle proposed the term "Minervian" for the project.

My own thinking greatly benefitted from conversations with Joseph Nye, Peter Hall, Susan Pharr, Bill Grimes, and many others during my time as Harvard Academy Scholar during 2004–06, as well as meetings in Paris with Karoline Postel-Vinay, Regine Serra, Nicolas Jabko, Cornelia Woll, and Zaki Laïdi. In Japan, discussions with Yoshihide Soeya around his work on Japan as a "middle power" also provided great inspiration to me. As well, Tsutomu Kikuchi's great wit and knowledge of EU–Japan and Japan–Canada linkages proved invaluable. In Canada and at G20 summits, Alan Alexandroff was a source of optimism and inspiration on the quest for global governance; he cunningly labeled the Minervian project as work "at the interstices of global governance."

Like a good Bordeaux wine, this project took more time to mature into a unified and thoughtful book. During this phase of thinking, writing, and rewriting, I would like to address my great thanks to the patient and hard-working contributors of the book.

Participants at the International Relations Workshop at UBC, led by my colleague Arjun Chowdhury, were great in refining the final products with their witty comments; I particularly wish to acknowledge Brian Job, Katia Coleman, Xu Hongcai, Yoel Kornreich, Konrad Kalicki, Linting Zhang, Chunman Zhang, and Michael Cohen.

This manuscript also benefitted from the candid questions and keen interest from students in my honors seminars (poli 390 and 490). Nothing is more invaluable for the development of ideas than engaging in deep exchanges with students. They always ask the right questions and see the gaps!

For the hard work of editing and unifying the chapters into a whole, I received great help from Madeleine Lyons, Teddy Harrison, and Bruce Lyth.

Atsuko Hatano (Tamura) provided great help in seeking and putting together comparative data and tables across Minervian actors. Her positive spirit and keen curiosity were wonderful assets.

In the end, none worked harder than Jessica Hedges-Chou in helping me shape and craft the final manuscript. Jessica's sharp mind, great dedication, and skills are all over this book.

Two other witty and playful persons played a great role in asking the "why" questions and in finding ways to slow the project, while providing a perpetual source of inspiration for me: thank you, Claire and Paul.

Finally, I dedicate this book to my wife, Yvonne, whose great talents, care, and wisdom are the source of all possibilities.

Notes on Contributors

Jennifer Chan is an associate professor in the Faculty of Education, as well as a faculty associate at the Centre for Japanese Research, Centre for Women's and Gender Studies, and the Institute for European Studies at the University of British Columbia. Her research focuses on gender, racism, multiculturalism, transnational social movements, human rights, and global governance. She is the author of *Gender and Human Rights Politics in Japan: Global Norms and Domestic Networks* (2004) and editor of *Another Japan Is Possible: New Social Movements and Global Citizenship Education in Japan* (2008).

Katharina P. Coleman is an associate professor in the Department of Political Science at the University of British Columbia. Her research focuses on formal international organizations and on issues surrounding the legitimate use of military force in the contemporary international system. Her regional area of expertise is sub-Saharan Africa. She has written articles and chapters on peace operations and the development of international norms, and she is the author of *International Organisations and Peace Enforcement: The Politics of International Legitimacy* (2007).

Elena Feditchkina is a Ph.D. candidate in the Department of Political Science at the University of British Columbia. Before embarking on her academic journey, she worked as a reporter in her place of origin, Eastern Siberia. Her research interests include the domestic and international politics of biodiversity protection and climate change policies, with a focus on Canada, New Zealand, Norway, the EU, and Russia.

Petrice R. Flowers is an associate professor in the Political Science Department at the University of Hawai'i at Manoa. She was an SSRC/JSPS postdoctoral research fellow at the University of Tokyo (2002–04) and a Fulbright Scholar in Japan and Korea (2009–10). Her current research is focused on a book-length project on refugees and human trafficking in Japan and Korea. She is the author of *Refugees, Women, and Weapons: International Norm Adoption and Compliance in Japan* (2009).

Daisaku Higashi is an associate professor in the Human Security Program at the University of Tokyo. He worked for the UN Assistance Mission in Afghanistan from December 2009 to 2010, and as a team leader for Reconciliation and Reintegration in Kabul. His doctoral dissertation at the University of British Columbia involved field research in Afghanistan and East Timor, and resulted in a UN DPKO published report, "Challenge of Constructing Legitimacy in Peacebuilding," as well as the book, *Peacebuilding: Field Research in Afghanistan and East Timor* (2009 – in Japanese), both of which informed the Japanese government's policies in support of the creation of a new reconciliation mechanism in Afghanistan in 2010.

Zaki Laïdi is a professor of international relations at Sciences Po Paris. He has published extensively on international relations and Europe as a global actor. He is the author of *A World Without Meaning* (1998), *The Great Disruption* (2006), and *Norms over Force: The Enigma of European Power* (2008). His forthcoming book *Limited Achievements: Obama's Foreign Policy* is one of the first books analyzing Barack Obama's foreign policy.

Joanne Lee is a senior legal officer with Australia's Department of Foreign Affairs and Trade. She was an adjunct lecturer and Ph.D. candidate in the ANU College of Law at the Australian National University (2004–12). From 1999 to 2004, she was a research associate for two research institutes at the University of British Columbia, providing legal and policy advice on the International Criminal Court, as well as participating in ICC negotiations at UN Headquarters as part of the NGO Coalition for the ICC. Her publications include "International Tribunals and the Criminalization of International Violence," in R. Price and M. Zacher (eds), *The United Nations and Global Security* (with Richard Price, 2004).

Ian Manners is a professor in the Department of Society and Globalization at Roskilde University. He works at the nexus of critical social theory, normative political theory, European integration, and the European Union in global politics. His recent publications include *The European Project: Politics and Law – History and Future* (edited with Rikard Bengtsson, Hans-Åke Persson, Ola Zetterqvuist, and Linda Gröning, 2012 – in Swedish), *Research Methods in European Union Studies* (edited with Kennet Lynggaard and Karl Löfgren, forthcoming), and *The Foreign Policies of European Union Member States* (edited with Amelia Hadfield and Richard Whitman, 2012). His article "Normative Power Europe: A Contradiction in Terms?" in the *Journal of Common Market Studies* was voted one of the five most important pieces on the EU of the decade by the members of European Union Studies Association.

Kim Richard Nossal is a professor of political studies and Director of the Centre for International and Defence Policy at Queen's University. He is the author of a number of works on Canadian foreign policy, including *International Policy and Politics in Canada* (with Stéphane Paquin and Stéphane Roussel, 2011).

Isao Sakaguchi is a professor in the Faculty of Law at Gakushuin University. He received his Ph.D. in international relations from the University of Tokyo. His current research focuses on international fisheries governance and private regimes. His recent works include *Global Environmental Governance and the Process of Regime Development: CITES, NGOs and States* (2006), "The Transformation of IWC Regime: Strategies of Activist NGOs and the Process of Norm Acceptance," *Kokusai Seiji*, 153: 42–57 (2008), and "Environmental Diplomacy of Japan: Middle Power, NGOs and Local Governments," *Kokusai Seiji*, 166: 26–41 (2011).

Henrik Selin is an associate professor in the Department of International Relations at Boston University. He is the author of *Global Governance of Hazardous Chemicals: Challenges of Multilevel Management* (2010) and co-editor of *Changing Climates in North American Politics: Institutions, Policymaking, and Multilevel Governance* (with Stacy D. VanDeveer, 2009) and *Transatlantic Environment and Energy Politics: Comparative and International Perspectives* (with Miranda A. Schreurs and Stacy D. VanDeveer, 2009). In addition, he has authored and co-authored more than 40 peer-reviewed journal articles and book chapters, as well as numerous reports, reviews, and commentaries.

Yves Tiberghien is an associate professor of political science at the University of British Columbia. He is also a faculty associate at the Centre for Chinese Research, at the Centre for Japanese Research, and at the Institute for European Studies at UBC, as well as a research associate at Sciences Po Paris and at the Asia Centre in Paris. He specializes in comparative political economy and international political economy with an empirical focus on China, Japan, and the European Union. He is currently working on a multi-year project on the battle for global governance, with a particular focus on the role of China, Japan, and Korea at the G20 and in global environmental issues, funded by the Social Science and Humanities Research Council of Canada. He is the author of *Entrepreneurial States: Reforming Corporate Governance in France, Japan, and Korea* (2007) and *L'Asie et le futur du monde* (2012 – in French).

Nicolas Véron is a senior fellow at Bruegel, the Brussels-based international economy think tank, and a visiting fellow at the Peterson Institute for International Economics in Washington, DC. His research focuses on financial systems and financial regulation around the globe, including current developments in the European Union. A graduate of France's Ecole Polytechnique and Ecole des Mines, his professional career has combined a variety of complementary experiences. His past positions include senior French civil servant, junior investment banker, CFO of a small listed company, and senior strategic consultant. He has co-authored *Smoke & Mirrors, Inc.: Accounting for Capitalism* (with Matthieu Autret and Alfred Galichon, 2006), and is also the author of several books in French.

1
Introduction: Minervian Actors and the Paradox of Post-1995 Global Institution Building

Yves Tiberghien

Since the early 1990s, humanity has faced unprecedented challenges of coordination and governance. In addition to traditional security dilemmas and the increasingly complex management of the global economy, we are challenged by a growing list of pressing global issues that cannot be addressed by market mechanisms alone. These issues include climate change, environmental and biodiversity preservation, global food safety, population health and pandemics, cultural preservation, human rights, and human security. The functional need for cooperation among key states, as well as the rising plethora of non-state actors, may be higher than ever in human history. In a nutshell, humanity is at a crossroads. It enjoys historically high levels of prosperity, peace, and interdependence. Yet, it will be able to preserve these levels only if it is able to provide for indispensable global public goods and minimize pressing global public risks (Attali 2011; Flahault 2011; Malloch-Brown 2011; Ruby 2010).

This book focuses on global institutions, defined broadly as a set of global rules, norms, treaties, or organizational frameworks that allow states (and other actors) to coordinate their actions in the context of fragmented sovereignty and the absence of a global government. The book develops an understanding of institutions that builds on the tradition that sees them as functional rules of the game, and as solutions to transaction costs and collective action dilemmas (North 1990; Williamson 1985). At the global level, transaction costs and levels of uncertainty are higher due to greater cultural differences and divergence in interests; the endeavor of global institution building is thus, paradoxically, both more essential and more difficult to achieve (Keohane 1984; Siebert

2009). The builders of institutions not only face the classic collective problem among as many as 195-odd states and numerous other significant actors; they also have to deal with the potential unevenness in the distribution of costs and benefits generated by new institutions and its security implications.

In the post-Cold War era, the challenge has been simplified by the removal of a lethal competition between East and West, and yet also complicated by the rapid diffusion power. Initially, during the period from 1990 to 2005, analysts and policy makers heralded a period of US unipolarity, marked by a renewed leadership in technology (the internet revolution) and the acceleration of globalization, as well as overwhelming military power and global dominance (Haas 2005; Ikenberry 2002; Walt 2005). Yet, this US hegemony quickly peaked with the challenges of Iraq, the global financial crisis of 2008, and the rise of large emerging nations, primarily China. The decade of the 2000s has seen the largest diffusion of economic power since 1945: together, the economies of advanced democracies of the OECD still represented 62% of the world's gross domestic product (GDP) in 1990 and 60% in 2000. But that share collapsed in the 2000s, reaching just 50% in 2011 (in PPP terms).[1] In nominal $, according to the World Bank's World Development Indicators, the US share of total world GDP shrank from a high of 31.4% in 2000 to 21.6% in 2011 (nominal $).

Ironically, however, the period of US renaissance in the 1990s did not correlate with a new leadership in global institution building. As Congress shifted inward after 1994 and the US presidency moved to unilateralism in 2001 under President G.W. Bush, the US chose not to convert its power into global institutions. After the mid-2000s, on the other hand, diffusion of power became more visible and, despite a new interest for global institutions by the time of the Barack Obama administration in 2009, global coordination clearly became more difficult. Today, global stability and the provision of global public goods call for a new strategy to enlarge the willing coalition (Brzezinski 2012), while the US hegemon must act under increasing budget constraints (Friedman and Mandelbaum 2011; Mandelbaum 2010).

This book is not about the United Nations as a whole, itself an ongoing and partially institutionalized effort at global governance with a much longer trajectory going back to 1945 and indeed to 1919 and the League of Nations (Weiss and Gordenker 1996; Weiss and Thakur 2010). Likewise, the book does not focus on global economic summits, such as the G8 or the new post-2008 G20 process (Alexandroff and Cooper 2010; Tiberghien 2012), or on the debate about an overhaul of global trade and financial system (WTO, IMF, BIS (Bank of International Settlements), FSB (Financial Stability Board) (Eichengreen 2011; Rodrik 2011).

This book focuses on one important episode of global institution building that took place against US opposition at the height of US unilateral dominance during the period from 1995 to roughly 2005 (but with some continuation until today): the advancement of global treaties, rules, and norms primarily in the areas of global environment, global rule of law, human security, and cultural diversity by a coalition of non-hegemonic actors.

The puzzle of non-hegemonic global institution building in 1990s and 2000s

In early 2001, international relations took an unusual turn. The US, the lone global superpower and seemingly indispensable leader in international institution building since the 1940s, had announced its withdrawal from the Kyoto Protocol on climate change a few months earlier. With this announcement, it was expected that Kyoto would die and that new negotiations would usher in a set of US-friendly institutions. Yet, by the end of July, all other economically advanced countries, except for Australia, had decided to ignore the US withdrawal and to press ahead with the implementation of the Kyoto Protocol. The European Union took the first step at its Gothenburg Summit in June, taking the decision to assume the role of climate hegemon and to lobby other countries in the process. Despite its tight economic integration with the US, Canada followed suit. Japan hesitated, torn between its close alliance with the US and clear economic interests on the one hand, and EU and civil society pressures on the other. By the end of July, however, Japan crossed the Rubicon and decided to ratify the Kyoto Protocol and thus participate in the creation of a new international institution in the absence of the US (Tiberghien and Schreurs 2007, 2010). Russia later joined the trio, enabling Kyoto to take force as international law in February 2005 (Harrison and Sundstrom 2010). A new major international institution was born, despite opposition by the global hegemon. Of course, subsequent meetings of the parties in Copenhagen (2009), Cancun (2010), and Durban (2011) have revealed the limits of this institution; the combined weight of the US and of emerging powers of the BASIC (Brazil, South Africa, India, China) axis proved too much for its initial setup. Nonetheless, the Kyoto process was significant both as an unusual advance in international relations and as a key building block for future institution building in the climate arena. As of 2012, it is important to note that nearly all countries have come to accept Kyoto norms, objectives, and discourses, even though they are not yet ready to accept immediate targets and costs. This Kyoto pattern was not an isolated one. The same process occurred with the ratification of the 1998 Statutes of Rome and the creation of the International Criminal Court (ICC) in 2002. While the US was initially involved in the drafting of the statutes and had been a signatory, it later decided to withdraw its signature and launch an active campaign against the ICC. Yet, despite the undisputed status of the US as the sole superpower and the unprecedented asymmetry of power in the world today, other participants (eventually including Japan in 2007) merely shrugged off the US opposition and pushed ahead (Bassiouni 1999; Broomhall 2003; Malone and Khong 2003; Sands 2003). Under the Obama administration, the US has dropped its anti-ICC campaign and now supports its use for selected cases (Ivory Coast, Libya), in essence acquiescing to its existence.

Meanwhile, Canada, Japan, Norway, and the EU have been advancing the concept of "human security" and lobbying for such notions to be integrated into policy deliberations at the UN level (Malone and Khong, 2003; Remacle 2005). The Ottawa treaty to ban personal landmines (1997 Convention on the Prohibition of the Use, Stockpiling, Production and Transfer of Anti-Personal Mines and on their Destruction) was signed, ratified, and implemented, despite opposition from the US. Again, the coalition driving the ban included Canada, key European countries, and Japan (Byers 2007; Cameron et al. 1998). In 2005, the process culminated in the adoption of the norm of "Responsibility to Protect" (R2P) during the UN general meetings.

In a different field, on October 20, 2005, 148 countries adopted a new cultural diversity treaty negotiated within the framework of UNESCO. The treaty, led by Canada and France, aims at helping nations protect their domestic cultures from homogenizing global economic forces and represents a major milestone in the achievement of this goal (Byers 2007; International Centre for Trade and Sustainable Development 2005). Only two countries opposed the treaty: the US and Israel. The treaty affirms the sovereign right of countries to protect and promote the diversity of cultural expressions, and insists its recognition by the WTO and other treaties. The US has argued that the treaty is vague and can be used to block trade in cultural goods and services. Other examples of attempts at international institution building include emerging norms of development assistance, assistance policies, humanitarian interventions, refugee rights, and human rights (Barnett and Finnemore 2004; Finnemore 2003; Weiss and Thakur 2010).

These cases exemplify *two important trends in international affairs* that took place during the key window of 1995 to 2005. The *first trend is an expansion of multilateral institution building* into new arenas. While the immediate post-Second World War period saw the creation of effective global institutions mainly in the field of economic cooperation and development (IMF, World Bank, WTO), security (disarmament treaties), and human rights (beginning with the International Declaration of Human Rights contained in the UN Charter), the 1990s and early 2000s saw the expansion of this trend into the arenas of environment, human security, and third-generation human rights (Reus-Smit 2004; Thakur 2006; Weiss and Thakur 2010). The development of these international institutions includes formal legal treaties, codes of conduct, and norms and practices that shape behavior. In this project, institutions are taken in their broadest sense and encompass the full spectrum of possibilities, ranging from norms and new agendas that frame international action to formal rules of the game, new international law, and rigid frameworks. Each chapter in this book addresses one kind of international institution as the object to be explained, but the array of institutions explored here covers the whole range from informal to formal.

The *second trend is a new political pattern in the creation of these institutions*. To the surprise of many, as the US decided that institution building beyond the realms of economy (trade, finance) and hard security (anti-terrorism, non-proliferation) was not in its interest and should be halted, other national and supranational actors joined forces to construct new institutions. This construction continued unabated despite, not only US opposition, but also the reluctance of other powers such as Russia and especially China. In the cockpit driving the continued trend, one can find what we call *Minervian actors*: in particular, an emergent European Union aiming to project a new common identity, a transforming Japan, and a Canada forcefully dedicated to multilateralism.

Minerva's rule

In the Roman (and Greek) pantheon, Minerva was the goddess of creativity, law and justice, and inventiveness. She was combative and effective, relying on craftiness rather than brute force like her father, the fearful Mars. In the Greek version, Athena accompanies many heroes such as Odysseus, Heracles, and Jason to victory through wisdom and guile. Because she encourages the cultivation of knowledge, art, craft, and law, she is a good symbol for the advancement of rules and institutions. She represents a pragmatic, yet powerful, effort at advancing human prosperity, civilization, and overall balance through tools and cumulated knowledge, rather than through a mere exercise of power. In international relations parlance, we take Minerva/Athena to represent the advance of institutions and governance.

Thus, under the label of *Minervian actors*, we refer to states or organizations such as the European Union that choose to commit significant resources and power (that is, not just discourse) to the advancement of global institutions and global governance. This approach presumes a specific intention and purpose behind this action, thus delineating a novel type of actor on the international scene. In the reality of the post-1995 world, we characterize the actions of Minervian actors as a non-hegemonic contribution to global governance, one that relies more on global and decentralized institutional incentives than on a unipolar power structure.[2] *The Minervian pole represents a group of states and non-state actors that support the creation of credible institutions, possibly backed by limited but effective use of economic resources or force.*

De facto, the set of countries analyzed in the book is limited to industrialized democracies, particularly Canada, Japan, and the EU, taken as a whole or in its parts. But "Minervian" universe is not limited to these jurisdictions. It is a broader term than, and analytically distinct from, "middle powers," which has been used since the late 1980s to describe nations such as Canada, Australia, Norway, South Africa, Mexico, or Brazil and has more recently been applied to Japan (Chapnick 2005; Cooper 1997; Finlayson 1988; Cooper et al. 1993; Pratt 1990; Soeya 2005; Wood 1988). Although Canada, Japan, and the EU have formed the backbone of the Minervian contribution to institution building, authors in this book draw attention to cases where participation by Norway, Switzerland, South Korea, and also South Africa and Mexico, is noteworthy. The Obama administration of the US has sometimes acted as a Minervian actor on a case-by-case basis since 2009, although the true nature of this behavior lends itself to debate (Laïdi 2010).

The Minervian moment in historical context

Historically, the United States has inspired and led the trend of global institution building in a classic hegemonic pattern (Gilpin 1981; Keohane 1984; Ikenberry 2010). President Wilson was the key thinker and political force behind the ill-fated League of Nations in 1919. Rooseveltian America established the foundations of post-war global institutions: the Bretton Woods monetary system, the International Monetary Fund (IMF), the World Bank, and the General Agreement on Trade and Tariffs (GATT). Likewise, the United Nations bore a strong

American birthmark. Eleanor Roosevelt, the former US First Lady, was the key actor behind the drafting of the UN Charter of Human Rights in 1947 (together with a French diplomat and a Canadian law professor). International law in trade and human rights developed thanks to US leadership.

The first rift between the US and its progeny dates back to the unilateral decision by President Nixon in 1971 to close the gold window, a resolution that ended the Bretton Woods monetary system and led to severe financial and trade tensions. While the Nixon era marked a shift in US attitudes toward global institution building, the US continued to exert leadership in the advancement of international human rights and international environmental treaties well into the 1990s. Initially, the US was well ahead of Europe in what is today seen as a key preserve of European leadership: global environment and climate change (Vogel 2003).

In the 1990s, the Clinton administration carried the Rooseveltian torch further and displayed significant leadership during the Kyoto negotiations in 1997 and the process that led to the creation of the International Criminal Court. But the then Republican-controlled Congress did not give a chance to the Clinton agenda. UN-bashing, already on the rise under the Reagan administration, had become central in the discursive landscape of Capitol Hill and achieved predominance under the Bush administration in 2001. The international agenda seemed in jeopardy across the board.

Around that time, leadership in new institution building appears to have shifted from the US to a group of countries committed to multilateral activism on a range of non-military agendas.[3] Countries such as Canada, European states, and Japan have emerged as the vanguard of this development, although their cooperation did not extend to all issue-areas and they are joined in their efforts by varying coalitions of other countries. In the post-Cold War period, these countries have taken increasingly common positions on global issues (particularly related to the environment, human security, and human rights); the sheer weight of this convergence pattern has facilitated instances of significant institutional change. On some issues, this "trilateral" cooperation is visible ex ante; on others it appears only in the final stages of institution building through a commonality in positions. It is also interesting to note that three other major rising powers, namely China, Russia, and India, have not yet played a driving role in the process of global institution building. Depending on the issue-areas, they have often lent support to the process (for example on the Cartagena

Biosafety Protocol), but have been neither first-movers nor essential actors. Does this new wave of institutionalization mark a significant shift away from great-power politics? Or does it embody the continuation of power politics through new means?

The EU as a global Minervian actor

One important assumption of this book relates to the European Union. Although the EU is made up of 27 (soon to be 28) countries with significant differences in international preferences and positions, it has increasingly acted as a coherent global actor since the early 1990s in the key issue-areas studied in this book: environment, human security, human rights, cultural diversity, and even accounting (Bretherton and Vogler 2006; Laïdi 2005; Manners 2002; McCormick 2007). Our central argument underscores this fact; the EU is often considered analytically as a single jurisdiction. This assumption would not hold for hard security or most economic issues (except trade) that are outside the focus of this book.

In his chapter on the Minervian setting for the European Union, Ian Manners emphasizes the growing common normative European identity across selected dimensions as a key factor behind this common behavior. As a result, many cases highlighted in this book reveal high levels of jurisdictional uploading to the European level, a more active European Commission, a more vocal European Parliament, and an expansion in the number and breadth of issue-areas under the responsibility of the European Council. The trend of Europeanization became particularly pronounced with the establishment of the Maastricht treaty in 1992, and was only attenuated by the 2004–07 enlargement waves, and, more seriously, the post-2009 euro crisis.

Nonetheless, most issues covered in this book fall under either national jurisdiction (foreign affairs) or areas of joint responsibility (environment, culture). Individual European states therefore remain important players throughout our analyses of multilateral institution building, but we find that the exact balance of responsibility between EU level and national level varies along a continuum and across cases. Cases such as Iraq post-war norms, R2P, landmines, and the UNESCO treaty find themselves on the low end of the Europeanization continuum, while environmental issues such as climate change, biodiversity, or chemical regulations operate within a higher degree of Europeanization.

Research questions

Two key questions lie at the core of our project to understand global institution building since the mid-1990s:

- What has been the role of Minervian actors (particularly Canada, the EU or individual European states, and Japan) in the intensification (in depth and scope) of multilateral institution building since the mid-1990s?
- Why have Minervian actors been willing and able to play this role?

The book focuses on two levels of analysis: it unpacks the Minervian trend at the global level by exploring the processes behind the formation of multilateral institutions (treaties, practices, and norms) in the post-hegemonic phase. In doing so, it demonstrates the key roles played by the EU, Japan, and Canada – individually and collectively, and in collaboration with non-state actors – in shaping these processes. At the same time, the book analyzes the domestic origins of this Minervian willingness to undertake the task of global leadership.

Substantive focus of the book

The book focuses on issue-areas where global governance has expanded during the 1990s and 2000s, namely *global environmental regulation, human security and international law*, the protection of *human rights* and *cultural diversity*. We also include one economic contrast case: *accounting rules*, although it is a case primarily concerned with regulation and law. The book excludes issues of hard security (including terrorism) and global economics (that is, trade and finance) where the international dynamic is different, relatively well understood, and entrenched in patterns established since the end of the Second World War. Our analysis is aimed squarely at understanding the new process of multilateral institution building that represents a substantial departure from the well-understood patterns that governed the post-Second World War international arena; the organizational form these institutions take or how their prescriptions may be implemented or enforced is not within the scope of this project.

Our case studies cover the construction of both formal treaties (Kyoto, ICC, UNESCO, landmines, chemical regulations) and less formal norms or coordinated behavior (R2P, Iraq post-war reconstruction, human security, accounting). The diversity of cases demonstrates a variety of coalition patterns (reviewed in Chapter 2): in some cases, the US is a major positive or negative player; in other cases, all Minervian players are acting in concordance (although rarely in open coordination), while in a third category of cases, they are divided. Finally, some negative cases are considered in Chapter 2 (such as international whaling and the post-2007 climate change negotiations), where Minervian actors either fight against each other or fail to generate new global institutions.

Conventional explanations

Traditionally, scholars of international relations would interpret the behavior of Minervian states through four lenses: realism, liberalism, constructivism, and domestic institutions and power alignments. We argue that realism carries only partial explanatory power, that liberalism carries limited explanatory power, and that constructivism needs to be supplemented with domestic explanations. Classic domestic explanations emphasizing domestic electoral institutions or distribution of power among societal actors are also off the mark.

From a realist perspective, we would theorize that Minervian actors participate in counter-hegemonic movements in the pursuit of economic and political interests. The process of institution building is an attempt to constrain the US and to amplify the voice of and maneuvering room for the EU, Japan, Canada, and others. A prototypical example of such a view is S.M. Walt's *Taming American Power* (2005). Walt argues that the unprecedented power of the US in world affairs worries other states. They develop various strategies to cope with this imbalance, of which Walt identifies eight: bandwagoning, regional balancing, bonding, penetration, balancing, blackmail, balking, and delegitimization. Walt argues that the development of multilateral institutions, such as the Kyoto Protocol or the Landmine Treaty, can be understood as an effort by other states to bind the US and to balance its overwhelming power:

> Indeed, building new institutions may even be an effective tactic when the United States refuses to play along. If the United States chooses not to engage in "international rulemaking", or if other states become convinced that the United States will reject some new convention no matter how it is written, they may decide to go ahead anyway, without further input from Washington. If their efforts succeed, the United States could end up being at least partly bound by the "power of the first draft." (151)

Walt also interprets institution building as an effort to counter US power by delegitimizing its position as a moral leader. Walt argues that other states choose to impose a political cost on US unilateralism by moving ahead with global institution building, even when other states know that the US rejection will make the new treaties largely ineffective. Thus, he writes:

> By negotiating, signing, and ratifying the Kyoto Protocol, the landmines convention, the Rome Statute on the International Criminal Court, and so on, the rest of the world is in effect saying to America: "Sure, you can do what you want, and we can't stop you. But we can make you look bad, and over time, more and more people will yearn for the day when the United States is not so powerful." (163)

In sum, Walt concludes that the process of moving ahead with Kyoto, the landmine treaty, and multilateral institutions has had a significant impact on the US image and capacity for leadership abroad (231).

A realist interpretation would also emphasize two additional, notable changes to the landscape: the end of the Cold War and the demise of the bi-polar world has weakened alliance cohesion. In addition, a perception of US economic dynamism in the 1990s provoked regulatory efforts by economic competitors.

This book shows that realism mostly misses the mark in explaining the behavior of Minervian actors (with a few exceptions discussed in Part II: The Competitive Mode), mainly because they do not extract much tangible direct benefit from their involvement in global institution building.

Through a liberal lens, we would interpret the actions of Minervian actors as self-interested contributions to the provision of common infrastructures for trade, prosperity, and welfare. Minervian actors recognize the necessity for international cooperation in the provision of public goods (for example, environmental protection, security, and so on) (Wood 1988). Possibly because of the absence of claims for global dominance, middle powers are able to focus their foreign policy away from great-power competition. In addition, as trading states with deep international linkages, they benefit directly from a stabilization of the global system through international institutions (Keohane 1984).

Global institution building is therefore a strategically attractive option to achieve solutions to problems that are inherently international in scope. Elements of this reasoning might be related to asymmetries in exposure to global environmental dangers, for example.

Thus, environmental degradation and resource dependence (by the EU and Japan) necessitates strong action. The problem, of course, lies in the puzzle of continued willingness to provide costly global goods when major players, such as the US and Australia, decide to free-ride. In this sense, the liberal explanation is less powerful in cases where cooperation has already broken down and cost distribution is asymmetric.

A third conventional approach is the constructivist school broadly conceived. Seen through such a lens, state preferences are influenced by socialization with other states, the actions of international organizations, or by global norms (Avant et al. 2010; Barnett and Finnemore 2004; Finnemore 2003; Keck and Sikkink 1998). These norms may be carried by civil society actors or by a diffused world society (Meyer et al. 1997). In this book, we acknowledge the power of norms and civil society actors as vectors, yet also emphasize that this explanation alone is insufficient. Why do such norms have a disproportionately high impact on Minervian actors, relative to other rich democracies like the US and Australia, and other democracies in general? What explains the differential penetration of such norms?

We may turn to domestic explanations, particularly the analysis of domestic institutions. Minervian actors may be spurred toward a multilateral institution building agenda because of an electoral system based on proportional representation and prone to produce coalition governments, or a particular foreign policy-making structure. Yet, the mix of Minervian actors includes countries with both parliamentary and presidential or semi-presidential systems, let alone a complex multi-level governance structure in the case of the EU.

The argument: three causal modes behind Minervian activism

This book argues that the behavior of Minervian actors in multilateral institution building since the 1990s must be analytically disaggregated. Minervian actors act for different reasons in different issue-areas, but there are clear patterns in their behavior. We argue that this behavior follows *three distinct causal modes,* only two of which are discussed in the existing literature.

By "modes" we mean the dominant causal processes by which particular issues were placed on domestic and international agendas. The modes serve as ideal types that identify causal patterns. We recognize that the actual process in each case is often interactive and can involve a variety of variables. Categorizing a case as exemplary of a given mode only denotes that this mode was the dominant one, not the exclusive one.

The competitive mode

The two well-documented hypotheses of economic/political realism and global civil society explain only a subset of considered cases. In the *first, competitive mode, Minervian actors support multilateralism primarily based on their perceived economic or political self-interests.* They support global institution building either to upload national constraints to the global level or according to counter-hegemonic motives against the US. This explanation is broadly compatible with the realist lens. In so doing, states sometimes join hands with global civil society actors or private firms; but this cooperation should not disguise their dominant economic or political interests behind the show of formal normative discourse.

The findings of the book show that this mode is only partially operative in a handful of cases: the UNESCO declaration of cultural diversity, the Cartagena Protocol on Biosafety, and the battle over international accounting standards (IAS). These cases tend to be relatively isolated and technical. High economic stakes engender the mobilization of interest coalitions that exert a strong voice over the policy pursued by Minervian states.

The normative mode

In the *second, normative mode, Minervian states support multilateralism because of the influence of norms and ideas* promoted by non-economic actors, such as global civil society, scientific and knowledge-based elites ("epistemic communities," Haas 1992), the staff of international organizations, or norms entrepreneurs (Ellickson 2001). The normative mode is a fluid and interactive process; it centers on a battle for meanings, identities, and national values. It builds upon the literature about social movements and the conditions for their success (Della Porta and Tarrow 2004; McAdam et al. 2001; Tarrow 1998, 2005). In general, the success of the normative mode is dependent on the relatively weak mobilization of adverse interest groups and comparatively low costs in terms of relations with the US. These intervening factors vary over time, and windows of opportunity may close after key events. This book emphasizes the multi-faceted character of normative coalitions across issue-areas. In some cases (for example, that of landmines), NGOs carry a lot of weight and are able to build alliances with domestic Minervian actors. In other cases, that of Responsibility to Protect, for example, key elite entrepreneurs and political leaders play a crucial role.

Yet, in other cases, experts and transnational scientific elites are the vectors of global norms that end up penetrating Minervian states after a process of scientific advancement, formation of meaning, and redefinition (in the case of CITES, for example). In all of these cases, we observe Minervian states to be permeable to global norms and global elites, owing to domestic allies, an open governance structure, and windows of opportunities for normative penetration. In many cases, the normative or ideational penetration follows a bottom–up process, but in some cases, such penetration can be conceptualized as a top-down elite development (Isao Sakaguchi (Chapter 8) demonstrates such a process in this volume).

The domestic leadership mode in interaction with public opinion

The *third key mode involves domestic political leadership* – that is, the projection of domestic agendas in Minervian countries onto the global agenda, usually involving multi-level coalitions. This projection involves coalition building, but political leaders are often acting as catalysts for the formation of NGO coalitions. This is a top–down mode where political leaders in key states are the prime movers. In many cases, individual leaders in Minervian states exploit zones of autonomy and use international agendas in an entrepreneurial way. They project a vision of global institution building and build multi-level coalitions that include NGOs and transnational scientific or bureaucratic elites, but they do so in the pursuit of political gains. Leaders aim to build their political reputation in front of domestic audiences, by demonstrating decisive action on the global scene. This mode assumes that leaders act on the basis of long-term political visions and not in the service of traditional economic interests. Furthermore, unlike the normative mode, this causal process is driven by the political elite, even though it may lead to the creation of an epistemic community or new grassroots coalition along the way.

In this mode, there is a natural interaction between the preferences of the electorate and the strategic calculations of political leaders. Public opinion forms the structural background and constraint to which political leaders respond. Yet, we also argue that public opinion constraints leave much room for political leadership, particularly in the area of foreign policy, which is often less salient than bread and butter domestic economic issues during elections. Leaders anticipate possible shifts in public opinion, especially when publicly held views and beliefs are not deeply entrenched. The calculations and bets (subject to political space available) of political leaders can shape state behavior on the international scene. Additionally, leaders can use the global scene as a dramatic platform; their actions on the international state will boomerang and shape domestic public opinion about themselves and the issues. Political entrepreneurship refers to actions that stretch electoral constraints, reshape coalitions, and exploit zones of autonomy. The significant variations in the behavior of leaders in Canada and Japan tend to demonstrate the large freedom of maneuver that leaders have with respect to global governance issues.

In the case of the EU, the exercise of political leadership encompasses several interactive levels. Thus, national leaders simultaneously play a global game and a EU game, calculating that their leadership on the global scene can augment their claim for leadership within the EU sphere. Schreurs and Tiberghien have argued that the EU's decentralized, multi-level, and continuously evolving institutional structure can, under the right conditions, generate a positive and reinforcing cycle of competitive leadership (Schreurs and Tiberghien 2007).

Methodology and country case selection

This book relies on the in-depth analysis of instances of global institution building to extract causal processes. It also uses two types of comparative analysis: comparison among countries within each chapter, and comparisons across issue-areas within causal modes.

The project focuses on the EU, Japan, and Canada, since they were the key players in most cases covered in the book. However, some thematic chapters briefly consider other relevant powers, depending on each case (such as South Africa, Brazil, and so on), as well as intermediate powers opposed to multilateralism (such as Australia). The goal is to situate the roles played by Japan, Canada, and the EU in comparison to like-minded and opposing mid-level democratic powers.

In addition, each chapter considers the role of the US in contrast (or sometimes in cooperation) to the Minervian actors.

Canada

For Canada, multilateralism has been a dominant foreign policy theme since the inception of the United Nations, especially in security matters and peacekeeping. This book demonstrates the key role played by Canada from 1995 to 2005 across many dimensions of global institution building. Yet, Canadian foreign policy is also marked by deepening economic integration with the US in the wake of NAFTA. How sustainable is a multilateral foreign policy that is perceived by the US government to contravene US interests or at least does not follow the US lead? Under what conditions does Canada choose to adhere to or to abandon multilateralism?

Byers (2007) and Nossal (Chapter 4, in this book) emphasize the particular political window that enabled the Canadian Minervian role between 1993 and 2006, as well as the disputed nature of this agenda within Canadian politics under the post-2006 Conservative government. Efforts by subsequent Liberal leaders, Stéphane Dion and then Michael Ignatieff, to extend the tradition of Jean Chretien and Lloyd Axworthy have failed to change the political direction. An increasingly entrenched Harper government has chosen to abandon most of the Canadian Minervian agenda, despite stable public support in its favor.

The EU and key European states

For Europe, the pursuit of global institution building is deeply embedded in its quest for a growing role as an international policy actor. To some extent, the global role of Europe is a finely constructed mythology (Manners 2010). This quest is intimately linked to the EU's own state-building ambitions, especially when public opinion reveals strong expectations for a common European foreign policy. Key members such as France, Germany, and the UK have become more willing to cede part of their sovereign rights and agenda-setting status in international negotiations; the situation is radically different from that of the 1980s. As the EU integrates its foreign policy, which actors shape the different components of the foreign policy agenda? Is the multilateral agenda the result of the capture of Europe's foreign policy voice by small states such as the Nordic countries and the Netherlands, or by civil society groups within these small states? Is it driven by Germany, which may find through this European agenda the long-sought reestablishment of a German voice in world affairs? Does it represent instead a point of equilibrium between the three big states, France, Germany, and the UK? Or is it the result of a supranational agenda led by the European Commission and the European Parliament? How do these competing forces negotiate a common path for the EU's future? Which is dominant, and under what conditions?

Japan

As for Japan, the pursuit of multilateral institution building lies on the crucial fault line of Japanese foreign policy: the tension between realism and idealism, particularly in the transformative period of the 1990s and 2000s (Curtis 2004; Davis 1993; Fukushima 1999; Hughes

2004; Inoguchi 2001; Kawashima 2003; Pempel 1998; Soeya 2005). On the one hand, the US–Japan alliance has provided the main anchor for Japanese foreign policy since the Yoshida doctrine of early 1950. On the other hand, since the 1950s, Japan has also professed an "UN-centered foreign policy," through which Japan has participated in projects aimed at global peacekeeping. In the 1990s, Japan worked hard to project a new image and demonstrate leadership by supporting the UN, being pro-active on human rights, development, disarmament, and environment, and most recently by contributing troops and generous aid to the reconstruction of post-conflict societies (for example, in Cambodia, East Timor, Afghanistan, Iraq). This ongoing tension between realism and the focus on the US alliance on the one hand and idealism, pacifism and a focus on the UN on the other goes back a long way in time. It is noteworthy to recall the critical role played by Nitobe Inazo in the creation of the League of Nations in the 1920s while Japan was veering toward imperialism.

In the 1990s, both tendencies appeared to be strengthening simultaneously, representing the concomitant strength of two opposing coalitions. On the one hand, as brilliantly argued by Michael Green (2001), Japan pursues a visibly realist policy in its relations with China and Russia. In the early and mid-2000s, under Prime Ministers Koizumi and Abe, various policy actors pushed for a stronger Japanese military accompanied by a strengthened US–Japan alliance. Some politicians tried to exploit discussions about constitutional revision to move toward a "normal" nation, with perhaps a stronger military. On the other hand, Japan continued to pursue a more multilateral and "idealist" foreign policy on a large number of issue-areas, showing a willingness to break from US positions at the UN and beyond, as demonstrated by the landmine treaty, Cartagena treaty, and support for the UN in general. This multilateral strand pushed Japan close to European foreign policy on many dimensions. This trend was visibly reinforced under Prime Minister Fukuda (2007–08) and the first two governments of the new Democratic Party of Japan (DPJ), led by Prime Minister Hatoyama (2009–10) and then Kan (2010–11).

The tension between these two trends plays out continuously and any equilibrium is unstable. In some instances, the pacifist coalition is granted particular policy goals in exchange for a low profile and the absence of overt anti-US coalition building. How durable is this pattern? Which actors end up shaping Japan's multilateral agenda and tipping the balance when the two strands of Japanese foreign policy stand in opposition to one another? These questions are particularly important, as Japan is frequently emerging as the crucial link or pivot for many new international initiatives.

The US: the elephant in the room

Given its global footprint and dominant role, the US is present in all issue-areas. Although issues of environmental and human security were not top priorities for US foreign policy during our period of interest, the US played an active role in all cases featured in the book. In many cases, the US chose to withdraw its support from the global institution building process or to oppose the direction taken by Minervian powers. Yet, the reality is often more complex than that: in cases such as the Kyoto negotiations or the ICC, US leaders and thinkers were at the forefront of institution building, even though they later faced domestic opposition. Thus, the book strives to account for the variety of US roles across cases and time periods.

Contributions of the book

This comparative study of global institution building by Minervian states is novel at theoretical and methodological levels. For international relations theory this book exposes three causal mechanisms through which so-called second-tier states push forward the creation of global institutions, even in the face of opposition from the global hegemon. The book demonstrates how these actors follow three distinct causal patterns of multilateral institution building and the differences between causal modes matters for the kinds of outcomes obtained. Additionally, our work deepens the literature on the impact of global civil society by analyzing its impact on the three key jurisdictions that have advanced the international agenda since the 1990s, and by investigating how the normative tone set by civil society is championed, negotiated, or exploited throughout the process of multilateral institution building. The book also demonstrates how states pursue a multilateral agenda with domestic political goals in mind.

From the standpoint of methodology, this book offers a case-by-case micro-level analysis of the relationships between NGOs, political leaders, mid-level states, and global change, particularly in the complex and little-understood area of international law. It also offers a systematic examination of European, Canadian, and Japanese international behavior across a dozen issue-areas.

The book proves that the advance of global governance is a multi-pronged phenomenon. The hegemonic or multi-polar competitive modes may shape the pursuit of global governance in hard security and in the economic realm. Yet, global governance may also advance in less visible arenas in time with a secondary, Minervian tune.

Précis of the book

The book is organized into five parts. Part I presents an analysis of Minervian power with a comparative chapter and two country-specific analyses. In Chapter 2, Tiberghien presents an overview of Minervian patterns and coalitions across issue-areas. The chapter identifies several clusters of cases and contrasts cases where all three main Minervian actors are aligned with cases where at least one is missing.

In Chapter 3, Manners argues that the political origins of the European Union's embrace of a global institution building agenda are to be found in the jurisdiction's shared internal (or "domestic") normative principles, which shape and inform its external policies. This agenda reflects the raison d'être of the EU itself: the pursuit of peace, prosperity, and progress over the past six decades. While the period 1984 to 1992 focussed on market building, the post-1990 period is defined by the EU's increasing concentration on progressive global institution building. The chapter concludes with a discussion of how constitutive and causal factors contribute to the EU's role as a Minervian actor.

Chapter 4 explains Canada's Minervian moment by way of an introduction to the Canadian multilateral identity. Nossal argues that we can best explain the rise of this policy orientation as a function of the permissiveness of global politics between 1990 and 2001, which saw the disciplines of the great-power rivalry of the Cold War dissipate and increasingly freed smaller actors like Canada to explore new patterns of global governance. The more proximate cause for the Minervian moment is found in Canada's domestic politics in the 1990s: the complete collapse of the Progressive Conservative party in the 1993 elections, the fragmentation of the Canadian party system, and the return of the Liberal party to a position of political hegemony that they then maintained for a decade. Yet, all this came to an end in 2006.

Part II of the book focuses on the competitive causal mode and explores the conditions under which Minervian commitment to global institution building is dominated by this more realist logic with two distinct case studies: the UNESCO declaration on cultural diversity and the battle over global accounting standards.

In Chapter 5, Chan argues that a hybrid model – a combination of the realist, interests-based paradigm and the bottom–up influence of normative discourse – of multilateral institution building best explains the introduction and ratification of the Convention on the Protection and Promotion of the Diversity of Cultural Expressions. While the Convention can be understood as a strategic counter-hegemonic attempt by the EU and Canada to regain control over cultural industries dominated by the US, its relative success could not be understood without analyzing the significant role played by global civil society.

In Chapter 6, Véron turns his attention to the endorsement of IFRS during 2000–02 by the European Union (later followed by Canada, with Japan adopting a more cautious approach). He argues that this constitutes a competitive response to the rapid spread in the late 1990s of US accounting standards. But it is a somewhat paradoxical case because the US wields considerable influence over the international accounting standard-setting body, and may indeed partly endorse IFRS in the near future. Accounting also includes important elements of the normative mode, based on the epistemic community of accountants that has played a key role in creating IFRS in the first place.

Part III analyzes the normative mode and the penetration of Minervian politics by coalitions of normative carriers (NGOs, epistemic communities, staff of international organizations). The four cases (landmines, CITES, responsibility to protect, and the peacebuilding norm) presented here demonstrate a variety of situations under this common framework.

In Chapter 7, Flowers demonstrates that the process that led to the championing of the Landmines treaty by Canada, Japan, and most European countries was an interactive one, which featured negotiations among transnational civil society, domestic interests, and state identity.

In Chapter 8, Sakaguchi explores the political dynamics of an older international regime, the Convention on International Trade in Endangered Species of Wildlife and Fauna (CITES). He describes the gradual emergence of a diffused normative community: a spontaneous network of self-motivated senior individuals who work as a body to sustain stability and to promote the self-development of the regime.

In Chapter 9, Coleman argues that the emergence of the "responsibility to protect" norm is a case of significant, though as of yet incomplete, norm building. The adoption of the norm at the 2005 World Summit illustrates the critical roles played by Canada and European countries, although the dominant causal process in this case cannot be dissociated from the important activities of eminent individuals and international bureaucrats.

In turn, in Chapter 10, Higashi focuses on the nascent UN peacebuilding norm and the resilience of that norm despite the US-led war in Iraq. After attacking Iraq in 2003, the Bush administration attempted to violate the peacebuilding norm and rebuild Iraq virtually single-handedly. However, a coalition comprising the UN Secretariat and Minervian actors initiated resistance against the hegemon. Facing a worsening situation in Iraq, the US subsequently backed down and asked the UN Secretariat to design key political procedures, such as establishing the interim government and conducting elections.

Part IV focuses on the most novel causal mode, the strategic process whereby political leaders in Minervian states use institution building to project values and seek political gain. This process of politically induced coalition building is explored in three cases: the regulation of chemical use, the International Criminal Court, and the 2010 Nagoya Biodiversity Protocol.

Selin's chapter (Chapter 11) applies the Minervian framework to global chemicals politics. He argues that the EU and Canada in particular have undertaken important intellectual and structural leadership roles in this case, pioneering many major policy expansions.

In Chapter 12, Lee focuses on the role of domestic political leadership, including the domestic political agenda driving Canadian and European interests, in the establishment of the International Criminal Court. She traces the impact of Canadian and European leadership through the subsequent worldwide treaty ratification campaign, which ensured that the Court would become more than just an idea.

In Chapter 13, Feditchkina focuses on the latest Minervian advance: the success of the Convention on Biological Diversity's COP 10 Meeting in agreeing to the so-called Nagoya Protocol on Access and Benefit Sharing, thanks to remarkable Japanese leadership, backed up by mild European support and strong actions by developing nations.

Finally, in Part V, Laïdi (Chapter 14) provides a rejoinder and contradictory view on the Minervian moment. After observing that the Minervian moment came to an end in the late 2000s, he argues that the Minervian cluster lacked unified foundations and was ill positioned to face the intensification of power politics since the late 2000s. Laïdi also views the EU as a problematic Minervian actor, given its internal multi-level games. The chapter offers the possibility of a vigorous debate to evaluate the Minervian impact.

Chapter 15 concludes with a review of the Minervian contribution, limits, and long-term legacy. It offers scenarios for the continuation of global institution building and sees the inclusion of emerging powers, such as China, as a sine qua non condition. Yet, preliminary results show that China can sometimes be open to a Minervian agenda.

Notes

1. OECD, *Perspectives on Global Development 2010 : Shifting Wealth*. Paris: OECD, 2010, figure 0.1, p. 15 (figures in PPP values, but figures at market exchange rates are quite similar).
2. This concept can be seen as humorous rejoinder to Kagan's 2003 typology of the world. ("Europeans are from Venus, Americans Are from Mars" Kagan 2003, 2004), even though empirical facts have shown this typology to be faulty.
3. Hence the concept of "civilian powers" (McCormick 2007; Telo 2005).

Part I
Minervian Settings

2
Varieties of Minervians: Scorecards and Patterns

Yves Tiberghien

What are the patterns and alignments of Minervian actors across issue-areas?*

This chapter provides an overview of empirical patterns observed in this book, as well as measurements on another related indicator: voting patterns at the United Nations. The findings show a degree of clustering among Minervian actors, as well as a significant gap between Minervians on the one hand and the US on the other; yet these findings are more robust on environmental issues (for example, climate, genetically engineered food) than security issues. Also, the patterns themselves provide only underlying structural background and cannot explain the actual behavior of actors in particular cases and periods. For example, Canada has shown a 180-degree change in behavior, while public opinion has remained relatively stable.

Varieties of patterns and outcomes across issue-areas

While the default pattern observed in this book is an alignment, in principle, of all three Minervian actors in favor of global institution building, against opposition by both the US hegemon and key rising powers such as China, India, and Russia (Brazil plays a more ambivalent role), the actual reality on the ground offers more variety. Tables 2.1 to 2.3 break up the patterns observed among Minervian actors into three categories: those where the three Minervian actors are lined up in favor of global institutions; those that exhibit only EU–Japan leadership (without Canada); and those where Japan is not even on board (irrespective of Canada's role). Table 2.4 focuses on cases where the Minervian circle was successfully expanded to include China, thus showing greater endurance.

Table 2.1 First pattern – three Minervian actors

	EU	Canada	Japan	US	China
Kyoto I	YES	YES	YES	NO	partial
ICC	YES	YES	YES	NO	NO
Landmines	YES	YES	YES	NO	NO
R2P	YES part	YES	YES	NO	NO-but
UNESCO	YES	YES	YES	NO	YES
Accounting	YES	YES	YES	YES part	Yes part
Chemical Regulations/ Conventions	YES	YES	YES	NO	YES

Table 2.2 Second pattern – EU–Japan configuration and gradual Chinese buy-in

	EU	Canada	Japan	US	China
Kyoto II	YES	NO	YES→NO	NO	Partial
Cartagena	YES	NO	YES	NO	YES
Biodiversity Nagoya	YES	NO	YES	NO	YES

A few cases not actually covered in the book are considered here. The first is the behavior of key actors in the International Whaling Commission (IWC), namely position on the whaling moratorium (Sakaguchi 2008a,b; 2011), ratification and position on the Cartagena Biosafety Protocol regarding genetically engineered seeds and plants (Bail et al. 2002; Falkner 2000; Newell and MacKenzie 2000; Tiberghien 2012), and the positions taken on the death penalty.

This pattern is the classic pattern and the dominant one observed in this book. It holds across different fields (human security, environment, culture, and even accounting), but only until 2006 did Canada play the Minervian role (Nossal, Chapter 4). On all of these issues, the Minervian actors line up against the US final position, although the US may have played an important or partial role in shaping the agreements, as discussed in the following chapters.

This second cluster reveals a significant subset of cases in which Canada has not acted as a Minervian actor, but has rather joined the US in opposing global institution building. In the case of Kyoto and climate change, Kyoto II refers to the post-2005 implementation of the Kyoto Agreement and the process of negotiations for a new treaty

Table 2.3 Cases of non-Minervian Japanese behavior

	EU	Canada	Japan	US	China
Kyoto II	YES	NO	YES→NO	NO	Partial
IWC (moratorium)	YES	YES	NO	YES	YES
Death Penalty	YES	YES	NO	NO	NO

after the Bali conference of 2007. Canada has not only failed to implement its commitment under the Kyoto Agreement, but it has also fully withdrawn in 2011 and has opposed deep commitments proposed during negotiations for a successor to that agreement. Similar behavior is observed in the two issue-areas related to biodiversity, namely the Cartagena protocol (not ratified by Canada) and the Nagoya negotiations (Feditchkina, Chapter 13). In these cases, Canadian behavior is heavily shaped by its deep economic integration with the US. Thus, Canada emerges as a hybrid actor, caught between its Minervian values and its North American identity.

In this third pattern, Japan is not supporting Europe as a Minervian actor and is taking a resistant approach. The cases include the post-2007 positions on Kyoto (except in 2009 under Hatoyama and possibly 2010 under Kan), as well as the well-known position on whaling, in which Japan has aligned with Iceland and Norway in resisting the moratorium that most other countries have supported. We may add as a comparative case the issue of death penalty: indeed, Japan, like the US (and China), has resisted banning the death penalty and continues to use it regularly (although some occasional individual justice ministers have refused approving any execution). This pattern shows that Japan retains some strong particularistic norms or national interests that can override its Minervian identity in some selective issue-areas.

A key additional question for understanding the impact of Minervian actors on world politics is whether the EU, Japan, and Canada have been successful in enlarging their circles beyond occasional alliances with Norway, Mexico, South Africa, and occasionally Brazil. Particularly, to what extent can China, the country slated to pass the US as the largest economy during 2016–18, be an ally of Minervian actors?

This table shows that, on most environmental topics, China, unlike the US, has actually ratified agreements championed by Minervian actors and has partly participated in the related socialization process

Table 2.4 Is China Minervian? Cases of successful Chinese engagement

	EU	Canada	Japan	US	China
Kyoto I	YES	YES	YES	NO	Partial
Kyoto II	YES	NO	NO	NO	Partial
Cartagena	YES	NO	YES	NO	YES
UNESCO	YES	YES	YES	NO	YES
Accounting	YES	YES	YES	YES part	YES part
Biodiversity Nagoya	YES	NO	YES	NO	YES
IWC (moratorium)	YES	YES	NO	YES	YES
Chemical Regulations/ Conventions	YES	YES	YES	NO	YES

(Johnston 2008; Tiberghien 2012). Although this buy-in on global norms and treaties has even extended to culture and accounting, it has not included human security (for example, landmines, ICC, even R2P). China remains skeptical of global norms and treaties that justify intrusion into domestic sovereignty on security-related issues (for example, hesitations related to the Libya UN resolution in 2011 and veto of the Syria UN resolutions in 2012).

In sum, these preliminary results point to a relatively robust Minervian coalition among the three main actors, although Japan, and even more so, Canada, have not joined the coalition on all issue-areas. This partial pattern points toward disputed Minervian identities. We should add that, on a case-by-case basis, key European countries have also held out or taken skeptical positions. For example, France has been slow and skeptical on issues such as the Convention on International Trade in Endangered Species of Wild Fauna and Flora (CITES regime, Sakaguchi, Chapter 8) and R2P. France retains an old power constituency that harks back to the day when it acted as a great power (similar to the US now). But the EU arena acts as a strong constraint on French behavior, either through institutional integration with more Minervian Europeans or through intense socialization processes in the case of intergovernmental issue-areas.

Minervians vs. the US: successes and failures

Tables 2.1 to 2.4 raise another interesting question: why hasn't the US been able to stop these various Minervian coalitions across so many issue-areas? The answers emerging from the cases of this book point to three probable factors. First, Minervian actors were good at building linkages with developing countries and gaining broad support in most cases. Second, Minervian actors acted on the basis of strong public support and often in alliance with non-governmental organization (NGO) networks. Thus, they were able to build broad legitimacy and to constrain the US ability to respond. Finally, in many issue-areas, the US probably chose to withdraw and not actively fight against the nascent institutions. The three exceptions to this are the ICC, Kyoto, and the Cartagena Biosafety Protocol, where US opposition was much fiercer and more pro-active. The outcome of those three battles points to a draw: the US lost on the ICC and eventually appears to bandwagon, albeit slowly. The US succeeded in gutting Kyoto and also pulled Canada and Japan to side with this position. Finally, the Cartagena battle points to a complete draw, with an ongoing battle between two norms: namely the precautionary principle embedded in the Cartagena protocol, and the principle of "substantial equivalence" embedded in the WTO agreement of 1994 (Falkner 2007; Tiberghien 2012).

One may also point out the issue-area of nuclear weapons, as one where the effort of Minervian actors (minus France and the UK) actually failed to produce an agreement in the face of the US position. In general, issues of high security and international economy are more impervious to the efforts of Minervian actors and are spheres where the US hegemony is more dominant. This is why Alan Alexandroff depicts the cases where Minervian actors succeeded in pushing global institution building as cases that lie at "the interstices of global governance."[1] In this category of Minervian failures, we can include the failure to craft a treaty on migration (in the face of divisions within the Minervian camp) and any effort to construct global rules regarding the death penalty.

Minervian voting behavior at the UN

Does the lineup of Minervian actors generally hold up across international issues, and is there a fundamental difference between Minervian actors and the US in all foreign policy questions? To explore this question, we turn to an analysis of voting behavior at the UN General Assembly (GA) over the past ten years. Although voting behavior at the UN cannot be equated to the commitment to the creation of new multilateral institutions explored in this book, we believe that it nonetheless can offer an interesting proxy to measure national attitudes toward multilateralism. This is especially true when we measure voting

Table 2.5 Voting coincidence with the United States at the UN General Assembly among selected states

	Canada	France	Germany	UK	Japan	ROK	Australia	China	India
2000	66	65	65	72	59	52	64	25	22
2001	57	60	55	63	48	45	56	17	18
2002	49	56	49	57	49	46	52	18	21
2003	48	51	47	57	39	38	58	13	20
2004	50	54	45	57	43	39	57	9	20
2005	49	53	45	55	47	39	58	13	19
2006	55	51	43	53	43	39	61	16	16
2007	55	49	39	51	37	33	55	9	15
2008	59	54	44	57	41	40	57	17	24
2009	80	71	66	72	58	58	77	27	30
2010	75	71	61	74	58	57	93	30	25

Source: US State Department, annual reports on voting coincidence with the United States at the General Assembly. Available from: http://www.state.gov/p/io/rls/rpt/index.htm

behavior relative to US behavior at the time of US reluctance toward multilateralism.

Interestingly, voting patterns at the UN General Assembly confirm the hypothesis of a growing concordance among European countries, Canada, and Japan. Table 2.5 presents succinct data on the degree of concordance between the US and several countries in UN General Assembly voting, measured as a percentage of agreement with the US. It shows that the voting patterns of Canada, Japan, and Germany have converged to very similar positions. For comparative purposes, we note that South Korea is also part of that cluster and exhibits a voting behavior that is extremely close to that of Japan.

These results are obtained from all plenary votes at the UN General Assembly over one whole year, excluding consensus resolutions. The US state department reports indicate that "voting coincidence percentages are derived by dividing the number of identical votes by the total of identical and opposite votes." Figure 2.1 illustrates the results of Table 2.5.

Table 2.5 and Figure 2.1 show that Minervian actors' voting behavior move in a close pattern that includes other countries, such as Korea and Australia. Their cluster stands in great contrast to the US position (the 100% line), and to large emerging powers, such as China and India (who vote very closely with each other). But the data highlight two additional patterns.

First, there is a robust gradation among the Minervian actors that holds relatively well. Japan and South Korea are consistently more divergent

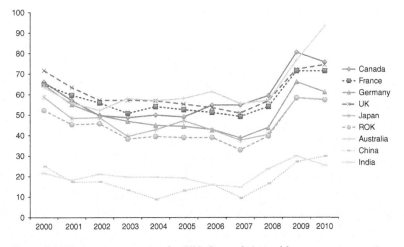

Figure 2.1 Voting patterns in the UN General Assembly: percentage voting coincidence with the US
Source: US State Secretary.

with the US than European countries and Canada. In 2007, their voting coincidence with the US fell below 40%. It stayed below 50% from 2001 to 2008, namely during the Bush administration. For Japan, the falling trend actually predates the Bush administration's retreat from multilateralism. Overall voting concordance with the US decreased from 67% in 1997 to 59% in 2000, 49% in 2002 and 37% in 2007. Unlike patterns in the mid-1990s, the US–Japan divergence extended to all major issues: Cuba, Palestine, disarmament, and human rights. These results contradict common assumptions about a solid US–Japan partnership at the United Nations. It reveals that Japan's Minervian identity is stronger than often assumed.

Canada's voting record deviated from the US position more often than the UK and France, and was very close to the German position for much of the period covered, but it rebounded to a higher level of coincidence after 2006. This signals the impact of the shift in government (Nossal, Chapter 4). As for European countries, the UK and France tend to vote more closely with the US than Germany; this pattern shows that there may be some spillover from the higher degree of cooperation among the US, France, and the UK at the UN Security Council, since all three are veto-holding permanent members. For comparative purposes, it is worth noting that Australia is consistently closest to the US, revealing a weaker Minervian identity. But Australia shows an important change in

2007, when the Kevin Rudd administration chose to return to multilateralism. Post-2007 Australia can be classified as Minervian.

Second, the Minervian voting behavior follows a general U-curve and indicates a steep drop in concordance with the US during the Bush administration. This reveals that the pattern has as much to do with US behavior as with Minervian preferences. In a way, the Minervian actors may have remained close to the previous internationalist agenda of the US (under the Clinton administration); it is the US that chose to depart from its previous behavior. There is a visible rebound under the Obama administration, although the gap remains with Minervian players.

Finally, we may note here the large gap between the US pattern of voting and China and India, even though the gap has narrowed under the Obama administration. This gap indicates that there is a way to go before we see a convergence of preferences and behavior between the Minervian clusters and these two important emerging powers that will shape tomorrow's world.

Note

* The author would like to acknowledge the great work by Atsuko Hatano (formerly Tamura) in putting together some of the data presented in this chapter.

1. Private conversation, February 2012.

3
The European Union as a Minervian Actor in Global Institution Building

Ian Manners

The political origins of the European Union's (EU) embrace of an agenda of global institution building are to be found in the internal (or "domestic") principles, which shape and inform its external policies. This agenda reflects the raison d'être of the EU itself: the pursuit of peace, prosperity, and progress over the past six decades. Hence while the period 1950 to 1969 focused on peace building and the period 1984 to 1992 on market building, the post-1990 period has seen the EU increasingly concentrate on progressive global institution building.

This chapter will first introduce the theories that provide our understanding of the EU as a Minervian actor, including both constitutive and causal theory. Then the chapter will look at the internal or domestic origins of the EU's norms, including economic, social, environmental, conflict, and political norms. Next, the chapter will consider the nine principles which shape the EU's external policy practices. Finally these practices will be the focus of a concluding discussion of Minervian power in action. This discussion will suggest that both constitutive and causal factors contribute to the EU as a Minervian actor in global institution building.

Theorizing the EU as a Minervian actor

Understanding the EU as a Minervian actor requires that we theorize its evolution both constitutively and causally. Constitutive theory contends that the subject of study is constituted or created within the context of a specific social relationship.[1] In contrast, causal theory contends that the object of study can be explained as a causal relationship between one factor and another.[2] From the perspective of constitutive theory, the evolution of the idea of the EU as a Minervian actor needs to be understood within the changing context of global politics. Hence the popularization of the idea of the EU as a "civilian power" during the 1970s must be understood within the context of the Cold War, with its constrictions on European political development.[3] Not only did the idea of civilian power constitute the self-image of the EU during the 1970s and 1980s, but it also survived the end of the Cold War, leading US commentators to distinguish between civilian, "Venusian" Europeans and military, "Martian" Americans.[4] In contrast, the idea of the EU as a normative, Minervian actor captures a preference for multilateralism and global institution building in the post-Cold War era.[5] What is constitutive about Minervian power is the way in which EU institutions, employees, and citizens start to conceive of themselves and behave as if they were normatively Minervian.[6] It may be possible to distinguish between some aspects of this constitutive self-image.[7]

Venus	Mars	Minerva
civilian	military	normative
feminine	masculine	metro sexual
international society	international anarchy	world society

Although such characterizations are clearly based on grossly simplified and essentialized stereotypes, they help clarify the aim of Minervians in global institutional building for a world society, rather than the Venusian emphasis on strengthening the international society of states, or Martian assumptions of international anarchy.[8]

From the perspective of causal theory, the evolution of the EU as a Minervian actor can be explained as the result of three determining factors.[9]

First, there is the role of political leadership reflecting domestic preferences within the EU member states, often reflected in intergovernmental bargaining in the Council of Ministers and at the European Council. The role of states, their governments, and leaders has long been an important factor in explaining the policies of the EU.[10]

Second, there is the role of competition between the EU and other international actors, as seen in the position taken by the Commission on the Doha trade negotiations in the World Trade Organization (WTO). The role of the supranational institutions of the EU, in particular the Commission, Court, and Parliament, has always been a central factor in explaining the policies of the EU.[11]

Third, there is the role of normative activism which goes beyond the actorness of the EU institutions or member states, for example in the EU's promotion of human rights agenda such as the international abolition of the death penalty. The role of cosmopolitical[12] or transnational factors has been of increasing importance in explaining the policies of the EU since the 1970s.[13] As the rest of the chapter will demonstrate, the combination of state/leadership, supranational/ competitive, and cosmopolitical/normative factors contribute to a causal explanation of the EU as a Minervian actor in global institution building.

Internal or domestic origins of the EU's norms

> The choice placed before Portugal is whether it resigns itself to staying in the group of the most conservative countries or if it embraces modernity.... This is an important step for Portugal towards becoming a more open, tolerant and just society. ... Portugal will now tackle abortion in the same way as most other developed European countries.[14]

The quotes from the former Portuguese Prime Minister José Sócrates illustrate the extent to which internal or domestic norms diffuse from other European countries, with positive allusions to "modernity," "open, tolerant and just society" in "other developed European countries." The internal or domestic origins of the EU's norms include the economic, social, environmental, conflict, and political norms which are part of the European experience of modernity and the construction of more open, tolerant, and just societies.

Internal or domestic economic norms in EU member states are marked by a belief in a social market economy featuring income redistribution, government intervention, and stakeholder capitalism.[15] These European economic norms are for more economic solidarity in comparison to most of the world. Comparative data illustrate how, over the past three decades average levels of EU inequality have remained significantly lower than most of the world, in particular China, Russia, and the US.[16] Clearly there are differences in Europe over this norm, with relatively higher inequality found in the UK and Italy compared to Denmark, Sweden, the Czech Republic, and Slovakia. A number of economists have pointed out that this discrepancy between Europe and Japan compared to the US and China is largely due to the income growth of the superrich – the top 1%, at the expense of the average worker.[17] These reports make clear the extent to which US median real wage and salary income has barely grown at all since 1966 and that even the "average US graduate fails to keep up with economy-wide productivity."[18] Such comparative data on inequality and relative poverty indicates that EU members share an internal or domestic norm for economic solidarity, particularly in comparison to China, the US, and Russia.[19]

Internal or domestic social norms in EU member states are regularly typified by the idea of a social model encompassing social legislation, social welfare, and social infrastructure investment.[20] Looking at comparative empirical data, European social norms support more social solidarity than in most of the rest of the world.[21] EU governments have the largest social support systems in the developed (OECD) world, alongside Switzerland, Norway, and Iceland. These figures also appear to give some indication of the inroads which neoliberalism has made in societies such as the Netherlands. Comparative data on social, educational, and health expenditure indicates that EU members share an internal or domestic norm for social solidarity, particularly in comparison to the non-European world.[22] An example of domestic social norms of solidarity motivating political leadership can be seen in the no votes to the EU's "Constitution for Europe" in France and the Netherlands, and the resulting calls for a more "social Europe."

Internal or domestic environmental norms in EU member states are frequently described with reference to "sustainable development" – an attempt to reconcile economic growth with protection of the environment in both the short and long term.[23] While many share these concerns for global warming and a more sustainable development, not all states around the world are able or willing to address one of the major causes of global warming – the emission of carbon dioxide. Comparisons of carbon dioxide emission levels over the past 25 years suggests that while EU per capita emissions are far above those of the developing world, they are less than half those of the US, Australia, and Canada.[24] In this respect the EU, New Zealand, and Japan lead the developed world in terms of carbon efficiency.

Internal or domestic EU member state norms for resolving conflict can be expressed as a commitment to a more "sustainable peace" – resolving both the structural causes and violent symptoms of conflict.[25] In order to make sense of the consistencies and contrasts of preferences for sustainable peace, it is worth comparing average levels of development assistance disbursed by the EU member states with other OECD donors.[26] Although development assistance is a very proximate means of looking at conflict resolution norms, together with comparable figures on military expenditure and UN peacekeeping forces, it suggests some internal or domestic European norms.

Following Norway and Switzerland, the EU provides the highest levels of OECD development assistance, although increasingly falling short of the UN target of 0.7% of the gross national product (GNP). Despite these mixed contributions, even the average levels of 0.4% of GNP for EU donors compare favorably with the OECD average of 0.33% of GNP, as well as with the Japanese and US levels below 0.3% of GNP.

Internal or domestic political norms in EU member states can be articulated through the notion of "cosmopolitical supranationality" – the principles of multilayered politics shaped by a vibrant international civil society, more equal rights for women, the pooling of sovereignty, and supranational law.[27] The question of the extent to which these preferences are shared or promoted, both within the EU and in the wider world, becomes particularly important here. In order to get an indication of European preferences for the multilateral processes of cosmopolitical supranationality, it is interesting to look at comparative data for participation in international law.[28] As such data illustrate, the average number of significant international treaties ratified by EU member states is the highest in the world, with only New Zealand, Brazil, Nigeria, Australia, and Russia coming relatively close. Although the ratification of such international treaties says very little about standards within the state, it is an important symbol of commitment, which may prove more important than the state had originally intended.

An example of domestic political norms motivating political leadership can be seen in the attempts by EU states in the Like-Minded Group to create and ratify the International Criminal Court in The Hague. While the UK and France were initially outside of this group and Germany was a strong advocate of the court, former German Chancellor Gerhard Schröder, former French President Jacques Chirac, and former British Prime Minister Tony Blair eventually supported its creation, with Britain offering to incarcerate accused war criminal Charles Taylor if he was convicted.[29]

EU principles and competition with other international actors

EU partnership and dialogue with third countries will promote common values of: respect for human rights, fundamental freedoms, peace, democracy, good governance, gender equality, the rule of law, solidarity and justice. The EU is strongly committed to effective multilateralism whereby all the world's nations share responsibility for development.[30]

The 2006 European Consensus on Development, announced in a joint statement by the European Parliament, Council, and Commission illustrates the extent to which the EU's external policy practices are shaped by the nine principles of peace, freedom, democracy, human rights, rule of law, equality, social solidarity, sustainable development, and good governance.[31] The promotion of such principles by the Council, Commission, Court, and Parliament is often controversial, with competition coming from other international actors. Competition is particularly intense with the "axis of ego," that is, the three key powers with permanent seats in the UN Security Council (here the US, Russia, and China), who consider themselves exceptional or super-powers and above international norms and law.[32] Thus, while the EU prime principle of peace, as well as core principles of freedom, democracy, human rights, and rule of law, are broadly accepted within the UN international system, the particular EU interpretation, indivisibility and application are often highly contested. The EU faces strong opposition in its promotion of the first, second, and third-generation rights of equality, social solidarity, sustainable development, and good governance.

The prime EU principle of sustainable peace emphasizes addressing the roots or causes of conflict, mirroring the European experience of ensuring that war "becomes not merely unthinkable, but materially impossible." The EU policy emphasis is placed on development aid, trade, interregional cooperation, political dialogue, and enlargement as part of a more holistic approach to conflict prevention. However, the EU's growing civilian and military operational capacities also have a sustainable peace mission with its focus on "peace-keeping, conflict prevention and strengthening international security in accordance with the principles of the United Nations Charter."[33]

The second EU principle is social freedom. Freedom within the EU operates within a distinctive socio-legal context. Thus, freedom is always just one of several rights held alongside other, equally important, principles such as democracy, rule of law, and human rights. Therefore, within the EU social freedom is circumscribed by the need to ensure that other principles are not compromised by unwarranted freedoms, such as anti-social behavior, hate crimes, inflammatory speech, and pornography. The wider implications of EU social freedom are significant, not least in references to "protection of children's rights" as a foreign policy objective, as EU extraterritorial legislation on "sex tourism" illustrates.[34]

The third EU principle is consensual democracy. Consensual democracy is the operating principle within the majority of EU member states and includes proportional representation (PR) electoral systems, coalition governments, and power sharing amongst parties. Similarly, the EU itself is a consensual form of polity, with PR and power sharing in the European Parliament, non-majoritarian voting in the Council (either Qualified Majority Voting or unanimity), and power sharing amongst all the member states. The EU has helped to spread consensual democracy into central and eastern Europe as part of the transition and accession processes.[35]

The fourth EU principle is associative human rights. Associative human rights include both individual human rights and collective human rights. These are associative because they emphasize the interdependence between individual rights such as freedom of expression and group rights such as religion or belief. The associative nature of EU human rights has developed since 1973 through the 1986 Declaration of Foreign Ministers of the Community on Human Rights and the 1991 Resolution of the Council on Human Rights, Democracy and Development.[36] All of these documents emphasize the universality and indivisibility of these associative human rights with consensual democracy, supranational rule of law, and social solidarity.

The fifth EU principle is the supranational rule of law. The EU principle of the rule of law is supranational in three senses – communitarian, international, and cosmopolitan. First, the EU principle of communitarian law promotes the pooling of sovereignty through the *acquis communautaire* – the supranational rule of law within the EU. Second, the EU principle of international law encourages participation by the EU and its member states in supranational law above and beyond the EU.[37] Third, the EU principle of cosmopolitan law advances the development and participation of the EU and its member states in humanitarian law and rights applicable to individuals.[38]

The sixth EU principle is inclusive equality involving a more open-ended and uninhibited understanding of which groups are particularly subject to discrimination.[39] Hence, the 2000 Charter of Fundamental Rights of the Union included references to the prohibition of "*any discrimination* based on *any ground* such as sex, race, colour, ethnic or social origin, genetic features, language, religion or belief, political or any other opinion, membership of a national minority, property, birth, disability, age or sexual orientation."[40] One weakness with the implementation of this principle is the extent to which discrimination based on nationality is still widespread in a majority of member states. This is particularly true of employment practices in consensual societies that promote homosociality.[41] The seventh EU principle is social solidarity. The extensive understanding of social solidarity became clear as the objectives of article 3.3 of the Treaty on European Union (TEU) refers to "balanced economic growth, [and] a social market economy, aiming at full employment and social progress," combating "social exclusion," as well as promoting "social justice and protection," inter-generational solidarity, and social solidarity among (and between) member states. The principle of social solidarity goes beyond inner-EU relations to inform and shape EU development and trade policies as article 3.5 of the TEU also illustrates when it refers to the Union's contribution to "solidarity and mutual respect among peoples, free and fair trade, eradication of poverty."[42]

The eighth EU principle is sustainable development, which places an emphasis on the dual problems of balance and integration. This EU principle is intended to provide a balance between uninhibited economic growth and biocentric ecological crisis: "it seeks to promote balanced and sustainable development" (preamble to the Charter of Fundamental Rights) and "shall work for the sustainable development of Europe based on balanced economic growth" (article 3.3, TEU). In parallel, the principle also involves the integration, or mainstreaming, of sustainable development into the policies and activities of the Union (articles 11 and 37 of the Treaty on the Functioning of the European Union, TFEU).[43] The EU seeks to promote these principles of sustainable development beyond Europe through its enlargement, development, trade, environmental, and foreign policies (articles 3.5 and 21.2 of the TEU).

The ninth EU principle is good governance emphasizing quality, representation, participation, social partnership, transparency, and accountability in "the democratic life of the Union" (article 11, TEU). The EU principle of good governance has two distinctive elements that have both significant internal and external consequences – the participation of civil society and the strengthening of multilateral cooperation. Since the Commission Presidency of Romano Prodi (1999–2004), significant emphasis has been placed on the promotion of good governance through the participation of civil society in order to encourage openness and transparency, as well as to facilitate democratic participation (article 11, TEU and 15, TFEU). In parallel, the unilateral invasion of Iraq has ensured that member states have strengthened their commitments to the promotion of "an international system based on stronger multilateral cooperation and good global governance" (article 21.2, TEU).[44]

Minervian Europe in action

The imperial unilateralism the Bush administration has pursued during the past five years has failed. Effective multilateralism, which European governments offer as their alternative, needs more active diplomacy. Strengthening international institutions, from the UN to the International Monetary Fund and World Trade Organisation, requires them to compromise on national status to accommodate rising powers.... [The EU Presidency] will need above all to show that European governments can reconcile national interests with broader international strategies, to pursue the "effective multilateralism" EU member states claim to support.[45]

The European fallout from the US invasion of Iraq in March 2003 was eventually to lead to an agreement on the December 2003 European Security Strategy emphasizing "effective multilateralism."[46] As William Wallace has observed, the EU Minervian approach offered an alternative to the failed Bush administration's strategy through effective multilateralism based on active diplomacy, a strengthening of international institutions and broader international strategies recognizing and embracing the normative activism of transnational groups. This section will focus on EU Minervian power in action by examining the way in which norms, principles, and practices drive global institution building. The EU exerts its Minervian normative influence through six mechanisms: contagion, information, procedure, direct transfer, overt presence, and through a cultural filter.[47]

Normative contagion almost entirely takes place through the diffusion of ideas from the EU to other political actors. An example of the EU's Minervian power through contagion can be found in the ways in which ideas and means of regional integration have diffused to other continents. Hence, ideas such as the creation of a "common high authority," "four freedoms," and even "single currency" are seen in other regions of the world as being so strong that they are worthy of imitation. Thus in both South America (Mercosur created in 1991, and UNASUR in 2011) and Africa (the move from the Organization of African Unity to the African Union in 2002) we see regional organizations being created in order to imitate the perceived worth of the EU.

As other chapters in this book illustrate, the diffusion of norms from the EU and its Minervian partners can be seen in action in the cases of the Kyoto protocol, the UNESCO declaration of cultural diversity, and the Ottawa landmines convention. The role of the EU in promoting the 1997 Kyoto protocol to the 1992 Framework Convention on Climate Change suggests that the "environmental imperative" drove the EU to "lead by example."[48] In the case of cultural diversity, the lead taken by the EU on issues of "cultural exception" since the 1994 Marrakesh ministerial meeting found form in the 2000 Council of Europe declaration on Cultural Diversity and the unprecedented adherence of the EU to the 2005 UNESCO Convention on the Protection and Promotion of the Diversity of Cultural Expressions as a regional organization of economic integration.[49] The third example of contagious diffusion suggests that the role of six EU NGOs from 1992 onwards was crucial in encouraging member states to commit to the International Campaign to Ban Landmines and agree to the 1997 Treaty of Ottawa.[50]

The informational diffusion of norms occurs through references to a range of strategic communications, such as new policy initiatives by the EU, and declaratory communications, such as initiatives from the presidency of the EU or the presidents of the Commission. An example of informational diffusion in the EU's normative power can be found in the December 2003 European Security Strategy with its reference to the "complex causes" of terrorism, including "the pressures of modernisation, cultural, social and political crises, and the alienation of young people living in foreign societies." The diffusion of such norms, both inside and outside the EU institutions leads to the spread of the idea that the EU might indeed be a Minervian actor, rather than an imperial one.

Four examples of EU strategic communications illustrate its normative impact: the October 2003 Commission communication, the December 2003 European Security Strategy, the September 2004 Human Security Doctrine, and the December 2008 Report on the Implementation of the European Security Strategy. The October 2003 Commission communication on "the choice of multilateralism" marked the first conscious step after the March 2003 unilateral invasion of Iraq to convey the centrality of the UN system to the EU: "effective multilateralism...means taking global rules seriously, whether they concern the preservation of peace or the limitation of carbon emissions; it means helping other countries to implement and abide by these rules; it means engaging actively in multilateral forums, and promoting a forward looking agenda that is not limited to a narrow defence of national interests."⁵¹

By December 2003 the European Council went further with a European Security Strategy (ESS), which announced the strategic objective of effective multilateralism: "[i]n a world of global threats, global markets and global media, our security and prosperity increasingly depend on an effective multilateral system. The development of a stronger international society, well functioning international institutions and a rule-based international order is our objective."⁵² The September 2004 Barcelona Report proposed a new human security doctrine for the implementation of the European Security Strategy including the principle of effective multilateralism which has three basic aspects:

[f]irstly, it means a commitment to work with international institutions, and through the procedures of international institutions.... Secondly, multilateralism entails a commitment to common ways of working including agreed rules and norms: creating common rules and norms, solving problems through rules and co-operation, and enforcing the rules.... Thirdly, multilateralism also has to include coordination, rather than duplication or rivalry.⁵³

The December 2008 Report on the Implementation of the 2003 ESS, in the section "Partnerships for Effective Multilateralism" argued that "the ESS called for Europe to contribute to a more effective multilateral order around the world. Since 2003, we have strengthened our partnerships in pursuit of that objective."

The procedural diffusion of norms takes place through the institutionalization of relationships between the EU and third parties, involving political partnership as found in interregional cooperation agreements, membership of an international organization, association agreements, or enlargement of the EU itself. Since 1995 these relationships with over 120 countries have systematically included an "essential elements" clause referring to human rights and democracy, although in cases such as India and Burma these prove extremely controversial.⁵⁴ Examples of procedural diffusion in the EU's normative power can be found in the 13 association agreements identified by the Commission's DG Trade in July 2005 – including Turkey, Macedonia, Croatia, Egypt, Israel, Jordan, Morocco, the Palestinian Authority, Tunisia, the Overseas Countries and Territories, Chile, the Euro-Mediterranean Association Agreement, and Albania. The EU's layers of institutionalized relationships include accession procedures, the European Neighbourhood Policy, and GSP+ arrangements. Although these relationships include a variety of different procedures, they all include discussion and diffusion of human rights, the environment, and core labor standards to varying degrees.

Examples of the procedural diffusion of norms include the essential element of effective implementation of UN core human rights conventions, International Labor Organization (ILO) core labor standards conventions, and key environmental conventions in the EU's relations with its European Neighbourhood Policy (ENP) partners.[55] Similarly, the arrangements applying a scheme of General Schemes of Preferences + (GSP+) for non-LDC (less developed countries) developing countries include the promotion of the principles found in the core UN and ILO human and labor rights conventions, as well as international conventions related to the environment and good governance.[56]

The diffusion of norms through direct transfer occurs when the EU is involved in humanitarian aid and technical assistance. The EU is able to directly transfer its norms through "conditionality clauses," but is equally likely to be the result of more "grass roots" engagement of EU agencies and support for NGOs on the ground. An interesting example of direct diffusion can be found in the April 2006 decision by Benita Ferrero-Waldner, External Relations Commissioner, to suspend payments to the newly elected Hamas government, but to increase aid to the Palestinian people through direct payments for aid to refugees and for fuel costs. Such direct diffusion is thus most obvious in development aid and peacebuilding activities, with examples such as Aceh, Darfur, and Palestine illustrating how these two policy areas are often deeply intertwined.[57] It can also occur through the Rapid Reaction Mechanism, humanitarian aid provided by ECHO, and the launching of a monitoring mission and an election observation mission in post-tsunami Aceh. Here the achievement of rule of law, human rights, and democracy were part of the overall peace process and humanitarian effort.

The overt diffusion of norms occurs as a result of the physical presence of the EU in third states and international organizations. Examples of overt diffusion include the role of Commission delegations and embassies of member states, or it may involve the presence of the Troïka of foreign ministers, the president of the Commission, or even monitoring missions like those deployed in the former Yugoslavia and Aceh. Attempts at the overt diffusion of human rights can be seen in the EU support for the creation of the UN Human Rights Council in 2006 and the more EU human rights mission to the Philippines in 2007.

Alongside Amnesty International and Human Rights Watch, the EU and its associated countries had pushed hard for the replacement of the discredited UN Human Rights Commission (HRC) by a new, strengthened UN Human Rights Council in 2006.[58] However within a year the overt presence of the EU at the UN was felt again as the EU members of the HRC threatened to pull out in order to prevent rights abusers on the Council, such as China, Cuba, Russia, Saudi Arabia, and Tunisia, from significantly weakening it.[59]

The final factor shaping and transforming the diffusion of EU norms is the cultural filter. The cultural filter is based on the interplay between the construction of knowledge and the creation of social and political identity by the subjects of norm diffusion. The chapters by Feditchkina (Chapter 13) and Sakaguchi (Chapter 8) on biodiversity illustrate the cultural filter at work. The refusal of the US to ratify the 2000 Cartagena Protocol on Biosafety, the 1992 Convention on Biological Diversity, or the 1997 Kyoto Protocol to the Framework Convention on Climate Change suggests that the local knowledge and identity construction regarding the environment is a powerful cultural filter. Furthermore the chapters by Flowers on landmines (Chapter 7), Coleman on R2P (Chapter 9), and Lee on the ICC (Chapter 12) suggest that the construction of sovereignty acts as a strong cultural filter to norm diffusion promoting global institution building. In all three of these cases Canada, Japan, and EU members eventually found themselves promoting global institution building, while facing great resistance from global opponents.

Conclusion

These six factors, together with the brief examples, illustrate the way in which EU Minervian power in action is shaped by both the causal elements of state/leadership, supranational/competitive, and cosmopolitical/normative, as well as the constitutive element of a EU normative self-image. This becomes more evident in the discussions of the merits of effective multilateralism as both a means and a goal.

National leaders use effective multilateralism as a tool to promote internal or domestic norms by state leaders, while the EU's supranational institutions see effective multilateralism as a means of overcoming internal divisions and of promoting an alternative global vision to that of the US.

In addition to these two causal factors, effective multilateralism also becomes a means by which transnational groups of normative activists seek to harness the EU to promote global institution building. They are able to play on the understanding of effective multilateralism as the constitutive expression of what the EU actually is – "a hybrid of supranational and international forms of governance which transcends Westphalian norms."[60]

It is this form of effective multilateralism embracing the active diplomacy of states, the strengthening of supranational and international institutions, and the engagement with the cosmopolitical and transnational activists that captures the EU as a Minervian actor in global institution building.

Notes

1. Frost 1996: 138; see also Wendt 1999.
2. Hay 2002: 32; Burnham et al. 2004: 27.
3. Duchêne 1972.
4. Kagan 2003.
5. Manners 2000a, 2002, 2010; Manners and Whitman 2003.
6. Diez and Pace 2011.
7. Manners 2000a: 29, 2002: 240; Manners and Whitman 2003: 391; Khanna 2004.
8. see Bull 1977; Diez and Whitman 2002; Diez et al. 2011 for these distinctions.
9. See Manners *forthcoming* for a discussion of these determining factors.
10. Wallace 1971, 1973.
11. Camps 1964, 1966.
12. A cosmopolitical approach "can thus be seen as an approach trying to combine communitarianism with cosmopolitanism... Traditional cosmopolitanism... relies on a discourse of individual rights; while communitarianism is based on a discourse of social rights which is often expressed in exclusive localism. Both run the risk of substituting ethics for politics." Kinnvall and Nesbitt-Larking 2011: 92. See Manners 2008: 47, 2011: 232 and 246, *forthcoming*.
13. Strange 1971; Webb 1977.
14. José Sócrates, Portuguese Prime Minister, quoted in Elaine Sciolino, "Portugal Votes to Soften Abortion Law," *International Herald Tribune*, February 11, 2007; and Peter Wise, "Portugal Takes Steps to Legalise Abortion," *Financial Times*, February 13, 2007.
15. Stjernø 2005; Manners 2006a: 21–22, 2007: 24.
16. Bengtsson et al. 2012.
17. Piketty and Saez 2006; Levy and Temin 2007; Sawhill and Morton 2007. See also "Special Report: Inequality and the American Dream," *The Economist*, June 17–23, 2006, 11–12, 24–26.
18. Dew-Becker and Gordon 2005; Levy and Temin 2007; see Krishna Guha and Alex Barker, "US Graduates Are not Immune to Income Inequality," *Financial Times*, June 5, 2007, 8.

19. Manners 2006a: 22; Bengtsson et al. 2012.
20. Michalski 2006; Manners 2006a: 23–24, 2007: 28.
21. Bengtsson et al. 2012.
22. Manners 2006a: 23–24; Bengtsson et al. 2012.
23. Baker 2006; Manners 2006a: 23–24.
24. Manners 2006a: 23–26; Bengtsson et al. 2012.
25. Peck 1998; Manners 2006a: 26–28, 2007: 31.
26. Manners 2007: 26–28; Bengtsson et al. 2012.
27. Beck 2003; Habermas 2003; Manners 2006a: 28–31.
28. See Manners 2006a: 31; Bengtsson et al. 2012.
29. Scheipers and Sicurelli 2007; Carola Hoyos, "us Warned not to Risk Rift with Europe Over Treaty," *Financial* Times, May 27, 2002; "France Puts US Under Pressure to Accept War Crimes Court," *euobserver.com*, March 24, 2005; Niki Tait, "War Crimes Trial Tests International Justice," *Financial Times*, June 4, 2007, 4; Lee *forthcoming*.
30. European Parliament, Council and Commission 2006: 3.
31. See also the Union's "values" and "the principles ... which it seeks to advance in the wider world" in articles 2, 3.5, and 21 of the Treaty on European Union.
32. Manners 2006b: 410.
33. Lucarelli and Menotti 2006; Bjorkdahl 2011; Richmond et al. 2011.
34. Manners 2009a.
35. Balfour 2006.
36. Jurado 2006.
37. Manners and Whitman 2003: 399.
38. Manners 2002: 241.
39. Petö and Manners 2006.
40. Article 21, Charter of Fundamental Rights of the Union 2000, 13; emphasis added.
41. Roper 1996.
42. see Bonaglia et al. 2006; Birchfield 2011; Manners 2009b.
43. See Baker 2006; Lightfoot and Burchell 2004, 2005.
44. See van den Hoven 2006, Manners 2009b.
45. William Wallace, "Europe Should Fill the Global Leadership Gap," *Financial Times*, September 27, 2006.
46. Ortega 2005; Whitman 2006, 2010.
47. Manners 2000a: 35, 2002: 244–45.
48. Manners 2000b: 39–49; Vogler 2005; Baker 2006.
49. Ferri 2005; Chan-Tibergien 2006.
50. Long 2002; Dover 2006.
51. Commission of the European Communities 2003: 3.
52. Solana 2003: 9.
53. Barcelona Study Group 2004: 16–17. See also Martin 2011 and Remacle *forthcoming*.
54. Jo Johnson, "eu-India Trade Pact Stumbles on Human Rights Rider," *Financial Times*, March 5, 2007; John Burton and Roel Landingin, "Rifts over Charter for ASEAN May Hit Regional Integration," *Financial* Times, July 31, 2007.
55. Commission of the European Communities 2004: 12–13, 32–35.
56. Council of the European Union 2005.

57. Manners 2007.
58. Mark Turner, "un Seeks to Mollify US Over Rights Council," *Financial Times*, March 11, 2007.
59. Frances Williams, "eu in Rift with Developing Nations over Human Rights," *Financial Times*, June 15, 2007.
60. Manners 2002: 240.

4
Canada's Minervian Moment: Global Activism and Domestic Politics

Kim Richard Nossal

Beginning in the early 1990s, just as the Cold War was coming to an end, the Canadian government began to embrace an active – and activist – foreign policy agenda, marked by an embrace of multilateralism that went well beyond Canada's traditional and historical attachment to international cooperation.[1] During this period Canada made a sustained effort to transform the norms, the institutions, and the leadership of the global system. The most prominent of these initiatives are among those examined in more detail in this volume: the Kyoto Protocol to the UN Framework Convention on Climate Change, the global ban on antipersonnel landmines, and the creation of an International Criminal Court. But, as I will show, Canada's transformative foreign policy agenda went well beyond these high-profile initiatives to include a range of initiatives that fit well into the "Minervian" analysis outlined by the editor.

However, Canada's embrace of a Minervian foreign policy was momentary. While we can see some early indications of a Minervian agenda in the final years of the Progressive Conservative prime minister, Brian Mulroney, the transformative agenda really flowered under Jean Chrétien, the Liberal prime minister who came to power after the October 1993 general elections. In the mid- and late-1990s, Chrétien, and his foreign minister from 1996 to 2000, Lloyd Axworthy, pursued a range of policy initiatives designed to entrench new norms, new patterns of global governance, and indeed new loci of global political leadership. The initiatives of the late 1990s were continued after Axworthy retired from politics in 2000, and embraced by Chrétien's successor, Paul Martin, when he took over as Liberal Party leader in November 2003, and as prime minister the following month. However, much of this Minervian behavior came to an end after the Liberals were defeated in the January 2006 elections and a new Conservative government under the leadership of Stephen Harper took office in February. Once in power, the Harper government abandoned the Minervian foreign policy agenda of the Liberals, even though it clearly remained popular among Canadians, at least when they were responding to pollsters" questions. But in the years since 2006, and particularly since achieving a majority in the 2011 elections, the Harper government consistently pursued a more muscular, "Mars-like" approach to global politics that was marked by the celebration of the use of force and a concomitant skepticism about the United Nations and multilateralism (Nossal 2013). The lack of enthusiasm that the Harper government has for Minervian-style multilateral engagement is palpable.

This chapter examines Canada's Minervian moment. It argues that we can best explain the rise – and decline – of this policy orientation by looking at three key variables. First, we have to see the Canadian foreign policy agenda as shaped by global systemic factors. There is no coincidence that Ottawa's embrace of a Minervian approach emerged as the Cold War came to an end, flowered in the mid- and late-1990s when the optimism about the possibility of a new global order was at its peak, and then was increasingly abandoned in the evolving global order after the attacks of September 11, 2001.

But while global systemic change was a necessary condition, it was not a sufficient condition. To explain Canada's enthusiasm for a Minervian approach to foreign policy during the brief post-Cold War era from 1991 to 2001, we also have to look at domestic politics, and the dynamic created by the embrace of this foreign policy agenda. I will argue that the transformation of Canadian politics in the early 1990s – and in particular the fragmentation of the national political party system that left the Liberal Party of Canada in a hegemonic position throughout the 1990s – was crucial for an understanding of the political "space" that was opened for the pursuit of a Minervian foreign policy.

Third, we also have to look at the idiosyncratic variable, for it mattered that Jean Chrétien led the Liberal Party, and it was significant that Chrétien selected Lloyd Axworthy as his minister of foreign affairs in 1996. When the necessary variable changed – when the relative freedom of the post-Cold War era was replaced by the tighter discipline of the post-9/11 era – the domestic space for a Minervian approach narrowed dramatically, giving rise to a barrage of criticism that increasingly delegitimized Chrétien's Minervian agenda. The Conservative Party of Canada that came to power in January 2006 had little sympathy for a Minervian approach; when the Conservatives achieved a majority in the May 2011 elections, it signaled the end of Canada's Minervian moment.

The rise and decline of Canada's Minervian agenda

While we associate Canada's transformative foreign policy agenda with the Liberal governments of Jean Chrétien (1993–2003) and Paul Martin (2003–2006), some of the roots of the Minervian agenda can ironically be traced to the Progressive Conservative government of Brian Mulroney, prime minister from September 1984 to June 1993. Certainly the good governance initiative embraced by Mulroney in the fall of 1991 represented a radical departure in Canada's human rights policy (Keating and Gecelovsky 2001), and foreshadowed the efforts by Mulroney's Liberal successors, Chrétien and Martin, to promote the export of political values such as democracy. Likewise, Jennifer Ross (2001) has argued that the roots of the "human security" agenda pressed by Axworthy in the late 1990s can be found in the Central American policies of Joe Clark, Mulroney's Secretary of State for External Affairs (as Canada's foreign minister was known prior to 1993). Finally, it should be noted that Mulroney was the first Canadian prime minister to press for a shift in the norm of Westphalian sovereignty: as early as November 1990, Mulroney was arguing that "The conventions of national sovereignty are becoming too narrow a base from which to resolve the broadening global and regional problems" (Michaud and Nossal 2001, p. 19). It was a theme reiterated by both Mulroney and Clark's successor, Barbara McDougall. But it was not until the general election of October 25, 1993 that we saw a marked shift in the foreign policy agenda.

The signal change was the embrace of policy initiatives designed to entrench new norms in global politics, to introduce new patterns and institutions of global governance, and indeed to challenge the locus of global political leadership. The most prominent of these initiatives are explored in greater length by other contributors to this volume: the global ban on antipersonnel landmines is discussed by Petrice Flowers in Chapter 7, and the creation of an International Criminal Court is examined by Joanne Lee (Chapter 12). Ottawa's policies on each of these initiatives confirms the essentially Minervian nature of the Canadian approach.

But Canada's transformative agenda under the Chrétien government went much further. First, Axworthy also sought to confront the dominance of the state-centric focus of national security by explicitly challenging the dominant norm of state sovereignty and embracing the concept of human security as a cardinal principle of Canadian foreign policy (Axworthy 2003, part 4).[2] He first articulated this approach less than a year after his appointment to the portfolio (1997), and polished it in the years afterwards, finally publishing it in April 1999 as a policy statement[3] – just as Canadian jet fighters were dropping bombs on targets in the Federal Republic of Yugoslavia to protect Kosovar Albanians from Serbian militias, and shortly before Canadian soldiers would join the Australian-led International Force for East Timor (INTERFET) intervention to protect East Timorese from Indonesian militias.[4] Canada also provided the impetus – and strong support – to the creation of an international blue ribbon panel to explore the ways in which state sovereignty could be re-interpreted to permit a more robust response to the kind of atrocity crimes witnessed in the 1990s. The report of the International Commission on Intervention and State Sovereignty, entitled *The Responsibility to Protect*, came out after Axworthy had left politics (International Commission on Intervention and State Sovereignty 2001; Axworthy 2003, pp. 179–89), but was endorsed by the Chrétien government and embraced enthusiastically by Paul Martin when he became prime minister in 2003.[5]

Importantly, throughout this period the Chrétien and Martin governments also posed a number of challenges to the hegemony of the United States. Between 1993 and 2006, Ottawa openly opposed American policy on a number of issues, both large and small.

In military affairs, Canada pushed against the US on antipersonnel landmines, on nuclear weapons, on ballistic missile defense (BMD), on the expansion of the North Atlantic Treaty Organization (NATO), and on the issue of regime change in Iraq after 9/11. Axworthy's bold and unorthodox landmines diplomacy – the so-called Ottawa Process[6] – was highly successful at delegitimizing antipersonnel landmines as a weapon of war, but ironically its success depended on alienating Washington.[7] In a similar vein, the Chrétien government was openly critical of nuclear weapons; Axworthy was an eager supporter of German efforts to get NATO to adopt a "no-first-use" policy in 1998 before, in his words, Canada "slammed into two brick walls" – the arrival of the Bush administration in January 2001 and the attacks of 9/11 (2003, pp. 360–65). Axworthy's opposition to nuclear weapons reflected a wider strain of antipathy toward space-based weaponry within the Liberal party; the Chrétien government consistently opposed the pursuit of a BMD program by the US. But perhaps the most important challenge to American leadership was the Chrétien government's decision to stay out of the US-led invasion of Iraq in March 2003, arguing that Canada would not participate unless there was Security Council authorization for the invasion.[8]

But the Chrétien government also challenged the US on non-military issues. As Jennifer Chan demonstrates in Chapter 5, Canada was increasingly at the forefront of what grew into a global movement to protect "cultural industries" from American-backed efforts to liberalize the global cultural marketplace, triggered by a dispute over *Sports Illustrated* (Sands 2001). On both Kyoto and the creation of the International Criminal Court,[9] Ottawa took a different approach from that of Washington (Bernstein 2002).

On Cuba, Chrétien went out of his way to oppose the US. While every Canadian government since 1960 had quarreled with the efforts of the United States to isolate the regime of Fidel Castro Ruz, the Chrétien government took the dispute to a higher level. Ottawa dramatically increased Canadian development assistance to Havana, and openly opposed legislation passed by the US Congress, colloquially known as Helms-Burton,[10] designed to increase the punishment of those who maintained business dealings with Cuba.

The Chrétien government even weighed in on the use of capital punishment in the US, with Axworthy calling on the then governor of Texas, George W. Bush, to grant executive clemency to Stan Faulder, a Canadian citizen in Texas who had been sentenced to death for a 1975 murder.[11] While a relatively minor incident, the Faulder case demonstrates the willingness of the Chrétien government to challenge the US on the norms of domestic punishment (and no doubt contributed in a minor way to the frostiness in Canada–US relations after Governor Bush became President Bush in 2001).

When Paul Martin took over as prime minister in December 2003, this transformative orientation in global policy continued. Martin embraced a foreign policy agenda that stressed new institutions of global leadership, notably his proposal for an L-20 group of leaders that would in essence challenge the G8 (Knight 2005, pp. 105–7), and his pressing for what can be seen as an outgrowth of Axworthy's human security agenda – the Responsibility to Protect. Moreover, Martin continued to oppose BMD and the war in Iraq, announcing in February 2005 that Canada would not be joining the BMD program – but not providing any reason or explanation for the decision other than to assert that BMD was "not in Canada's interests."[12] In addition, Martin made American opposition to Kyoto a key plank of the Liberal party's platform for the January 2006 election, going so far as to openly try to shame the administration of George W. Bush at an international conference in December 2005. He publicly excoriated the Bush administration for its refusal to embrace Kyoto, calling on Americans to heed the "global conscience" on climate change (choosing not to mention the fact that Canada was much further away from meeting its Kyoto targets than the US was). In a further snub to Bush, Martin arranged a special photo opportunity with Bill Clinton.[13] With the defeat of the Martin Liberals in the January 2006 elections, much of the Minervian foreign policy of the previous decade came to an end. After the Conservative government under Stephen Harper took office in February 2006, there was considerable continuity in some areas of policy, such as defense policy (Nossal 2007a). But in those areas of foreign policy we can identify as Minervian, there was little evidence that the Harper Conservatives had any interest in pushing a Minervian agenda. On the contrary, the Harper government backed away from a key initiative that had been embraced by both Chrétien and Martin – the Kyoto accords. Even though the Conservatives had only a minority in the House of Commons, and even though all the opposition parties were openly supportive of Kyoto, Harper left in no doubt that he had no intention of meeting the commitments under the protocol embraced by the Liberals when they were in power, arguing that the Kyoto targets were impossible to meet (Schwanen 2006). And while the Conservatives openly opposed the US on some key issues, such as rejecting outright the American contention that water between Canadian islands in the Arctic constituted an international strait, the mood of the Canada–US relationship changed dramatically. To be sure, in office Harper offered little support for the American mission in Iraq, but the Conservative government did nothing to oppose or question American hegemony. Most importantly, after February 2006, there were no new global governance initiatives from Ottawa comparable to the kind of initiatives embraced by both the Chrétien and Martin governments. In short, if Canada was one of the leading Minervian actors in the 1990s, that Minervian enthusiasm did not survive the change of government that occurred in 2006.

Explaining Canada's Minervian moment

When Lloyd Axworthy articulated his "doctrine" in the mid-1990s (1997) – and when he reflected on those years in his 2003 book, *Navigating a New World* – he focused on the importance of the changes in the international system as galvanizing factors that prompted the need for a "new" approach. Growing global inequities, the "spectre of ecological disaster," "messy internal ethnic conflicts," threats of different sorts from international terrorists and drug dealers – all these, Axworthy argued, created a vacuum and "an obvious demand for more effective international teamwork to meet all these challenges" (2003, pp. 2–3).

While Hampson and Oliver are correct to note that Axworthy's premise that the end of the Cold War had changed the nature of international politics was questionable (1998, pp. 382–85), there is little doubt that the Canadian agenda was affected by the changes that came with the end of the rivalry between the US and the Soviet Union. Axworthy may have felt that the new global order created a *demand* for a different kind of global politics; but we can see in retrospect that that order created an essential *permissiveness* in global politics between 1990 and 2001. As the disciplines of the great-power rivalry of the Cold War dissipated, smaller actors like Canada were increasingly freed to explore new patterns of global governance and new ways of relating to the emerging hyperpower. It was possible to cross the US – or to question American global leadership – in ways that would have been either unthinkable in the Cold War era.

However, the end of the Cold War was a necessary, but not sufficient condition for the embrace of a Minervian foreign policy. The sufficient condition is to be found in the nature of domestic politics in Canada in the 1990s that saw the complete collapse of the Progressive Conservative party in the 1993 elections, the fragmentation of the Canadian party system, and the return of the Liberal party to a position of political hegemony in the 1990s. The dominance of the Liberal Party in Canadian politics throughout the 1990s and the fragmentation of opposition voices allowed the idiosyncratic preferences of the key political leaders – the prime minister and the minister of foreign affairs – to dominate.

The idiosyncratic factor is of crucial importance in understanding the kind of foreign policy pursued by the Canadian government in the 1990s. The fact that Jean Chrétien led the Liberals during this period mattered; a Québécois, Chrétien not only had a historically grounded distrust of military force in world affairs,[14] but also, and more importantly, a profound understanding of the Canadian body politic and a keen capacity to use that understanding to advance the electoral interests of the Liberal Party. He understood, for example, the degree to which anti-American sentiment, which is deeply entrenched in Canadian political culture, particularly in urban English-speaking Canada, could be manipulated for electoral advantage. Even if Chrétien did not think in "Minervian" terms, he understood that an essentially "Minervian" foreign policy – one that articulated new patterns of multilateralism and global governance in a way that would diminish the role of the US as a global hegemon – would be deeply appealing to anti-American sentiment in Canada.

Likewise, the fact that in 1996 Chrétien appointed Axworthy as foreign minister mattered. A member of the Liberal party's so-called left wing, Axworthy brought to the portfolio a strong and long-standing strain of antipathy to the United States. His distrust of the United States as a hegemonic power had been consistently articulated throughout his political career, and thus it was not surprising that, once in a position to give effect to these views, Axworthy's inclinations would have led him to pursue policies that challenged the global primacy of the US.

Moreover, a Minervian foreign policy fitted well with the Liberal government's primary domestic policy goal in the 1990s: reducing the federal deficit and managing the national debt that had ballooned as a result of undisciplined deficit spending in the previous two decades. The pursuit of a policy of a highly personalized diplomacy of robust multilateralism – encouraging the creation of new institutions of global governance and new patterns of global regulation – was perfect for this: it allowed Ottawa to appear highly active in global politics while at the same time it was dramatically cutting the more "traditional" (and expensive) tools of statecraft, such as the diplomatic establishment, the armed forces, the intelligence community, and development assistance.[15] Thus, it is not surprising that a foreign policy that focused primarily on the personal initiatives of the foreign minister, and was thus extremely inexpensive, won the support of other ministers around the Cabinet table.

Finally, a policy of robust Minervian multilateralism allowed the Chrétien government to feed – and gain politically from – a mythology that had been increasingly entrenched in Canadian political culture over the Cold War era. According to Don Munton and Tom Keating, multilateralism had been used by a succession of Canadian governments for political/electoral purposes: to encourage in Canadians a certain benign view of their country's role in the world, and then to gain electoral support for reinforcing that view in action.[16] By the early 1990s, that view – that Canada was the world's primary peacekeeper, that it was exceedingly generous in devoting its resources to the world's poor, that it always sought to do good in global affairs, that it always pursued multilateral solutions to problems and never embraced unilateralism – was deeply entrenched in Canadian political culture. The fact that such views were almost entirely mythological was beside the point; the existence of these views permitted the Chrétien government to play to such mythology in its foreign policy in the 1990s, and, in the words of Denis Stairs, "to indulge in inflated and self-serving rhetoric, a rhetoric clearly designed to appeal to the preferences and prejudices of a population indoctrinated by its own myths" (2003b, p. 503).

I have termed this Canada's "ear candy" approach to foreign policy (Nossal 2005b). In other words, Canadian politicians tended to describe Canada's global terms in glowing and sweet-sounding terms, designed to convince Canadians that their government was doing something worthwhile in their name, even though there was little of substance actually being done. But the sugar high produced was addictive: the more their politicians fed them feel-good rhetoric about Canadian foreign policy, the more Canadians appeared to expect such rhetorical excesses from their government – and, as importantly, to be entirely unsatisfied with more honest, realistic, or sober assessments of the options available to Canada in the real world of world politics. Moreover, the dynamic quickly became circular: politicians themselves became addicted to telling Canadians about their role in international affairs in terms that they knew would generate political support.

However, this domestic dynamic was eventually affected by the intrusion once again of systemic factors – the events of 9/11. These attacks had a profoundly transformative impact on global politics, bringing the post-Cold War era to an end. In the post-9/11 era, some of the discipline on smaller states that had been lifted during the post-Cold War era was reimposed. In Canada, one of the domestic effects of the events of 9/11 was to galvanize a much more concentrated criticism of the Chrétien government's foreign policy than Axworthy's initiatives had generated in the 1990s.

Much of the criticism of the Chrétien government's foreign policy in the 1990s came from the academic community, and tended to focus on Lloyd Axworthy (Hampson et al. 2001; Welsh 2004, p. 170), or attributing foreign policy outcomes to Axworthy personally. Hillmer and Chapnick, for example, term Canada's pursuit of "an ambitious doctrine of intrusive internationalism" during this period as the "Axworthy Revolution" (2001, p. 67). For their part, Fen Osler Hampson and Dean F. Oliver refer to the "Axworthy doctrine," providing what remains as the most thorough and balanced critique of Axworthy's approach. Hampson and Oliver were not unsympathetic analysts: they paid tribute to "Axworthy's careful articulation of foreign policy principles" and the "complex, interlocking set of assumptions and foreign policy objectives" he embraced. In their view, "Axworthy's Canada" was

a charter member of what we might call the "moral minority," that distinguished (and self-styled) group of states and organizations whose "moral multilateralism" is predicated on their faith that the enunciation of a new set of global norms will lead inexorably to the creation of a just and more equitable international order. (Hampson and Oliver 1998, p. 381)

And yet, while Hampson and Oliver argue that there was much to be defended and supported, there were nonetheless "yawning contradictions" in some of Axworthy's "pulpit diplomacy" and the "incautious moralizing" that tended to mark foreign policy during this era on the one hand, and the dramatic decline in the resources actually devoted to international affairs on the other (1998, pp. 382, 405).[17] Two of the main elements of the "Axworthy doctrine" also came under fire: his notion of human security,[18] and for his appropriation of the idea of "soft power," first articulated by Joseph S. Nye, Jr (1990).[19]

But ironically it was after 9/11 – long after Axworthy had left office – that the foreign policy approach he had championed attracted wider and more sustained criticism. One particularly influential critique was Andrew Cohen's *While Canada Slept: How We Lost Our Place in the World*, published in 2003. *While Canada Slept* was a devastating critique that argued that the Chrétien government had gutted Canadian international capabilities to such an extent that Canada's voice no longer mattered in global politics as it once did (2003). One might argue with Cohen's golden-age assumptions, but his book was a bestseller, attracting considerable media and public attention. Because of that, his argument had a powerful impact on foreign policy discourse in Canada: not by accident did Paul Martin subtitle the 2005 *International Policy Statement* – his own vision of foreign policy designed to distinguish himself from his despised predecessor – "A Role of Pride and Influence in the World" (Canada 2005).

One of the reasons Cohen's book resonated as it did was because it appeared amidst a growing welter of criticism directed at Chrétien's foreign policy. For example, Denis Stairs of Dalhousie University published a series of biting critiques of Canadian foreign policy. In 2001, playing on Theodore Roosevelt's invocation to "speak softly and carry a big stick" and Isaiah Berlin's metaphor of the bent twig,[20] Stairs wrote caustically that Canada's foreign policy approach in the 1990s was to "Speak Loudly and Carry a Bent Twig" (2001).[21] In 2003, Stairs worried that "Canadians have grown alarmingly smug, complacent, and self-deluded in their approach to international affairs," thanks in large part to the "active encouragement of their leaders" (2003a). Later that year, he argued that greater realism was needed in Canadian foreign policy and that the expectations that had been so inflated during the Chrétien years needed to be lowered: "The grandiose and self-serving rhetoric so common now in our foreign policy pronunciamentos could be quietly abandoned in favor of more honest (and hence, more cautious) accounts of what is likely to be feasible in the real world" (2003b, p. 491). Stairs also advocated a more discriminating and less ideological approach to multilateralism, arguing that "'Multilateralism if helpful' is a better dictum than 'multilateralism every time'" (2003b, p. 499). One of Canada's leading military historians, J.L. Granatstein, also stressed the need to address the deteriorating relationship with the United States instead of "preach[ing] a moralistic, soft-power human-security policy to the world, in effect making Canada's weakness-is-strength into an Orwellian virtue" (2003, p. 12). His more fully developed critique of Canada's Liberal period – *Whose War Is It?* – appeared in 2007.

Of particular note was the rising number of critical voices of former senior officials. Michael Hart, a former senior trade negotiator, excoriated the Chrétien government for ignoring the importance of Canada–US relations in favor of a "romantic quest to exercise 'soft' power" (2002–03, p. 38). Lewis Mackenzie, a retired general who had commanded UN forces in Yugoslavia in the early 1990s, and who was by this time hardly non-partisan, having run for the Progressive Conservatives in the 1997 federal election, criticized the Chrétien government for making foreign policy "on the fly," ignoring the advice of the military (2003). Allan Gotlieb, a former deputy foreign minister and Canadian ambassador to the US, characterized the Chrétien period as one of "romanticism," and called for a rejection of a "feed-good foreign policy" and a return to greater realism (2004, 2005). Another former Canadian ambassador to Washington, Derek Burney, dismissed the initiatives of this era as nothing more than what he called a "Let's pretend" foreign policy (2005). (Roy Rempel, who was to become a foreign policy adviser to Stephen Harper, took up Burney's theme; outlining what he called Canada's "pretend foreign policy" during this period, he entitled his book *Dreamland* in order to underscore what he argued was the unreal world in which Canadian foreign policy makers were living (2006).)

To be sure, there were some who celebrated the Minervian foreign policy agenda. One of the staunchest defenders of the agenda was Paul Heinbecker (2004a, 2004b, 2007, 2010), a senior official in the Department of Foreign Affairs and International Trade; as an assistant deputy minister in Ottawa in the late 1990s, and as Canada's permanent representative to the United Nations between 2000 and 2003, he had been heavily involved in the formulation and execution of numerous aspects of Canada's Minervian foreign policy, including serving as the head of Canada's delegation to the Kyoto negotiations.

Likewise, Jennifer Welsh of the University of Oxford presented a strong Minervian argument in her 2004 book *At Home in the World,* which outlined a powerful argument that Canada should become what she called a "Model Citizen" in contemporary global politics (2004, especially chapter 6). Indeed, Welsh's vision so captivated Paul Martin that he engaged her to participate in the writing of the review of international policy his government undertook in 2004 and 2005. Welsh's vision is clearly evident in the overview booklet of the 2005 *International Policy Statement.*

In a similar vein, John Erik Fossum and his colleagues applied the Dutch notion of *gidsland* – or "mentor state" – to Canada (and several other states besides) (Fossum 2006; Bosold and von Bredow 2006). Joost Herman defines *gidsland* (literally "guiding nation") as "a nation that progressively guides other countries locked in pitiful nationalist struggles for power, dominance, and religious zeal to the proper international behaviour consisting of respect for the international legal order, the rights of men, and free trade as the best way of ensuring prosperity for all." This notion, deeply embedded in the history and practice of Dutch foreign policy, sees the possibility of a country acting "a role model for other states by teaching them how to behave properly on the international scene, how to become 'good' states" (Herman 2005, p. 863).

These debates had a paradoxical impact. On the one hand, the criticism leveled at Chrétien had an impact at the elite level, and had a particular impact on Martin, for as he took office he signaled that he would pursue a very different foreign policy than Chrétien. He promised to mend relations with the US, indicating, for example, support for ballistic missile defense. And in some areas Martin did pursue different policies, dramatically increasing spending for the military and engaging Canada in a new combat mission in Afghanistan.

However, it is equally clear that by 2003, the ear candy dynamic had worked well. All indications of public sentiment in Canada suggested that the Minervian policies embraced by the Chrétien Liberal government were exceedingly popular in Canada: overwhelmingly Canadians applauded Chrétien's decision not to participate in the invasion of Iraq; overwhelming numbers of Canadians endorsed multilateralism, the International Criminal Court, and Kyoto; there was virtual unanimity in Québec in support of a refusal to join BMD.[22] Thus Martin found it politically irresistible to continue many of Chrétien's policies, embracing the transformative foreign policy agenda with a passion, putting the responsibility to protect at the forefront of his agenda, looking for ways of changing global leadership by plumping for an "L-20" summit of global leaders, privileging Kyoto, refusing to join ballistic missile defense, and allowing anti-Americanism to creep into his election campaigns (Nossal 2007b, pp. 74–75). But as this was occurring, there was an important shift in the domestic party structure in Canada. In December 2003, the same month that Martin took over as prime minister, one of the parties that had emerged out of the fragmentation of the Progressive Conservative Party in the early 1990s – the Canadian Alliance – formally merged with the rump of the Progressive Conservative Party to form the Conservative Party of Canada, ending a long struggle to "unite the right," as it was called, in an effort to stop the vote-splitting that ensured the continuation of Liberal hegemony. In March 2004, Stephen Harper was elected as the leader of the new party.

This had a profound impact on Canadian politics. With the "right united," the vote-splitting that had occurred in the 1993, 1997, and 2000 elections largely disappeared. Moreover, Harper's skills in French, combined with the revelation in February 2004 that the Liberals under Chrétien had been running a corrupt sponsorship scheme in the 1990s, changed party fortunes in Québec. As Table 4.1 demonstrates, in the 1997 elections, Reform candidates in Québec received a scant 0.3 percent of the popular vote, while the Progressive Conservatives under the leadership of Jean Charest, a Québécois who had been in Brian Mulroney's cabinet and who was one of the two surviving Progressive Conservative MPs of the 1993 election, won five of the province's 75 seats. By 2000, however, Charest was gone, having left federal politics to take over the leadership of the Québec Liberal Party and become premier of Québec. But the newly formed Canadian Alliance increased the share of the popular vote in Québec dramatically, which kept going up in both 2004 and 2006 as Liberal fortunes tanked.

As Table 4.1 demonstrates, these changes in voting patterns in Québec, combined with shifts in other parts of the country, resulted in the slow but progressive abandonment of the Liberal Party by Canadian voters. In 2004, the Liberals were reduced to a minority in the House of Commons; in January 2006, the Conservatives under Stephen Harper were elected with a minority. In October 2008, the Conservatives were returned with another minority. In the May 2011 elections, the Conservatives won a majority, and the Liberals suffered a dramatic defeat, falling from 77 seats at dissolution to just 34 seats. Likewise, the Bloc Québécois was abandoned en masse by Québec voters, who turned in large numbers to the New Democratic Party (NDP). The NDP's 59 members from Québec propelled the party into second place, supplanting the Liberals as the official opposition. And while there is no evidence that a concern over foreign policy played any part in the

Table 4.1 Changing party Fortunes in Québec, 1997–2011. Percentage of popular vote in Québec (number of seats)

Election	Reform Party	Canadian Alliance	Progressive Conservative	Conservative Party	Liberal Party	Bloc Québécois	New Democratic Party
1997	0.3% (0)	–	22.2% (5)	–	36.7% (26)	37.9% (44)	2.0% (0)
2000	–	6.2% (0)	5.6% (1)	–	44.2% (36)	39.9% (38)	1.8% (0)
2004	–	–	–	8.8% (0)	33.9% (21)	48.9% (54)	4.6% (0)
2006	–	–	–	24.6% (10)	20.8% (13)	42.1% (51)	7.5% (0)
2008	–	–	–	21.7% (10)	23.7% (14)	38.1% (49)	12.1% (1)
2011	–	–	–	16.5% (5)	14.2% (7)	23.4% (4)	42.9% (59)

Source: Andrew Heard, Simon Fraser University (www.sfu.ca/~aheard/elections/).

dramatic shifts in voter preferences between 2004 and 2011, there is little doubt that, with Harper in power, Canada's Minervian foreign policy had come to an end.

Conclusion

I have argued that Canada's membership in the Minervian club was interrupted by the change of government in 2006. Canada's enthusiasm for the Minervian agenda arose because with the end of the Cold War there was an opportunity for foreign policy makers in smaller powers to seize the opportunity to forge new patterns of global power and authority, often challenging the global hegemonic role of the US – paradoxically at the very moment that the US was reconstructing itself as the "indispensable country," as both Madeleine Albright, the US Secretary of State, and President Bill Clinton liked to put it. There was nothing deterministic about this process, however: in some countries, political leaders seized that opportunity. In the Canadian case, we need to look at domestic politics to understand how and why the Liberal government of Jean Chrétien embraced the Minervian agenda so enthusiastically, an enthusiasm that continued under Chrétien's successor, Paul Martin.

Of crucial importance in this process was the changing nature of Canadian party politics, which saw the Liberal Party gain a dominant position electorally at precisely the same time that the global system was changing. This gave Liberals the freedom of maneuver to embrace the foreign policy orientations of Lloyd Axworthy, a politician on the party's left wing who was deeply skeptical of power politics, military force, and the dominant global power of the United States. Of equal importance was that Axworthy's leader was a Quebecker who likewise had a strong anti-American streak, was profoundly anti-military, and was willing to use foreign policy issues to entrench and advance his party's partisan electoral interests.

The impact of these factors can perhaps best be seen from what happened when there was a change in both the international system and domestic Canadian politics. When the permissiveness of the post-Cold War era diminished after 9/11, the Canadian government attracted more and more elite criticism, which in turn increasingly delegitimized the foreign policy that had worked so well in the 1990s. And when the Canadian party system experienced a profound shift – for reasons that had little to do with foreign policy – the net effect was to bring Stephen Harper and the Conservative Party to power, and to extinguish Canada's enthusiasm for a Minervian agenda.

Notes

1. Canada's historical attachment to multilateralism is best surveyed in Keating 2002.
2. Also Stoett 1999; McRae and Hubert 2001. For critiques, see Paris 2001, Hay 2000.
3. Canada 1999. After Axworthy's departure from politics in 2000, this document was quickly "disappeared" from the Department of Foreign Affairs and International Affairs "Human Security" website. However, it was posted to a number of other sites, where it remains available: for example, www. summit-americas.org/Canada/HumanSecurity-english.htm
4. On Kosovo, see Nossal and Roussel 2000; on Timor, see Hataley and Nossal 2004.
5. Martin's *International Policy Statement* (Canada 2005, Diplomacy booklet, 20ff) embraced five different global responsibilities. For a critique, Nossal 2005a, 2005b.
6. See Tomlin 1998; Cameron et al. 1998; Lenarcic 1998; Gwodzdecky and Sinclair 2001. For Axworthy's own account, see Axworthy 2003: 126–55.
7. Axworthy's rejection of an American request for an exemption for the Demilitarized Zone in Korea meant that the ban on landmines was total.
8. "PM Says Canada Won't Fight in Iraq," *CBC News*, March 18, 2003: www. cbc.ca/news/story/2003/03/17/chretieniraq030317.html; also Noble 2003, Barry 2005.
9. See Axworthy 2003: 200–13; Robinson 2001.
10. P.L. 104–114, Cuban Liberty and Democratic Solidarity (Libertad) Act of 1996.
11. When Faulder was finally executed in June 1999, Axworthy issued a statement that indicated that the Canadian government "deeply regretted" the execution. Canada, Department of Foreign Affairs and International Trade, "Execution of Joseph Stanley Faulder: Comments by the Government of Canada," *Press Release*, No. 145, June 17, 1999.
12. See www.rcinet.ca/rci/en/chroniques/7563.shtml
13. *Globe and Mail*, Toronto, December 9, 2005.
14. For a discussion, see Haglund 2006.
15. The decline in Canada's international capacity during this period is covered most succinctly by Cohen 2003.
16. Munton and Keating 2001, Munton 2002–03.
17. See also Nossal 1998–99.
18. See, for example, Owens and Arneil 1999; Paris 2001.
19. For critiques of Axworthy's application of this concept, see Hampson and Oliver 1998: 388–92; Nossal 1998; Cooper and Bercuson 1999.
20. Berlin (1972) saw nationalist movements as violent responses to oppression, like a bent twig that snaps back to hit one in the face.
21. See also Stairs et al. 2003; Bercuson and Stairs 2005.
22. See the public opinion polls cited by Young 2007: 16; on Québec and BMD, see Haglund 2006.

Part II
The Competitive Mode

5
UNESCO versus the World Trade Organization: Will Cultural Diversity Trump Free Trade?

Jennifer Chan

> The Parties, in conformity with the Charter of the United Nations, the principles of international law and universally recognized human rights instruments, reaffirm their sovereign right to formulate and implement their cultural policies and to adopt measures to protect and promote the diversity of cultural expressions and to strengthen international cooperation to achieve the purposes of this Convention.
>
> Article 5, Convention on the Protection and Promotion of the Diversity of Cultural Expressions

On October 20, 2005, 148 countries adopted a new cultural diversity convention within the framework of UNESCO. The treaty, in force since March 2007, recognizes the dual (culture/trade) nature of cultural goods and services and affirms the rights of states to adopt measures to promote cultural diversity. Negotiated within the relatively short span of four years, it was hailed as a moral victory by most governments and non- governmental coalitions. Only two countries opposed the treaty: the US and Israel. Four countries – Australia, Honduras, Liberia, and Nicaragua – abstained. As of January 2012, 120 states as well as the European Union have adopted the Convention on the Protection and Promotion of the Diversity of Cultural Expressions.[1]

This chapter looks at the political process that led to the creation of this convention, especially the roles played by Canada, France, the EU, and Japan. In accordance with the three causal modes forwarded in this book about Minervian power, I examine how the case of the Convention on the Protection and Promotion of the Diversity of Cultural Expressions (hereafter known as the Convention) is best explained by a realist paradigm. The Convention can be seen as a strategic counter-hegemonic attempt by the EU (led by France) and Canada to regain control over cultural industries dominated by the US. The economic interests of France and Canada were represented by their culture and foreign ministries, as well as the Ambassadors to UNESCO. However, due to political sensitivity and the threat of a cultural trade war at the level of the WTO, the issue of cultural diversity was primarily framed in a normative rather than a materialist way by an international non-governmental coalition of professional cultural associations. It is this strategic alliance of statist and sub-state actors that makes the Convention a particularly nuanced case study of the Minervian competitive logic. State actors were important in defining and putting the issue of cultural diversity on the global agenda, but the non-governmental International Network on Cultural Diversity largely carried out the painstaking work of convention adoption and ratification. The domestic political alignment of Minervian actors might have played a role as well. As Nossal argues in his chapter on Canada's Minerva moment in this volume (Chapter 4), Canada's active global role in multilateralism occurred under Liberal leadership under prime ministers Jean Chretien and Paul Martin. The leadership role played by Canada in the lead-up toward the adoption of the Convention certainly fell under this period of liberal leadership.

The chapter is organized in four parts. The first section situates the case study within a larger literature on cultural trade and globalization, and takes a look at the convention itself, highlighting its objectives, principles, definitions, rights, and relationships to other international legal instruments. The second section uses a realist hypothesis to analyze the alliance led by the French and Canadian governments to pursue the UNESCO convention. The third section then examines the crucial supportive role of global civil society. I conclude with a discussion on the outstanding issues of ratification and the implementation of the convention.

Promoting and protecting cultural diversity

> Without cultural pluralism, we choke.
>
> Gilberto Gil, Brazilian Minister of Culture[2]

According to Caves (2000), the global market of "creative industries" is estimated to be worth around US$ 800 billion per year. Many scholars have pointed out the paradox of global expansion and increasing homogeneity. McChesney (2000) and Grant and Wood (2004) argue that around five to ten firms, mostly US-based, usually dominate the world market, regardless of whether it is in the business of book publishing, film, music, or media in general. In the case of Canada, despite government cultural policy measures such as limits on foreign ownership, content regulation, preferential treatment of Canadian rights holders, funding programs, and government cultural agencies, foreign firms and products dominate the Canadian cultural market. The question of whether culture should be exempt from agreements on trade liberalization became inevitable. Some have argued that cultural products should be distinguished from other goods (Grant and Wood 2004). First, they are public goods whose production cost is independent of the number of consumers. Hence, market prices often far exceed marginal cost. Second, since they are "experience" goods, they are not as substitutable as regular goods, and both information and competition are far from being perfect as is assumed in the traditional efficient market equilibrium. Third, the high fixed costs nature of these industries favors large, established firms, making the entry of individual or small competitors extremely difficult. To these "curious economics" of cultural goods, one can add the more fundamental opposition between the principle of comparative advantage, emphasizing efficiency, and that of cultural diversity, centered on the fundamental freedom of expression.

The debate over cultural exemptions within trade agreements began nearly two decades ago. At the conclusion of the Canada–US Free Trade Agreement (FTA) in 1987, Canada managed to have its cultural industries, except those "which would have been inconsistent with the Agreement," exempt (Neil 2003, p. 102). In 1993, similarly, the European Union opposed the inclusion of cultural goods and services in the final Uruguay round of the General Agreement on Tariffs and Trade, the forerunner of the WTO. In 1994, when Canada signed the North American Free Trade Agreement (NAFTA), it again negotiated the right to exempt cultural industries from most terms of the agreement and to "continue to support its cultural industries as long as the measures it uses are otherwise consistent with the pre-existing Canada/US Free Trade Agreement."[3]

Since 1995, however, negotiations on cultural trade have been back through the General Agreement on Trade in Services (GATS) within the WTO. Realizing how difficult it is to negotiate a true cultural exemption clause in international trade agreements (Canada, for example, was forced to grant the United States a retaliation clause that limits the real scope of the cultural exemption clause) and being aware of the intense pressures being applied to culture in proliferating multilateral and bilateral trade negotiations, a global movement has been fighting for a legally binding global convention on cultural diversity under the auspices of UNESCO since the late 1990s. The Convention on the Protection and Promotion of the Diversity of Cultural Expressions, adopted almost unanimously in October 2005, built upon the 2000 Council of Europe Declaration on Cultural Diversity as well as the 2001 UNESCO Declaration on Cultural Diversity. The preamble of the Convention reiterates the core ideas within the earlier Declaration that cultural diversity is a heritage of humanity, indissociable from democracy, a root of development, human rights, cultural rights, accessible to all, and fosters creativity and dialogue among cultures.[4] The central objectives include the protection and promotion of the diversity of cultural expressions; recognition of the distinctive nature of cultural activities, goods and services as vehicles of identity, values and meaning; recognition of the link between culture and development; strengthening international cooperation to enhance the capacity of developing countries; and reaffirmation of the sovereign right of states to maintain, adopt, and implement cultural policies (Article 1). The eight guiding principles guarantee that all measures aimed at protecting and promoting the diversity of cultural expressions shall respect human rights and fundamental freedoms, sovereignty, equal dignity for all cultures, international solidarity and cooperation, complementarity of the economic and cultural aspects of development, sustainability, equitable access, and openness (Article 2).

"Cultural diversity" refers to the manifold ways in which the cultures of groups and societies find expression and "protection" means the adoption of measures aimed at the preservation, safeguarding and enhancement of the diversity of cultural expressions (Article 4). Two of the most debated provisions pertain to the rights and obligations of Parties and relationships to other instruments. Article 6 stipulates the right of states to adopt:

(a) regulatory measures aimed at protecting and promoting diversity of cultural expressions;
(b) measures that, in an appropriate manner, provide opportunities for domestic cultural activities, goods and services among all those available within the national territory for the creation, production, dissemination, distribution and enjoyment of such domestic cultural activities, goods and services, including provisions relating to the language used for such activities, goods and services;
(c) measures aimed at providing domestic independent cultural industries and activities in the informal sector effective access to the

means of production, dissemination and distribution of cultural activities, goods and services;

(d) measures aimed at providing public financial assistance;

(e) measures aimed at encouraging non-profit organizations, as well as public and private institutions and artists and other cultural professionals, to develop and promote the free exchange and circulation of ideas, cultural expressions and cultural activities, goods and services, and to stimulate both the creative and entrepreneurial spirit in their activities;

(f) measures aimed at establishing and supporting public institutions, as appropriate;

(g) measures aimed at nurturing and supporting artists and others involved in the creation of cultural expressions; and

(h) measures aimed at enhancing diversity of the media, including through public service broadcasting.

Finally, Article 20 specifies, "Parties shall take into account the relevant provisions of this Convention" even though "nothing in this Convention shall be interpreted as modifying rights and obligations of the Parties under any other treaties to which they are parties." The adoption of the Convention in October 2005 despite vehement US opposition should be considered a triumph. The European Commission hails the text as the basis of a new pillar of world governance in cultural matters.[5] Despite its shortcomings, the Convention provides a legal tool for states to provide legitimate measures to protect its cultural industries.

The greatest unknown about the impact of this new convention, however, pertains to its relationship to other treaties. According to two international law experts, there are two extremes in this area. At one extreme, there is Article 103 of the UN Charter, which stipulates that: "In the event of a conflict between the obligations of the Members of the United Nations under the present Charter and their obligations under any other international agreement, their obligations under the present Charter shall prevail." At the other extreme, there are those clauses that stipulate that "this Convention shall not affect the rights and obligations of States Parties deriving from other international agreements or international law."[6] NGO networks including the International Network on Cultural Diversity and the campaign for Communication Rights in the Information Society (CRIS) have warned that the Convention should not be subordinated to the WTO. The convention, entered into force in March 2007, has the same legal value of all other international sets of rules and, according to Mohamed

Lotfi M'rini, professor of international trade at the University of Laval in Canada, can "weaken the power of the general agreement on services at the WTO," even though it would not be applicable to the rights and obligations contracted by countries under bilateral or multilateral trade agreements, such as the North American and the Central American free trade agreements (NAFTA and CAFTA), in which the United States is the central player.[7] The current dispute mechanism through a Conciliation Commission has no real juridical standing and it remains unclear how such issues will be solved once the convention takes effect.

Binding the hegemon: state networks for cultural diversity

It follows that if the concept of cultural diversity was able to carry weight, it is because it responded to, in a realistic and efficient fashion, a question that had been well-defined: how can we ensure that free trade, undertaken by the World Trade Organization, does not end up being a white-wash of cultures subjected to the law of the marketplace nor a breaking down of political structures meant to support creativity? With this second corollary question: how can we fight the good fight against cultural hegemony and the consolidation of industries without stifling the dynamic flow of trade or inciting protectionist acts or isolationism.

Jean Musitelli, 2006, former ambassador, permanent delegate of France to UNESCO (1997–2002), and member of the group of international experts in charge of the pre-project of the Convention on Cultural Diversity (2003–04).[8]

The Convention was a result of nearly a decade of state lobbying and civil society mobilization against US cultural hegemony. Between 1998 and 2005, three main positions on the issue of cultural diversity emerged: 1) a pro-Convention majority position, led by a Franco–Canadian partnership, supported by the EU, Japan, India, Korea, Mexico, Brazil, South Africa, and most other developing states; 2) a middle-of-the-road position held primarily by Japan, which was supportive of the Convention but with reservations; and finally 3) an anti-Convention position, led by the US and Australia, which considered the Convention as anti-free trade. The French and Canadian governments, through their cultural and foreign ministries, successfully took leadership in using a new international instrument in the form of a UNESCO convention to circumvent US domination within the WTO. This strategic partnership was further buttressed by an active non-governmental coalition of diverse cultural professional organizations that pushed the agenda beyond a cultural trade framework. By 2005, cultural diversity was seen as a basic human right, worthy of global protection.

Perceptions of US economic prowess, manifest in proliferating bilateral and regional free trade agreements since the 1990s, have led to regulatory efforts by its economic competitors. By the late 1990s, it became clear that the cultural exception doctrine was an insufficient protection. To escape the deadlock, the French proposed in 1998 the concept of "cultural diversity" (Musitelli 2006). According to the former ambassador of France to UNESCO, the concept signaled a departure from the defensive "cultural exception" doctrine, enlarged the issue to a universal dimension, and transformed it into a rule, rather than the exception, "by making the rebalancing of culture/commerce a pillar of construction of the new international judicial order destined to regulate globalization" (Musitelli 2006). The "Copernican revolution" from exception to diversity would be led by a Franco–Canadian engine (Musitelli 2006).

In 1998, under the leadership of the Canadian Minister of Heritage, Sheila Copps, an informal group of over 40 culture ministers formed the International Network on Cultural Policy (INCP) at a meeting in Ottawa. In December that year, Prime Ministers Jean Chrétien (Canada) and Lionel Jospin (France) published a joint communiqué "On the Importance of Cultural Diversity in a Global Economy." In February 1999, the Cultural Industries Sectoral Advisory Group on International Trade (SAGIT), an advisory committee to the Canadian Minister of International Trade, tabled a report entitled "Canadian Culture in a Global World: New Strategies for Culture and Trade." The Group recommended that Canada work to promote:

> A new strategy that would involve negotiating a new international instrument that would specifically address cultural diversity, and acknowledge the legitimate role of domestic cultural policies in ensuring cultural diversity...Canada could initiate a new international instrument, which would lay out the ground rules for cultural policies and trade, and allow Canada and other countries to maintain policies that promote their cultural industries.[9]

Paris had a strategic two-step plan: first, a declaration of principle, followed by a constraining legal instrument (Musitelli 2006). The plan was realized through intense Franco–Canadian cooperation

(Paris–Quebec and Paris–Ottawa nexus in parallel) between 1999 and 2001 when the UNESCO Declaration on Cultural Diversity was adopted. In 1999, a mandate was given to the Director General of UNESCO to set up a working group on cultural diversity. UNESCO organized a colloquium "Culture, the Market and Globalization" attended by both Ministers of Culture, Catherine Trautman and Sheila Copps. Later in November that year, the two Ministers of Culture presided over a round table on "Culture, Creativity in a Globalized World" with 55 Ministers of Culture. The final declaration foreshadowed the current convention by proclaiming the right of states and governments to freely establish their cultural and audio-visual policies (Musitelli 2006).

In April 2000, the French Prime Minister Lionel Jospin and Quebec Premier Lucien Bouchard made a joint declaration reaffirming,

> their commitment to linguistic and cultural diversity, convinced that the richness of the world and future of our civilization depend upon recognized and respected differences, ... consider that cultural goods and services, reflections of a society's national identity and values, are unique in nature and consequently require a special status with respect to the laws of free trade, and reaffirm that it is the right, responsibility and duty of countries and governments to ensure their potential to preserve and develop their ability to define and implement cultural policies, including audio-visual policies, in order to preserve cultural diversity.[10]

Later, in September 2002, French president Jacques Chirac put forward the idea for a convention on cultural diversity at the World Summit on Sustainable Development in Johannesburg. The idea was gaining ground, helped in particular by the support of all the member states of the European Union and the Organisation internationale de la Francophonie. Six months later, in February 2003, the French Minister of Culture, Jean-Jacques Aillagon, led a delegation to the office of the UNESCO Director General to commit him to beginning the preparatory work on the convention (Musitelli 2006).

By the early 2000s, there was undeniable momentum to draft an international convention on cultural diversity. There were, however, two very different conceptions of cultural expressions and cultural goods. A majority group, led by Canada, France, and the EU, supported by countries including Korea, Mexico, and South Africa defends the principle of international legislation confirming special treatment for cultural goods and services as vehicles of identity, values, and meaning. Here, it is important to note French leadership in the European context. The European Union converted to diversity rather slowly (Musitelli 2006). On the one hand, the UK was suspicious of a French-led project that smacks of protectionism. On the other, institutions in Brussels cared little about culture in promoting Europe's competitiveness and did not want a potential UNESCO–WTO fight (Musitelli 2006). Only in 2003 did the European Commission issue its first communication on the subject "Towards an International Instrument on Cultural Diversity."[11] The convention was negotiated jointly by the European Commission, on behalf of the Community, and the Council Presidency, on behalf of the member states. The European Community's involvement in negotiations on a normative text at UNESCO was the first of its kind. The European Union was able to participate for the first time and speak with a single voice as a key player in the UNESCO negotiations. The European Parliament, and above all its Committee on Culture, followed these negotiations closely and supported the Community's approach throughout the process.[12] In the case of Canada, although the initial impetus came from Quebec, the issue was soon taken up by the federal government, as evidenced in the leadership of the Minister of Heritage, Sheila Copps, in as early as 1998.

A second position on cultural diversity, led by the US, Australia, and Japan, sees the text as an attempt to maintain protectionist policies in a sector that should be open to free trade.[13] The majority position is not hard to comprehend. Both France and Canada have long supported national cultural policies that help foster the cultural sector. Despite measures such as limits on foreign ownership, content regulation, preferential treatment, funding programs, and government cultural agencies, American firms and products dominate the Canadian and European cultural market. In Canada, 97% of films, 81% of English-language magazines, 79% of music, and 45% of books are foreign owned.[14] Both the French and Canadian governments worry that the cultural exemption clauses within bilateral and multilateral trade agreements including NAFTA and the WTO are not reliable long-term solutions, as there is continuous pressure for states to make voluntary efforts toward maximum trade liberalization and opening up sectors for commitments.

The United States considers state cultural policies of many countries discriminatory. It was the leading voice of dissent during the negotiations for the Convention and voted "no" on the adoption of the Convention. For Louise Oliver, the US Ambassador to UNESCO, the convention on diversity restricts, rather than promotes, the freedom of expression:

> It is therefore with regret that we stand in opposition today to this Convention because of those who have indicated a clear intent to use this convention to control – not facilitate – the flow of goods, services, and ideas ... In addition, this Convention as now drafted could be used by states to justify policies that could be used or abused to control the cultural lives of their citizens – policies that a state might use to control what its citizens can see; what they can read; what they can listen to; and what they can do ... We have been clear that the Convention cannot properly and must not be read to prevail over or modify rights and obligations under other international agreements, including WTO Agreements.[15]

According to Richard Martin, co-head of the US delegation, "this convention is actually about trade ... clearly exceeds the mandate of UNESCO." Further, he called the convention's text "deeply flawed and fundamentally incompatible with (the agency's) obligation to promote the free flow of ideas by word and image."[16] For Dana Gioia, Chairman of the National Endowment for the Arts and a member of the US delegation, "culture resides within people, within their community, the individual artist and the individual artist community," and "what this Convention does in a very simple way is nothing ... to protect individual or minority cultural rights but advocates government control of expression, artists and audience."[17] Media commentators view the convention as an attempt to legitimize cultural protectionism to restrict exports of American products, particularly Hollywood movies and television programs.[18] During the negotiations, the US repeated demands for bracketing of the words "protect," "protection," "cultural goods and services," and "cultural contents and expressions."[19] It also expressed its formal objection to the definitions of cultural expressions, cultural activities goods and services, cultural industries, cultural policies and protection, as well as provisions in Articles 6.2.b and c regarding the "rights of Parties at the national level" to adopt measures.[20]

Although the US failed to garner the support of other member states to stop the Convention, it did manage to water down perhaps the most important clause on the relationship between the Convention and other treaties, rendering its impact uncertain. The 2004 preliminary draft of the convention included an option that would have granted limited normative priority to cultural protection, but this option was ultimately dropped, leaving Article 20(2) as the operative provision in case of conflict with another treaty ("Nothing in this Convention shall be interpreted as modifying rights and obligations of the Parties under any other treaties to which they are parties."). Hence, according to one international law expert, the convention might be referred to as part of the context for the purpose of interpreting WTO rights and obligations, but not as a carved-out treaty that can "trump" them; and this is not inconsistent with existing WTO Appellate Body jurisprudence.[21] At the last minute of the debates, the US also managed to lobby the Indian government to add the so-called Indian clause, allowing non-ratifying countries to ignore the validity of the convention, thereby rendering its effectiveness uncertain.[22]

Japan, strong in its exports of cultural products from anime to manga and popular culture, took a middle-of-the-road position. The presence of a Japanese Director General at UNESCO might have made strong Japanese governmental opposition to the Convention difficult. The basic stance of the Japanese Ministry of Education, Culture, Sports, Science and Technology (MEXT) was to approve of the Convention, while taking the freedom of movement of cultural goods and services into consideration.[23] It agrees with the convention's central notion that cultural goods are expressions of cultural identities, and hence deserve to be preserved and supported by states.[24] Indeed, Japan has traditionally attached great significance to its cultural heritage, and more recently paid much attention to its cultural diplomacy. At a gathering in 2006, the Japanese Minister of Foreign Affairs, Taro Aso, made an impassioned appeal to the country's young artists concerning their role in creating a good image of Japan through exporting its cultural products:

> With all due respect to Mickey and Donald, whether you look at J-pop, J-anime, or J-fashion, the competitiveness of any of these is much more than you might imagine...What you in the content business are doing is work that you yourselves have chosen to do, not work that someone – least of all people at the Ministry of Foreign Affairs – has asked you to do. It is that fact that is bringing about a steady increase in the number of fans of Japan. We have a grasp on the hearts of young people in many countries, not the least of which being China...And that is why I say

that you are the people who are the new actors involved with bringing Japanese culture to the world ... Japan also boasts many newer forms of culture that have a high degree of appeal. This would be pop culture, including anime, music, and fashion among others, and the Ministry of Foreign Affairs is really going all out to "market" this, so to speak ... I think we can safely say that any kind of cultural diplomacy that fails to take advantage of pop culture is not really worthy of being called "cultural diplomacy" ... And so, I am speaking to you here today to urge you to join with us in polishing the Japan "brand." [25]

Although Japan supported the Convention over all, at times it expressed reservations, often together with the US, against certain provisions including Article 6.1 on the rights of parties to adopt measures at the national level. It also formally expressed reservations against Article 8 on "measures to protect cultural expressions," especially those "on its territory [that] are at risk of extinction, under serious threat, or otherwise in need of urgent safeguarding." [26] The government of Japan might have been concerned about potential claims made by minority groups such as the Ainu on the protection of their cultures. [27] It is important to note that the issue of "vulnerable forms of cultural expression" was completely unacceptable to several countries including the US and Canada, and the chair replaced "vulnerable" with "at risk of extinction," [28] thereby heightening the bar for those eligible for state support.

Other countries, including India, Korea, Mexico, and Brazil – all strong exporters of films and television soap operas – supported the majority position led by Canada and France/EU. In particular, Korean civil society actors led by the Coalition for Diversity in Moving Images lobbied its government strongly in favor of the Convention. [29] Since the late 1960s, Korean law mandated that local cinemas screen domestic films for a minimum of 146 days per year. Implemented in 1993, the quota system has had a clearly positive impact on the Korean film industry. Between 1993 and 2005, ticket sales for Korean movies increased 200% and market share increased from 15.9% to 46.9%. The number of moviegoers grew from roughly 58 million in 1999 to 130 million in 2004. Korean filmmakers have also won critical acclaim at major international film festivals. Although movies from the United States and elsewhere continue to have significant access to Korean audiences (60% or more of the screen time), the screen quota policy has been the target of the Motion Pictures Association of America and the negotiations for the US–Korea free trade agreement. [30] In November 2004,

Table 5.1 State positions on the proposed Convention on the Protection and Promotion of the Diversity of Cultural Expressions

States	Roles and Positions
I) Pro-Convention majority position	Led by Franco-Canadian partnership, supported by the EU, Japan, India, Korea, Mexico, Brazil, South Africa, and most other developing states.
France	• proposed the concept of cultural diversity to replace the defensive "cultural exception" doctrine; • French president Jacques Chirac put forward the idea of a convention on cultural diversity at the World Summit on Sustainable Development in Johannesburg in 2002; and • led a delegation to the office of the UNESCO Director General to commit him to beginning the preparatory work on the convention in 2003.
Canada	• spearheaded the International Network on Cultural Policy with over 40 culture ministers; • formed the Cultural Industries Sectoral Advisory Group on International Trade to the Canadian Minister of International Trade, which recommended the negotiation of a new international instrument on cultural diversity;
EU	• UK was skeptical of a French-led position; and EU was initially concerned about potential UNESCO-WTO fight over the issue of cultural protection; • slowly but finally converted to the Franco-Canadian majority position; issued its first communication "Towards an International Instrument on Cultural Diversity" in 2003; and negotiated for the Convention as a single voice.
Korea, Mexico, and Brazil	• middle income countries with important cultural industries rallied around the majority Franco-Canadian position. For example, the Korean government saw the Convention as an important legal tool to ward off intense trade pressures from the US to half its screen quota.
Developing countries led by South Africa and India	• on behalf of the interests of developing countries, South Africa and India co-chaired a working group on articles pertaining to international cooperation, preferential treatment, and an International Fund for Cultural Diversity.
II) Middle of the Road Position	Supported the Convention but with reservations
Japan	Japan supported the Convention over all but expressed reservations about "measures to protect cultural expressions" due to concerns about potential claims made by minority groups such as the Ainu on the protection of their cultures

Continued

Table 5.1   Continued

States	Roles and Positions
II) Against the Convention	Led by the US and Australia
US	• sees the Convention as counter to free trade and freedom of expression; • challenges the mandate of UNESCO to negotiate a convention on the trade of cultural industries; and • also sees the Convention as legitimizing cultural protectionism against US products.

the US ambassador to Korea, Christopher Hill, said at a lecture on the roadmap to a free trade agreement at Korea University that the Korean government and people had to choose between an FTA and Korea's screen quota system.[31] The Korean government saw the Convention as an important legal tool to ward off intense trade pressures from the US to halve its screen quota. In January 2006, days before the official US–Korea FTA negotiations opened, Korea announced the reduction of its movie theatre screen quota system by 50 percent, effective July 2006. [32] The final bilateral FTA agreement stipulates Korea's "commitment to lock in all other content requirements at the least restrictive level allowed under current law, including the motion picture screen quota."[33]

Developing countries overall supported the majority position (Francophone African countries were aligned with the French position, for example), but insisted on the development aspects of the Convention. A working group co-chaired by South Africa and India worked on articles 12–18 on international cooperation, preferential treatment, and an International Fund for Cultural Diversity. While these provisions were kept in the Convention, the language was significantly watered down. Draft Article 7 on intellectual property rights and piracy was deleted. There is no longer any obligation on States to provide preferential treatment for artists and cultural goods and services from developing countries; instead, "developed countries shall facilitate cultural exchanges with developing countries by granting, through the appropriate institutional frameworks, preferential treatment" (Article 16). The African group had also put forward a proposal to make contributions to the proposed Cultural Diversity Fund mandatory, with a right for nations to take a reservation against this provision on ratification, but now contributions to the Fund are voluntary

(Article 18).[34] Table 5.1 summarizes the positions taken up by various state actors.

Global civil society mobilization for cultural diversity

> Cultural diversity is a fundamental right and that countries should assure its preservation and promotion. It believes it is crucial that countries and governments be entirely free to adopt the policies necessary to support the diversity of cultural expression and the viability of enterprises that produce and disseminate this expression; that international trade agreements fully respect these policies; that the application of such policies not be subject to reprisals.
>
> Coalition for Cultural Diversity mission statement, June 2000[35]

Although the Convention on the Protection and Promotion of the Diversity of Cultural Expressions was primarily driven by competitive state interests, the speed and extent of adoption of the Convention could not be fully explained without understanding the crucial, supportive role of global civil society. The past decade saw new patterns of institution building at the international level. As in the cases of the landmine ban and children's rights, global civil society lobbied states such as Canada and Sweden to push for rapid ratification of international treaties or norms.[36] National non-governmental coalitions on cultural diversity were first developed in France and Canada, followed by a global network.

The non-governmental French Coalition for Cultural Diversity, previously known as the Cultural Watchdog Committee, was created in 1997 to combat the OECD's Multilateral Agreement on Investment (MAI). It includes 50 professional cultural associations in cinema, performing arts, publishing, music, graphic arts, plastic arts, and multimedia) and defends cultural diversity endangered by international commercial negotiations.[37] Similarly, the Canadian Coalition on Cultural Diversity was created in 1998 by professional cultural associations in Québec in the midst of the growing opposition to the MAI. The Coalition, which receives financial support from the Québec Government through the departments of Culture and Communications, International Relations, and Industry and Trade, now includes 38 associations throughout Canada that represent artists, independent producers, broadcasters, distributors, and publishers working in the fields of publishing, film, television, music, performing arts, and visual arts.

After the aborted talks on the MAI in 1998, the two national NGO coalitions lobbied the governments of Canada and France to make a joint declaration on the importance of cultural diversity in the world economy:

> Both governments agree to promote ... cultural and linguistic plurality and ensure that cultural goods and services are fully recognized and treated as not just any merchandise. ... They will cooperate closely with international multilateral organizations, to ensure that questions dealing with cultural policy and diversity receive the attention and the importance they deserve in relation to economic and trade issues.[38]

In 1999, the International Network for Cultural Diversity was created with non-governmental organizations in 70 countries and cultural ministers in 53 countries. In September 2000, members of INCD met in parallel at the INCP annual conference in Santorini, Greece and concluded that "market forces alone cannot ensure cultural diversity at the national and international levels"; "states have a right and responsibility to implement policies and programs that support diverse artistic and cultural activities"; and that only a new international instrument could "give a permanent legal foundation for cultural diversity" (Neil 2003, p. 7). By the time the drafting of the convention began in 2003, an International Liaison Committee of Coalitions for Cultural Diversity (ILC-CCD) was established to facilitate cooperation and the development of joint positions and actions among the existing national coalitions for cultural diversity. By 2006, the ILC-CCD now brings together 38 national coalitions representing some 400 cultural professional organizations from Argentina, Australia, Austria, Belgium, Benin, Brazil, Burkina Faso, Cameroon, Canada, Chad, Chile, Colombia, Congo, Ecuador, France, Gabon, Germany, Guinea, Hungary, Ireland, Italy, Ivory Coast, Republic of Korea, Mali, Mexico, Morocco, New Zealand, Nigeria, Paraguay, Peru, Senegal, Slovakia, Spain, Switzerland, Togo, Tunisia, Uruguay, and Venezuela. Some of these coalitions on cultural diversity built upon the larger national and regional civil society efforts to monitor free trade agreements. For the Latin American coalitions, for example, the culture campaign is an integral part of the Hemispheric Social Alliance that started with the NAFTA negotiations. Before the ILC-CCD was established, the non-governmental International Network on Cultural Diversity was already created in 2000 with now more than 400 organizations from 71 countries, including the United States, in parallel with the cultural minister-centered International Network on Cultural Policy.

As drafting efforts began, the INCD teamed up with Free Press and the campaign for Communication Rights in the Information Society to form the watchdog Media Trade Monitor to follow the negotiations. Although there are differences in the positions between the governmental and non-governmental networks (INCD, in its earlier draft, for example, favored a more open definition of culture and cultural diversity),[39] the international NGO networks largely supported the majority Canada–France position on the convention. Article 11 does acknowledge the fundamental role played by civil society in protecting and promoting cultural diversity. Non-governmental coalitions such as the Media Trade Monitor and International Network on Cultural Diversity (INCD), however, would have liked to see a stronger emphasis on the protection and promotion of cultural diversity within countries, especially indigenous cultures (now figured only in the preamble, Article 2 "Guiding Principles" and Article 7 "Measures to Promote Cultural Expressions") and intellectual property rights and piracy (now only in the preamble).[40] INCD further criticizes that the convention contains neither concrete obligations nor specific targets. The clauses on international cooperation remain as obligations to which states "shall endeavour to" adhere.[41] After the Convention was signed in 2005, the work of INCD has focused on individual state ratification and follow-up monitoring.

Conclusion: when does cultural diversity trump free trade?

It is now time for the cultural diversity movement to step back and consider whether the Convention has value as a political tool. While it has not achieved the outcome we had hoped for, is there sufficient benefit in confirming the right of States to implement cultural policies to justify organizing a campaign to have it approved and ratified? Will the Convention be a useful organizing tool in the ongoing work? Can it become a rallying point for civil society groups and governments that remain concerned about how the trade and investment agreements are being used to stifle cultural policies and local artists and cultural producers?

Gary Neil, INCD, May 2005[42]

This chapter explored international institution building by new powers in a new area beyond security, development, and human rights. The adoption of an international convention on cultural diversity despite US opposition should be considered as an important moment in international relations. Canada became the first state to ratify the Convention in December 2005 and France joined in June 2006. Japan did not take up a leadership role in the process even though it was in support of the Convention. To date, it has not yet ratified the Convention.

Unlike in other recent areas of international norm setting such as women's rights and children's rights where NGOs took the lead in framing the rights language without states necessarily realizing its political or economic interests (Chan-Tiberghien 2004), in the case of the cultural diversity convention, the leading states were clearly driven by their own economic interests. In this view, the outcome of the Convention is best explained by a realist paradigm of multilateral institution building. The Convention can be seen as a strategic counter-hegemonic attempt by France (supported by the EU) and Canada to regain control over cultural industries dominated by the US. Global civil society acts as pressure group to bring about speedy and near universal adoption of the Convention.

Can one interpret the convention as a result of particular political alignments of domestic interests? Undeniably, domestic interests groups in Canada, France, and the EU lobbied strongly for the Convention. In the EU, the European broadcasting union, European federation of employers' associations – representing over 3,500 theatres, theatre production companies, orchestras, operas, ballet and dance companies, and other professional organizations in the performing arts in Europe – and the European Arts Entertainment Alliance, composed of the International Federation of Musicians, International Federation of Actors, and EURO-MEI (representing creative, technical, and administrative workers in the entertainment sector) were all in favor of the UNESCO Convention on the protection and promotion of the diversity of cultural expressions. However, these interest groups were not the most politically connected/powerful groups and did not primarily act through the domestic political system. Rather, their power in this case came from their ability to form transnational coalitions and to gain voice through these linkages.

As in most other cases of international conventions, the devil is in the implementation. Many supporters of the Convention have noted that the final draft falls short of original intentions and does not have strong enforcement mechanisms.[43] At the Cultural Diversity Ministerial Forum of the Asia-Pacific Region on May 11 2012, the General Secretary of the International Federation of Coalitions for Cultural Diversity, Charles Vallerand, emphasized again that the Convention is more a platform for dialogue and that "collaboration is based on goodwill and a voluntary commitment". There is no such thing in this Convention as "trade disciplines" and "legally binding dispute settlement mechanisms."[44] The United States can retaliate by cutting its monetary contribution to the organization, which is 22 percent of the UNESCO budget. It has also stepped up its efforts in signing bilateral trade agreements with developing countries in which these countries give up their rights to preserve and support their own unique audiovisual and information services, including film, television, and music. The case of the US–Korea Free Trade Agreement serves as a warning example of how the Convention is unable to safeguard Korea's screen quota system. States and NGOs are now closely monitoring implementation work in fear of US pressures against ratifying the Convention through bilateral trade agreement stipulations.

On December 18, 2006, the European Community, joined by 12 member states (Austria, Denmark, Estonia, Finland, France, Lithuania, Luxemburg, Malta, Slovakia, Slovenia, Spain, and Sweden) deposited their instruments of ratification at the UNESCO headquarters in Paris. On the day of adoption, President Chirac paid tribute to the contribution of the Organisation internationale de la Francophonie as well as the European Union, which played a major role in the drafting of this text and its successful outcome.[45] The Convention took effect in March 2007. A network of state and non-state actors has managed, within the span of a few years, to stage a diplomatic success story. Cultural diversity is no longer simply a French or Canadian problem. It has become a pillar of global governance.

Several lessons could be drawn from this case study of the Convention. First, when non-hegemonic states are blocked by political institutions dominated by the hegemon (in this case at the World Trade Organization by the US), they might attempt to circumvent by creating new international instruments. In this case, France and Canada were successful in lobbying for the Convention. Second, however, it is important to note how cultural diversity is couched as a universal value and norm beyond its material interests. Framing the issue at hand beyond mere economic, political, or military interests so as to gain global legitimacy became a strategic exercise. Third, in certain issue-areas such as cultural diversity, a coalition of Minervian governmental and non-governmental actors might increase the chance of success to bind the hegemon in a new normative framework. It is too early to tell whether the Convention leaves a long-term legacy on US–Minervian-actor relationships. For example, there is still no evidence of the US challenging any state using the Convention's parameters to protect its cultural industries within the WTO. Other scholars, such as Nossal in this volume (Chapter 4), have also argued that the change of political leadership in Canada with the dominance of the Conservative Party since 2006 has brought a decline in Canada's leadership in global governance. While the support of Prime Minister Stephen Harper for the Convention might be lukewarm at best, the non-governmental Canadian Coalition on Cultural Diversity remains globally active. Future research can look at the legacy of the Convention, the impact of diminishing support of states such as Canada, and the role of the International Network on Cultural Diversity as a global watchdog institution.

Notes

1. http://portal.unesco.org/la/convention.asp?KO=31038&language=E
2. "US, Japanese Calls For Cultural Treaty Change Meet With Resistance," Intellectual Property Watch, http://www.ip-watch.org/weblog/index.php?p=111&res=1024_ff&print=0
3. Canadian Cultural Industries Sectoral Advisory Group on International Trade 1999.
4. For full text of the Convention, see http://portal.unesco.org/culture/en/ev.php-URL_ID=11281&URL_DO=DO_TOPIC&URL_SECTION=201.html
5. http://ec.europa.eu/culture/portal/action/diversity/unesco_en.htm
6. Ivan Bernier and Hélène Ruiz Fabri for Quebec's Ministère de la Culture et des Communincations, 2006, "Implementing the UNESCO Convention on the Protection and Promotion of the Diversity of Cultural Expressions," http://www.cptech.org/unesco/
7. Julio Godoy, "UNESCO Adopts Convention to Protect Diversity," October 20, 2005, http://mediatrademonitor.org/node/251
8. Musitelli 2006, http://www.diplomatie.gouv.fr/fr/IMG/pdf/0701-MUSITELLI-EN.pdf
9. http://www.dfait-maeci.gc.ca/tna-nac/canculture-en.asp
10. http://www.cdc-ccd.org/Anglais/Liensenanglais/who_we_are/coal_position_eng.html
11. http://ec.europa.eu/comm/avpolicy/ext/multilateral/unesco/index_en.htm
12. http://www.europa-eu-un.org/articles/en/article_6630_en.htm
13. "Diversite culturelle, une convention bien fragile," Gilles Cloutier et al., October 2005, http://www.magazineforces.com/news.html?L=0&nid=107 and Armand Mattleart, "Cultural Diversity Belongs to Us All," Le Monde diplomatique, November 2005, http://mondediplo.com/2005/11/15unesco
14. Canadian Cultural Industries Sectoral Advisory Group on International Trade 1999.
15. For the full statement by Ambassador Louise V. Oliver, Permanent Delegate of the United States of America Explanation of Vote of the United States on the Convention on the Protection and Promotion of the Diversity of Cultural Expressions, http://66.102.7.104/search?q=cache:os-O5kMbB9AJ:www.

usunesco.org/texts/GenConf33_Amb_Intervention_CD_Vote.pdf+Louise+
Oliver+and+cultural+diversity&hl=en&ct=clnk&cd=1&client=safari
16. Julio Godoy, "UNESCO Adopts Convention to Protect Diversity," http://
www.ipsnews.net/news.asp?idnews=30714
17. "UNESCO Cultural Diversity Convention: The U.S. View," http://fpc.state.
gov/fpc/54039.htm
18. George Will, "Dimwitted Nod to Diversity," October 12, 2005, http://
www.washingtonpost.com/wp-dyn/content/article/2005/10/11/
AR2005101101320.html
19. http://www.cdc-ccd.org/coalition_currents/Fev05/coalition_currents_en_
fev05.html
20. Oral Report by the Rapporteur of the Third Intergovernmental Meeting of
Experts, http://portal.unesco.org/culture/en/ev.php-URL_ID=26852&URL_
DO=DO_TOPIC&URL_SECTION=201.html
21. Tomer Broude, "Comment: Cultural Diversity and the WTO: A Diverse
Relationship," November 21, 2005, http://www.asil.org/insights/2005/11/
insightcomment051121_000.html
22. Julio Godoy, "UNESCO Adopts Convention to Protect Diversity," October
20, 2005, http://www.ipsnews.net/news.asp?idnews=30714
23. http://www.mext.go.jp/b_menu/shingi/bunka/
gijiroku/019/04120201/001/005.pdf
24. http://www.mext.go.jp/b_menu/shingi/bunka/
gijiroku/019/04120201/001/003.htm
25. "A New Look at Cultural Diplomacy: A Call to Japan's Cultural Practitioners
Speech by Minister for Foreign Affairs Taro Aso at Digital Hollywood
University," April 28, 2006, http://www.mofa.go.jp/announce/fm/aso/
speech0604-2.html
26. Oral Report by the Rapporteur of the Third Intergovernmental Meeting of
Experts, http://portal.unesco.org/culture/en/ev.php-URL_ID=26852&URL_
DO=DO_TOPIC&URL_SECTION=201.html
27. The issue of definition of "minority" culture was discussed during the fifth
preparatory meeting for the Convention on August 27, 2004, http://www.
mext.go.jp/b_menu/shingi/bunka/gijiroku/019/04120201.htm
28. INCD May 2005 newsletter, http://www.incd.net/docs/NewsletterMay2005.
htm
29. http://screenquota.org/home2/default.asp
30. "Letter from the International Network on Cultural Diversity to the Office
of the US Trade Representative," March 24, 2006, http://www.incd.net/
US-Korea%20FTA%20-%20Submission%20of%20INCD%20et%20al.htm
31. "korea Must Choose between FTA and Screen Quota: US Ambassador,"
http://www.bilaterals.org/article.php3?id_article=908
32. Luke Eric Peterson, "Culture Treaty Couldn't Save Korea from Hollywood,"
February 16, 2006, http://mediatrademonitor.org/node/274
33. Office of the United States Trade Representative "Trade Facts: Free Trade
With Korea, Summary of the KORUS FTA," April 2007 http://www.casbaa.
com/doc/KORUS_FTA_Fact_Sheet.pdf
34. Sasha Constanza Shock, "CRIS/Media Trade update on UNESCO Draft
Convention on Cultural Diversity," http://www.crisinfo.org/content/view/
full/691

35. http://www.cdc-ccd.org/Anglais/Liensenanglais/framewho_we_are.htm
36. See Cameron et al. 1998 on the global movement to ban landmine and Chan-Tiberghien 2004 on the global movement to ban commercial sexual exploitation of children.
37. http://www.coalitionfrancaise.org/eng/
38. http://www.cdc-ccd.org/Anglais/Liensenanglais/who_we_are/coal_position_eng.html
39. International Network for Cultural Diversity Proposed Convention. www.incd.net, accessed on August 17, 2006.
40. See http://mediatrademonitor.org/node/254 and http://www.incd.net/docs/NewsletterMay2005.htm
41. http://www.incd.net/docs/NewsletterMay2005.htm
42. http://www.incd.net/docs/NewsletterMay2005.htm
43. http://www.incd.net/docs/NewsletterMay2005.htm
44. http://www.cdc-ccd.org/Le-forum-ministeriel-sur-la
45. http://www.ambafrance-us.org/news/statmnts/2005/chirac_unesco102005.asp

6
A Double-Entry Minervian Case: The Battle over International Accounting Standards

Nicolas Véron

Economics and hard security issues generally appear to escape the Minervian logic of institution building. They most often give rise to institutions that are dominated or strongly influenced by the US, such as the IMF or NATO, or to no institutions at all. Specifically in the area of financial markets, Wall Street and the US public authorities, most prominent among them the Securities and Exchange Commission (SEC), have tended to set the agenda and to pioneer new developments worldwide, both in financial innovation and in regulatory processes. This trend has been observed since the aftermath of the Second World War, which marked London's eclipse as a global financial center.

The landscape of global finance is changing fast however, and perhaps the extension of Minervian patterns to capital markets is ineluctable. Before the 2008 financial crisis, the twentieth anniversary of London's "Big Bang" deregulation in 2006 emphasized the City of London's phoenix-like rise as an alternative global center to New York, and was accompanied by much soul-searching in the US banking and public policy communities about the negative effects of the 2002 Sarbanes–Oxley Act on the competitiveness of the country's financial markets.[1] Since then, the threat of Asian competition against established Western financial centers has become ever more concrete. The share of US companies in the cumulated market value of the world's 500 largest listed corporations was 57 percent in March 2003 and has since declined considerably, reaching 40 percent at the end of 2011. The total share of European companies declined much less, from 28 to 25 percent in the same period after a high point of 34 percent in 2007, and that of emerging-markets companies surged from 4 to 23 percent. Japan declined from 7 to 5 percent, and Canada and Australia together rose from 4 to 6 percent over the same period.[2] In this context, accounting standards provide a unique, and perhaps frontier, case of Minervian development in one of the most crucial infrastructures of financial markets. Financial statements are the key vector of information in financial markets. The requirements that govern their preparation, particularly accounting standards, are not just a norm for neutral measurement. They can and often do influence economic behavior. Changes made to standards typically create new groups of winners and losers. One example, which gave rise to much controversy in the US, is that allowing stock options to be booked as an expense effectively resulted in fewer stock options being granted.[3] Similar real-world effects can be observed for virtually all standards that govern the preparation of financial statements. However, the power to determine accounting standards should also not be overstated. Rather than introduce novel and autonomous dynamics of change, the effect of new standards is generally limited to, as in the case of stock options, raising consideration for elements of accounting to which the market-place previously paid insufficient attention, but this is a significant power nevertheless. As the old financial maxim goes, *"you manage what you measure"*; in an increasingly complex economy, the decision made over what to measure becomes more difficult and critical, and the power attached to standard-setting authority increases (Véron et al. 2006).

This chapter is devoted to the emergence of International Financial Reporting Standards (IFRS) as a global phenomenon since 1999–2000. This development has a clear Minervian character. Until the early 2000s, accounting standards were developed under almost exclusively national frameworks. US accounting standards or, as they are called, Generally Accepted Accounting Principles (GAAP), were the key international reference. International Accounting Standards (as IFRS were called at that time) had emerged under a "normative" mode fostered in an internationally cooperative manner by the accounting profession, but their practical impact was limited. The endorsement of IFRS by the European Union, announced in 2000 and formalized in 2002, triggered a rapid series of developments that transformed them into the dominant body of accounting standards worldwide in only a few years. Canada decided to adopt IFRS some time after the EU, as did Australia, Brazil, Israel, South Korea, and many other jurisdictions around the globe. Japan has been more cautious and has adopted an intermediary stance between that of Europe and Canada and that of the US, with a rather slow convergence of its national accounting standards toward

IFRS, but also a more pro-active attitude that allows its domestic listed companies to adopt IFRS as an alternative to the local standards.

This striking sequence of events, which took many participants by surprise, broadly fits the competitive mode of Minervian institution building. It should be noted that the EU, Canada, and Japan did not act in a specifically coordinated manner in adopting IFRS and that Australia was more pro-active than Japan in this development. But the EU, the key player in this case, chose IFRS to counter the hegemonic reach of US GAAP and foster what it considered a more balanced structure for norm creation. The counter-hegemonic motive of the EU decision is illustrated by the numerous claims made by the European Commission since 2000, that IFRS are superior to US GAAP as high-quality accounting standards, and encouragement for other countries to also adopt the European model.

The case of accounting standards, however, is also ripe with specificities that distinguish it from other Minervian issue-areas. First, the institution predates the accounting scandals of the early 2000s, and, more importantly, escapes traditional global institutional categories. IFRS accounting standards are shaped by a private-sector organization currently named the International Accounting Standards Board (IASB), whose origins date back to 1967. The IASB has only weak links with national governments even though, as discussed below, a Monitoring Board of government representatives was added to its structure in 2009 and is not based on an international treaty. As we shall see, the combination of this private-sector structure with extensive *de facto* policy-making powers granted by the endorsement of IFRS in many jurisdictions has, as we shall see, led to tensions that have not yet been fully resolved. Second, although the story of IFRS adoption fits the competitive mode, the US has played a key role in shaping both the IASB as an institution and IFRS as a body of standards. The relationship between the hegemon and the IASB is therefore characterized by a combination of cooperation and competition, which is not found to the same extent in most other issue-areas covered in this book.

The chapter starts with a brief summary of the historical developments that led to the endorsement of IFRS (or of standards modeled almost entirely on them) in a growing number of jurisdictions. The following section investigates why some countries have been willing to abandon their standard-setting power in favor of the IASB. Finally, the chapter offers a brief review of the key challenges to the IASB and IFRS implementation, which raise questions about their sustainability, even in the jurisdictions (such as the EU) that have already endorsed the international standards.

Tedious as this issue-area may appear at first sight, the implications of accounting standards are significant. First, there are ramifications for global growth. The cross-border convergence of accounting standards promises comparability of company financial statements across jurisdictions. This should result in a better allocation of international capital and reduction in the cost of capital, as has effectively been observed in the EU (Li 2010). This in turn should result in enhanced growth and job creation. Second, the European Union has effectively assumed global leadership on IFRS, and the international community's perception of its leadership capability would be damaged in the event of failure. More generally, the IASB is a striking example of an international institution shaped in large part by the private sector, and therefore its fate has implications not only for Minervian power development but also for the role of the private sector in global governance (Véron 2007).

The emergence and spread of international accounting standards

Accounting and standardization before IFRS

Financial accounting started in northern Italy in the late Middle Age. The so-called double-entry bookkeeping method, by which credit and debit operations are simultaneously recorded, appeared at the same time as capitalist enterprise itself, when merchants started to assemble into "companies" and entrust their operations to hired managers who had no ownership of the business. During the Industrial Revolution large companies started expanding overseas; this was particularly true for British companies, who spread into what was to become the colonial Empire. This led to a much-increased need for reporting and supervision of remote operations that were often run by untrustworthy managers. The introduction of limited liability for joint-stock companies in the 1860s also vastly accelerated corporate expansion and specialization. Simultaneously, accounting practices became more elaborate and complex, but they long remained primarily directed at internal control, for the use of head-office managers and directors rather than for external shareholders or the public. Even listed companies provided the public with information that was generally scarce, often of dubious quality, and difficult to compare from one company to the other.

The next step was a move toward public disclosure and standardization of financial information, and originated in the US. Following the stock market crash of October 1929 and the ensuing scandals and outcry, the landmark securities legislation of 1933 and 1934 created a national framework that still largely underlies US accounting regulation and has been replicated in many countries. The New Deal legislation set up the Securities and Exchange Commission as the regulator of all national capital markets, made independent external audit compulsory for all publicly listed companies, and paved the way for the emergence of a formally identified set of GAAP. Therefore, both the modern concept of accounting standards and the requirement for statutory audits, as we know them, were born directly from the stock market crisis. By the mid-1950s US GAAP had been constituted as a full body of rules, and has been constantly updated since then. In 1973 the SEC transferred the task of accounting standard-setting from the accounting profession to the Financial Accounting Standards Board (FASB), a newly created private-sector body.

Different accounting traditions evolved in other industrialized countries in accordance with their diverse capitalist systems. By the end of the twentieth century, all developed and most developing countries had formally adopted national accounting standards and issued laws mandating their use by a wide array of companies incorporated in the country, including all listed ones. But even in the late 1990s, national accounting standards still differed widely from one country to another.

The birth and development of international accounting standards

International accounting standard-setting traces its origins back to February 1967, when Henry Benson, a prominent British accountant who had just been elected President of the Institute of Chartered Accountants in England and Wales established an Accountants International Study Group with his Canadian and US counterparts. This group then gradually developed a doctrinal framework (Benson 1989), and later formed the basis for the creation, in 1973, of the International Accounting Standards Committee (IASC) by a wide array of accounting bodies from Australia, France, Germany, Japan, Mexico, and the Netherlands, in addition to Canada, the United Kingdom (with Ireland), and the United States. The IASC's stated aim was to issue international standards of reference that would guide the convergence of national standards over time. Benson was elected the IASC's first chairman and opened its offices in London.

In the ensuing years, the IASC prepared and published a number of documents that together constituted an increasingly comprehensive body of rules. These were eventually completed in 1998 and released as a set of 39 so-called core International Accounting Standards. Simultaneously, the IASC's governance evolved to accommodate a growing and increasingly diverse stakeholder base, gradually opening up to international public institutions, the European Commission, and FASB, the US standard-setting body. In the late 1990s, it became clear that a more structured governance framework that could provide greater independence from the accounting profession was needed. At the insistence of the SEC, and because other constituents had failed to agree on a better alternative, the new governance framework, which was enshrined in a statutory "Constitution" adopted in 2000, was closely modeled on that of FASB (Camfferman and Zeff 2007). It established the Delaware-incorporated IASC Foundation, governed by a group of 22 trustees (renamed the IFRS Foundation in 2010), and the London-based International Accounting Standards Board, which is hosted by the Foundation. At the same time, the standards themselves were re-branded as International Financial Reporting Standards instead of International Accounting Standards as they had been known before, even though (as if to further confuse outsiders) existing IAS standards, such as the much-debated IAS 39 standard on financial instruments, kept the same denomination.[4]

The IASB prepares and adopts the standards and their accompanying texts and interpretations, while the IFRS Foundation is responsible for raising the necessary yearly funds for the functioning of the IASB and its staff. A significant development was the creation in 2009 of a "Monitoring Board" of public authorities, including the European Commission, the SEC, and the Japanese Financial Services Agency, to which the IFRS Foundation's Trustees have voluntarily accepted to grant a veto on their own appointments and re-appointments. The 2011 budget was approximately US $40 million, to which the "Big Four" accounting firms (Deloitte, Ernst & Young, KPMG, and PricewaterhouseCoopers) contributed US $2.25 million each. Apart from the Big Four, funding is organized on a jurisdiction-by-jurisdiction basis (individual countries and the European Union), with diverse funding schemes across jurisdictions.[5]

EU adoption and global spread

The IASB develops standards but has no power to ensure their endorsement in national (or international) legislation, implementation, and enforcement. This is where nations and governments come in.

As recently as 2000, no major developed country had required the use of IFRS as compulsory. Indeed, only a few had allowed their use for public financial statements as an alternative to national standards. US GAAP were generally seen as the dominant reference for national accounting standards, even though a number of countries had drawn on the IASB's technical work to draft their own national standards. Since then, the situation has changed dramatically. Among the world's 500 largest publicly listed companies, the share of those which use IFRS has risen from about 5 percent in 2003 to an estimated 50 percent in 2012 (Véron 2011). In less than a decade, IFRS have become the most utilized system of accounting standards worldwide.

The single watershed event behind this dramatic shift was when the European Commission formally proposed in 2000 the adoption of IFRS as the sole set of standards for the publication of consolidated accounts by publicly listed companies from 2005. This was swiftly (by EU standards) confirmed in a regulation of the European Parliament and European Council of July 19, 2002, which set out an endorsement process by which the IASB's standards and interpretations would be given legal currency in all EU member states. In the next sections, I come back to the reasons behind this remarkable development, relate it to the Minervian framework, and outline the challenges that are likely to result from it in the near future.

The adoption of IFRS in the EU has triggered a series of similar moves all around the world, including, but not only or even principally, in the other Minervian actors. Even though some of these jurisdictions were gradually harmonizing their accounting standards with IFRS before, it is highly unlikely that this would have led to complete convergence without the momentum provided by the EU decision (Posner 2006).

The EU's immediate neighbors, such as Norway, Switzerland, Turkey, and Israel, have almost entirely shifted to IFRS. So have Australia, Brazil, Hong Kong, Singapore, South Korea, and many other developed or emerging countries. Canada's adoption of IFRS, completed in 2011, was made especially significant by its proximity to the US and its widespread familiarity with US GAAP before that transition. India and China have converged their accounting standards with IFRS to a large extent, even though significant differences remain in both cases.

Japan's approach has been more cautious than that of Europe, Canada, Australia, or even China, but it has also engaged in a gradual process of convergence toward IFRS. In early 2005, the Accounting Standards Board of Japan started a formal discussion with the IASB with simultaneous work on several standards and regular meetings between the two bodies. More recently, Japan has authorized its domestic listed companies to opt voluntarily for IFRS as an alternative to the use of national accounting standards.

The evolving US involvement

The US authorities have built significant influence over international accounting standard-setting, especially since the 1990s. The key driver behind the IASC's work during that decade was the prospect of a formal endorsement by the International Organization of Securities Commissions (IOSCO), in which the SEC is considered the largest source of influence. The incentive for the IOSCO backing was a central factor behind the IASC's adoption of all SEC proposals in the overhaul of its governance framework during 1999–2000, though the eventual endorsement by IOSCO in 2000 was more qualified than the international standard-setters would have hoped for (Camfferman and Zeff 2007). Furthermore, since 2001, American members such as Thomas Jones and James Leisenring have been particularly influential in the proceedings of the IASB.

While these developments were taking place, however, the international environment was changed, first by the Enron bankruptcy in December 2001, and later by other accounting scandals that erupted in 2002 following the bursting of the late 1990s stock market bubble. Before this wave of controversy, specific American standards had been occasionally criticized, but US GAAP as a whole were widely considered, in the US and elsewhere, to the best available set of accounting standards. But Enron's collapse shattered this perception: it exposed the shortcomings of some detailed US GAAP rules, most notably those on consolidation, which gave Enron enough leeway to hide its now famous "special-purpose entities" off its balance sheet, packing them with real debts backed by flimsy assets.

A new situation emerged, in which IFRS – recently bolstered by their European endorsement – could be seen as an alternative to US GAAP. Some observers, such as Robert Litan at the Brookings Institution, advocated free regulatory competition between the two sets of standards (Benston et al. 2003). In February 2002, a Senate Committee investigating the Enron debacle heard the testimony of then-IASB Chairman David Tweedie explicitly criticize the rules-based approach prevalent in US GAAP, contrasting it with the more principles-based stance adopted by the IASB (Véron et al. 2006). Shortly thereafter, the Sarbanes–Oxley Act specifically mandated the SEC to study how a principles-based system (such as IFRS) could be introduced in the United States.[6]

This sequence of events still frames the present, and at the time of writing (mid-2012), unsettled, relationship between the IASB and the US. On the one hand the US is still home to the largest capital markets; they have built significant influence over international accounting standard-setting, and the IASB and its trustees see eventual IFRS recognition in the US as a key aim. On the other hand, US leadership in worldwide capital markets has been eroded since 2007, not least by the financial crisis, and the IASB can be tempted to treat the US as just another constituency that may adopt its standards. The first set of factors explains the feeling, widespread in Continental Europe, that the IASB is subservient to its main US interlocutors, the SEC and FASB. The second set results in a number of US stakeholders advocating the adoption of IFRS for the sake of global convergence.

Since the early 2000s the IASB and FASB have been seeking to narrow the differences between IFRS and US GAAP – a process they call "convergence," but which in fact is very different from the unilateral convergence of, say, Australian or South Korean accounting standards toward IFRS. This process was first enshrined in the so-called Norwalk Agreement of September 2002 and detailed in a FASB–IASB Memorandum of Understanding in February 2006.[7] On some issues FASB has adopted standards identical or near-identical to existing IFRS (for stock option expensing, for example); on other issues the IASB has adopted standards identical or near-identical to existing US GAAP rules; and on yet other issues the two bodies have jointly developed entirely new projects. But the process has been fraught with difficulties and is no longer expected to lead to complete convergence, as some US GAAP rules remain firmly embedded in the US national context and cannot easily be transposed to other environments, while the IASB claims to issue principles-based standards for global use.

In parallel with the IASB–FASB convergence process, the US authorities and their international counterparts, most prominently the EU, have long discussed the scope for mutual recognition. They started from an asymmetric situation, as the EU has long allowed listed companies to report under US GAAP with no requirement to "reconcile" their financial statements with IFRS (that is, to explain all differences between statements under US GAAP and IFRS). By contrast, the SEC forced all companies listed in the US to reconcile their financials with US GAAP until this requirement was dropped in late 2007. But as of late 2012 and after multiple public debates and consultation, the SEC has not yet made a decision to adopt IFRS for US domestic issuers.

Why did it happen?

Having exposed the key facts and milestones of the development and spread of international accounting standards, I now focus on the forces that appear to have caused the aforementioned advances or have made them possible, and examine how these forces correspond to the Minervian modes of institution building. In this analysis, two different sequences of events should be distinguished, separated by the EU's landmark decision to adopt IFRS during 2000–02.

The early years: normative institution building by the accounting community

The first sequence is the birth of international accounting standard-setting in the late 1960s and early 1970s, its continuation in the 1980s and early 1990s, and the finalization of a comprehensive set of standards and a reformed governance framework in the late 1990s. This sequence is accurately described as the development of common norms, first as a shared basis of acceptable practices, and later as a reference for local standard-setting by the worldwide epistemic community of accounting professionals.

Beyond the accounting profession, international standard-setting was also a response to the needs of market participants, whose activities assumed an increasingly cross-border character in the 1960s and early 1970s. This was primarily the case for the multinational corporations that emerged at that time and for whom the use of markedly different accounting standards from one country to another appeared costly, unnecessary, and potentially dangerous as it multiplied the risks of error or malpractice. Furthermore, on the investment side it was a time of increasing cross-border mobility as investors moved funds from one developed country to another to chase the best opportunities. For international investors, it was desirable to be able to assess companies' economic performance on the basis of comparable information whatever their country of incorporation, and international accounting standards were an attractive proposition to achieve that goal.

The IASC's establishment also offered US stakeholders an opportunity to broaden the debate, with a double advantage: first, to make sure that other countries would not diverge too markedly from the demanding conceptual framework that was being built in the US; and second, to somewhat loosen the SEC's embrace on all things accounting by giving a hearing to external voices. Schematically, the accounting philosophy adopted by the IASC puts emphasis on balance-sheet items (assets, liabilities and equity) as a basis for the determination of revenues and costs, and is thus very close to the one formed by FASB shortly after its creation in 1973. When, in the late 1980s, the IASC eventually completed its own conceptual document – the Framework for the Preparation and Presentation of Financial Statements – it largely based itself on FASB's Concepts Statements.

Simultaneously, because unencumbered by the highly litigious US environment, the IASC could issue standards that were more principles-based than the detailed, prescriptive US GAAP rules that had evolved over the years. This was also in harmony with the British tradition of emphasizing "substance over form" in accounting choices, which resulted in short, principles-based standards enabling the exercise of judgment in assessing diverse real-world situations. The IASC was also more independent than FASB was from special interest groups based in the US, which made it useful for the SEC to overcome local opposition to certain accounting reforms on several occasions. A recent example of this dynamic is the reform of the accounting treatment ("expensing") of stock options; its prior adoption by the IASB was used by the SEC to impose it in the US in 2004–05 despite fierce political opposition, most prominently from the high-technology sector.

In short, until its endorsement by the EU, international standard-setting combined the following features. On the one hand, it somewhat corresponded to the Minervian Normative Mode of institution building, but with the significant difference that the epistemic community on which it rested was not made up of NGOs or traditional actors within "civil society," but of the accounting profession and other participants in worldwide capital markets. On the other hand, it very much followed the pattern of other international initiatives that were shaped by the US interest in fostering an open environment based on the rule of law throughout the non-Communist world. However, public authorities were not instrumental in the IASC's creation and affirmed their interest only at a later stage.

Most important to note is that until the EU's decision during 2000–02, and notwithstanding a few relatively insignificant exceptions in developing countries, international accounting standards had not been elevated to the level of publicly enforceable rules. This also holds true after their endorsement by IOSCO in 2000, which still left national regulators the possibility of imposing so-called reconciliation requirements.[8] Therefore, in all jurisdictions that would use the option, the use of IFRS could not be seen as an alternative to national standards but just as an additional, and therefore costly, reporting requirement. In other words, the main impact of IFRS was to provide a shared reference for the legally binding work of national accounting standard-setters, but that was too loose to produce genuine harmonization and comparability of financial statements across borders.

Europe's endorsement of IFRS and the shift to competitive mode

Europe's decision during 2000–02 to endorse IFRS was a radical one: a rare example of EU countries in effect delegating sovereignty to a global body without taking the intermediate step of organizing the corresponding function at EU level. To understand it, one must look back to the steps that predated the decision.

In the 1970s there had been much talk about harmonizing accounting standards across Europe. These efforts resulted in two landmark directives (European-level framework legislation), the first about annual (individual) corporate accounts in 1978 and the second on consolidated accounts in 1983. These texts, coupled with market pressure, led to some convergence of heavily state-bound accounting systems such as those of France and much of southern Europe, with intermediate systems such as Germany's. This led toward a more investor-oriented philosophy for practices and standards as already existed in the English-speaking world. However, the convergence that took place remained well short of harmonization, let alone unification of standards, and it stalled in the 1980s. In the absence of a European standard-setting authority and any enforceable process to drive convergence, standard-setting remained a national task that was only marginally impacted by the two directives.

A critical development occurred in the 1990s, when it became clear all across Europe, and particularly in Germany, that prominent corporations and high-growth companies were attracted to listing their shares on the New York Stock Exchange (NYSE) or on NASDAQ.[9] To do this, such issuers had to comply with US securities legislation and therefore publish sets of financial statements using US GAAP, under close oversight by the SEC, alongside the ones they published before using the accounting rules of their home country. This highlighted the extent of the differences between US GAAP and most continental European standards, and generally made US GAAP appear more rigorous and demanding. The turning point was reached when Daimler-Benz, the Stuttgart-based industrial giant, became the first German company to list its shares (or more accurately, American depositary receipts) on the NYSE in October 1993. The SEC forced Daimler to reclassify 4 billion Deutsche Mark (DM) in pension provisions as extraordinary profit for 1992, and for 1993 the company had to publish a loss under US GAAP of

DM 1.8 billion (around €950 million) while its accounts using German standards showed a net profit of DM 615 million (€315 million). Following this and other cases, the opinion became widespread that accounts in US GAAP could provide investors with higher-value information than accounts prepared in accordance with most national European rules.

The flow of secondary listings of European companies on US markets accelerated during the second half of the 1990s, including in the technology sector as a consequence of very high valuation levels. This led to European fears that the most dynamic parts of the European corporate world would be increasingly subject to US rather than European regulation and legislation, a concern that was only accelerated by the late 1990s technology bubble, when NASDAQ appeared as the preferred venue for hot new international listings. Therefore, policy makers felt an urge to counter the "flight" to the high-quality US GAAP environment by adopting better standards in Europe, which would bring credibility to the European market environment and simultaneously preserve a voice for national governments and EU institutions in the preparation and adoption of the rules.

This defensive concern dovetailed with Europe's own integration agenda, which had lagged somewhat in the area of financial markets and was made more visible by the adoption of the Euro, effective since January 1999. The renewed interest in Europe's financial integration triggered a series of market developments, including the first project for a combination between the London Stock Exchange and Deutsche Börse in 1998, and soon afterwards the merger between the Paris, Brussels, and Amsterdam bourses to form Euronext (which merged with the NYSE in 2007). The European Commission eventually pushed an ambitious set of legislative and regulatory initiatives, the Financial Services Action Plan, which it adopted in May 1999.

Although the Action Plan did not explicitly endorse IFRS it included the aim of, "moving towards a single set of financial statements for listed companies."[10] This same objective was repeated at the EU's Lisbon European Council meeting in March 2000, which, apart from notoriously setting the goal for Europe to become "the most competitive and dynamic knowledge-based economy in the world" by 2010, also specified 2005 as the deadline for the EU-wide unification of accounting standards. Eventually, in June 2000, the Commission announced its preference for International Accounting Standards. The European Commission then decided to adopt the standards by means of a regulation, or legislation that is directly applicable as national law in all EU member states, and thus more immediately efficient for harmonization than the directives adopted in the 1970s that required "transposition" into national legislation by each EU member state. After its ratification by the European Parliament and Council (comprised of the then 15 member states' governments), the regulation was officially adopted on July 19, 2002.

In short, the above decision path can be summarized in three steps, which explains the apparent paradox that the EU adoption of IFRS was both a surprisingly bold public policy initiative, and a move whose intent was primarily defensive, thus legitimizing its depiction under the Competitive Minervian Mode.

First, the completion of the Single Market Programme and of Economic and Monetary Union, coupled with the "irrational exuberance" and vibrant market development of the late 1990s, persuaded governments that they could no longer adhere to purely national accounting standards. A common accounting language was needed.

Second, for several reasons the idea of creating EU-wide standards attracted no decisive support. One reason was the failure of directive-led accounting harmonization in the 1970s and 1980s. Another was the lack of appetite in some countries, including the UK, to reinforce the power of EU institutions in a matter as crucial as accounting standards. From the point of view of the City of London, IFRS adoption provided a means to achieve desirable accounting harmonization, while still "keeping Brussels at bay" – not to mention the advantage of having the standard-setter already located in the City. Furthermore, it was doubtful that the EU could assemble the technical capabilities, skills, and efficient processes that would enable it to issue standards that could compete with IFRS and US GAAP on the same level of quality. Finally, and perhaps most decisively, the rapid pace of global integration of financial markets made many participants doubt that creating a new set of standards with primarily European scope would make any sense at all.

The third step, then, was straightforward. If the EU could not contemplate standards of its own, then it had only two options left: either totally surrender accounting sovereignty to FASB through the flight of the best companies toward US GAAP, as was spontaneously happening (pre-Enron); or just partially surrender it to the IASB. It is hardly surprising that Europeans chose the second option rather than the first.

Nevertheless, the initial degree of consensus around the decision was as remarkable as it would prove short-lived. The regulation was approved in March 2002 in the European Parliament by 492 votes out of 526, and then unanimously by the Council in June. Only later did controversy, most prominently about the IAS 39 standard on financial instruments, reveal how much sovereignty member states had abandoned in the process – accounting standards were important as a *de facto* policy-making instrument, and the IASB was essentially independent from European special interests. For better or worse, the landmark EU adoption of IFRS was resolved by leaders who, at least in some cases, had failed to recognize the wider political implications of their decision. This observation rules out application of the Minervian Political Leadership Mode to accounting standard-setting, as there is no indication that IFRS were being shaped by uniquely European political priorities (Posner and Véron 2010).

A work in progress

Despite the specificity of accounting standards compared with other issue-areas analyzed in this book, the Minervian framework and its Competitive Mode provide a convincing description of Europe's landmark decision to adopt IFRS during 2000–02, which led to IFRS adoption or recognition in a significant number of jurisdictions and probable future adoption in still more jurisdictions, that could one day even include the US. However, this dynamic could still be reverted.

Two major pitfalls may disrupt the previously exposed trends. The IASB's legitimacy as a global standard-setter may be contested; inconsistent IFRS implementation may lead to a low degree of comparability of financial statements across national (or sectoral) borders, thus undermining the very justification of the shift to international standards.

The challenge to the IASB: legitimacy

Strong as it presently looks, one should not forget the international accounting framework's essential frailty. The IASB is a small-sized private-sector organization with unresolved funding problems and limited legitimacy outside its continued capacity to develop good-quality financial reporting standards. International accounting standard-setting is not underpinned by an international treaty, and there are no current plans to create one. The IASB's relationship with the Monitoring Board remains ambiguous, and the Monitoring Board is itself an ad hoc body whose global representativeness is lopsided (Véron 2011).

IFRS adoption has many distributional effects that result in winners and losers, and politicians have increasingly taken notice. The global financial crisis, especially in its initial phase in 2007–08, has put IFRS to the test and resulted in much controversy about the alleged pro-cyclical role of "fair value" (or "mark-to-market") accounting in the credit bubble, and then in the market downturn (Laux and Leuz 2010). Political controversy surrounding international accounting standard-setting is unlikely to disappear.

The IASB has only gradually discovered the full extent of the responsibility that its success has imposed upon it. Until around late 2002, when European companies started to realize in earnest that they had to prepare for the shift to IFRS accounting, the IASB's proceedings were followed by only a small group of specialized accountants. Now, the IASB must understand the interests of its various constituencies – multinational corporations, audit firms, investment banks, fund-management companies, various public authorities in the EU, China, the US and elsewhere, international organizations, central banks, and many others still. It needs to strike the right balance between these interests in order to fulfill its mandate and ensure its own survival.

The IASB experienced its first major political battle with the European debate over the IAS 39 standard on financial instruments in 2003–04. This standard extended the scope of financial assets and liabilities to be accounted for at "fair value," which contrasted with the existing national standards in most countries that allowed accounting at historical cost, or no accounting at all in the case of financial derivatives. IAS 39 was opposed by many European banks, which were used to sector-specific accounting standards with a number of prudential provisions that increased the banks' ability to survive crises but made them less than transparent vis-à-vis investors. Faced with the banks' fierce lobbying, the IASB stonewalled and escalated the discussion into a decisive test of its independence. Eventually, the IASB did not amend its standard, and in November 2004 the EU endorsed a version from which a few paragraphs were "carved out" so that their implementation would be only optional for EU-listed banks.

But such independence came at a price, and could not be sustained forever. Many of the IASB's former friends in Europe were somewhat estranged by the rigidity it displayed in this episode. The pattern was almost completely reversed in October 2008, at the height of the financial crisis following the bankruptcy of Lehman Brothers, when the European Union effectively imposed a change in IAS 39 that was reluctantly adopted in a rush by the IASB, without complying with its normal due process. Since this episode, the IASB has maintained a difficult relationship with the EU institutions, resisting further attempts at interference in the standard-setting but conceding on other dimensions, including the appointment of Europeans to key positions. Hans Hoogervorst, a Dutchman, was appointed in 2011 as David Tweedie's successor as chairman of the IASB, and a Frenchman, Michel Prada, was made chairman of the IFRS Foundation's Trustees.

In parallel, the IASB also has to maintain its independence vis-à-vis other jurisdictions and stakeholders in order to retain its worldwide legitimacy. This is especially significant with regards to the United States. From this point of view, the convergence process with US GAAP, as heralded in the Norwalk Agreement of 2002 and ensuing joint IASB–FASB documents, has been riddled with ambiguities. FASB derives strong public legitimacy from its backing by the SEC, itself a mighty public agency under close oversight by the democratically elected US Congress – something for which the IASB has no equivalent to show. FASB is also a larger body, with more staff and arguably more experience than the IASB. Moreover, many individuals who spent a large part of their career at FASB hold prominent positions in the IASB's own staff. Therefore, the discussion is heavily tilted toward the IASB being led to adopt US GAAP rules rather than FASB embrace of IASB principles. This situation carries the risk of a negative net effect on IFRS quality.

Other risks to the IASB's legitimacy abound. The IASB must prove it is not overly influenced by the largest global accounting firms, even though it needs to draw on their unique pool of knowledge. It must fight disengagement by market participants, many of which have criticized IASB choices as leading to abstract accounting with a weak connection to the economic reality of business operations. And it must avoid paralysis: the risk of becoming overly cautious and therefore incapable of addressing the challenges of the day.

Finally, the ancillary issue of funding for the international accounting standard-setter is mostly unresolved. Before 2001, national accountancy bodies provided most of the funding for the IASC, but in the 1990s this was rightly considered incompatible with the requirement for independence. In 2001, a transitory funding framework was put together for an initial period of five years, and then extended until 2008. In March 2006 the trustees decided on principles for the eventual funding framework, but this has proved difficult to put in place.[11] Under this framework, the IASB faces the challenge of raising its revenue through individual jurisdictions without becoming hostage to the corresponding national governments, or the European Commission in the case of the EU (Véron 2011).

The challenge to individual jurisdictions: consistent implementation

Even if the IASB asserts its legitimacy, there is no guarantee that IFRS implementation will succeed. IFRS are mainly principles-based standards that do not enter into prescriptive rule making, or at least do so less than US GAAP. This means there can sometimes be several different ways of implementing them in concrete situations. The IFRS Interpretations Committee, which is attached to the IASB, has until now adopted a fairly limited conception of its role, with an average of only four to five interpretations issued every year since 1997, and has rejected many demands for interpretations. It also refuses to give detailed implementation guidance in cases that the IASB thinks should be governed by individual, decentralized judgment. This latter point is a consequence of the heterogeneity of implementation contexts, as Gilbert Gélard, then one of the IASB's 14 members, noted: "IFRS cover the world, which is heterogeneous from many points of view.... Global standard-setting is bound to be somewhat general, and wary of the forced uniformity that would result from too detailed rules" (2006).

Such restraint by the standard-setter can lead to fragmentation along sectoral or, more dangerously still, national boundaries. In the absence of guidance from the IASB, companies and auditors may be tempted to turn to some third-party authority to secure their judgments and reduce legal uncertainty, be it the national securities regulator, the now-idle national standard-setting body (which, in most cases, has not been dismantled), industry groups, or other sources. Even though European companies have implemented IFRS for several years now, national specificities remain in their implementation.

Against the serious risk of fragmentation, there are several correcting mechanisms, but all have their limits, and whether their cumulated effect will be enough is still unclear. First, auditors have among their tasks the enforcement of uniform implementation in all countries, but the generally decentralized governance of the "Big Four" networks makes it difficult to ensure complete consistency. Second, there is market pressure from investors, financial analysts, and industry organizations to promote uniformity of implementation, but many investors and analysts are reluctant to sustain over time the analytical effort that would be required to put sufficient pressures on companies to ensure comparability. Third, the EU countries have identified the risk of fragmentation and created some tools to fight it, through coordination of national regulators, creation of a database of past decisions, common standards of enforcement, and meetings involving all stakeholders to exchange best practices, but while dialogue is undoubtedly useful, the thorniest divergences of implementation may not be eliminated this way. Despite the creation of the European Securities and Markets Authority (ESMA) in 2011, EU member states have stopped short of a centralization of IFRS enforcement that would ensure consistency. Finally, the SEC might serve a useful purpose as a reference for implementation.

The US securities regulator has not yet endorsed IFRS use for domestic issuers, but it does oversee financial statements prepared using IFRS and published by foreign companies listed in the US. Donald Nicolaisen, as the SEC's Chief Accountant, made it clear in April 2005 that "securities regulators, including the SEC, need to ensure that compliance [of European companies' financial statements with IFRS] is enforced. The SEC...may find it necessary from time to time to weigh in on particular accounting interpretations" (2005). Because of the SEC's clout and skills, its pronouncements on the implementation of IFRS carry more weight than those of any other national securities regulators. But the risk remains that SEC-issued implementation guidance could give rise to political opposition in Europe, and to mismatches and biases due to the differences between US and European legal and accounting cultures.

Of course, the challenge of IFRS implementation is not specific to the EU, and similar difficulties may be experienced in all jurisdictions that use IFRS. However, because the EU has taken leadership in IFRS adoption, the way it addresses this challenge in the years to come will be particularly crucial.

We are still in the early phase of IFRS adoption, and the resilience of what has been achieved to date has not yet been fully tested. Many difficulties in implementation have been papered over by the use of "first-time adoption" options left to companies for their first-time application of IFRS. Accounting standards provide a striking embodiment of the Competitive Minervian Mode in an economic issue-area, but the jury is still out as to the eventual outcome.

Notes

1. See for example, Interim Report of the Committee on Capital Market Regulation, November 30, 2006 (on www.capmktsreg.org); and "Sustaining New York's and the US' Global Financial Services Leadership," report jointly commissioner by Mayor Michael R. Bloomberg and Senator Charles E. Schumer, January 2007 (on www.mikebloomberg.com or www.senate.gov).

2. Author's calculation based on FT Global 500 rankings, available online at: http://www.ft.com

3. In the year of transition toward IFRS use, a study by PricewaterhouseCoopers found that the proportion of executive incentive awards accounted for by stock options fell sharply, from 36 to 21 percent. *Financial Times*, "IFRS Put Damper on Share Option Schemes," August 11, 2005.

4. Here I follow the common practice of using the collective "IFRS" to refer to the entire body of standards and interpretations, that is, all individual texts named IAS, IFRS, and the so-called SIC and IFRIC interpretative rules (or "interpretations") once they have been approved by the IASB. I also frequently use the acronym "IASB" as shorthand for the entire standard-setting organization that encompasses the IASB, the IFRS Foundation (formerly IASC Foundation) as well as the IFRS Interpretation Committee (once known as IFRIC) and the IFRS Advisory Council (formerly Standards Advisory Council), which were also created in 2001.

5. The detail of funding from each jurisdiction is provided in the IFRS Foundation's annual report.

6. See SEC (2003). The report disputes the principles-based nature of IFRS, and proposes limited reforms to the US accounting framework.

7. The Norwalk Agreement of September 2002 was given this name as it was signed in FASB's home city of Norwalk, Connecticut.

8. Companies publish reconciliation requirements to explain the differences between their financial statements prepared in accordance with international standards on the one hand, and national standards on the other.

9. Some continental European companies had already listed in New York in the decades before, but the trend intensified in the 1990s.

10. European Commission Press Release, May 11, 1999.

11. "Principles for a New Funding System," blueprint approved by the IASC Foundation's Trustees in their March 2006 meeting; available at: www.iasb.org

Part III
The Normative Mode

7
The Ottawa Process: Domestic Interests, Transnational Civil Society, and State Identity

Petrice R. Flowers

The 1997 Convention to prohibit the production, use, transfer, and stockpiling of antipersonnel landmines (also known as the Ottawa Convention or Mine Ban Treaty) is a landmark accomplishment for two key reasons (Williams and Goose 1998; Lawson and Tomlinson 1998; *Landmine Monitor*[1]). First, the speed with which treaty negotiations took place is unprecedented in international relations. Second, the negotiation process itself was remarkable because transnational non-state actors were an integral part of the process. Although both of these points have been the subjects of excellent scholarly inquiries (Price 1998; Anderson 2000; Rutherford 2001), few have attempted to understand the comprehensive role of three Minervian actors – Canada, the European Union, and Japan – in the Ottawa Process. The Ottawa Convention was negotiated, ratified, and entered into force without the support of the United States and despite objections from the largest producers of antipersonnel landmines. How was it possible for Canada, the EU, and Japan to overcome US objections to a comprehensive ban on antipersonnel (AP) landmines? Why would these three actors undertake this course of action, given the risks to their relations with the United States?

Traditional international relations theory focuses on power politics to explain relations between states. In this view, great powers dominate the building and maintaining of international institutions. The inability of powerful states to control the outcome of the Ottawa Process disputes the realist contention that international institutions are merely a reflection of states' material power. The bottom–up, normative mode of explanation offers broad variation in the types, numbers, and combinations of factors that explain global institution building in a particular issue-area. These factors may vary, based at least in part, on the domestic political context.

Instead of the three primary normative aspects of domestic interests, transnational civil society, and state identity offering three competing explanations, I suggest that the relationships between the three is essential to understanding this story, which is a story of process and interaction.

The landmine case is the first in which advanced democracies with significant but non-hegemonic power have successfully carved out a niche in advancing global institution building without the support of the hegemonic power, the United States. The processes of negotiating and ratifying the Mine Ban Treaty demonstrate the importance of a normative mode of global institution building that depends on transnational civil society and norm entrepreneurs, among others, in both using and shaping meaning and identity in bottom–up processes of global institution building. These normative processes are rooted in domestic political, social, and economic circumstances, but they were formed in a historically contingent international context that offered the opportunity for Minervian actors to actively embark on an identity-based international political agenda.

The remainder of this chapter is divided into four sections. The first section sketches the theoretical framework, defines the key variables, and explicates the potential policy impact and limitations of each variable. The second section provides the essential background about the growth of the movement to ban landmines, from the initial calls for a Convention on Certain Conventional Weapons (CCW) Review Conference to the Ottawa Process. The third section analyzes Japan, Canada, and key European states' move toward supporting a ban. Japan represents a "hard" case with weak non-governmental organizations and a government that was strongly identified with and supportive of the US position. Japan remained on the sidelines of the Ottawa Process until finally signing the ban in 1998. The Canadian case is characterized by strong, pro-active NGOs that took the lead on demanding that Canadian values be reflected in foreign policy and in defining those values. Germany, France, and the UK followed different trajectories toward supporting a ban, but their NGOs were the leaders of transnational civil society organizations that played a critical role in creating the ban. The final section considers the possible implications of this model on building global institutions in the future.

Domestic interests, transnational civil society, and state identity

States with relative agreement between the ministries of foreign affairs and defense were early supporters of a comprehensive ban on landmines. States with significant economic interests in producing and exporting landmines, as well as those whose identities are closely tied to traditional conceptualization of security based on relative gains, were opposed to a comprehensive ban. The Minervian states fell somewhere between these two extremes; their interest in creating foreign policies based on a broader understanding of security facilitated their transformation to supporters of a total ban on AP mines. By considering the roles of domestic interests, transnational civil society, and state identity in an interactive process we can better account for how both domestic and international determinants of state interest shape identity and state actions on this issue. Because the Ottawa Process was not state centric or consensus based, it provided a context that allowed for the interaction of non-state actors, international organizations, and states, and for the consideration of broad sets of domestic interests alongside traditional state interests. Transnational civil society's reframing of the issue of antipersonnel mines was essential in getting and keeping the issue on the international agenda and in shaping state identity through socializing (or "teaching") states on understanding the issue (Price 1998; Wendt 1994). Transnational civil society is partly comprised of domestic organizations and can play a key role in shaping state–society relations; they often served as an intermediary between the two during the Ottawa Process. As in the case of Japan, this role can be extremely important in situations where state–society relations are strained. Domestic interests cannot explain all policy choices, especially those that seem to contradict or conflict with state interests (Finnemore 1996), but states do have to respond to domestic interests in order to maintain power and legitimacy. This case is particularly interesting because of the role that domestic organizations play in transnational civil society, which makes the relationships between transnational and domestic civil society organizations as important as each of their relationships with states. Finnemore and Sikkink's (1998) two-level norm game is a good starting point for considering the complex relationship between domestic interests and transnational civil society; this is essential to understanding the extent to which each contributes to an explanation of the success of the Ottawa Process. Consideration of broader domestic interests that include the expectations of the public and are represented by state and non-state actors is fundamental. This approach recognizes that although the constructivist contention states that interests and identity are not always derived from within the state, at times they are. More often, however, they are a complex negotiation of the two.

Many studies of international norms primarily focus on the role of non-state actors such as NGOs, norm entrepreneurs, and epistemic communities in the transmission of norms (for example, Klotz 1995; Finnemore 1996; Keck and Sikkink 1998; Crawford 1993). In these studies, norm adoption is often found to be closely related to the activities of non-state actors such as transnational activists, international organizations, transnational advocacy networks, or sometimes a combination of these. Yet non-state actors are only partially responsible for norm adoption; these processes are also dependent on other domestic actors, including government institutions. Cortell and Davis point out two national-level factors that are important determinants of the effects of international norms at the level of domestic political processes: "the domestic salience or legitimacy of the norm, and the structural context within which the domestic policy debate transpires" (Cortell and Davis 2000, p. 66). The landmine case illustrates that adoption of international norms often hinges on support from domestic actors at least partially determined by the degree of conflict with relevant domestic interests, and that domestic salience and domestic structural context are interconnected. The idea that identity and legitimacy are important motivators, sometimes as important as economic interests, is also relevant to this case; it calls into question state motivations for refusing to accept the US position and moving ahead with building global institutions.

The three variables in this interactive process that produced state commitments to the Ottawa Convention are: domestic interests represented by domestic NGOs and government actors, transnational civil society, and state identity. In analyzing this interactive process I focus on two key questions: how does each variable impact policy decisions? What are the limitations of each variable's impact on policy decisions? Domestic actors include both supporters and opponents of the Convention, with the primary advocates being domestic NGOs and individual government actors who sometimes serve as norm entrepreneurs (as in the case of Canada's Lloyd Axworthy and Japan's Keizo Obuchi). Government actors, including key ministries and agencies, can be supporters or opponents depending on the interests of the institutions that they represent. NGOs can play a pivotal role where international and domestic norms conflict; this role is strengthened when NGOs enjoy broad public support that allows them to mobilize public opinion in their favor. The manner in which governmental actors affect decisions depends on the issue and on the actor, but in general, government actors dominate agenda setting. If a pivotal government actor is a norm entrepreneur, s/he can affect the political opportunities available to NGOs and provide access that enables NGOs to get their concerns on the national agenda. This access does not, however, guarantee NGO success. On the other hand, there are also scenarios where no such actor emerges and we see a more typical political struggle between institutions with conflicting interests. In the case of landmines the key conflict is between ministries of defense and foreign affairs. The impact of various governmental actors can be limited in terms of their power vis-à-vis other actors, and by their ability to mobilize ideational support of the public by framing the issues in ways that resonate and elicit widespread public support. NGOs face more material and ideational limitations on their potential to impact policy decisions. Their influence can be limited by a lack of authority, legitimacy, and access (Price 2003). In addition, NGOs may suffer from unsuccessful issue framing that does not resonate with the public and other potential supporters.

Transnational civil society organizations can fill in gaps where domestic NGOs fall short; this can be especially helpful in dealing with reluctant states. By socializing states, agenda setting at the international level, shaming or calling on states to account for decisions, these organizations can persuade even reluctant states to participate in building and strengthening institutions. As is the case with domestic NGOs, these organizations have to deal with issues of legitimacy, authority, and access, but a great many of them are bolstered by their status in the United Nations and other international institutions as representatives of the people, ties to powerful states, and a growing consensus within the international community that NGOs and civil society are important actors for the promotion of democracy and other values internationally (Keck and Sikkink 1998; Anderson 2000; Hubert 2000; Thakur 2006). Potential limitations on transnational civil society's ability to influence policy are similar to those that domestic NGOs face, with the addition of opposition from powerful states and other international actors as well as the possibility that their issues may not enjoy support among domestic constituencies in key states.

States' identity concerns seriously impact those issues on which states choose to act and the substance of that action. A state is more likely to act on issues that will impact its legitimacy at home or abroad as well as those issues that are central to a state's own understanding of self or the self it wishes to establish or project. Price (2004) reminds us that identity pressures play a role in shaping state interests and are therefore a significant aspect of global institutions such as international treaty law. Some states such as Canada and Japan had both domestic and international motivations for implementing their foreign policy with state identity concerns in mind. In Canada's case, there was a conscious effort on the part of the public to demand that the government enact policies that more accurately reflected Canadian values and substantiate Canada's identity as an international moral leader. In Japan there was a general need to articulate a normative core that would define Japanese foreign policy priorities and offer a more coherent vision of Japan's role in the world. Part of the goal in creating such a normative vision was to move Japan toward a more active role in international politics in general and improve its chances of gaining a permanent seat on the UN Security Council. The EU states faced a different challenge posed by their pursuit of a collective identity and the need to integrate their individual state identities into a coherent unit. The larger international context in which the Mine Ban Treaty was negotiated is one where the absence of a constructive or at least a coherent hegemonic interest presented the Minervian actors with the opportunity to project their state identities (Anderson 2000). In choosing to create a global institution banning landmines, the Minervian actors were embarking on an identity-based agenda that would strengthen their own legitimacy as international actors while building a lasting global institution based on shared values.

Growth of the movement to ban landmines

The use of antipersonnel landmines, primarily as a defensive weapon to deter removal of antitank mines, began during the First World War. Their use was not questioned until the 1970s, by which time they were increasingly being used as strategic offensive weapons (Politis 1999). In the 1970s attention to the devastation that landmines cause put the issue on the international agenda, which resulted in the ratification of the 1980 Convention on Certain Conventional Weapons, with Protocol II focused on the use of landmines. CCW attempts to protect civilians by prohibiting the use of landmines in civilian areas. However, loopholes and other shortcomings weakened the prohibition. Internal armed conflicts were not covered by the ban, and even in international conflicts, the country where the mines were placed was responsible for their removal; this was usually hindered by lack of resources. Finally, Protocol II did not regulate production and transfer of mines

(Politis 1999; Roberts 1998). Thus NGOs working in mine-infested areas continued to see new victims of landmines well after conflicts had ended. These organizations witnessed how landmines inhibited refugees from returning home and post-war reconstruction efforts (Roberts 1998). Thus NGOs began to argue that the damage caused by landmines could be adequately addressed only by a total ban on the weapons. In order for this to happen, framing the issue of landmine use would have to shift from being understood and dealt with as a military issue to a humanitarian one. This work was the domain of NGOs; in October 1992, US and European human rights and humanitarian aid organizations began pursuing the goal of ending the use, production, trade, and stockpiling of antipersonnel landmines (Roberts 1998).

   NGOs played a crucial role in getting the issue of antipersonnel mines on the international agenda and mobilizing international concerns. In 1993, ten years after the CCW entered into force, France called for a CCW Review Conference under pressure from Handicap International, a French NGO. When the United States announced a moratorium on exporting AP mines – giving a boost to the international ban campaign – the time was ripe for a review conference. The CCW Review Conference finally occurred in September 1995, and NGOs presented the delegates with 1.5 million signatures calling for a ban on AP mines. In the time between France calling for a review conference in 1993 and the conference, taking place in 1995, the International Campaign to Ban Landmines (ICBL) had made major strides in building a movement. In 1994, under pressure from their national ban campaigns, both Sweden and Italy called for a ban on AP mines. In May 1993 the first international NGO Conference on AP mines was held in London; 70 representatives of 40 non-governmental organizations attended the conference. The second NGO conference, held in 1994, marked the start of support from various UN agencies. The conference was co hosted by UNICEF and held in Geneva; participation doubled. The third NGO Conference was held in Phnom Penh, Cambodia, in June 1995, just three months before the CCW Review Conference. The founding of the Cambodia Campaign to Ban Landmines in August 1994 and the fact that Cambodia hosted the third NGO Conference indicated that this movement was not just one of first-world activists advocating for what is largely a third-world problem. Another milestone was reached in March 1995, when Belgium became the first country to ban use, production, trade, and stockpiling of AP mines; Norway followed suit in June of that same year.

   The momentum of the third NGO conference, which had 450 participants from more than 40 countries, left activists hopeful that the CCW

Review Conference would produce an agreement to ban landmines. Political wrangling, the rules of the negotiating process, and a blocking coalition led by the United States and supported by Japan resulted in a less-than-desirable agreement by the end of the conference. Disappointed by the inability to secure a ban on AP mines, a group of countries that supported a ban – later known as the core states – and NGOs attended a meeting before the Review Conference ended. At this meeting they agreed to meet in Canada the next year to continue working toward a ban. The Ottawa Process, which led to the Ottawa Convention banning the use, transfer, production, and stockpiling of AP mines, was initiated in October 1996 when the Canadian government hosted the conference titled "Towards a Global Ban on Anti-Personnel Landmines." Fifty countries, twenty-four observer states, NGOs, and UN agencies, among others, attended the conference. To the surprise of many, then Canadian Foreign Minister, Lloyd Axworthy, issued a challenge that they return to Ottawa in December 1997 – a mere 14 months later – to sign a ban (Williams and Goose 1998). Despite the failure of the CCW Review Conference to produce a ban, the energy and dedication of the core states kept the movement going by supporting a ban and giving NGOs access to government actors and the negotiation process. [2] Furthermore, since the negotiations in the Ottawa Process did not have to conform to consensus rules, there was less of an opportunity for the United States and other powerful opposition states to block progress toward a ban.

Building the ban

Of the three Minervian actors, Japan was the last to sign and ratify the Ottawa Convention. A very strong norm entrepreneur, Keizo Obuchi, and state identity triggered the shift in Japan's position, from supporting the US argument for a limited ban to supporting a total ban. Obuchi's high-profile role in the government – first as foreign minister, then as prime minister – actually increased NGO actors' credibility, and in turn their public support. Domestic NGOs also drew from the rhetorical frames, increasing willingness and ability of transnational civil society to pressure the government. Because Japanese NGOs have limited access to political power and little chance to directly affect government decisions, they were heavily dependent on Obuchi's support and public opinion. Lack of consensus among government institutions on this issue was also important. While Japan's Ministry of Foreign Affairs supported a ban, the Defense Agency was hindered by not having full ministerial status and divisions between uniformed officials who opposed the ban and civilians who supported it (Osa 1998). In the interactive process between transnational civil society, domestic interests, and state identity, the latter two had the greatest impact on the Japanese government's decision to sign and ratify the Convention.

Canada perhaps provides the case with the most dynamic relations between domestic interests, transnational civil society, and state identity. In contrast to Japan's NGOs, Canadian NGOs enjoyed a strong position vis-à-vis the government. This was enhanced in 1993 when the Liberal Party included a promise to adopt a broader understanding of security to guide Canada's foreign policy as part of their campaign platform. NGOs pushed them to go even further and develop policies that reflected Canadian values. NGO strength on this issue was based partly on public support that allowed them, and not the government, to claim to represent Canadian values. The government's willingness to eventually include NGOs in policy discussions and international meetings further increased NGO credibility among the Canadian public and influence over the government (Warmington and Tuttle 1998). Once NGO representatives were allowed to attend international meetings as part of the official Canadian delegation, they were poised to contribute their legitimacy, credibility, and access to government officials (Canadian as well as non-Canadian) to transnational civil society. These NGOs were not always welcomed at international meetings, and they were certainly disappointed with the outcomes of the initial meetings in which they participated, but their involvement from a very early stage meant that they had already worked through many of the difficulties with government actors and institutions that Japanese NGOs were only beginning to deal with in 1997. The exchange between Canadian NGOs, with their support from the Canadian public and transnational actors, and Canadian government actors made it more likely that there would be a broader base of support for an international ban within the government, despite tensions between the Ministries of Foreign Affairs and Defense. Thus, when Foreign Ministers Ouellet and Axworthy emerged as supporters of a ban, they had an opportunity to take the initiative on the international level.

There was broad-based, early support in the EU for an international ban; this support stretched from the European Commission to strong national-level support in small, medium, and large EU member states. Although many EU states were supportive of a ban, they differed from Canada on the appropriate avenue to pursue such an outcome. In contrast to the Canadian position of calling for an independent process that gave NGOs a seat at the table (Hubert 2000), France, Britain,

Germany, Spain, and Finland viewed the Conference on Disarmament (CD) – which had a traditional state-centric approach – as the legitimate forum within which to pursue a ban. Germany, Britain, and France each took different routes to supporting the ban. In Germany there was early convergence of interests among state and non-state domestic actors, leading to Germany's 1996 ban on landmines. Its position as a core state, one of the original states supporting a total ban, lent legitimacy to the movement to ban landmines both at the state level and at the level of transnational civil society. It seems that the lack of domestic disputes precluded the development of high-profile advocates that might have grown out of a more contentious domestic process of moving toward a ban. In the cases of France and Britain, neither was a core state but their domestic NGOs played key roles in establishing the transnational civil society movement to ban landmines. In both cases, the high profile of domestic NGOs in transnational civil society was not enough to secure government support. France is a bit closer to the Canadian case insofar as the government was willing to listen to domestic NGOs and take their requests to push for a CCW Review Conference seriously. The French government did push for the Review Conference in the early 1990s, but did not support a total ban. Indeed, France did not support a total ban on landmines until after the Socialists came to power in 1997. French NGOs, especially Handicap International, had access to government actors who were often responsive to NGO concerns. In Britain there was a clear divide along party lines; even though British NGOs played a key role in establishing the ICBL and Britain was home to Princess Diana, the highest-profile supporter of a ban, the government did not lend its support to a ban until the Labour Party gained power in 1997. The state's close identification with the United States, opposition of both the ministries of foreign affairs and defense to a ban, and Conservative rule solidified government opposition to a ban and left little room for domestic NGOs, transnational civil society, or normative concerns to penetrate policy making. After Labour gained power the government announced its intention to destroy its AP mine stockpiles by 2005 and apply a unilateral moratorium on the use of AP mines until this date, and pursue a ban within both the Ottawa Process and the CD.

The European Commission took positions that were supportive of a ban even before the CCW Review Conference; however, they maintained that a more comprehensive ban should come from the CCW Review Conference and Council on Disarmament. The diversity of EU member states' positions on the issue probably constrained just how far the Commission could go in its support of a ban. The remainder of this section is divided into three sub-sections; each focuses on one of the three variables and demonstrates how the variables functioned during the Ottawa Process.

Transnational civil society

The key to policy change based on normative concerns involve defining which values will guide policy, and effectively articulating the identity that will be reflected. Transnational civil society played a central role in defining and articulating these concerns at the systemic level and in shaping state identity. Though much of the literature focuses on how transnational civil society organizations impact states, these organizations also influence domestic NGOs. Despite their central role, the relationship between transnational civil society and domestic NGOs involved in working toward a ban has not been analyzed. It is often assumed that on a given issue there is a harmony of interests and close working relationship between domestic NGOs and transnational civil society that makes it possible for the latter to work from outside while the former works from inside state borders toward the same goal. For this assumption to be accurate would require a state–society relationship that allowed NGOs to operate within an independent civil society.

In Japan, for example, the momentum of the landmine ban treaty negotiations rested on NGOs to a great extent, but given their generally very weak status in Japan, one would not expect NGOs to be able to exert sufficient influence to change the government's position. Because these groups are by definition "outsiders," they usually do not have access to networks of power in Japan (Swartz and Pharr 2003).[3] These two things hold when discussing the NGO sector as a whole, but they sometimes break down when we consider a specific organization. Groups with extensive field experience that also enjoyed good relations with the government, such as the Japanese organization Association for Aid and Relief (AAR, formerly Association to Aid Refugees), used their connections to gain support from influential people. One of those individuals was Yasuhiro Nakasone, who had served as both prime minister and director general of the Defense Agency. Nakasone still exercised "enormous influence on both political circles and the Defense Agency. Members of the Liberal Democratic Party [the party in power] admitted that Mr. Nakasone's support for a total ban had a great impact on the government's final decision" (Osa 1998, p. 174). Through the

1996 election of Yukihisa Fujita (a former board member of AAR) to the Diet, NGOs gained an ally who was willing to popularize their concerns about the landmine issue within the government. Support within the Diet increased when the Japan Parliamentarian League to Promote a Ban on Antipersonnel Mines was formed in June 1997, with Osa appointed Secretary-General of the group (Kitagawa 2005).

Though the Canadian ban campaign emerged in a difficult domestic context for Canadian NGOs, they still enjoyed smoother relations with the government than their Japanese colleagues. Due to budget cuts and the political nature of the issue, Canadian NGOs were reluctant to get involved with mine ban advocacy, but in 1993 a few of them started responding to ICBL criticism of Canada's lack of action. By fall of that year, these organizations had established formal objectives and requested a meeting with the government in which they sought a substantial role in the development of a Canadian foreign policy that reflected Canadian values (Warmington and Tuttle 1998). In this case NGOs, not the government, were first to respond to criticism from transnational civil society. This case suggests that domestic NGOs, like states, may have to be persuaded to adopt the position advocated by transnational civil society actors. It is difficult for domestic NGOs to ignore calls for state response to an issue from transnational civil society actors. Often domestic NGOs mobilize transnational networks to exert pressure from outside on reluctant states (Keck and Sikkink 1998). However, when transnational civil society is engaged on an issue that existing domestic NGOs should be involved in but are not, those domestic organizations risk loss of credibility. This may damage NGOs' credibility by calling into question their ability to speak on behalf of a large domestic constituency and use that as leverage vis-à-vis the government; they may also face criticism from that constituency. This can be especially damaging in a place like Canada with a strong and independent civil society, and can open the possibility for the government to dominate particular issues. In this case, domestic NGOs that should be pressing the state for change end up legitimizing the state's lack of response. We see the same scenario in Japan insofar as the irresponsive state is heavily criticized by transnational civil society. In Japan, there was a natural constituency of supporters among those who held pacifist and anti-militarist beliefs but these groups had not been effectively mobilized for the campaign to ban landmines. Weak domestic NGOs can use this situation as an opportunity to step up the pressure on the government, but their energies are better spent on using the increased attention to build a domestic constituency and support for their cause.

Identity

Where interest in identity and values was guiding foreign policy, the goal was not necessarily to project a state's identity for the purpose of creating a new hegemonic discourse based on Canadian or Japanese values. Instead, there was strong belief among domestic populations that their values and identity would create a more humane, sustainable, less conflict-ridden foreign policy. This assumption can be attributed to the population wanting to redress their lack of influence over Cold War-era foreign policy. Not only were people denied access to foreign policy decision making, but the policies of their states were also guided by a worldview that seemed, at least after the fact, to produce and perpetuate conflict. Thus identity-based foreign policy promised an opportunity for non-state actors to influence foreign policy and gain legitimacy among the population and in turn use that influence to establish the identity that would guide policy; this was particularly important for the Minervian actors in creating global institutions. Identity – cultural (for example, Anglo-Saxon) and community (for example, NATO) – was a challenge in different cases. Because states were already members of various (security) communities and other relationships that shaped state identity, demands from domestic constituencies that foreign policy reflect Canadian, Japanese, or European values became a part of the ongoing process of identity formation. Wendt (1994) argues that state identity is sustained by political practices and is always changing. What we see in the Ottawa Process is a change in the practices that constitute identity. The UK has strong cultural and community ties with the United States that definitely influenced its late adoption of the Ottawa Convention. Japan's security alliance with the United States had the same effect. On the other hand, despite being a close ally of the United States and a member of NATO, Canada constantly asserts its independence by attempting to distinguish itself from the United States. I am not suggesting that these three actors are creating new identities in response or opposition to the United States, but am highlighting the fact that the United States figures prominently in their identity formation by virtue of being a powerful actor in institutions through which they have formed collective identities.

According to Obuchi, when he first became foreign minister and realized that deaths from AP mines in places like Cambodia were increasing rather than decreasing, he knew that Japan had to sign the Convention.[4] However, until it signed the treaty in 1998, Japan remained outside the ban camp. Japan's strong support of the US position was based on its commitment to the US–Japan Security Treaty. The treaty has shaped Japan's post-war foreign and domestic policy; it is such a central part of the US–Japan relationship that in the past the Japanese government ignored domestic opposition to the treaty and continued to renew its commitment. During the discussions on instituting an international ban on landmines, Japan was faced with the challenge of pro-actively shaping its post-Cold War foreign policy while still maintaining its relationship with the United States. In short, Japan had yet to articulate an effective identity or normative core to guide its post-Cold War policies. The criticism it faced after the first Gulf War made it clear that a passive stance on tough issues was no longer acceptable – Japan would have to actively reaffirm its relationship with the United States and demonstrate its commitment through decisive action. Being a consumer of the US security umbrella meant making new commitments in a changed international context, but the basis of these new commitments would shift from Cold War-era concerns with security to normative concerns that had been ignored. In the end, Obuchi insisted that the international trend toward banning landmines and Japan's commitment to international peace led to his decision to support the ban.

Although transnational civil society actors were not able to impact the Japanese government directly, the one opening to apply pressure was based on Japan's identity concerns. At first, these concerns were utilitarian and focused on maintaining a "good image." Eventually the identity concerns became part of a more complex understanding of Japan's interest in human security, understood in this context as foreign policy based on humanitarian concerns that broaden the state's concept of security. As one member pointed out in the February 13, 1998 meeting of the Foreign Affairs Committee, if Japan entered the Convention as one of the original 40 countries to ratify and therefore shared responsibility for bringing the treaty into effect, it would be afforded international prestige and power, especially because this would mean opposing the United States on a security issue. This enhanced international status and moral authority would also allow Japan to take a leading role in the region and persuade other Asian countries to ratify. Yet the framing of these two issues illustrates a deep conflict between Japan's desire to be an independent leader in world politics, especially in Asia, and dependence on the United States for its security. This conflict actually delayed ratification.

Domestic interests

NGOs and government actors often represent competing interests, and they both require the support of broad domestic constituencies to legitimize pursuit of these interests. In all of the cases discussed here there was eventual agreement on the importance of instituting a ban on landmines. The nature of the ban – partial or total – and how to achieve it was a more contentious issue. Because of transnational civil society efforts, most states agreed that an international ban on landmines was necessary. However, most did not support a total ban that would prohibit the production, use, transfer, and stockpiling of AP mines, preferring instead a more limited ban. This made it easy for government actors and domestic NGOs to work together on the landmine issue. Each side believed that since they basically agreed on the need for some limits to be put into place to protect civilians, they could convince the other to come around to their way of thinking.

Mines Action Canada (MAC) accepted a government offer to appoint a representative to the official Canadian CCW delegation shortly after the moratorium was announced. MAC's representative was involved in daily discussions with the Departments of Foreign Affairs and National Defence regarding the negotiations, and was also asked to speak on Canada's behalf during negotiations. The experience convinced NGOs that the traditional consensus diplomacy would block any significant changes to the CCW (Warmington and Tuttle 1998). Despite the disappointment, NGOs learned valuable lessons from this insight into the world of international diplomacy that helped them deal even more effectively with the government and create a vision for pursuing a total ban. When the CCW Review Conference failed to produce a ban, the Canadian government announced that it would host a meeting of pro-ban states. MAC was involved in planning this meeting scheduled for October 1996; by this time MAC included more than 40 NGOs and had developed credibility as a reliable and authoritative source of information among Canadian media. The organization was part of the official Canadian delegation throughout the Ottawa Process, as well as a participant in official bilateral meetings to inform governments in the Asia–Pacific region of the Process, and in these roles MAC was given the opportunity to put the skills learned from the CCW Review Conference to use. Despite this privileged position, especially when compared to Japanese NGOs, government and NGO opinions often conflicted during the process. A high level of public support remained crucial, especially when disagreements arose between NGOs and the Canadian government. Even when their efforts were frustrated, NGOs that had the opportunity to work closely with the government gained valuable experience that they could use to improve their overall strategy.

While Canadian NGOs were building expertise and public support for a ban, some government actors were becoming advocates for a ban and allies for NGOs. During a conversation with a Canadian Broadcasting Corporation reporter in November 1995, then Foreign Minister Ouellet stated his opinion that Canada should destroy its stockpile and declare a total ban on the production, export, and use of AP mines. In the end, Ouellet's statements and the changes in policy that it precipitated took control of the mine issue away from the Department of National Defence, opening political space for further changes. Upon Ouellet's retirement, Lloyd Axworthy became foreign minister. By the time Axworthy took his position, the Department of Foreign Affairs and International Trade's Non-proliferation, Arms Control, and Disarmament Division (IDA), the bureaucratic home of the mine issue, had come to view AP mines as a policy priority. This response and encouragement from his senior policy advisor, a holdover from Ouellet, led Axworthy to designate the AP mine issue as an immediate policy priority. Axworthy was also pro-active in establishing a partnership with NGOs. By the summer of 1996, IDA, having officially taken the lead on preparations for the Ottawa conference, held weekly conference calls with ICBL to plan the meeting, and MAC was invited to join Canada's official delegation. "To encourage other governments to do likewise, Canada agreed to increase the number of delegates that could be accredited to the Ottawa session by one if the national delegation included an NGO" (Tomlin 1998, pp. 192–98).

The Mine Advocacy Group (MAG), a British NGO, was one of the cofounders of the International Campaign to Ban Landmines. Despite this early involvement and the establishment of a nationwide network of NGOs, the UK Working Group on Banning Landmines, neither domestic nor transnational civil society organizations had a discernible impact on the British government's position on banning landmines. Immediately after the Labour party prevailed in the May 1997 elections, the UK's policy on landmines shifted dramatically. The government announced its intentions to destroy all stockpiled AP mines by 2005, apply a moratorium on using AP mines until 2005 or until announcement of an international ban, and negotiation of a ban within the Ottawa Process while continuing to work for a ban within the Conference on Disarmament. Despite the change of position, the British government was still committed to working within the traditional framework to achieve a ban.

French NGOs were international leaders in the process that began before Ottawa and that eventually resulted in the Mine Ban Treaty. Initially, French NGOs not only brought the issue to the government's attention, but they also educated government actors and shaped government action and official positions through this teaching role. The French NGO Handicap International (HI), one of the founding organizations of the International Campaign to Ban Landmines and the organization responsible for convincing the French government to request a CCW review conference, served as the main link between different constituencies in France throughout the Ottawa Process. As part of its efforts to publicize the landmine problem, HI worked to educate both the public and government officials and to publicize NGO activities related to mine clearance and victim assistance (Chabasse 1998). The organization began establishing contacts with the French Foreign Affairs Ministry and high-ranking officials after returning from an October 1992 meeting in New York of the six organizations that would become the founders and steering committee of the ICBL. In response to overwhelming interest from the French media and government, HI organized a second landmines conference in February 1993 that it used as an opportunity to teach the interested parties about the landmine issue. It was also used to network transnationally by inviting representatives of the French government; the Mines Advisory Group (a coalition of NGOs from the UK); and US senator Patrick Leahy, a ban advocate who sent a letter to HI, "encouraging the association to convince the French government to convene a meeting for the revision of the 1980 Convention on Certain Conventional Weapons" (Chabasse 1998, p. 62).

French NGOs got a boost when Xavier Emmanuelli, a friend of several NGO leaders, became Secretary of State for Humanitarian Affairs. His position provided NGOs with access to information on meetings and the decision process and relayed information from NGOs to highly placed government officials. As in Canada, there were cleavages between domestic institutions on this issue – the President and one of his Ministers supported a ban while the military hierarchy defended the use of mines. The French government used the first Ottawa conference in October 1996 to announce two shifts in its position on AP landmines: a draft act banning manufacture and sales of landmines that would require the Ministry of Defence to submit an annual report on progress in destroying stockpiles, and the statement that the government relinquished the use of mines except "in the case of absolute necessity to protect its forces," for which it was publicly criticized by the ICBL (Chabasse 1998, pp. 64–65).

The Socialist win in the June 1997 French elections led to even more rapid evolution in the French position toward a ban. The prime minister supported a total ban and long-term pro-ban officials were appointed to the positions of Minister of Defence and Minister for Co-operation and Development. Having a pro-ban minister at the head of the Defence Ministry made it possible to finally establish the domestic consensus necessary for France to take an official position supporting a total ban. At the meeting in Brussels that same month, the French government announced that it would sign the Ottawa Convention and that it would ban all use of antipersonnel mines by the end of 2005 or when the Convention entered into force, whichever came first (Chabasse 1998). With a strong, clear position on the issue, France took a leading role at the negotiations in Oslo.

Conclusion

The lack of a clear agenda in the post-Cold War international context offered an opening for the three Minervian actors to focus on identity concerns and respond to identity pressures from the international community. This context allowed each to pursue foreign policy priorities that reflected their identities and contributed to building global institutions that reflected their shared interests. In each case, domestic interests, transnational civil society, and identity were essential in decisions to sign on to the Mine Ban Treaty, but no single one of the three variables can account for support for a total ban on landmines in all cases. The Canadian case demonstrated the most dynamic interaction between the three variables. Although there was not a consensus for support of a total ban within the Canadian government when Lloyd Axworthy initiated the Ottawa Process, resistance was overcome by domestic NGO access to the government through Axworthy and his office, transnational civil society and state identity concerns. Despite European NGOs forming the core of transnational civil society active on the landmines issue, conflict between ministries of foreign affairs and powerful defense ministries kept both France and the United Kingdom from supporting a total ban until 1997. Japan as well finally came around to supporting the Mine Ban Treaty in the same year. Keizo Obuchi, a high-profile norm entrepreneur lent access and legitimacy to domestic NGOs but Japan did not support a total ban until late in the Ottawa Process after identity pressures made supporting the US position a threat to Japan's international legitimacy.

Despite the diversity of the dominant variable in each case, Canada, Japan, France, and the United Kingdom shared an interest in creating foreign policy with normative foundations that would reflect state identity.

These cases demonstrate that the struggle to define meaning and identity is an essential part of the process of global institution building. Just as opposition from strong government ministries within a resistant state does not guarantee a state's continued opposition, the existence of strong transnational civil society organizations that teach states how to understand issues or domestic NGOs committed to an issue is not enough to ensure support for emerging global institutions. Legitimacy of domestic NGOs and transnational civil society will help them gain support from domestic constituencies and this can help them make a credible claim to access agenda setting and policy making. Their cause will be furthered when influential government actors become norm entrepreneurs. Under these conditions, interests and identities of even reluctant states will be reconstituted to support building global institutions.

Although I have not conducted the same kind of systematic analysis of negotiations of the Convention on Cluster Munitions (CCM), the CCM case is useful in helping us reflect on the question of whether Minervian actors will continue to play a significant role in building global institutions that address security issues. The CCM is a treaty designed to address an issue similar to AP mines – that is, indiscriminate weapons that continue to kill and maim civilians long after war has ended. The CCM entered into force on August 1, 2010 after a process modeled on the Ottawa Process this time led by Norway (itself one of the first two countries to adopt a total ban on landmines even before the Ottawa Process began) and named the Oslo Process after Norway's capital city. As was the case in discussions on banning landmines, the United States, Russia, China, and India were the primary actors in a blocking coalition.

There are some notable differences between the role that particular states played during the negotiations of the Mine Ban Treaty and the role that those same states played in the CCM negotiations. In the CCM case, Japan was one of the original signatories of the Convention and was the fourteenth state to ratify it; thus, it helped move the treaty toward entering into force. Japan has also worked to promote universal ratification of the treaty by encouraging non-signatories to join the CCM and engaging in other outreach activities. Canada, also one of the original signatories, has yet to ratify the CCM. Canada was an active participant in the Oslo Process; however, conflict between the ministries of Foreign Affairs and Defence as well as concern about its relations with the United States seems to have stalled any move toward ratifying the treaty (Blanchfield 2011a, 2011b).

The European Union as an institution took a stronger, more unified role on the CCM than it did on the Landmine Treaty. In advance of the

December 2008 signing convention, the European Parliament passed a resolution that called on all EU member states to sign and ratify the treaty.[5] When the signing convention opened, 21 of the 27 EU member states signed the convention. The UK took the initiative when prior to a May 2008 meeting in Dublin, Prime Minister Gordon Brown announced that the UK would stop using cluster bombs. The UK signed the treaty at the 2008 convention and ratified it on May 20, 2010; it was not one of the first 30 states to ratify. The French position on the ban evolved from its opposition in 2005 to signing the treaty in December 2008 and being one of the 30 countries to bring the treaty into force by ratifying it on September 25, 2009. Germany, one of the other key Minervian actors and one of the core states on the Landmine Treaty, was also one of the initial 30 states to sign the treaty and bring it into force. This brief summary demonstrates that two of the Minervian actors, Canada and Japan, have acted significantly different on the CCM than they did on the Mine Ban Treaty. Japan has become even more pro-active and although it is still concerned about its relationship with the United States, it has continued to play the role of Minervian actor on the CCM. Canada's actions on the other hand seem to support the contention that since 2006, the country has ceased to be a Minervian actor (see Nossal, Chapter 4).

With the economic rise and increasingly important international political roles of the BRIC countries – Brazil, Russia, India, and China – there is some speculation about the possibility of these states becoming Minervian actors. On the issue of weapons in general, and cluster bombs in particular, there is no chance of that. Three of the BRIC countries – Russia, India, and China – are firmly in the blocking coalition and the fourth, Brazil, has also neither signed nor ratified the convention.

Notes

1. Available online at www.hrw.org/hrw/reports/1999/landmine
2. The early core group states that supported a total ban on landmines were Austria, Belgium, Canada, Ireland, Philippines, Mexico, Netherlands, Norway, South Africa, Switzerland, and later Colombia and Germany.
3. It is important to acknowledge, however, that the status of NGOs has been improving since passage of a new non-profit law in the mid-1990s. See Pekkanen 2000; Schwartz and Pharr 2003.
4. Peace and Security Committee Meeting March 12, 1998; Foreign Affairs Committee Meeting September 25, 1998.
5. See the European Parliament website: www.europarl.europa.eu/sides/getDoc. do?language=en&type=IM-PRESS&reference=20081114ST042065 accessed March 2, 2012.

8
The Resilience of CITES Regime and Diffused Normative Community

Isao Sakaguchi

CITES, or the Convention on International Trade in Endangered Species of Wild Fauna and Flora, was established in 1973 to prevent species extinction that is occurring due to excessive international trade. CITES is a thought-provoking case of multilateral institution building because even though its post-Cold War development was driven by actors who derived power from a norm, salient social movements were not found in the process as seen in the case of anti-landmines. Instead, senior officials and experts who had internalized the principal norm behind CITES, namely, conservationism, pursued a top–down pathway to influence the construction of CITES.

Wildlife conservation has become a highly confrontational issue due to an irreconcilable ideological conflict that pits a sustainability-focused *conservationism* norm against a *preservationism* norm driven by the principle of non-consumption. Although there are many influential preservationism-minded activist NGOs that originated in Western society, as exemplified by anti-whaling groups, most environmental treaties, including CITES, are founded on conservationism. Unsatisfied with the existing regimes, preservationist forces have attempted to transform them; through these efforts they have already successfully effected the transformation of the International Whaling Commission into a preservationism-minded body (Sakaguchi 2008a).

CITES also became highly politicized in the late 1980s due to a highly publicized contention over the African elephant. The species experienced an estimated decline in continental population, from 1,343,340 in 1979 to 609,000 in 1989, because of rampant poaching and the illegal ivory trade. This massive population decline ignited a *Save the Elephant* campaign, which was supported by a variety of NGOs, including the Environmental Investigation Agency and the Friends of Animals.

131

The campaign tilted national opinion in most Minervian states (except in Japan) against the ivory trade, and gave political leaders from these countries a strong motive to support the movement. At the Seventh meeting of the Conference of the Parties to CITES (hereafter abbreviated as COP 7) in 1989, seven parties, including Kenya, Tanzania, and the US, aiming to curtail illegal poaching and ivory trading proposed the inclusion of all African elephant populations in Appendix I of the Convention, which would effectively ban commercial trade of the species. Australia, Canada, members of the then European Community (EC), and the US voted for the ban, while Japan, as the main importer of raw ivory, was opposed (Sakaguchi 2006, pp. 97–131).[1]

This comprehensive ban triggered regime destabilization for CITES. Because successful management programs geared toward sustainability had resulted in exceptionally sound, and even excessive elephant populations, in some Southern African countries, the comprehensive ban was adopted not as a (semi-) permanent policy, but specifically as a stopgap measure to check poaching and illegal trade that had become uncontrollable in *other* range states. However, pro-ban countries and preservationism-minded NGOs maneuvered to ensure the policy's permanency, which created strong mistrust among the parties and, consequently, polarized the CITES signatories. But in contrast to the IWC case, neither a turbulent regime change[2] nor regime decay has occurred; at COP 10 (1997), despite US opposition, the elephant populations of Botswana, Namibia, and Zimbabwe were moved back under Appendix II to allow the resumption of strictly controlled trade in ivory and other products. This reconstruction of the CITES regime according to the original norm of conservationism facilitated the maturation of a cooperative relationship among Minervian actors: Canada, Japan, the European Union (EU), and its member countries, together with some African range states. Because of the COP 10 proceedings, CITES was able to recover its balance before falling into total dysfunction. Moreover, in the process of resolving the contested issue, the parties adopted a number of rules designed to guide institutional decisions, and in so doing established a deeper convention for honoring agreed-upon rules. The parties have become more thoroughly socialized[3] by the regime, contributing to CITES' institutional robustness.

This chapter aims to explain the resilience of the CITES regime, with special focus on the role played by Minervian actors. Some important questions, which I discuss in the chapter, concern how and why the economically powerless Southern African countries were able to prevail in their efforts to achieve the resumption of trade in elephant products. In particular, why was it that not only Japan but also Western Minervian actors stood together to support the downlisting of the African elephant populations from Appendix I to Appendix II, even in the face of extremely negative public opinions?

Minervian actors and the diffused normative community

This chapter demonstrates that in a relatively mature regime such as CITES, which has to a certain extent succeeded in socializing parties, the norm in question approaches stage 3 (norm internalization) of its *norm life cycle* as proposed by Martha Finnemore and Kathryn Sikkink; parties' conformity to or compliance with rules does not generally require external pressure (1998). This does not mean that rule-following behavior by parties is automatically guaranteed. When the development of a norm is between stage 2 (norm cascade) and stage 3, or when an internationally shared norm has not yet been embedded deeply enough in domestic civil societies, political interventions such as the initiative to list and retain the African elephant under Appendix I of CITES occasionally hinder and sometimes paralyze multilateral cooperation. Though any regime at one time or another will face such a moment of turbulence, in most cases it survives and regains stability in the long term, as the CITES case illustrates. However, as there is a strong research bias among social constructivists to focus on newly proliferated norms that are still in stage 1 (norm emergence) and stage 2 of the norm life cycle, this period of development has remained opaque (Finnemore and Sikkink 1998). It is crucial that we examine initial stages, but we also need to better understand how regimes, following departure from stage 2, overcome disruptive factors and reproduce convergence in actors' expectations for the long term. Because it is a relatively older convention, studying the CITES case allows us to begin addressing this gap in our understanding of norm entrenchment, thus providing valuable theoretical implications for the study of post-Cold War global institution building.

Unfortunately, insofar as many institutions created in the post-Cold War era have relatively short institutional histories and are therefore still far from stage 3 of the norm life cycle, the Minervian framework has not yet developed the tools necessary to fully grasp the homeostasis or self-developing process of a somewhat matured regime. In the creation of a new regime, outstanding norm entrepreneurs take the lead to persuade and pressure passive or reluctant countries to accept newly invented norms, but in a relatively matured regime, whose founding norms are widely accepted by parties as appropriate, the political process tends to be more driven by voluntarism or the habit of socialized elites (Finnemore and Sikkink 1998). In order to analytically capture the spontaneous cooperation among socialized elites, I introduce a new concept: the *diffused normative community* or *DNC*.[4]

A DNC is composed of self-motivated, often senior, individuals who have accepted or internalized core norms of the regime as appropriate standards of behavior. Equipped with a loose, often informal, network that does not yet possess a command channel or hierarchical relations, a DNC functions as a spontaneous organ for the maintenance of regime stability.[5] The majority of a DNC's members are incumbent or former governmental officials, and staff of international organizations, and also includes experts from research institutes and NGOs. A DNC is usually invisible to outsiders, and it may appear dormant in peaceful times; having no formal body or established center to coordinate their activities, even the constituents themselves may not be conscious of its existence. However, once a regime is faced with destabilizing factors, the network of members is activated in order to prevent regime disruption or regime change.

Thus, in relatively matured regimes, the Minervian normative mode functions top–down as well as bottom–up. The open polity of Minervian actors promotes voluntary transnational elite networking. They are therefore likely to constitute the core of DNC. Based on this identified top–down pathway, I will demonstrate that the development and further establishment of the CITES regime was the effect of a conservationism DNC reacting to disruption caused by preservationist forces. The CITES case offers a good illustration of how a regime composed of socialized actors can reproduce the convergence of actors' expectations, and how socialized Minervian actors contribute to building a resilient and robust regime.

Origin of the CITES regime and its basic framework

CITES is unique in that an *advisory NGO*, the International Union for the Conservation of Nature (IUCN), played a decisive role in regime formation. During the 1960s, IUCN drafted the treaty text, and revised it several times in response to views and opinions provided by concerned countries. Advisory NGOs mainly target elites in governments, international organizations, and firms, while *activist NGOs* are characterized by their strong grassroots orientation, and therefore bottom–up influence (Steinar and Gulbrandsen 2003). IUCN is known as the most authoritative advisory NGO with the largest network in nature conservation, as well as being a pioneer for sustainability. It is a decentralized organization that facilitates networking among conservationists in various sectors (Holdgate 1999); as such, it comprises an essential component in a conservationism DNC.

In the early 1970s, the IUCN's treaty-drafting effort was supplemented by a US and Kenyan initiative to strengthen the text. The treaty was finally adopted in 1973 and came into force in 1975. That the United Nations Environment Program (UNEP) commissioned the IUCN to administer the CITES Secretariat until the IUCN withdrew from the position in 1984 deserves special mention (Sakaguchi 2006, pp. 71–72). Furthermore, at COP 1 (1976) the parties adopted a resolution stipulating that scientific input or biological data must be provided by the IUCN, and trade data by Trade Records Analysis of Flora and Fauna in Commerce (TRAFFIC). TRAFFIC was established as a specialist group within the IUCN Species Survival Commission (SSC) in 1976 to monitor wildlife trade and later became a partnership program between the IUCN and the World Wide Fund for Nature (WWF). CITES therefore became dependent on the advisory NGOs for the provision of both biological and trade-related data (Sakaguchi 2006, pp. 70–77).

CITES regulates international trade mainly by determining the listing of species under either Appendix I or Appendix II. Appendix I is a list of species threatened with extinction by international trade in which commercial trade is banned. Appendix II lists species that are not necessarily threatened with extinction but that may become so unless trade is closely controlled; only an export permit authorizes the commercial trade in species listed in Appendix II. At COP 1 (1976), the parties adopted the so-called *Bern criteria* as an operational guideline to determine the appropriate categorization of a given species into either Appendix. Support by two-thirds of all parties is required for the modification of Appendices I or II (Wijnstekers 2001).

With regard to membership to CITES, it is important to note that the so-called *Gaborone Amendment*, which permitted membership by regional economic organizations, was adopted in 1983. Though not yet fully operative, the EU then began to behave as if it was a *single* state by taking joint action in voting based on the procedures of the Council of Ministers. By this set of procedures, the European Commission, led by experienced CITES experts, first recommends a proposal. If it gains at least two-thirds majority support based on weighted voting, the proposal becomes a common position, and if not, the result is abstention.[6] With its growing membership the EU has emerged as a key voter, especially on position issues. It was the EU that ultimately enabled the downlisting of African elephants at COP 10.

Ivory trade ban and the destabilization of CITES

The ban adopted at COP 7 resulted in significantly decreased levels of poaching in most range states, and rescued some tourism industries, which are the primary source of foreign currency revenue in Kenya and Tanzania. For that reason most range states supported the continuation of the ban. The Southern African countries, on the other hand, continued to suffer from overpopulation and devastation of habitat, as well as loss of potential trade revenue, which had been reinvested in their conservation activities. Caught in an ironic bind, the Southern African states considered the ban as punishment for having sustained their elephant populations so well.[7] These distinct domestic contexts therefore resulted in a point of conflict between the interests of pro-trade and pro-ban range states.

In 1991, in preparation for the resumption of the ivory trade, Botswana, Malawi, Zimbabwe, and newly independent Namibia signed the Agreement for the Establishment of the Southern African Center for Ivory Marketing (SACIM) to manage trade in ivory securely. The SACIM countries collectively, and South Africa independently, submitted a downlisting proposal at COP 8 (1992). Significantly, as certain populations did not fit the Bern criteria for Appendix I, the COP 7 moratorium decision stipulated a proposal for establishing a Panel of Experts system to make it easier to downlist sound populations from Appendix I to Appendix II (Sakaguchi 2006, pp. 97–131). The Panel of Experts established for COP 8 determined that South Africa and Zimbabwe satisfied both the biological and trade control criteria set for downlisting, but it found serious shortcomings in Botswana's trade control and a shortage of data on the Namibian population. Malawi did not meet either criterion. However, because Japan, a potential importer, still lacked effective trade controls, the Panel recommended that until both exporting and importing countries had strict trade controls firmly in place, trade should be limited to non-ivory products (mainly hides) for which poachers rarely hunt elephants due to technical reasons (Sakaguchi 2006, pp. 156–60).

COP 8 was hosted by Japan in Kyoto. During 1980s Japan was notorious for its bad records in CITES. For example, while receiving approval to host the next Conference of the Parties, Japan retained 14 reservations at the time of COP 7, the largest number among the parties, to the CITES listing decisions. The rather surprising decision to host COP 8 came from Japan's Ministry of Foreign Affairs. Enhancing the state's engagement in global environmental diplomacy in hopes of improving the country's overall international reputation, the ministry became concerned about the criticism against Japan at CITES.[8] To save Japan's honor as a host country, it halved the number of reservations to seven by COP 8. Since then Japan has become an active participant, and, together with other like-minded actors, has pushed CITES toward sustainable use (Sakaguchi 2011; Mofson 1996, pp. 120–50).

The Panel report was presented at COP 8, but most parties were not inclined to honestly discuss the Panel's recommendation. In deliberation about the downlisting proposals, Kenya, Tanzania, and Zambia, all in a close relationship with Western preservationist NGOs at that time, ignored the Panel's report completely and accused the SACIM countries of attempting to reinstate the ivory trade. The countries of West and Central Africa, under strong diplomatic pressure from France, also came out against downlisting. The French delegation was led by Pierre Pfeffer, director general of Société Nationale de Protection de la Nature (SNPN)[9] and leader of the *Amnistie pour les Elephants* campaign in France. *Amnistie pour les Elephants* had turned French national opinion almost unanimously against the ivory trade (Sakaguchi 2006, pp. 98–99).

The government of the UK also faced strong pressure from pro-ban NGOs, and it proclaimed in the Parliament, without waiting for the Panel's report, that it would oppose all elephant downlisting proposals. At COP 8, Tony Baldry, Secretary of State for the Environment, made a strong statement against resuming trade even in non-ivory products. The UK statement shocked Peter Dollinger, chairman of the Panel and head of the Swiss delegation; previous to the UK statement, he had urged the parties to respect the downlisting criteria adopted at COP 7. Dollinger, an SSC regional member and an old CITES participant since COP 1, was one of the core members of the conservationism DNC. At the COP 8 the EC as a whole, upon hearing the broad opposition of range states, adopted a common position against downlisting (Sakaguchi 2006, pp. 162–66).

In a surprise move, the US – despite its leadership in the effort at COP 7 to categorize African elephants under Appendix I – accused pro-ban countries of ignoring the Panel's report, and questioned the participants on whether CITES would become a treaty that encourages wise use of wildlife resources, or be marked by protectionism and unsound management. The SACIM countries eventually withdrew their proposal, and even worse, stated their intention to review their future participation in CITES. South Africa was also forced to withdraw its own proposal without it being discussed at all (Sakaguchi 2006, pp. 167–70).

The parties' failure at rational deliberation of the elephant proposals had a spillover effect that impacted the entire integrity of the CITES regime. A lack of convergence among the actors' expectations over the elephant issue engendered more divisive attitudes regarding other broad proposals. An unusually large number of proposals (almost half!) – especially those backed by the same pro-ban NGOs, mainly tropical timber proposals and Atlantic bluefin tuna proposals – were forced to be withdrawn without being discussed, whether or not they met the listing criteria. This occurred because a number of parties began to suspect a hidden agenda – that the proposals might comprise a project to institute a permanent ban on trade. CITES, pressured by preservationism forces, was on the brink of institutional dysfunction (Sakaguchi 2006, pp. 170–73).

Structural reform of CITES and emergent cooperation by Minervian actors[10]

Despite the disaster at COP 8, the SACIM countries initiated a reform of the structure of CITES, with the help of Minervian actors. In August 1991, SACIM convened a workshop on the future of CITES at the Gonarezhou National Park in Zimbabwe. Almost 20 participants, who came from various Minervian actors and IUCN as well as the SACIM countries, discussed potential measures to reform CITES and bring it strongly in line with the idea of sustainable use. The hidden but prima-facie agenda was securing the resumption of the ivory trade. Although they did not officially represent their governments or organizations, most of participants had long been serving as delegates or observers to the CITES conferences. At the same time, they were also either working for or were associated with the main supporting organizations of the CITES regime: the CITES Secretariat and the IUCN. It was in this context that the conservationism DNC, composed of self-motivated individuals, was activated to protect the CITES regime.

Introducing the Minervian participants, David Brackett, director general of the Canadian Wildlife Service (CWS) and SSC chairman joined the DNC. When his plan to participate became publicized, Canadian activist NGOs angrily criticized him and claimed that most of the workshop invitation list resembled a "Who's Who" of opponents to the CITES protective listing of the African elephant.[11] In response to this, Brackett had no choice but to proclaim that the meeting had "no connection" with the ivory trade.[12] Later, as the appointed chairman of the COP 10 Committee I, Brackett was an important figure that helped the SACIM countries by ordering the proceedings in a way that favored them. This was a personally risky initiative for him to undertake, as it was not acknowledged by his government.

Yoshio Kaneko was an ex-official of the CITES Secretariat up until COP 7 and since then had been working as an adviser to the government of Japan. Willem Wijnsteker had been in charge of wildlife trade legislation in the European Commission since 1978, and was deeply involved in forming the Commission's recommendations to listing proposals. He was also well known as the author of the official CITES legal reference, *The Evolution of CITES*, and was appointed CITES secretary-general in 1999 (Wijnstekers 2001).

Peter Schei had headed the Norwegian delegation since COP 2 (1979), and was also associated with IUCN as an SSC regional member. At COP 10 he was appointed by Brackett as chairman of a working group mandated to draft a final amendment for the proposals to categorize the African elephant under Appendix II. Robert Jenkins was an official with the Australian National Parks and Wildlife Service (ANPWS) and also a member of SSC/Sustainable Use Specialist Group (SUSG).

The Gonarezhou workshop produced several influential documents, including *New Criteria for Listing Species on CITES Appendices*, and *The Case for a New Convention on International Trade in Wild Species of Flora and Fauna* or *CITES II*, which radically denounced CITES as an "imperialist treaty." Their goal was to deal with the perceived deficiencies of the present CITES by transforming the regime into a new convention that was more closely aligned with modern conservation concepts of sustainable development. In effect, the SACIM countries aimed to bring about change in CITES from the inside (Mofson 1996, pp. 106–8), with help of like-minded experts based out of Minervian actor states. Despite their failure at COP 8, they persisted in gradually eroding the preservationist forces and, often working behind the scenes, enabled the Southern African countries to pass their downlisting proposals at COP 10.

As a first step in this process, the SACIM countries, led by Zimbabwe, submitted several resolutions to COP 8, all of which were first formulated at the Gonarezhou workshop. For example, the resolution on the benefits of trade was introduced and adopted by consensus. It intended to correct the bias in CITES against trade as a negative influence on conservation. Three Minervian actors – Canada, the EC, and Japan – expressed support for the resolution. The resolution intended to correct the perceived imperialist inclination of CITES was also adopted by consensus, which obliged proponents to consult with range states before formal submission of proposals (Sakaguchi 2006, pp. 174–76).

One of the most important resolutions submitted by the SACIM countries at COP 8 concerned new listing criteria. Their goal was to replace the vague Bern criteria with more objective numerical criteria using a threshold approach. The basic ideas were entirely imported from the new listing criteria in the SSC Red List. George Rabb, chairman of the SSC Steering Committee and a member of SUSG, realized that the new Red List criteria could be also utilized as CITES criteria, and he sent a listing criteria specialist to the Gonarezhou workshop to help the SACIM countries with this project. The work of drafting the new criteria was commissioned to IUCN after COP 8, and the new numerical criteria were adopted *unanimously* at COP 9. It was widely believed that the criteria would make it more difficult to list species in Appendix I and easier to delist species, such as African elephant (Mofson 1996, pp. 147–48). The SACIM initiative to reform CITES was, in principle, successful, receiving strong support from conservationism-minded officials sent from Minervian actors and experts of IUCN.

Paving the way for downlisting

COP 8 was marked by lack of mutual trust, especially among range states. The EC, under Portuguese presidency, was deeply worried during the conference about escalating disruption to the CITES regime, and called for more dialogue on the controversial issue of elephant conservation. Robin Sharp, head of the UK delegation at both COP 8 and COP 9, took the lead, together with his counterpart at SACIM, Nigel Hunter, a Botswanian delegate at COP 8 and COP 9, and also an SSC regional member.

Based on the suggestion of Hunter, in November 1992 the EC sent a mission led by Sharp to Southern and East African countries to confer with representatives. Throughout the meetings, it became clear that East African support for the ban simply reflected their distinct conservation needs, not a preservationist mindset. On behalf of the EU, which was reorganized from the EC in 1993, the UK organized a dialogue in September 1994 at Kasane, Botswana, with the aim to alleviate the misunderstanding and tension that had surfaced during COP 8 (European Community 1992). Sharp recalls preparing for the meeting as a lonely exercise that received little support from the UK Department of Environment, and he was even criticized by the Department for spending too much time on African problems. Yet he persisted in his efforts simply because of his own convictions.[13]

Seventeen range states, the EU, Japan, the US, TRAFFIC, and the SSC/African Elephant Specialist Group (AESG) sent representatives to Kasane. Holly Dublin, AESG chairperson, was well equipped to facilitate the dialogue as she was personally acquainted with the majority of African representatives. As many AESG African members also worked for conservation authorities at home, through AESG the conservationism DNC was connected with African range states, while SSC worked as a bridge to connect Minervian actors with the group (Sharp 1997, pp. 111–19).

COP 9 was held in November 1994 in Florida. South Africa proposed to move its population back to Appendix II, restricting trade solely to "non-ivory" products. In the deliberation, Dollinger, as chairman of the Panel of Experts, reported that South Africa's proposal met the downlisting criteria *completely*. Therefore, failure to adopt it would be tantamount to determining that there was no chance of passing any downlisting proposal as far as the African elephant is concerned, however sound a population and management system a range state had in place. In short, the regime's premise of conservationism would be virtually nullified (Sakaguchi 2006, p. 190).

A series of behind-the-scenes meetings of the range states took place during COP 9, and were chaired by David Western, who was appointed director of the Kenyan Wildlife Service (KWS) after COP 8. Former chairman of AESG, he became an indispensable key actor in hammering out an African solution for COP 10. In that instance, CITES once again benefited from the spontaneous cooperation of the conservationism DNC members (Sakaguchi 2006, pp. 113–14, 187–96, 209–28). Western was gravely concerned about the polarization of CITES. Acknowledging that Kenya had benefited the most from the comprehensive ban, he still believed that all the parties should be subject to the CITES criteria. However, no other range states were prepared to take part in a discussion. Astonishingly, one after another, the Central and West African countries, subdued by France before COP 9, stated that there was no room for compromise. So once again range states failed to examine the input of the Panel of Experts, despite all of the efforts made at Kasane (Sakaguchi 2006, p. 191).

Western subsequently held an informal meeting with representatives of the UK, the US, New Zealand (as Standing Committee chair), and the CITES Secretariat. They were all seriously concerned about the potential destabilization of the CITES regime. It is interesting that all of the parties at the meeting had strongly supported the uplisting decision at COP 7. Now infused with a sense of crisis, a wide spectrum of parties, irrespective of their positions at COP 7, threw in their support for the efforts of the Southern African countries.[14]

As a first step to prevent the destabilization of CITES, in a backdoor meeting Western suggested that the parties support South Africa's controversial proposal to downlist its white rhino population to Appendix II, solely for trade in live animals and safari trophy hunting. Excessive poaching for horns had reduced the continental population to a dangerous low of 3,800 in 1984. In contrast, the population in South Africa, once reduced in 1895 to no more than 20, had increased to 3,234 in 1984 and to 6,376 in 1994. He believed that adopting the rhino proposal would demonstrate the general willingness of the parties to accept downlisting as long as the species in question was managed well and met the criteria, no matter how much pressure activist NGOs exerted. At the backdoor meeting the Kenyan project was supported by all of the range states, the EU, and the US. Later it was officially adopted, by an astonishing margin of 66 to 2.

The white rhino case illustrated the power of African consensus. The delegates from Western countries were caught in a dilemma, between extremely negative public opinion at home and what they perceived to be the right thing to do at CITES. For both the EU member countries and the US, African consensus is required to support the domestically unpopular downlisting of African elephants. Therefore, Western proposed a plan to convene inter-conference dialogue meetings with the aim of facilitating an African consensus in a relaxed atmosphere free of pressure from NGOs and donors (specifically France). His suggestion was supported unanimously behind the scenes by representatives of the range states, the UK, the EU, and the US.

When it came to the official open session, South Africa's elephant proposal received full support from Minervian actors such as Australia, Canada, and Japan. Germany, on behalf of the EU, and the US admitted that South Africa met all of the downlisting criteria but declared their will to abstain on the vote due to the absence of African consensus. Shortly afterward, South Africa withdrew its proposal, as planned, and expressed its appreciation for the "friendship" expressed by the parties (Sakaguchi 2006, pp. 192–96).

It became clear at COP 9 that most of the parties still shared the conservationism norm in principle, and consequently parties' expectations resumed convergence on a variety of proposals, as they set about deliberating each one in terms of listing criteria and scientific inputs.

As a result, CITES pulled back from the brink of collapse at COP 9 and moved toward recovering its stability (Sakaguchi, 2006, pp. 199–200). Importantly, at the Standing Committee held during COP 9, two Minervian actors, Japan and the UK, were nominated for chair of the next term, by Senegal and Trinidad Tobago respectively. Though the US preferred the UK, Japan was elected by consensus, as Sharp declined to be a chair (CITES 1994).

The critical moment at COP 10 and afterward

For the CITES regime to fully regain its stability, it was critical that the COP 10 successfully resolve to downlist sound elephant populations. And to achieve this, it was necessary that the African range states reach a consensus. As one of the efforts to promote African consensus-building, the first African dialogue took place in Dakar in November 1996 with 31 range states in attendance. At the request of the range states, the meeting had been organized by the IUCN with financial support from Minervian actors (Canada, Japan, and the UK) and the US. Two experts, Dublin and Tom Milliken (of TRAFFIC), facilitated the dialogue. At this meeting the participants expressed concern about external pressures that restricted their policy options and, in the "spirit of Dakar," as they put it, they agreed that it was desirable to keep out external intervention and build an "African consensus" on elephant proposals (Sharp 1997, pp. 111–19).

COP 10 was to take place in June 1997 at Harare, Zimbabwe. In preparation, three SACIM countries (Botswana, Namibia, and Zimbabwe) submitted separate but similar downlisting proposals with an ivory quota to be shipped solely to Japan. The Panel of Experts reported that the populations of the three countries were healthy and well managed, but reported deficiencies in Zimbabwe's control over the semi-worked ivory trade and Botswana's control over ivory stock. The Panel also reported deficiencies in Japan's control over retail ivory market. The Panel concluded that resumption of the ivory trade would not damage the populations of the three countries, but that it might allow ivory from other range states to flow illegally into those countries and stimulate poaching elsewhere if the reported deficiencies were not dealt with satisfactorily.

The IUCN organized a second African dialogue meeting in Darwendale, Zimbabwe, a few days before COP 10. Some of the most intense discussion focused on how to correct the deficiencies reported by the Panel. Both the proponents and Japan actively addressed this issue and promised to take effective measures to close any potential loopholes. Lack of time made it impossible to build consensus on ivory export, so that issue was carried over to COP 10, but the Darwendale meeting produced an African agreement at least in resumption of non-ivory products.

When the COP 10 sessions started, Western exerted leadership behind the scenes and fashioned a compromise among the Southern and East African countries to allow the three countries a "one-time" experimental ivory quota, provided that deficiencies reported by the Panel were adequately dealt with (Sakaguchi 2006, pp. 215–21). Both Canada and the EU were inclined to support the idea of an experimental ivory quota while Japan, not being able to participate in the backdoor meetings, remained dissatisfied.[15] The US delegation, headed by Ronald Barry since COP 9, was given strict instruction by the White House not to support any downlisting proposals for the African elephant, though he was personally very sympathetic to the downlisting proposals.

The official deliberation on the African elephant downlisting proposals submitted by Botswana, Namibia, and Zimbabwe started in Committee I in the second week of COP 10, which was chaired by Brackett, participant of the Gonarezhou workshop. The range states requested the establishment of a working group to receive final inputs from the West and Central African range states, which during COP 10 were once again held in check by France and given strict instructions to oppose downlisting in any form. The majority of statements given were in favor of downlisting, although several countries, including Australia and the US, spoke in opposition. Significantly, the Netherlands, on behalf of the EU, stated that the EU position against downlisting had changed, and they wanted to participate in the working group to find solutions for problems reported by the Panel. Canada joined the EU in voicing their wish to take part in the working group. Rather abruptly, the prospects had changed. The dramatic shift in the EU official position raised the probability that downlisting at COP 10 could be achieved (Sakaguchi 2006, pp. 223–26).

Despite the statement made by the Netherlands, in reality the EU as a whole has not been antagonistic to downlisting from the beginning. The European Commission in particular, led by Wijnsteker, took a strong stance respecting the downlisting criteria set at COP 7. For example, at COP 9 it recommended supporting South Africa's downlisting proposal as there was no scientific reason to keep the elephant population in Appendix I. The Commission's recommendation failed to gain more than two-thirds weighted majority at COP 9, as France, Germany, the

Netherlands, and the UK all stood against downlisting. Interestingly, at a senior delegate level, even representatives of the opposing EU members (except France) were sympathetic to downlisting, as the case of the UK illustrates.[16] African consensus is a requirement for these EU members to support downlisting proposals. Thanks to the dialogue process, African range states came to COP 10 with a united position to allow the three countries to resume trade at least in non-ivory products.

Brackett suggested the appointment of Schei, another participant of the Gonarezhou workshop, as chair of the working group. In the course of their discussions, Ghana and Côte D'Ivoire argued that they could not support any proposal unless conservation revenue could be guaranteed through the "non-commercial" disposal of their ivory stocks. In response, the UK, on behalf of the EU, promised that the EU would provide conservation funds. Recalling how past disunity had threatened CITES, Robert Hepworth, head of the UK delegation, worried that failure to adopt the downlisting proposals would poison the atmosphere of the convention. At COP 10, it was Hepworth who persuaded his government and ultimately gained permission to support downlisting. It was a difficult decision for the government, as it violated the manifesto of the Labour Party.[17]

After considerable wrangling, the African range states finally reached a consensus in the working group. The proposals for the final amendment drafted by the working group were presented, and the amended proposals of Botswania, Namibia, and Zimbabwe, were adopted by 74 to 21 with 24 abstentions, 72 to 22 with 24 abstentions, and 77 to 23 with 20 abstentions, respectively. The relatively large number of abstentions came from the EU. In a meeting to form an EU common position, the European Commission strongly recommended supporting the final amendments. Due to the UK support, it gathered nearly two-thirds majority support. However, besides France, both the Netherlands and Germany again failed to support the recommendation despite clear recognition by the delegations that the populations of the three countries did not qualify for Appendix I status. Because of a margin of a few votes, abstention became the EU common position (Sakaguchi 2006, pp. 227–48). Despite the EU abstention at the final moment, the overt support it gave in its statement at Committee I created the perception that downlisting would not fail, even in the eyes of reluctant parties.

The controversy over African elephants subsided at COP 10. As post-COP 10 developments illustrate, CITES became more robust as it underwent similar challenges from preservationist forces. At COP 11 (2000) and COP 12 (2002), a proposal to return all the elephant populations of the Southern African countries to Appendix I was submitted.[18] Interestingly the proposal was opposed on the basis of its lack of any evidential foundation not only by nearly all of the range states, but also by both the EU and the US, thus illustrating their unwavering determination to respect the listing criteria (Sakaguchi 2006, pp. 285–90).

Through the settlement of the highly conflictive downlisting issue, parties gained an appreciation of how critical rule-respecting behavior is for achieving and maintaining long-term cooperation for the purpose of the CITES regime, which was prevention of species extinction. In other words, they have more fully internalized the basic norm of the CITES regime. As a result, CITES developed into a robust and rigorous regime.

Conclusion

The post-Cold War development of the CITES regime traced in detail in the chapter demonstrates the power of conservationism DNC networking, in which the Minervian actors played indispensable core roles. The Minervian actors, except for Japan (it also had economic interest in the ivory trade), have clearly been motivated by the conservationism norm rather than economic interest or political gain. It is also important to recognize that most of the key figures who helped to restore stability to the CITES regime acted not on governmental instructions or pressure from bottom–up forces, but according to their own convictions. These convictions were based on what they believed to be appropriate or right in light of the conservationism norm and rules that were the foundation for CITES, as illustrated by the negotiations among the participants of the Gonarezhou workshop.

The case study demonstrates that in analyzing the Minervian action of multilateral institution building, we need to take full account of the norm life cycle. In a relatively mature regime that is approaching stage 3 of the norm life cycle (norm internalization), the Minervian normative mode works not only from bottom–up but also from top–down, through a DNC that functions like an agency to reproduce regime stability and to promote regime development. Minervian actors are likely to seek multilateralism in such a mature regime as well as in a nascent regime, more actively than hegemonic powers or undemocratic powers due to the property of their open polity and moderate power status (Tiberghien, Introduction).

This case study also shows a new possibility in post-Cold War global institution building: Minervian and US partnership through a DNC.

What was salient is the unexpectedly sympathetic attitude taken by the US. This happened because the US delegation, composed of experienced officials, was also involved in the conservationism DNC. Barry, for example, has participated in the US delegation since COP 4 (1983). As a member of the conservationism DNC, the US, together with the Minervian actors, supported the African dialogue process after COP 9. During COP 10, Barry even lent unofficial support to the East and Southern African compromise in a backdoor meeting.[19] At the level of delegation, even the US sought rule-conforming behavior rather than unilateralism.

Observing from a wider viewpoint, some might question why IWC, with a far older history, has failed to prevent preservationism from capturing the regime. Significantly, the "moratorium" resolution adopted in 1982 stipulated that based upon the best scientific advice and by 1990, IWC would consider the establishment of "other" catch limits. However, once pressured by extremely negative public opinion and pro-ban NGOs, many non-whaling Minervian actors as well as the US decided to ignore the resolution and chose to comply with public opinion (Miyaoka 2004, pp. 74–97; Sakaguchi 2008a). This occurred, first, because IWC is a single species treaty solely for cetaceans while CITES is a multi-species treaty that covers all wildlife, including timber and fisheries species. Issue linkage makes rule-ignoring behavior more risky because of the negative spillover effect, as seen at CITES COP 8.[20] This sort of issue linkage did not exist in IWC, which facilitated the actors' rule-ignoring behavior. Second, the conservationism DNC in IWC lost its sphere due to the dramatic change in the IWC constituent members. IWC saw a sharp increase of parties, from 15 in 1977 to 37 in 1982. Most of them were preservationism-minded non-whaling countries that did not share whaling countries' traditional logic of appropriateness.

Though the conflict over the African elephant has been settled, recently CITES is faced with a new challenge: how to deal with fisheries species. This contentious issue was elevated by the turmoil over the Appendix I listing proposal of Atlantic bluefin tuna, submitted by Monaco to COP 15 (2010). In response to the pandemic failure of specialized international fisheries bodies to prevent depletion of resources under their jurisdictions, more and more environmental NGOs have initiated ocean campaigns. The CITES efforts to regulate trade in fisheries product was also gradually strengthened since COP 10, and resulted in the listing of sturgeon, European eel and several shark species under Appendix II. During these proceedings, the collaboration between CITES and the Food and Agriculture Organization (FAO) of the United Nations was strengthened, and the listing criteria were also amended to add a special criterion for fisheries species (Sakaguchi 2008b). However, at COP 15, all of the fisheries proposals, including those concerning bluefin tuna and several shark species, were rejected without being examined on the basis of the listing criteria and population data and despite FAO's positive recommendation for some of them. Japan, led exclusively by the Fisheries Agency on fisheries proposals, played the central role in rejecting CITES involvement in fisheries at COP 15, while both the EU and the US have been in favor (Ishii 2011). Although this new dispute has not yet generated a divisive effect on other non-fisheries proposals, CITES is under another trial of its institutional robustness.

Notes

1. Japan voted against the original proposals but abstained from voting on the final amendment presented by Somalia (Sakaguchi 2006, pp. 122–26).
2. Changes in principles and norms signal a regime change, whereas amendments to rules and decision-making procedures are changes that occur within a regime (Krasner 1982, pp. 186–89).
3. Socialization is defined here as a process by which social interaction leads novices to endorse expected ways of thinking, feeling, and acting (Johnston 2001).
4. Despite the same elite-orientation, a DNC is not identical to the concept of the epistemic community. A DNC generates its influence from normative embeddedness rather than scientific knowledge or scientific authority (Haas 1992).
5. Anne-Marie Slaughter also focuses on spontaneous but more visible governmental networks (Slaughter 2004).
6. Author's interview with David Morgan, Brussels, February 18, 2001.
7. *The Herald*, June 13, 1997.
8. For example, Japan pledged to expand its environmental aid to 1 trillion yen at the UNCED in 1992, and also hosted COP 3 of the UN Framework Convention on Climate Change in 1997 (Sakaguchi 2011).
9. SNPN is the CITES Scientific Authority in France.
10. Most of the description of this section is based on confidential information from a person who was involved in the Gonarezhou workshop.
11. *Toronto Star*, August 4, 1991.
12. *Toronto Star*, August 22, 1991.
13. Author's interview with Robin Sharp, London, March 13, 2001.
14. Author's interview with David Western, Nairobi, March 5, 2001.
15. Author's interview with Ronald Barry, Washington, DC, November 7, 2000.
16. The delegation of Germany at COP 9 and COP 10 was headed by Gerald Emonds, a long-time CITES participant since COP 1. Emonds clearly

recognized the sound management of several southern African countries, and at COP 9, on behalf of EU, expressed its will to help the African dialogue process. According to Chris Shürmann, an experienced official of the Dutch Scientific Authority to CITES, the Scientific Authority recommended that the government support the downlisting at COP 9 and COP 10. However, higher-ranked politicians had overruled their recommendations.

17. Author's interview with Robert Hepworth, Gigiri, Kenya, March 7, 2001.
18. The population of South Africa was also returned to Appendix II at COP 11.
19. See note 15.
20. Barry, addressing the position taken by the US, clearly stated in the interview with the author that issues come and go but relations last longer, and that they cannot alienate other parties whose cooperation is constantly needed (Sakaguchi 2006, p. 268). On the effect of issue linkage of environmental issues, see Oberthur and Gehring 2004.

9
Minerva's Allies: States, Secretariats, and Individuals in the Emergence of the Responsibility to Protect Norm

Katharina P. Coleman

In September 1999, reflecting on the Rwandan genocide and NATO's Kosovo campaign, UN Secretary-General Kofi Annan challenged the UN General Assembly (GA) to come to terms with the question of humanitarian intervention. He sparked intense debate, but consensus proved elusive as ardent supporters of humanitarian intervention clashed with staunch defenders of state sovereignty. One year later, Canada announced a new initiative designed to bridge the impasse: the International Commission on Intervention and State Sovereignty (ICISS). The Commission's 2001 report sought to reframe the issue of humanitarian intervention in terms of an international "responsibility to protect" civilians from large-scale loss of life or ethnic cleansing if their own states proved unwilling or unable to do so (ICISS 2001a). Despite initial setbacks, this notion – often referred to as R2P – has achieved considerable international recognition, culminating in its unanimous endorsement (in modified form) at the 2005 UN World Summit. Although important components of the ICISS report were sacrificed to secure this endorsement (Coleman, forthcoming) and serious challenges to the norm's implementation remain, this was a remarkable case of international norm building. R2P shaped contemporary debates about military intervention in Darfur (for example, Williams and Bellamy 2005), was reaffirmed by the Security Council in 2006 (UNSC 2006, §4), and in 2011 the Council invoked R2P in its responses to crises in Côte d'Ivoire and Libya (UNSC 2011a; UNSC 2011b; UNSC 2011c).

The emergence of R2P cannot be explained without reference to Minervian actors, notably Canada, the UK, and other European states.

However, members of international secretariats, eminent private individuals, and key non-Minervian states including South Africa and Mexico also played a crucial role.[1] This coalition was brought together by a shared normative commitment: although several actors (including Minervian ones) had strategic interests in promoting R2P, ultimately they were united by their principled support of the idea that state sovereignty should not prevent international intervention to halt massive and systematic human rights abuses. In contrast to other instances of Minervian norm building (for example, Flowers, Chapter 7), however, it was not grassroots mobilization that drove the norm-building process but the commitment of key national policy makers, distinguished diplomats, and high-ranking bureaucrats.

Thus this chapter highlights the significance of Minervian actors operating in the normative mode, but it illustrates a remarkably elite-driven version of this dynamic and it stresses the potentially crucial importance of coalitions with other actors – Minerva's allies. It proceeds in four sections. The first examines the positions of the key Minervian actors at the outset of the R2P debate and highlights their shared normative motivations. The second focuses on the first phase of the emergence of a global R2P norm, the formation and operation of the ICISS. This phase was notable for its insulation from interstate politics: Canada sought to shield the Commission from the direct influence not only of norm opponents but also of fellow Minervian actors. By contrast, private individuals, foundations, and members of the UN secretariat – notably Secretary-General Annan – were indispensable allies. The third section focuses on the politics of reintroducing R2P into international diplomatic circles. Eminent individuals and international bureaucrats dominated the beginning of this phase, but toward its end interstate politics gained increased importance and alliances between Minervian actors became crucial. The conclusion reflects on both the implementation of the R2P norm since 2005 and the implications of this case study for the argument of this book.

Starting the process: the 1999 UN General Assembly debate

The alliance between Minervian powers and international bureaucrats that was to prove crucial in developing the R2P norm was already apparent in the 1999 GA debate about sovereignty and humanitarian intervention. Secretary-General Annan launched the debate, but without Minervian support for the concept of humanitarian intervention it would have ended in a reaffirmation of the inviolability of state sovereignty.

In opening the GA debate, Annan argued that a new international norm in favor of intervention was already developing (UNGA 1999a), and indeed the end of the Cold War had wrought considerable changes on state practices and international discourse. Annan's predecessor, Boutros Boutros-Ghali, declared in 1992 that "the time of absolute and exclusive sovereignty ... has passed" in an increasingly interdependent world (Boutros-Ghali 1992, §17). The multiplication and ambitious mandates of early post-Cold War UN peacekeeping operations suggested more permissive attitudes toward state sovereignty, but ultimately it was the failures of UN peacekeeping that galvanized support for a new norm. The 1994 genocide in Rwanda, executed in the presence of a UN peacekeeping mission (UNAMIR), became a rallying cry for proponents of humanitarian intervention. As Annan put it, "the genocide in Rwanda will define for our generation the consequences of inaction in the face of mass murder" (UNGA 1999a).

Nevertheless the notion of humanitarian intervention remained deeply controversial in 1999, and divisions were sharpened by NATO's 78-day-long Kosovo campaign, launched without express Security Council authorization on March 24, 1999. NATO defended its actions as a necessary response to a humanitarian catastrophe, but for its opponents the campaign illustrated the danger of unbridled interventionism in the name of human rights and reaffirmed the need to protect state sovereignty.

Thus Annan's opening speech elicited strong negative reactions in the GA. Algerian President Bouteflika, who held the Organization of African Unity's (OAU) rotating Chair, insisted that African states remained "extremely sensitive to any undermining of our sovereignty ... because sovereignty is our final defense against the rules of an unjust world" (UNGA 1999a). China declared itself "opposed to the use of force under any pretext" and warned that if the notion of humanitarian intervention were endorsed, "the sovereignty and independence by which some small and weak countries protect themselves would be jeopardized and international peace and security would be seriously endangered" (UNGA 1999e). Several other states pointedly rejected Annan's suggestion that the rules of intervention were already changing. Egypt warned, "these ideas and suggestions deal with concepts that are not yet established" (UNGA 1999f). Russia insisted that any evolution in international norms "should be done through collective discussion ... not as a fait accompli and not working from scratch: it should be based on valid rules of international law," of which state sovereignty is a central tenet (UNGA 1999c).

Annan also failed to win clear US support. The United States endorsed the concept of humanitarian intervention, but was not committed to building stronger international norms about it. The United States had rejected British calls for international guidelines on intervention in the immediate aftermath of the Kosovo campaign in order to avoid restricting its freedom of action (Wheeler 2001, p. 564), and had little interest in further negotiations on the issue. President Clinton's speech to the GA stressed flexibility: the international community should prevent mass killings and displacement "whenever possible," but its "response in every case cannot and should not be the same" and would "depend on the capacity of countries to act and on their perception of their national interests" (UNGA 1999c). Clinton thus defended UN intervention, intervention by regional organizations, and occasional US inaction: "We cannot do everything, anywhere." The status quo, although muddled by controversy and confusion, allowed for all these options and was thus acceptable to the United States. It would not be a major ally in norm building on this issue.

It was Minervian actors – notably Canada and key European Union members such as the UK, France, and Germany – that provided crucial support for the notion of a humanitarian intervention norm. In each of these states, public attitudes toward humanitarian intervention were generally positive but there was little organized grassroots demand for a new international norm. It thus fell to political elites to decide whether to take advantage of their permissive domestic conditions in order to champion a new norm on the international stage, and they did so for both strategic and normative reasons.

Canada's position had roots in the Rwandan genocide, to which it had a special connection through UNAMIR's Canadian Force Commander, whose testimony helped generate public support for the principle of humanitarian intervention – but not a strong demand for Canada to promote a new international norm on the issue. However, key Canadian policy makers were also affected by the genocide, including Foreign Affairs Minister Lloyd Axworthy, for whom a report on the lack of international response became "a template that would guide my four and a half years in Foreign Affairs" (2003, p. 160). The Kosovo crisis further galvanized Axworthy into supporting an international effort to develop a norm of humanitarian intervention. Canada participated in the Kosovo campaign, and 64 percent of Canadians supported it (Everts and Isernia 2001, p. 232), but for Axworthy,

> Kosovo raised difficult questions pertaining to humanitarian inter-
> vention and the meaning of sovereignty. While there was strong
> endorsement of the need to intervene to protect people from the

widespread abuse, there was equally strong criticism of the way the actions in Kosovo contravened fundamental articles of national sovereignty without explicit authorization from the UN Security Council. The time has come to face these issues. (2003, p. 190)

Canada thus emphatically endorsed Annan's call for renewed international debate about humanitarian intervention (UNGA 1999f). This position was not purely altruistic. As Nossal notes (in Chapter 4), Canada pursued an intensely multilateralist foreign policy in the 1990s. The 1996–97 Ottawa Process on antipersonnel landmines had established Canada as a leading player in international norm diplomacy, and this success inspired not only the Foreign Affairs ministry (Axworthy 2003, p. 156) but also the Canadian public: a 1998 poll suggested that 82 percent of Canadians believed Canada had increased its international influence and that 62 percent were prouder of Canada's international record than they had been a decade earlier (Hampson and Oliver 1998, p. 379). Thus moral leadership was both domestically popular and perceived as a source of international status. The shared belief among policy makers and the public in a coincidence between Canadian interests and the pursuit of Canadian values put Canada in a position to lead an international initiative on humanitarian intervention.

The UK also emphatically supported a new humanitarian intervention norm during the 1999 GA debate (UNGA 1999b). This position reflected broad popular endorsement of the principle of humanitarian intervention: in a 2002 poll, 75 percent of British respondents supported using British troops to halt civil wars abroad (CCFR and GMF 2002b). It also reflected the ruling Labour Party's 1997 commitment to an "ethical" foreign policy[2] and the lessons the British government drew from NATO's Kosovo campaign. The UK had been the campaign's third largest military contributor, and the government had defended it as "justified as an exceptional measure to prevent an overwhelming humanitarian catastrophe" (Shinoda 2000, p. 518). The British public had largely agreed: a May 1999 poll found 80 percent of respondents agreeing that "someone had to do something about Kosovo on humanitarian grounds" and 66 percent agreeing that "Britain was right to join in the NATO actions against Serbia" (Taylor, undated). However, other countries had been more skeptical, and this had proved costly. Russian and Chinese veto threats caused NATO to launch the campaign without an explicit UN mandate, and this dramatically heightened the burden of public justification on participating states. British policy makers concluded that better international "guidelines" for humanitarian intervention were necessary (Blair 1999). These would make it more difficult for Security Council members to veto genuine humanitarian interventions and make such interventions easier to defend internationally even if they lacked a Security Council mandate (Wheeler 2001, p. 565). The UK saw this as advantageous both because it supported humanitarian intervention in principle and because it saw itself as more likely to launch an intervention in the future than to seek to prevent one.

France also supported the elaboration of an international norm on humanitarian intervention. French public opinion was firmly committed to humanitarian intervention: a 1998 poll found 78 percent of respondents approving of the use of French troops to "contribute to bring peace in a region of the world" and 87 percent in support of using French troops to "assist a population in distress (famine, civil war)" (Everts and Isernia 2001, p. 189). This allowed Prime Minister Lionel Jospin to emphatically support the principle of humanitarian intervention at the 1999 GA debate: "State-instigated violence has spawned serious humanitarian crises over the past few years... This is unacceptable. Consequently, we must uphold the principle of international intervention, under United Nations auspices, to assist the victims" (UNGA 1999a). Like the UK, France also had strategic reasons for its stance, derived from its experience of NATO's Kosovo campaign. France was the campaign's second largest military contributor and after an initial wariness the French public strongly approved of the intervention (Everts and Isernia 2001, p. 192). However, French policy makers were uncomfortable operating through NATO, which they perceived to be dominated by Anglo-Saxon powers (Daalder and O'Hanlon 2000, p. 80). The UN Security Council was a more favorable forum for French influence thanks to the diversity of its member states and France's permanent seat, and French policy makers believed that an international norm of humanitarian intervention would reaffirm the centrality of the Security Council in such operations. Thus Jospin insisted: "The role of the Security Council... is more vital than ever... To be sure, there have been circumstances when an urgent humanitarian situation dictated we should act immediately, but such an approach must remain the exception... Our fundamental rule is that it is for the Security Council to resolve crisis situations" (UNGA 1999a).

German political elites also had both normative and strategic reasons for supporting the elaboration of an international humanitarian intervention norm. Germany's historically grounded reluctance to deploy its troops abroad coexisted with a commitment to humanitarianism. A 2002 poll found public approval of the use of German troops to halt civil wars abroad almost 20 points below French and British rates, but at 58 percent, this approval rate was still ten points higher than among US respondents (CCFR and GMF 2002a; 2002b). Moreover, when asked about "purely" humanitarian operations such as troop deployment for famine relief, 83 percent of respondents indicated approval (CCFR and GMF 2002b). The Kosovo campaign brought the tensions between these principles to a head. Chancellor Gerhard Schroeder defended the intervention as a necessary response to a humanitarian crisis (Krieger 2001, p. 404), but public support for the German military's first combat mission since 1945 proved brittle, falling from 60 percent in April 1999 to 52 percent in May, in part because of continued questions about the intervention's legitimacy (Rudolf 2000, p. 136). A stronger international framework for humanitarian intervention would address such legitimacy concerns for future operations and thus facilitate German participation in them. At the 1999 GA, therefore, Foreign Minister Fischer not only affirmed that "non-interference in internal affairs must no longer be used as a shield for dictators and murderers" but also insisted on the need to "further develop the existing United Nations system" in order to ensure that "a practice of humanitarian interventions [would not] evolve outside the United Nations system" (UNGA 1999e).

Thus diverse strategic calculations and an overarching normative commitment to the principle of humanitarian intervention united Canada and key European states in support of Annan's 1999 call for a re-examination of the issues of sovereignty and intervention. However, the Minervian coalition was not wholly united in this support. Although other European states also supported this call (for example, Italy, see UNGA 1999e), the EU as a body lagged behind its most powerful member states. In the 1999 GA debate Finland, speaking for the EU, shied away from fully endorsing the principle of humanitarian intervention (UNGA 1999c). Japan also declined to openly support humanitarian intervention. Like Germany, it faced historical constraints on its ability to use force internationally but was re-evaluating its role on humanitarian issues. It had emerged as a strong supporter of the concept of human security and a growing contributor to UN peacekeeping operations, with increasing domestic support for revising Japan's constitution to enable it to undertake these tasks (Murata 2003, pp. 41–44). The Japanese government even acknowledged NATO's Kosovo campaign as "an unavoidable measure for humanitarian purposes" (Murata 2003, p. 44). However, overt support for a humanitarian intervention norm remained impossible due to divided domestic public opinion and the skepticism of Japan's neighbors about both humanitarian intervention and Japan's evolving military role. Thus Japan skirted the issue at the 1999 GA debate (UNGA 1999d, UNGA 1999g).

Yet given the acute skepticism of many developing states, even a fully united Minervian coalition could not have swayed the 1999 GA debate in favor of endorsing humanitarian intervention. Developing states were not united in this opposition. Indeed, in July 2000 the newly formed African Union (AU) endorsed "the right of the Union to intervene in a Member State...in respect of grave circumstances, namely: war crimes, genocide and crimes against humanity" (Kioko 2003, p. 807). This was a result of several trends. At the level of public opinion, the Rwandan genocide had highlighted the potential consequences of non-intervention: a 2005 poll found 65 percent of respondents in eight African states believing that the UN should "authorize force to stop human rights violations such as genocide."[3] At the elite level, the early post-Cold War era saw the toppling of many entrenched authoritarian regimes, and several of the new leaders condemned the OAU for condoning the human rights abuses of their predecessors (Kioko 2003, p. 813). Support for the principle of humanitarian intervention remained far from universal, but it was sufficient to produce the 2000 AU position and led some African states to advocate for a re-examination of the developing world's stance on the issue. In 2000, for example, South Africa urged the Non-Aligned Movement "to acknowledge Africa's needs...humanitarian intervention as a concept should therefore be developed to provide for international action in the face of genocide and crimes against humanity."[4] However, the GA was not a propitious forum for engaging in a constructive dialogue that explored the diversity and potential overlap of states' positions. On the contrary, the 1999 debate tended to polarize states: "fervent supporters of intervention on human rights grounds, opposed by anxious defenders of state sovereignty, dug themselves deeper and deeper into opposing trenches" (Evans and Sahnoun 2002). One Minervian actor, Canada, concluded that the pursuit of a new humanitarian intervention norm had to take on a new shape.

The Independent Commission on Intervention and State Sovereignty

Canada announced its ICISS initiative in September 2000. The Commission was tasked to "wrestle with the whole range of questions – legal, moral, operational, and political – rolled up in this debate [between state sovereignty and intervention], to consult with the widest possible range of opinion around the world, and to bring back a report that would help the Secretary-General and everyone else find some new common ground" (ICISS 2001a, p. vii). Canada invited Australian diplomat Gareth Evans and Algerian diplomat Mohamed Sahnoun to act as ICISS co-chairs and appointed the remaining ten commissioners in consultation with them. The first full ICISS meeting was held in Ottawa in November 2000 and was followed by a series of consultations with NGOs and other actors. The ICISS drafted and revised its report in light of these consultations, the information produced by its own research team, and discussions at formal and informal ICISS meetings. The final report was presented to Kofi Annan on December 18, 2001 (ICISS 2001b, pp. 342–43).

The report presented a complex package of recommendations. It sought to overcome the deadlock between proponents of humanitarian intervention and defenders of state sovereignty by reframing the issue as a responsibility to protect populations from serious harm that rests in the first instance with their states and only passes to the international community if these states are unwilling or unable to fulfill their role. The report also acknowledged concerns that a humanitarian intervention norm would provide powerful states a license for military intervention without addressing the root causes of conflict or the deleterious effects of intervention. In response, it argued that the responsibility to protect included not only a responsibility to react to human suffering but also the responsibilities to prevent conflict and to rebuild after military interventions. It also proposed a "just cause threshold" limiting intervention to cases of large-scale loss of life or ethnic cleansing, as well as four "precautionary principles" (right intention, last resort, proportional means, and reasonable prospects of success), which it argued would confine intervention to "extreme and exceptional cases" (ICISS 2001a, pp. 31–37). Finally, the report addressed the question of "right authority" by arguing that UN Security Council authorization should be sought for any military intervention, that Permanent Members should restrict their veto usage on these issues, and that authority might pass to the GA or to regional organizations if the Council failed to react to a crisis. This reaffirmed the centrality of the Security Council stressed by France and Germany, among others, without ruling out action without a Council mandate, which was important to the UK, the United States, and many African states.

In the context of this book, two features of the ICISS are particularly notable. First, the ICISS deliberately did *not* involve a Minervian coalition. Since the Commission was designed to bridge the gap between

Western and non-Western states, Canada made a strenuous effort to ensure that it was not seen as the instrument of a coalition of developed countries. The first step to conveying this message was selecting a diverse set of participants. Six of the twelve ICISS commissioners (including one co-chair) hailed from non-Western countries. The ICISS Advisory Board consisted of seven diplomats from the developing world, four individuals affiliated with international organizations, and only four Western policy makers. The ICISS research team was multinational and headed by a Zimbabwean and a US national. The second step was to hold geographically dispersed consultations: the ICISS met with NGOs and other actors in Ottawa, Geneva, London, Maputo, Washington D.C., Santiago (Chile), Cairo, Paris, New Delhi, Beijing, and St. Petersburg. Finally, Canada did not allow the initiative to be funded by Western states but shared most of the costs with five major independent foundations (ICISS 1999b, pp. 341–50).

This drive for diversity should not be overstated. Canada retained substantial influence over the ICISS, appointing its members, providing its secretariat and the largest single contribution to its budget, and chairing the Advisory Board through Lloyd Axworthy, who had just left his position as Canadian Foreign Minister. Minervian ties were also maintained. Former British Foreign Secretary Robin Cook served on the Advisory Board, the UK and Switzerland made small financial contributions to the ICISS, and the commission held a roundtable consultation with French government officials in Paris on May 23, 2001 (ICISS 2001b, p. 378). Regular ICISS briefings "to interested governments" also kept lines of communication with Minervian actors open (ICISS 2001b, p. 343). However, contacts among Minervian actors were deliberately discreet because Canada recognized that at this stage of the norm-building process an activist Minervian coalition would be counterproductive. The ICISS was indisputably a Canadian initiative, but it was politically crucial to stress that there was "nothing precooked" about the Commission's report, that is, that neither Canada nor any of the other Western states was driving its findings.[5]

The second critical ICISS feature was its links to Secretary-General Annan, which continued the alliance noted during the 1999 GA debate. Annan provided both the official starting point and the formal end point of the endeavor. The ICISS presented itself as a response to Annan's "compelling pleas to the international community to... 'forge unity' around the basic questions of principle and process involved" in the issue of humanitarian intervention (ICISS 2001a, p. vii). Axworthy consulted Annan before launching the initiative, obtaining both his endorsement of the Commission and his commitment to receive its final report (Axworthy 2003, p. 191). The endorsement further allayed criticism that the ICISS was a purely Western initiative, and Annan's willingness to receive the report diminished the risk that the Commission's report would be ignored. As ICISS co-chair Gareth Evans explained (2006), "[i]t is one thing to develop a concept like the responsibility to protect, but quite another to get any policy maker to take any notice of it."

Annan's motivations were largely normative. He had served as the UN's Under-Secretary-General for Peacekeeping during the Rwanda genocide and as Secretary-General responded emphatically to criticisms of the UN's inaction: "All of us must bitterly regret that we did not do more to prevent it ... On behalf of the United Nations, I acknowledge this failure and express my deep remorse."[6] Annan became a firm supporter of humanitarian intervention under exceptional circumstances. Already in 1998, he argued that "even national sovereignty can be set aside if it stands in the way of the Security Council's overriding duty to preserve international peace and security."[7] His position on NATO's 1999 Kosovo campaign was remarkably nuanced. As Secretary-General he could not condone an intervention launched without a Security Council mandate, but he also refused to condemn it: "It is indeed tragic that diplomacy has failed, but there are times when the use of force may be legitimate in the pursuit of peace" (Weller 1999, p. 498). Annan ensured that his subsequent call for renewed international engagement with the concept of humanitarian intervention could not be ignored by launching it almost simultaneously in the Security Council, the *Economist* magazine, and the GA.[8] He seemed determined to establish the principle of humanitarian intervention as part of his legacy as Secretary-General, and his active support for ICISS stemmed from this commitment. His role in this initiative underlines that international bureaucrats can be crucial allies of Minervian coalitions seeking to build new international institutions.

From concept to international recognition: the road to the World Summit

Despite its high-level support, the R2P concept only narrowly escaped international oblivion: "it was almost suffocated at birth by being published in December 2001, in the immediate aftermath of 9/11, and by the massive international preoccupation with terrorism, rather than internal human rights, that then began" (Evans 2006). In this new political context, Canada abandoned its original plan of introducing the ICISS report at the 2001 GA session and simply submitted it to Secretary-General Annan instead. It also devoted foreign ministry staff and resources to promoting R2P, but while the concept gained some prominence among academics and international lawyers, it made little headway in international diplomatic circles. The 2003 US-led invasion of Iraq dealt a further blow to the R2P's chances of international acceptance by deepening fears of abuse of the concept of humanitarian intervention not only in developing states but also among Minervian actors. Thus the July 2003 Progressive Governance Summit failed to endorse R2P in part because of opposition from Germany.[9]

International bureaucrats and a handful of prominent individuals propelled R2P back onto the international agenda, with Minervian actors – including Canada – taking a back seat. The process began in 2004 with Annan's High-Level Panel on Threats, Challenges and Change (HLP). Announced in the shadow of the US-led invasion of Iraq, the sixteen-member Panel had a broad mandate to "examine today's global threats and provide an analysis of future challenges to international peace and security" and to "recommend changes to ensure effective collective action" to address them (HLP 2004, p. 119). It conducted extensive regional consultations and issue workshops and over the course of six formal meetings drafted a report that was submitted to Annan on December 1, 2004. Among many other provisions, the Panel "endorse[d] the emerging norm that there is a collective international responsibility to protect ... in the event of genocide and other large-scale killing, ethnic cleansing, or serious violations of humanitarian law which sovereign Governments have proved powerless or unwilling to prevent" (HLP 2004, p. 66).

In the context of this book, the relative absence of Minervian powers at this stage is notable. The idea of the HLP emanated from Annan and UN Under-Secretary-General for Political Affairs Kieran Prendergast, whose Department elaborated the Panel's structure and terms of reference (NUPI 2006, p. 14). Annan convened the panel, closely followed its progress, and made clear that one of its tasks was to clarify the "norms and guidelines concerning humanitarian intervention."[10] He also appointed the HLP members, including former ICISS co-chair Gareth Evans, who emerged as one of the panel's key members and was instrumental in persuading it to endorse R2P (NUPI 2006, p. 26). Evans served more in his individual capacity than as representative of the Australian government, whose recent lack of leadership on human security issues disappointed him (Evans 2005). His influence on Panel deliberations eclipsed that of R2P's most ardent state supporter. Canada submitted a "non-paper" recommending R2P to the Panel, but its influence was limited. As one HLP secretariat member commented, the Panel "didn't need a Canadian non-paper to know what R2P was. We had Gareth Evans on the Panel."[11] Evans's allies on R2P eventually included British panelist Lord David Hannay, Norway's Gro Harlem Brundtland, Japan's former UN High Commissioner for Refugees Sadako Ogata, and Tanzania's former OAU Secretary-General Salim Ahmed Salim. Like Evans, all four were on the HLP in their individual capacity rather than as state representatives, though they exerted considerable influence in their home countries. The HLP's secretariat, a small team of professionals headed by Stephen Stedman that was charged with briefing the panel on the major issues before it and preparing draft reports, also had a strong normative commitment to R2P.

The Panel's principal R2P skeptics included Egypt's Amr Moussa, China's Qian Qichen, and Russia's Evgenii Primakov. Their objections were partly addressed by compromise, most notably by stressing the need for Security Council authorization of humanitarian interventions.[12] However, normative persuasion also played an important role. The Panel discussion on R2P took place in Africa and was put in the context of the grave threats posed by civil wars and the UN's uneven responses to them, including its failure in Rwanda. R2P proponents deliberately kept the discussion pragmatic:

> one tactic we would fall back on if it seemed that people were getting too wrapped up in the sovereignty and first principles [was] to engage them in a very practical conversation that started "well, if something like what occurred in Rwanda breaks out tomorrow in Burundi and you're seeing tens of thousands of people slaughtered, do we want a repeat of what happened in April 1994?" And nobody on the panel was going to say yes. It becomes a much more practical "OK, so we agree that there are circumstances where everybody around this table will want a forceful response – then how do we think about it? Is there any other better way of thinking about it than what Gareth [Evans] has come up with?"[13]

Salim's support for R2P was also crucial because it denied R2P critics the only alternative moral high ground, which was the position of defenders of the sovereignty of vulnerable developing states: "it was very difficult for the sovereignty hawks to try to position themselves as the voice of the little guys when the African representative is basically very supportive of the proposition."[14] Thus although reservations were expressed, the Panel did not reject the concept of R2P, which allowed Secretariat members to keep it in subsequent drafts of the Panel report. Encountering no decisive opposition, it remained in the final draft.

The HLP report provided the basis for the discussion of security issues in Annan's own report, *In Larger Freedom* (ILF), which was released in March 2005 to structure interstate diplomacy leading up to the September 2005 World Summit. Like the HLP, the ILF was a UN Secretariat initiative ostensibly removed from interstate politics. However, Minervian actors and their non-Western allies played a more active role at this stage because interstate diplomacy necessarily furnished the parameters of the ILF's recommendations. The UN Secretariat monitored states' reactions to the HLP report closely in order to assess what positions the Secretary-General would be able to take and defend. Thanks in part to lobbying from Canada and its Minervian and African allies, there was enough support for R2P to make its consideration a viable though controversial proposition. As the contemporary Canadian Ambassador to the UN noted, "Canada and like-minded states certainly made it possible for Kofi, politically, to continue his strenuous advocacy as Secretary-General for R2P."[15] ILF thus endorsed R2P – with one strategic alteration: unlike the ICISS and the HLP, it separated the concept of R2P from the issue of guidelines regarding the use of force because informal consultations revealed that opposition from all permanent Security Council members except the UK would prevent consensus on such guidelines.

In April 2005, over three years after the ICISS report was published, R2P finally became the subject of high-level multilateral diplomacy in the form of negotiations about the Outcome Document of the 2005 World Summit. Predictably, states were divided on the issue. Canada led the pro-R2P coalition, supported by both Minervian actors and other states. The European Union had rallied around R2P and formally confirmed its collective endorsement of the concept at the beginning of the negotiations (EU@UN 2005). It remained united in its support for R2P throughout the negotiating process and became especially effective when the UK assumed the EU presidency in July 2005. Japan formally but unenthusiastically "embraced" R2P in April 2005, noting its preference for a focus on human security and stressing the need for conflict prevention (Kenzo 2005). A key non-Minervian member of the coalition was the AU, which had signaled its support for R2P in the March 2005 "Ezulwini Consensus" (Bellamy 2006, pp. 160–61). Other states were relatively neutral or only mildly supportive. Several developing states found themselves able to embrace R2P once it had been decoupled from a discussion of criteria for using force that might promote Western interventionism (Wheeler 2005, p. 3). The United States opposed any language that implied an obligation to intervene or precluded action without Security Council consent, but was in principle open to R2P thanks largely to the 2004 report of the Task Force on the United Nations led by George Mitchell and Newt Gingrich (Bellamy 2006, pp. 162–63; Bolton 2005). Opposition to R2P remained formidable, however. Russia and China remained skeptical, and India, Pakistan, and Egypt adamantly opposed R2P because of its perceived curtailment of state sovereignty. In June 2005, the Non-Aligned Movement "reiterated [its] rejection of the so-called 'right' of humanitarian intervention ... [and] observed similarities between the new expression 'responsibility to protect' and 'humanitarian intervention'" (Rahman 2005). A World Summit consensus on R2P thus seemed highly unlikely.

Ultimately, however, the Outcome Document did include a section on the "responsibility to protect populations from genocide, war crimes, ethnic cleansing and crimes against humanity" (UNGA 2005, p. 30). The text was a compromise. There was no outright recognition of an international responsibility to intervene militarily in order to stop the listed crimes, and a string of caveats surrounded the possibility of collective action. The need for the GA to "continue consideration" of the responsibility to protect "bearing in mind the principles of the Charter and international law" was stressed, extending an open invitation for R2P opponents to revisit the issue. Even the section's title was a compromise between states advocating a straightforward endorsement of the ICISS concept and others resisting any reference to the far-reaching report. Critics charged that "the 2005 consensus was produced ... by bargaining away key tenets of the ICISS's recommendations" (Bellamy 2006, p. 167; see also Wheeler 2005), but even this limited outcome was a hard-won victory that Minervian powers were instrumental in achieving. Canada lobbied hard for R2P, contributed substantially to drafting the relevant language in the Outcome Document, and played a key role in maintaining the unity of the pro-R2P coalition. Its commitment was crucial in the final days of negotiation, when "what carried the vote over the line was some very effective last minute personal diplomacy with major wavering-country leaders by Canadian Prime Minister Paul Martin" (Evans 2006). The UK also played a key role within the pro-R2P coalition both in its own right and as the EU's president.

However, the impact of Canada's Minervian allies should not be overstated. The UK's influence was diminished: as Gareth Evans noted (2006), the support of states involved in Iraq "was not particularly helpful ... when it came to meeting [the] familiar sovereignty concerns." Germany was distracted by its hope of obtaining a permanent Security Council seat and Japan, which was not enthusiastic about R2P to begin with, was similarly preoccupied. Minervian actors also still struggled to overcome the distrust of R2P in the developing world. Under these conditions, "the support that mattered ... was persistent advocacy by sub-Saharan African countries, led by South Africa [and] a clear – and historically quite significant – embrace of limited-sovereignty principles by the key Latin American countries" (Evans 2006). Sub-Saharan African states largely remained united behind the Ezulwini consensus, with South Africa proving a particularly strong R2P advocate and Rwandan support giving the concept a special moral status. In Latin America, Mexico emerged as a crucial R2P supporter. These states made World Summit endorsement of R2P possible by disarming the criticism that it was a purely Western concept. The ambassadors from Australia and New Zealand also emerged as major personal defenders of the R2P concept. The fact that the Summit was dealing with a vast range of issues also played a role. As one secretariat member put it, "R2P by itself would never have been endorsed in a resolution of the General Assembly. But the fact that it came in a huge package, where many countries were focused on other things, and had other battles to fight ... it got through in the end."[16]

The final crucial factor in explaining the World Summit's endorsement of R2P is the agency of the UN Secretariat. Two main Secretariat teams worked on the World Summit negotiations, one focusing on security issues under Stephen Stedman's leadership and the other concentrating on development issues under Robert Orr's direction. Negotiations began as a consultation exercise in which facilitators appointed by GA President Jean Ping held discussions with Member States and generated successive draft documents reflecting the state of negotiations. Since capturing an emerging consensus is more an art than a science, facilitators – and the Secretariat members who assisted them – enjoyed considerable leeway in producing these drafts (NUPI 2006, p. 54). Secretariat support for R2P (both in itself and as a potential bargaining chip) played a key role in the concept's persistence through this phase of negotiations.[17] In August 2005, however, newly arrived US ambassador to the UN John Bolton insisted on line-by-line text negotiations, which were carried out by successively smaller working groups of countries created by Ping (NUPI 2006, p. 56). The Secretariat enjoyed less direct influence in this phase, though its input remained substantial as facilitators sought help in reaching compromises within these groups.

The Secretariat re-emerged as a critical actor in the final days of negotiations, when working groups failed to reach consensus and the danger of an unproductive Summit loomed. On the eve of the Summit, large sections of the draft Outcome Document remained contested, including parts of the R2P section. That night Ping, Orr, Stedman, and their staffs worked through the entire draft to produce a compromise package that Ping then submitted to the Summit on a "take-it-or-leave-it" basis.[18] The facilitators' text on R2P remained intact in this process, effectively overruling the remaining state objections. This was the text that the Summit unanimously endorsed on September 16, 2005.

Conclusion

It is impossible to explain the emergence of the R2P norm without reference to Minervian actors, but it also cannot be explained solely with reference to these actors. Because there were profound North/South divisions on the issue, a coalition of developed states could not champion the norm alone. Thus Canada deliberately downplayed the influence of other Minervian powers on the ICISS and depended heavily on developing state allies during the World Summit. Elite non-state actors also played a crucial role throughout the process. Kofi Annan propelled the issue of humanitarian intervention onto the diplomatic agenda in 1999, provided crucial political support to the ICISS, created the HLP, and placed many of its recommendations on the World Summit's agenda through his *In Larger Freedom* report. Within the HLP, Gareth Evans was instrumental in promoting R2P, as was the HLP secretariat. During World Summit negotiations, UN Secretariat members helped ensure that R2P remained in successive drafts of the Outcome Document and was part of the package ultimately presented to states for their decision. None of these actors could have successfully promoted R2P in isolation: it was their cooperation that made R2P's emergence possible. In the context of this book, therefore, this chapter serves to highlight that, at least in some circumstances (for example, on issues creating North/South divisions) Minervian actors must enter coalitions with non-Minervian entities to be effective international institution builders.

The motivations of these actors were diverse, but the overarching mode of institution building was normative in a largely elite-driven way: key decision makers came to see a correspondence between national or organizational interests and normative commitments to improving international responses to massive human rights abuses. Moreover, while the promotion of R2P provides ample evidence of tactical maneuvering, bargaining, and outright pressure politics, normative reasoning was never out of the picture. From Annan's initial challenge through the ICISS and the HLP meetings to the World Summit negotiations, the moral question of how to respond to another genocide such as the one in Rwanda resonated widely, and undercut proponents of the normative status quo.

Yet while Minervian actors and their allies achieved a remarkable success in formulating R2P and then securing its World Summit endorsement, serious challenges to the norm's implementation remain. The Security Council's reaction to the World Summit affirmation of R2P fell considerably short of a ringing endorsement: it merely "reaffirm[ed] the provisions of...the 2005 World Summit Outcome Document regarding the responsibility to protect populations from genocide, war crimes, ethnic cleansing and crimes against humanity" in an April 2006 resolution broadly focused on the protection of civilians in armed conflicts (UNSC 2006, §4). The Council's simultaneous failure to decisively address the escalating crisis in Darfur prompted doubts about its commitment to R2P and therefore the norm's practical viability. As HLP member Lord Hannay commented in 2006, "If the people of Darfur cannot be protected...then the responsibility to protect will look pretty sick."[19] Given this chapter's focus, it is noteworthy that Hannay suggested the following remedy: "The Secretary General has to play a key role. China and Russia are dragging their feet, China perhaps because it has not really made its mind up about what place it wants in the world. Ban is close to China and that might help." Yet a 2009 comprehensive Secretary-General's report *Implementing the Responsibility to Protect* had little apparent impact (UNGA 2009). In 2011, however, R2P resurfaced dramatically in Security Council decisions. On February 26, the Council cited R2P in its resolution imposing sanctions on Libya and referring the Libyan situation to the International Criminal Court (UNSC 2011a). The Council referenced R2P again when it authorized the imposition of a No Fly Zone on March 17 (UNSC 2011b). Less than two weeks later, the Council invoked R2P again in authorizing the use of "all necessary means" to protect civilians and the imposition of sanctions on Laurent Gbagbo and his key supporters in Cote d'Ivoire (UNSC 2011c).

The Libya and Côte d'Ivoire decisions were not caused by a sudden conversion of Security Council members to the R2P norm, and the Council's inability to act on R2P principles in other situations (including Syria) highlights the persistent limits to the norm's implementation. Nevertheless, the 2011 resolutions are significant in two respects. First, they demonstrate that key Council members deemed the R2P norm to be sufficiently entrenched in the contemporary international system to be usefully invoked as (part of) a justification for robust international intervention. Second, regardless of Council members' reasons for invoking R2P, doing so has set a precedent and further entrenched the norm in international discourse, if not necessarily practice. Thus although the norm-building initiative launched by Minervian actors and their allies in 1999 is far from complete, it is one step closer to its goal.

Notes

1. See Chapter 1 on the possibly "extending circle" of Minervian actors.
2. Robin Cook's speech on the government's ethical foreign policy. *Guardian Unlimited*, May 12, 1997.
3. "Africans Want UN to Curb Human Rights Abuses," *Angus Reid Global Monitor*, July 5, 2005.
4. "Keeping Peace by Force," *Sowetan* (South Africa) April 14, 2000.
5. "Canada Launched Commission to Support Intervention when Lives Threatened," *Canadian Press Newswire*, September 14, 2000.
6. "Inaction by UN Cited in Report on Rwanda Killings," *Boston Globe*, December 17, 1999, A2.
7. "Secretary-General Reflects on 'Intervention' in Thirty-Fifth Annual Ditchley Foundation Lecture," *UN Press Release*, June 26, 1998.
8. "In Statement to Security Council, Secretary-General Says Plight of Civilians in Armed Conflict Can No Longer be Neglected," *UN Press Release*, September 16, 1999; Annan 1999.
9. "British PM Urges Tougher Stance against Brutal Regimes," *Agence France Presse* July 15, 2003.
10. Interview with Stephen Stedman, Research Director of HLP Secretariat in 2003–04 and Special Advisor with the rank of Assistant Secretary-General to Secretary-General Kofi Annan in 2005. By telephone, February 16, 2007.
11. Confidential interview with a former member of the HLP Secretariat, June 2006.
12. In section 272, however, the HLP did allow for post hoc authorization of interventions by regional organizations. Interview with Stephen Stedman, February 16, 2007.
13. Interview with Stephen Stedman.
14. Interview with Stephen Stedman.
15. Interview with Ambassador Allan Rock, Canadian ambassador to the UN in 2004–06, July 11, 2007.
16. Interview with Sebastian Graf von Einsiedel, member of the UN Secretary-General's Executive Office in 2005, June 29, 2006.
17. Confidential interview with a member of the UN Secretariat's negotiation team for the World Summit, July 2007.
18. Interview with Stephen Stedman, February 16, 2007. See also NUPI 2006: 58.

19. "Paul Reynolds. No Honeymoon for New UN Secretary-General," *BBC News* October 9, 2006. Security Council resolution 1706 (August 31, 2006) referred to "the responsibility of the Government of the Sudan to protect civilians under threat of physical violence," but gave little indication of robust international intervention.

10

The Battle of the Peacebuilding Norm after the Iraq War

Daisaku Higashi

Introduction

Peacebuilding has become one of the dominant issues in current world politics. As we witness challenges in Iraq, Afghanistan, Sudan, the Democratic Republic of Congo, Haiti, Kosovo, East Timor, and Libya, there is no doubt that peacebuilding – whether it's called post-conflict reconstruction, nation building, or by any other term – has been a critical agenda for multinational efforts in international security. As Doyle and Sambanis argue, "One of the most important challenges for the international community is how to rebuild state polities in the aftermath of civil war" (2000, p. 779).

In this chapter, I argue that there is a new norm on peacebuilding, which the International Organizations (IOs), predominantly the UN, established through their multiple practices of post-conflict reconstruction after the end of the Cold War. I will also acknowledge the key role that Minervian actors played in endorsing this peacebuilding norm. I argue that the norm comprises three key components: (1) the central role of the UN through Security Council authorization in conducting peacebuilding activities; (2) national elections legitimatized by International Organizations, mainly by the UN; (3) local agreements that produce an inclusive political process for creating new governments. It is important to recognize that the "bottom–up process" created the peacebuilding norm – multiple practices of the UN missions responding to the demand on the ground. In this process, the EU, Canada, and Japan – corroborating with UN Secretariats – greatly contributed to the development of this peacebuilding norm by identifying the UN's central role in peacebuilding and dispatching their military and civilian personnel to multiple-functioned UN missions. The key reason Minervian actors support these missions is that they share the view that the legitimacy offered by UN Security Council authorization is almost indispensable for peacebuilding, as the unilateral approach could be seen as neo-colonialist. As a result, the UN's central role in all peacekeeping missions has been recognized as necessary for both normative and practical reasons in succeeding in peacebuilding.

The Iraq war and the subsequent nation-building process have prompted an examination of the robustness of this peacebuilding norm. The Bush administration not only invaded Iraq without explicit UN authorization, but also attempted to violate the norm by rebuilding Iraq in a virtually unilateral way. However, when faced with the worsening situation in Iraq – especially the devastating attack on the UN's Baghdad headquarters in the summer of 2003 – the UN Secretariat and some Minervian actors, especially Germany and France, who originally opposed the Iraq War in 2003, began serious actions to resist the hegemon; they challenged the Bush administration to return to the peacebuilding norm and give the central role to the UN. The US refused those requests at first, but being unable to handle the political insurgents and deteriorating security in Iraq, the administration subsequently asked the UN Secretariat to design key political procedures. These procedures included establishing the interim government and conducting two national elections in 2004, and illustrated a substantial shift in US policy and a return to the peacebuilding norm defined above.

This is an excellent case that demonstrates that a norm created by the UN's "bottom–up process" can resist a substantial challenge by the hegemon, even on a core international security issue. The case also shows that despite the coalition of the UN Secretariat and Minervian actors not having sufficient powers to change the policy of a hegemon by themselves in the short-term, the coalition can establish a normative mechanism which will apply long-term pressure and push the hegemon to return to the international institutional mechanism that is consistent with the prevailing norm, particularly when it faces fiasco in its unilateral policies.

My argument will proceed in five steps. First, I will define the peacebuilding norm and its key components. Second, I will discuss the roles that the EU, Canada, and Japan played in developing the norm. Third, I will argue that the US violated this peacebuilding norm with an unauthorized intervention by attempting to conduct nation building in Iraq virtually single-handedly. Fourth, I will explain how both the UN Secretariat and Minervian states resisted the challenge by the US. Fifth,

I will account for how the coalition of the UN Secretariat and Minervian actors succeeded in pushing the US to change its policy and ask the UN Secretariat to design and assist in rebuilding Iraq. In conclusion, I assert that this change of policy by the US has had a historic implication on the activities of peacebuilding: it confirms that even the most powerful states cannot succeed in nation building single-handedly.

What is the peacebuilding norm?

The 1992 report by the then-UN Secretary-General Boutros Boutros-Ghali, "An Agenda for Peace," defines peacebuilding as efforts to "identify and support structures which will tend to strength and solidify peace in order to avoid a relapse into conflict" (1992, p. 32). Following this, I contend that there is a "peacebuilding norm" that has been created by numerous practices by IOs since the end of the Cold War. The norm has three key components.

(1) The UN'S central role authorized by the UN Security Council

Since the end of the Cold War, the UN has played a central role in rebuilding territories wracked by violent conflicts (Caplan 2005, p. 1). The tasks of the UN missions have covered not only economic and humanitarian assistance but also political transitions, such as demobilization, democratization (electoral assistance, institution building), and creating bureaucracy (Sens 2004, p. 146).

The personnel who led these multinational missions demonstrate that the UN has been playing a leading role in peacebuilding. In the majority of cases, the heads of peacebuilding administrations were special representatives appointed by the Secretary-General of the UN. For example, the head of UNTAC in Cambodia was Yasushi Akashi, a special representative to the Secretary-General; the head of the UNTAET in East Timor was Sergio de Mello; the head of UNAMA in Afghanistan was Lakhdar Brahimi. In general, no person was authorized to have greater power than the special representatives of the Secretary-General in these internationally run administrations.

(2) Elections legitimatized by IOs

An expectation has emerged that an election is a key element in forming a new government after conflict. The fairness of the election process is crucial in persuading people to accept the new government. Out of 25 countries and regions in which the UN conducted peacebuilding from the end of the Cold War to 2003, more than 20 UN missions were assigned to pursue democratization, including electoral design, assistance, and management (Sens 2004, p. 154).[1] To ensure the legitimacy of elections, it is very common for IOs, predominantly the UN, to conduct or monitor the elections. Without the IOs' commitment, the election might be in danger of being perceived as biased because partisan factions or occupiers may operate it.[2]

(3) Local agreements that produce inclusive political process in creating new governments

It is crucial for a peacebuilding effort to have not only the legitimacy conferred by the UN Security Council, but also indigenous legitimacy obtained by local political processes. In many cases, "peace accords" or "peace agreements" by combating factions are an initial step to confer indigenous legitimacy on the transitional process. In Cambodia, the Paris Peace Accord in 1991 became the basis that invited all major combating factions into the peacebuilding process (Paris 2004, p. 82). In Sierra Leone, the "Lomé Accord" was reached by the Kabbah government and the Revolutionary Unitary Front (RUF) – a notorious insurgent group in July 1999. The accord defined amnesty for all parties and rebels as well as power sharing between the Kabbah government and the RUF, thus creating a political process that all factions could join; it is considered one of the most successful cases of past peacebuilding supported by the UN peacekeeping operations (Hayner 2007). In East Timor, popular consultations in 1999, in which approximately 80 percent of East Timorese voted, resolved independence of the region from Indonesia; it became the basis for constructing a new nation with almost all factions in East Timor (Paris 2004).[3]

I argue that one of the reasons why this norm (UN leading role, elections legitimized by the IOs, and local agreements that create inclusive political process) is so robust is that the UN efforts in peacebuilding have enjoyed a much higher success rate than the nation-building attempts by the current hegemonic state, perhaps because the UN enjoys greater legitimacy both internationally and domestically; it also has a tendency to create more inclusive political processes compared with the hegemon, also attributing to its perceived legitimacy. Pei and Kasper (2003) examined all attempts at nation building (16 cases) by the US since 1900. He concluded that out of 16 cases, only four cases succeeded in establishing democratic government 10 years after US intervention, and these four cases were Japan (1945), West Germany (1945), Grenada (1983), and Panama (1989). Surprisingly, 12 out of 16 US nation-building projects completely failed in establishing lasting democracy (Pei 2003, p. 2).

On the other hand, the record for UN peacebuilding efforts is significantly better. The RAND Corporation examined 16 nation-building cases in the aftermath of conflicts since the Second World War and concluded that "two-thirds of UN nation-building operations can be categorized as successful at this time."[4] It is for this reason that in May, 2003, just after the US invasion of Iraq, Pei insisted that "the long-term prospects for nation building in Iraq would likely be enhanced if the effort were managed by the United Nations," primarily because, "the United Nations-led rebuilding effort would be viewed as more legitimate" (2003, p. 7).

As Pei points out, the UN has a significant advantage in legitimacy, compared with unilateral nation building. What is the definition of legitimacy? According to Frank, "legitimacy exerts a pull to compliance which is powered by the quality of the rule or the rule-making institution and not by coercive authority. It exerts a claim to compliance in the voluntarist mode" (1990, p. 26). Why then, is legitimacy so crucial for peacebuilding? Hurd argues that because these interventions, including peacebuilding, often resemble "the kind of overt regional imperialisms, they leave participants vulnerable to criticism as 'neoimperialists'" (2002, p. 44). In order to avoid these criticisms, the general response has been to invoke the myth of collectivity, which is "essential for the legitimacy of the United Nations" (Hurd 2002, p. 48).

Following Hurd's argument, I assert that the first key component of the peacebuilding norm (the UN's leading role as authorized by the UN Security Council) reflects the need for the peace-builders to obtain *international legitimacy* in the eyes of both the international community and local people in host territories. This international legitimacy relies on the successful completion of two stages. The first is to obtain *international support* from the member states, as indicated by the provision of funds and personnel to the mission. The second is to create higher credibility or legitimacy *in the eyes of the local people, including political leaders*. Without the legitimacy and central role of the UN, the outsider's intervention would be much more likely to be perceived as colonialist or simple aggression (Pei 2003, p. 5). My research in Afghanistan and East Timor revealed that the overwhelming majority of respondents of my opinion survey insisted that they want the UN to play a central role in commanding peacekeeping forces, not the US or multinational forces (Higashi 2008, 2009).[5]

The second and third key components of the peacebuilding norm, national elections legitimized by the IOs and local agreements that produce inclusive political process, are required to increase the indigenous acceptance in more direct ways. The various political processes used to justify peacebuilding efforts (peace accords, popular consultations, Loya Jirga, and so on) become key tools for peace-builders who need wide acceptance from the local populace. National elections often function as a final stage of conferring this indigenous legitimacy to a new government. In sum, both international legitimacy and indigenous legitimacy are critical for success in peacebuilding.

The contribution of Minervian actors to the peacebuilding norm

Minervian actors – such as the EU member states, Canada, and Japan – played a key role in enhancing the norm of peacebuilding, which was established by the UN's multinational practices. Minervian actors not only established the idea of the "central role of the UN" in peacebuilding, but also showed their support by making major financial contributions and dispatching military and civilian personnel to UN-mandated peacebuilding missions.

As Tardy argues, the EU states have been strong supporters of the UN and have embraced "the centrality and legitimizing power of the UN Security Council" (2005, p. 51). In 2003, the EU and the UN adopted the "Joint Declaration on UN-EU Cooperation in Crisis Management," which emphasized that "the United Nations and European Union are united by the premise that the primary responsibility for the maintenance of international peace and security rests with the United Nations Security Council, in accordance with the United Nations Charter."[6] The declaration stated that the EU and the UN agreed to establish a joint consultative mechanism to strengthen the UN missions in peacebuilding and crisis management as a whole. By reiterating their principles, the EU states played a significant role in codifying the peacebuilding norm, particularly at a time when the UN's legitimacy was being challenged by the formally unauthorized intervention in Iraq.

In terms of financial responsibility, the EU states are major contributors to UN missions in the world; the EU states have a 39 percent share in the total UN peacekeeping budget (Tardy 2005, p. 51). As for the personnel contribution, the EU states dispatched substantial numbers of staff to UN-mandated peacebuilding (Tardy 2005, p. 52). For example, EU states contributed 85 percent of the Stabilization Force (SFOR) in Bosnia, which was established in 1996 to maintain security in the region (Bowman 2003). The major contributors to SFOR were France (2,280), United Kingdom (1,890), and Germany (1,720) in 2002

(Bowman 2003, pp. 8–10). In Kosovo, the EU provided approximately 36,000 members for the Kosovo Force (KFOR), over 80 percent of the Force's total strength.[7] Canada identifies itself as one of the foremost proponents of UN peacebuilding.[8] In 1996 – at a very early stage of UN peacebuilding operations – Lloyd Axworthy, Minister of Foreign Affairs, formally launched the "Canadian Peacebuilding Initiative" and attempted to play a crucial role in defining the significance of peacebuilding.[9] Axworthy appealed to the UN General Assembly in 1998, "For Canada, the universal values set out in the UN Charter have acted as our moral compass in setting our global agenda. The United Nations system has served as the instrument in achieving our goals."[10]

Following its promise at the UN General Assembly, Canada has continued to dispatch its staff to UN-mandated peacebuilding missions throughout the world. Canada contributed 1,500 personnel in Bosnia, 1,600 military staff in Kosovo, and 600 military personnel in East Timor.[11] In sum, the EU and Canada may be categorized as "supporters" or even "advocates" of the peacebuilding norm, which was created by the practices of UN-led peacebuilding. This recognition was significantly reinforced by their objections to the US-led nation building in Iraq.

Peacebuilding is one of the main areas into which Japan has been attempting to expand its international role, especially in the security dimension, which has been taboo since the Second World War. At the public debate on peacebuilding in the UN Security Council in 2005, Mr. Oshima, the Japanese ambassador to the UN, strongly emphasized the Japanese intention to participate in the UN's peacebuilding efforts: "One of the priority issues in my country's international assistance policy is its support for 'consolidation of peace and nation-building' in countries emerging from conflict."[12] Japan dispatched 600 members of the Japan Defense Force to the Cambodia UN mission in 1993; marking the first time Japan had dispatched army personnel overseas since the end of the Second World War.[13] A further 680 members of the Japan Defense Force were dispatched to East Timor to participate in UN operations in 1999, and it was the biggest deployment by the Japan Defense Force at that time. The Japanese government currently defines the activities of peacebuilding as "its new flag (or goal) as a peace-seeking nation."[14] Although Japan has been ambiguous in its position advocating the UN-led peacebuilding, as it supported US-led nation building in Iraq, Japan for the most part has supported the fundamental role of the UN in peacebuilding.

In sum, the Minervian actors played a key role in enhancing the peacebuilding norm by emphasizing the importance of the UN-led framework and illustrated this through their participation in multiple UN missions. On the other hand, the US policies on peacebuilding have been deeply influenced by the positions of the different administrations. The Clinton administration basically supported, or at least acquiesced to, UN-led peacebuilding (Bowman 2003). However, the Bush administration drastically changed US policies. After initiating the invasion of Iraq in 2003, the Bush administration attempted to take a completely new approach to peacebuilding with its largely unilateralist agenda for the rebuilding of Iraq.

The Bush administration's challenge to the peacebuilding norm

After President Bush was inaugurated in 2001, the neoconservatives – whose agenda is typically explained by the platform of "Project for the New American Century" signed by Vice President Dick Cheney, Secretary of Defense Donald Rumsfeld, and Deputy Secretary of Defense Paul Wolfowitz in the first Bush administration – evinced a strong ideology to downplay the role of the UN. This ideology was deeply reflected in their plan for nation building in Iraq. While administration officials were not very much impolitic in official statements, Richard Perle, a prominent neoconservative and chair of the Defense Policy Board, declared that the "UN was dead" when the UN Security Council did not authorize the US invasion of Iraq in March 2003. He insisted, "Saddam Hussein's reign of terror is about to end. He will go quickly, but not alone: in a parting irony, he will take the UN down with him" (Perle 2003).

Neoconservatives made it a priority to form a new regime in Iraq without the UN's central and political role. Another neoconservative, Stephen Schwartz (2003), wrote an article titled, "UN Go Home," one week after the Hussein regime collapsed. He insisted that the last thing the US should do was ask the UN to play a leading role in shaping a new Iraq: "The United States must not permit the U.N., with its terrible record in the Balkans, among the Palestinians, in Africa, in Cambodia, and elsewhere, to inflict its incompetence and neuroses on the people of Iraq" (Schwartz 2003, p. 10).

It took only one month for the US-led coalition to complete its invasion of Iraq and occupy the state. Shortly thereafter, the US started to push members of the UN Security Council to adopt a new resolution regarding the rebuilding of Iraq. After a serious debate in the Council, the UN Security Council adopted Resolution 1483 on May 22, 2003. Under strong pressure from the US, the resolution stated the US-led occupation "Authority" had the "effective administration of the territory"; the Coalition Authority was officially granted the central power to rebuild Iraq.[15]

It is obvious that with Resolution 1483, the US attempted to violate the first key component of the peacebuilding norm: *the UN's leading role*. The resolution conferred the leading role of rebuilding Iraq on the US-led occupying power, not the UN. It was the first time in UN history that the UN Security Council authorized an occupying power, not UN missions or missions by IOs, to "have absolute responsibility to rebuild a state."[16]

The authority of Bremer

The absolute power of the Coalition Authority was clearly demonstrated by the head of the Coalition Provisional Authority (CPA) in Iraq, Paul Bremer, who was appointed administrator of the CPA in May 2003. He articulates his power in his book: "I would be the only paramount authority figure – other than dictator Saddam Hussein – that most Iraqis had ever known" (2006, p. 4). He believed that he was empowered with "all executive, legislative, and judicial functions in Iraq" (2006, p. 13).

Responding to the idea of the Bush administration, Bremer had a clear plan to establish the new government. He wrote a memo to the Secretary of Defense on June 3, 2003, insisting the CPA would work to (1) appoint the interim government in two months; (2) start a constitutional process at the end of July; (3) let the Iraqis write a new constitution in six months; and (4) hold national elections within a year; "A tall order, but a worthy goal," he described (2006, p. 84). The first Bremer plan can be explained as shown in Figure 10.1.

In order to achieve this plan, Bremer established the Iraqi Governing Council in July 2003. Bremer appointed all 25 members of the Governing Council; thus it was largely viewed as puppet body for the US agenda, but the CPA asserted that the Governing Council could function as an interim governmental body (Bremer 2006, pp. 90–103).

I assert that the first Bremer plan and the creation of the Iraqi Governing Council appointed by Bremer were serious attempts to violate the second and third key component of the peacebuilding norm: *national elections legitimatized by IOs, and local agreements that produce inclusive political process in creating new governments*. The CPA planned to control the whole political process, such as creating an interim government and conducting national elections.

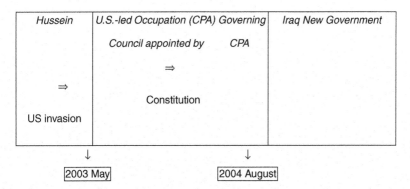

2003 May   2004 August

US occupation started.   National elections conducted by CPA

Figure 10.1 The first Bremer plan

The story appeared clear. The Bush administration wanted to establish a new Iraq without the UN's political role. It was a serious attempt to violate the peacebuilding norm that had prevailed until the Iraq war based on the accumulated efforts by the international communities, led by the Minervian actors.

Resistance to the hegemon

As the political insurgents resulted in the deterioration of the security conditions in Iraq, the UN Secretariat, led by Secretary-General Kofi Annan and Under-Secretary-General Kieran Prendergast, began resisting the US policy in Iraq. Slowly they started to push the Bush administration back to the original norm of peacebuilding, which they were convinced was more legitimate. And some Minervian actors, notably France, Germany, and Canada, which opposed the US invasion of Iraq, strongly endorsed the resistance of the UN Secretariat; they formed a coalition with the Secretary-General to ask the US to return to the peacebuilding norm. Although the group of Minerva states was split into the supporters and the opponents of the Bush Iraq reconstruction policy, the UN Secretariat, headed by Kofi Annan, confronted the Bush administration so bluntly that one UN Secretariat defined it as "the biggest resistance of the UN Secretariat to a superpower on the security issue since the birth of the UN."[17]

The resistance of the UN Secretariat against the US occupation started with the most serious attack on the UN in its history. At approximately

4:30 PM local Iraqi time on August 19, 2003, a flatbed truck carrying 1,000 kilograms of high explosives detonated outside the UN headquarters in Baghdad. It killed 22 UN staff, including Sergio de Mello, Special Representative of the Secretary-General.[18] This suicide attack caused Annan and many others in the UN Secretariat to realize that the UN should withdraw from Iraq unless they could play a substantial political role, commensurate with the risk to UN staff.[19] It was clear that the United Nations played only a marginal role in Iraq before the attack. Prendergast, the Under-Secretary-General of Political Affairs and key Secretariat who designed UN policy in Iraq at that time, explained,

> [After the August 19 attack] we had a sustained debate over quite a long period about what was our proper profile, what was our proper presence, what role were we playing? As far as I could see, politically we were playing an extremely marginal role. I do not believe that we were being consulted by the CPA about any matters of substance.[20]

As Secretary-General, Annan had a unilateral right to stop the dispatch of UN humanitarian workers due to security concerns. In September 2003, he decided to reduce the number of international staff in Iraq from 800 to 80.[21]

Three weeks after the August 19 attack, Annan and Prendergast not only decided to reduce the number of staff, but also started to push the US to change its policy in Iraq. On September 13, 2003, Annan called the foreign ministers of the five permanent members (P5) of the UN Security Council to Geneva.[22] In this meeting, he proposed his own plan and demanded the US and the Coalition change its Iraq policy. Before this meeting, the Bush administration had already proposed a new UN Security Council resolution to establish a multinational force, but the resolution still assumed the First Bremer Plan, in which the CPA would have primary responsibility to create a constitution and conduct an election.

Opposing the ideas of the US, Annan and Prendergast proposed an alternative plan (Figure 10.2) with the objective of handing over sovereignty to a "new interim government" that would have more inclusive participations by broad Iraqi political groups, followed by the constitutional process, elections, and then the formation of a new permanent government.[23] The plan implied that the whole process would be assisted by the UN as a key player, suggesting that the rebuilding of Iraq needed to be conducted by Iraqis, supported by the UN, but not by the CPA. This plan shows the determination of the UN Secretariat to push

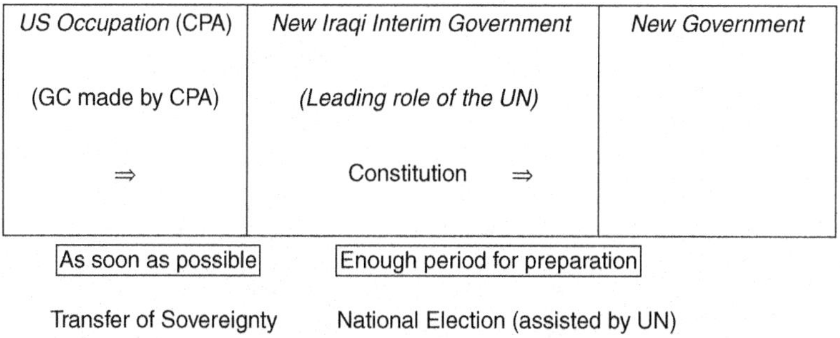

US Occupation (CPA)	New Iraqi Interim Government	New Government
(GC made by CPA)	*(Leading role of the UN)*	
$\Rightarrow$	Constitution $\Rightarrow$	

|As soon as possible| |Enough period for preparation| |

Transfer of Sovereignty   National Election (assisted by UN)

Figure 10.2 The Annan proposal

the US back to the peacebuilding norm even in Iraq. There is a sharp contrast between Bremer's first plan and Annan's proposal.

At the September 13 meeting in Geneva, Annan demanded that the P5 states take this proposal into consideration in the new resolution. In front of the foreign ministers of the P5 states he asserted that,

> The UN Security Council Resolution 1483 placed the UN in a very difficult position. Special Representative [Sergio] Vieira de Mello was unable to fulfill the role the UN should have played... We cannot repeat this error... Especially now, we must be sure to pass the correct resolution, as the bad resolutions kill people.[24]

The UN Secretariats who embraced the values of the peacebuilding norm were convinced that the CPA-led reconstruction would fail because of the lack of legitimacy. The Iraqi-led process assisted by the UN mission would have more legitimacy and acceptance both inside and outside Iraq.

Assistance for Annan from other member states

Of course, the UN Secretariats alone cannot confront the hegemon; the proposal relied on the support of the Minervian actors who decided to join in the confrontation with the Bush administration. France and Germany, the key partners in the UN Security Council that opposed the US invasion of Iraq in 2003, announced an "amendment to the U.S. draft" of the new resolution to incorporate the Annan proposal.[25] In the amendment, France and Germany declared, "We fully agree with the Secretary-General's proposal of a timetable. In our view, if we want the process to be welcomed and supported by the Iraqis and the countries of the region, the UN through the Secretary-General should play *the key role*, not the Authority."[26] France and Germany explicitly backed up the Annan alternative.

However, the Minervian states are split in two: The UK, Italy, and Spain, which supported the US invasion of Iraq at that time, basically endorsed the Bush policy of rebuilding Iraq and dispatched a substantial number of forces to assist the US occupation in Iraq. On the other hand, Germany, France, and Canada, which opposed the US invasion in the first place, demonstrated their opposition to the US Iraq policy and never dispatched military personnel to Iraq. These countries, which had endorsed the UN missions for peacebuilding, strongly recommended that the US to return to the original peacebuilding norm with the conviction that the UN must be more legitimate in conducting a post-conflict reconstruction. Germany's ambassador to the UN emphasized, "We were fully in agreement with what he [the Secretary-General] had said.... The problem was to fulfill these conditions in order to enable the Secretary-General and the UN to play again *the central role* in the reconstruction of Iraq."[27]

The position of Japan – which is, in this case, similar to that of UK – was between the two stances: although Japan officially supported the US attack on Iraq and its rebuilding, behind the scenes, Japan continued to request that the Bush Administration return to the UN. On the one hand, Japanese government decided to deploy more than 600 military personnel to Iraq by insisting that the operation was "humanitarian assistance."[28] The Japan Defense Agency stated that "the dispatch of the Japan Defense Force to Iraq [would] contribute to enhancing the relationship with the United States, the only ally of Japan."[29] On the other hand, Koizumi, Prime Minister of Japan at that time, recommended that President Bush ask the UN to play a more central role. When Bush came to Japan in October 2003, Koizumi asked Bush to use the UN in more substantial ways to democratize Iraq because "the UN has more legitimacy than the U.S."[30]

Supported by some Minervian actors, notably France, Germany, and other UN Security Council members such as Peru and Mexico, Annan and Prendergast seriously attempted to reshape US policies in Iraq. Responding to Annan's plan backed by Germany and France, the US proposed a new draft of the resolution on October 2, 2003.

Disappointingly for Annan, the substance of the US plan had not changed; the CPA was still responsible for creating the constitution and conducting elections in Iraq. Reading the new draft by the US, Annan respondedtothemedia,"Theresolutionhasjustbeenreleased. ... Obviously it's not going in the direction I had recommended."[31] Prendergast took action. UN Secretariats gathered in Prendergast's room and wrote a new draft of Annan's speech for the luncheon meeting on the same day. In front of the 15 representatives of states of the UN Security Council, Annan spoke with a harsh tone:

> If the Coalition Authority had concluded that the best way forward was to keep their original ideas on political transition, the occupying power had a difficult job ahead and was shouldering an enormous burden. In this case, the UN could not play an effective political role: *Either the CPA or the UN* should be in charge of the political process ... Attempting to blur the role of the two is a cause for confusion and could expose the United Nations to risk that is not justified by the substance of its role.[32]

Annan concluded that the United Nations would be ready to assume a political role at a later stage, if it were to become clear that "only the UN could do so."[33] The evocative speech by Annan, who tends to be calm and friendly to the US, was broadcast as "the most significant and unprecedented revolt of the United Nations against the United States in the history of the UN."[34] Prendergast explained the objective of the speech:

> The Secretary-General should say "no" more often; there is a temptation sometimes on the part of the Security Council to give the Secretary-General and the UN Secretariat a mandate which is unimplementable, and we should say if it is unimplementable ... in this particular case, we wanted to know what, exactly, are we being asked to do? Is it sufficiently important to risk the lives of our staff?[35]

Germany and France expressed their strong support of Annan's harsh criticism of the US Iraq policy. De la Sablière, the French Ambassador to the UN, responded,

> It was the UN which was able to help Iraqi people to find their own solution in this transition period, not the CPA or occupying power ... The United Nations has enough experience to help Iraqis to create new constitutions and conduct elections with legitimate mechanism.[36]

The coalition of the UN Secretariat and Minervian states, especially France and Germany, made an unprecedented attempt to change the core security policy of the US. However, the US did not accept the words of the coalition. The Bush administration adamantly persuaded the UN Security Council members to adopt Resolution 1511, without substantial changes, on October 16, 2003. The Resolution clearly demonstrated the limitations of the coalition of the UN Secretariat and Minerva actors: they could not change the US policy simply through their own persuasion. Annan and Prendergast decided to withdraw all international UN staff from Baghdad on November 4, deciding that the UN could not play a cosmetic and risky role in Iraq anymore.[37]

The peacebuilding norm pushed the US back to the UN

Although the Bush administration refused the request by the UN Secretariat and some Minervian states in October 2003, it eventually changed its Iraq policy and asked the UN to play a critical role in forming an interim government and conducting elections. This dramatic change was mainly caused by US failure of nation building in Iraq, reinforced by the continuous requests by the coalition of the UN Secretariats and Minervian actors. This process suggests both the limits and the significance of the international peacebuilding norm supported by the UN Secretariats and Minervian actors: although this norm may not be able to change US policy in the short term, the combined pressures of these forces might establish a "bottom–up" mechanism by which the hegemon is encouraged to return to the international framework over a long period, especially when the hegemon faces huge difficulty.

The sudden change of US policy was announced on January 19, 2004, in the bilateral meeting between the CPA, headed by Bremer, and UN Secretariat, headed by Annan and Prendergast, at the UN Headquarters. Before this meeting, the Bush administration faced a critical impasse: brutal insurgency, which was destroying Bremer's nation-building plans, as well as political oppositions from Iraqi fractions including Ayatollah Sistani – the most powerful Shiite religious leader in Iraq. Bremer said in the meeting with Annan that Ayatollah Sistani and his supporters did not accept CPA's electoral plan, and he asked the UN to dispatch an electoral investigation team to Iraq with the aim of designing an alternative plan. Annan responded that the UN would not return to Iraq if it was only to encourage Ayatollah Sistani to follow the US plan, but said that if the US was ready to accept a UN alternative, he would consider dispatching investigators to Iraq.[38] After the meeting, Bremer acknowledged his enthusiasm for the involvement of the UN:

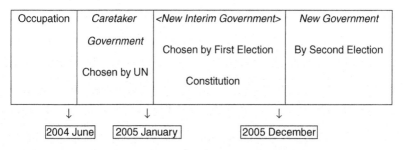

Occupation	Caretaker Government Chosen by UN	<New Interim Government> Chosen by First Election Constitution	New Government By Second Election

|2004 June| |2005 January| |2005 December|

UN (Brahimi) negotiated First National Election   Second National Election

Designed and assisted by UN Designed and assisted by UN

Figure 10.3 Brahimi proposal

"I think the encouraging news from today was that the Secretary-General agreed to consider this request very seriously."[39] It appeared that the US had finally recognized that to gain the support of the Iraqi political factions, the US needed to ask for help from UN, which had more legitimacy in the eyes of Iraqis.

In February 2004, Annan dispatched Brahimi, a special advisor of the Secretary-General on the Middle East, to Iraq. Brahimi met more than 200 leaders of various factions in Iraq, including Ayatollah Sistani, and announced an alternative proposal for rebuilding Iraq (see Figure 10.3).

In the Brahimi plan, the first interim government was a "caretaker government" organized by much broader range of Iraqi leaders, and Brahimi would assist in its formation to enhance a more inclusive political process. This caretaker government was to conduct the first national election in January 2005, which would produce a "new interim government." This interim government would adopt the constitution and conduct the second national election in December 2005 to create a new formal government.[40]

I assert that this "Brahimi plan" followed the original peacebuilding norm because the UN would play a leading role in creating a caretaker government and designing and assisting in the two national elections (the first and second key components). It also called for creating both a "caretaker government" and the "interim government," which would be elected by the Iraqi people and have more inclusive representations by the different Iraqi political groups (the third key component).

Following the Bush administration's acceptance of the plan, Brahimi led the process of selecting the cabinet members of the "caretaker government" in June 2004. The UN electoral teams also played a major role in the formation of the Independent Electoral Commission in Iraq (IECI).[41] The team worked with the IECI to design a proportional representation system for national elections and assist in both the January and December elections in 2005.[42] In short, in terms of choosing the caretaker government and conducting two elections, the UN played a central role in Iraq. And without the political role of the UN, the CPA, headed by the US (hegemon), could not advance the political process in creating a new government in Iraq.

Why did the US change its policy? There seem to be three fundamental reasons. First, the security conditions in Iraq had harshly deteriorated. The average daily number of attacks by insurgents jumped from 8 in June 2003 to over 30 in November of the same year.[43] The worsening security began to seriously threaten the US plan to rebuild Iraq.[44] Second, the Iraqi leaders of political factions rejected the CPA plan. Shiite people, who make up between 60 and 70 percent of the Iraqi population, were opposed to the election conducted by the CPA and very consistent in demanding that the UN play a central role in conducting elections. Thus, the Shiite members of the Governing Council, headed by Abed al-Aziz al-Hakim, sent a letter to Annan at the end of 2003 and asked the UN to oversee the elections in making a constitutional government.[45] This incident demonstrated that the US was lacking the legitimacy required to pull the different Iraqi factions to follow the CPA-led process. Larry Diamond, the former senior advisor to the CPA, noted that the US occupation had "a serious legitimacy problem," and that pattern changed only when the Bush administration "finally turned to the UN for help" (2004, p. 45). The third possible reason is the impact of the Iraqi situation on the presidential election in 2004. By asking the UN to play a key role, the Bush administration could sell two points to the American people on the election trail: (1) the transfer of sovereignty to the caretaker government; and (2) two scheduled elections to create the formal government. Fixing the political schedule became possible due to the support of Iraqi factions for the Brahimi plan. Although it is not largely recognized both in the US and the world, the Bush administration would not have achieved even the creation of an interim government by the end of June 2004 and two elections by the end of 2005 if it had not asked the UN to play a central role.

Iraqi political process has been fragile. After the formal government was established in the end of 2005, the political uprising became so harsh that many experts argued that Iraq had begun a situation of civil war; but as US forces changed its tactics in 2007 and started the Awakening Movement, which invited more than 100,000 Sunni insurgents to the Awakening Councils that provided them about 300 USD per month in exchange of stopping attacks, the security situation was calm down after 2008; all US forces withdrew from Iraq in the end of 2011.[46]

Conclusion

In this chapter, I have argued that there is a peacebuilding norm created by the UN's multiple practices after the end of the Cold War. The norm appears to be robust as illustrated by the three key components that have been applied to the recent major peacebuilding efforts, such as in East Timor, Sierra Leone, and Sudan. Although the US attempted to change this norm in Iraq, the norm was strong enough that the UN Secretariat and Minervian states pushed the US, eventually successfully, to return to the original norm and to follow the procedures designed by the UN Secretariats. I have asserted that this change of policy by the US has had a historic impact on the activities of peacebuilding: it confirms that even the most powerful states cannot succeed in nation building single-handedly.

This process has interesting theoretical implications for the Minervian project. The international norms such as peacebuilding, or the international mechanisms such as the Kyoto Protocol have faced substantial resistance from the hegemon. However, triggered by serious needs on the ground (in this case, the failure of Iraqi nation building), the hegemon might join the international mechanism pushed by UN Secretariats and supported by Minervian actors. Thus, it is critical for Minervians to create new international institutions, which can apply consistent pressure to the hegemon to join in the future, much as the peacebuilding norm eventually garnered US support.

Notes

1. Data comes from Appendix 9.1. The Appendix lists UN missions that had the assignment of democratization including electoral assistance. Additionally, the Iraq and DRC missions started electoral tasks after 2004.
2. The research by the author in Afghanistan and East Timor suggests that an overwhelming majority of people in Afghanistan and East Timor prefer the election to be conducted by both the local government and the UN, rather than by the local entities single-handedly, because the UN can give the "credibility to the elections" (Higashi 2008, Appendix: Q 29; Higashi 2009, Appendix: Q 28)

3. Also see BBC News, September 4, 1999.
4. RAND News Release 2005, "RAND Study Says UN Nation Building Record Compares Favorably with the U.S. in Some Respects."
5. See Higashi 2008 (Afghanistan) Appendix, Question 14 & Higashi 2009 (East Timor) Appendix, Question 7. The sample of the survey is 260 in Afghanistan and 319 in East Timor.
6. Joint Declaration on UN–EU Cooperation in Crisis Management adopted on September 24, 2003.
7. EU News February 10, 2002.
8. Ministry of Foreign Affairs and International Trade Canada: Evaluation of the Peacebuilding and Human Security Program 2000.
9. Ibid.
10. Ibid.
11. Ministry of Foreign Affairs and International Trade Canada: Canada & Kosovo, Bosnia, East Timor, Afghanistan.
12. Statement by Permanent Representative of Japan on Peacebuilding, May 26, 2005.
13. Japan Defense Agency Homepage: Activities of Japan Defense Force in International Community.
14. Statement by Director of International Peace Cooperation at Ministry of Foreign Affair in Japan, November 1, 2006.
15. UN Security Council Resolution 1483, May 22, 2003.
16. Author's interview with Salim Lone, the former director of communication working for UN Baghdad Headquarters, on March 18, 2004.
17. Author's interview with one UN Secretariat with condition of anonymity in 2004.
18. Report of Secretary-General December 5, 2003, p. 4.
19. Author's interview with Prendergast, May 26, 2006.
20. Author's interview with Prendergast, March 6, 2004.
21. Report of Secretary-General December 5, 2003, p. 6.
22. Ibid., p. 14.
23. Ibid., p. 14.
24. NHK Documentary 2004. The contents of this documentary, which was directed by the author are supported by interviews with top leaders such as Annan, Prendergast, Brahimi, and Negroponte (US Ambassador to the UN at that time) as well as minutes of critical meetings.
25. France and Germany "Amendment to the US draft" 2003.
26. Ibid. Emphasis added.
27. Author's interview with Pleuger, the German Ambassador to the UN, March 5, 2004. Emphasis added.
28. Asahi Newspaper. July 18, 2006.
29. Japan Defense Agency Homepage, "What Can We or Japan Defense Agency Do for Iraqi Reconstruction?"
30. Author's interview with a journalist who shared a dinner with Koizumi in 2004.
31. UN Homepage, "Secretary-General off the cuff," October 2, 2003.
32. NHK Documentary 2004, based on the minutes.
33. Ibid.
34. Asahi Newspaper. November 7, 2003.

35. Author's interview with Prendergast, March 9, 2004.
36. Author's interview with De La Sablière, French Ambassador of the UN, March 12, 2004.
37. Report of the Secretary-General, December 5, 2003.
38. Author's interview with Kofi Annan in March 2004.
39. Bremer Press conference on January 19, 2004.
40. The Brahimi recommendation presented to the UN Security Council on February 23, 2004.
41. UN Homepage: Iraq Electoral Fact Sheet.
42. Ibid.
43. Ibid., p. 22.
44. *New York Times*, November 15, 2003.
45. Hakim Letter on December 23, 2003.
46. Simon, Steven. 2008. "The Price of Surge: How U.S. Strategy Is Hastening Iraq's Demise." *Foreign Affairs*, 87 (3), 57–76.

Part IV
The Political Leadership Mode

11
Minervian Politics and International Chemicals Policy

Henrik Selin

Introduction

The global community of international organizations, states, and non-governmental actors has engaged in sustained cooperation on hazardous chemicals since the 1960s, establishing a host of international institutions for chemicals management. Tens of thousands of chemicals are used regularly in industrial manufacturing, in agriculture, in consumer products, and in human health protection. Modern chemistry provides numerous societal benefits, but chemicals production and use also come with risks. At high doses, many chemicals are lethal. Studies have also linked low-dose exposure to hazardous chemicals with disruption of endocrine functions, immune system impairments, and functional and physiological effects on reproduction capabilities in animals and humans (Arctic Monitoring and Assessment Programme 2009, 2010). International and domestic management efforts seek to minimize environmental and human health risks from hazardous chemicals while recognizing the many positive aspects of the chemicals revolution.

This chapter applies the Minervian framework to international chemicals politics and examines the roles of Canada, the European Union (EU), and Japan on chemicals policy making and management. It argues that the EU and Canada have demonstrated critical leadership on international chemicals management and pioneered many major policy expansions on hazardous chemicals, especially since the early 1990s. Japan has traditionally been more passive in international forums, but has frequently supported policy developments championed by the EU and Canada by, for example, signing and ratifying major treaties relatively quickly. The three Minervian actors have also been motivated by somewhat different sets of interests, and the chapter discusses major domestic and regional factors shaping actions taken by Canada, the EU, and Japan in the context of the Minervian framework.

In short, many actions by Canada, the EU, and Japan have been driven by a combination of modes one and three of the Minervian framework's three causal modes of policy change. Canada and the EU have demonstrated leadership in response to concerns about adverse human health and environmental effects from hazardous chemicals (mode three of policy change). In Canada, Arctic pollution and indigenous politics were major leadership drivers in the 1980s and 1990s. During the same time, the EU was also motivated by regional environmental and health reasons in its regulatory push (including for the Arctic). More recently, EU actions have also been motivated by economic concerns about the competitiveness of European firms. As a result, the EU has acted to upload its relatively stringent standards to the international levels to harmonize requirements for firms across countries (mode one of policy change). Japan has been less active than Canada and the EU, but pollution issues are still domestically important.

The chapter starts by setting the case of international chemicals management in the context of the volume's overall theoretical focus on Minervian politics, institution building, and different modes of policy change. Next is a presentation of the main components of the chemicals regime. This is followed by an examination of some of the main institutional developments on chemicals policy and management from the 1960s to the present, also noting key positions taken by Canada, the EU, and Japan. After this, the international roles of Canada, the EU, and Japan, as well as factors that have shaped their interests and actions on critical issues, are discussed in turn. The chapter ends with a few concluding remarks on past, current, and future Minervian politics in the areas of international chemicals management.

Minervian politics and international chemicals management

International political, scientific, and technical meetings on hazardous chemicals are typically well attended by many countries, and also a host of intergovernmental and non-governmental organizations (Selin 2010). Predominantly since the 1980s, major industrialized countries including the United States, Canada, Japan, Australia, New Zealand, and the EU member states have joined China, India, Brazil, South Africa, and other major developing countries in expanding political goals, policies, and technical standards for international chemicals management. However, participation is not synonymous with leadership, which involves a deliberate strategic effort to champion new policy ideas and build necessary coalitions for policy change.

Leadership, undertaken by states and organizations, is often critical for successful international institution building. Such leadership may be exercised in many different forms, including its intellectual and structural manifestations (Young 1991). An intellectual leader relies largely on the power of ideas, norms, and knowledge to shape the way other participants conzeptualize issues and policy alternatives. Intellectual leaders often seek particular policy outcomes by trying to secure acceptance of new ideas, norms, and knowledge. Structural leadership is exercised through the use of material resources, such as financial, technical, and scientific resources, necessary for assessment and policy making. Of course, these two forms of leadership can be combined. In fact, it is common for environmental leader states to combine their intellectual leadership with different kinds of material support for policy change.

On international chemicals issues, Canada and the EU have demonstrated much intellectual and structural leadership, especially since the early 1990s and onwards. They have exhibited these forms of leadership by advocating for policy expansions in combination with hosting international political and scientific meetings. Canada and the EU have initiated and sponsored major international environmental scientific assessments, appointed national experts to international organizations, and funded their work of preparing background documents and policy proposals. In contrast, the United States and Australia, for example, have participated in most of the same meetings, but have commonly been less willing to lead. As such, Canada and the EU have frequently promoted new policies in a political vacuum left by the relative inaction of other major countries (Downie 2003; Selin 2003; Selin and Selin 2008).

Canadian and European intellectual and structural leadership has been motivated by multiple factors, which are discussed in this chapter in more detail. In brief, Canada and the EU share a desire to reduce the extensive transboundary transport of emissions to northern latitudes. Hazardous chemicals are also politically and publicly important human health and environmental issues in Canada and the EU, and their international actions are reflecting their relatively tough domestic and regional chemicals legislation. In Canada, chemicals policy is also closely linked with sensitive domestic issues regarding Arctic indigenous peoples' rights. In the EU, environmental leader states working closely with the European Commission and the European Parliament have raised regulatory standards and removed hazardous substances from commercial goods (Selin 2007; Selin and VanDeveer 2006).

Political efforts by countries to "trade up" their relatively high national environmental standards to the international level can also be driven by economic interests and aspirations (Vogel 1997). As environmental leader states seek to raise global standards, they, in part, hope to expand restrictions on domestic firms to competitors operating in other parts of the world, thereby leveling the playing field between domestic and foreign companies competing in highly competitive and globalized markets. Recent EU chemicals policy expansions have important international market ramifications. Specifically, whereas many earlier international standards for consumer and environmental protection were *de facto* set in the US because of the relative stringency of early US regulations in combination with the size of the US economy, the EU is increasingly replacing the US as the main actor setting international product and assessment standards on hazardous chemicals (Selin and VanDeveer 2006; Schreurs et al. 2009; Kelemen and Vogel 2010).

International chemicals policy

Adopting a global political goal, governments at the World Summit on Sustainable Development (WSSD) in 2002 agreed that by 2020 chemicals should be "used and produced in ways that lead to the minimization of significant adverse effects on human health and the environment" (United Nations 2002, §23). Global and regional institutions have been developed in response to the realization that many chemicals issues are fundamentally international. A large number of chemicals are commonly traded between firms and countries, together with a growing number of goods containing chemicals. Emissions of chemicals also frequently cross national borders. In addition, many efforts to raise awareness about hazardous chemicals and develop better domestic policies and management practices depend on international support. The chemicals regime is structured around three global conventions, various regional agreements, and includes participation by many organizations (Selin 2010).

The global Stockholm Convention regulates the production, use, trade, disposal, and emissions of persistent organic pollutants (POPs), a category of particularly toxic and long-lived chemicals. It was adopted in 2001 and entered into force in 2004. By 2012, 175 countries and the EU were parties to the Stockholm Convention, which covered 22 POPs.

More will be added in the future. The production and use of pesticides and industrial chemicals listed in Annex A are generally prohibited, but parties may apply for country-specific and time-limited exemptions. Annex B lists pesticides and industrial chemicals subject to restrictions where only specified uses are allowed. Annex C lists by-products of production and combustion processes regulated through the application of best available techniques and best environmental practices. The import and export of regulated chemicals are permitted only for substances subject to use exemptions or for the environmentally sound management and disposal of discarded chemicals.

The Rotterdam Convention is a global agreement regulating the international trade in certain pesticides and industrial chemicals through a prior informed consent (PIC) procedure. It was adopted in 1998 and entered into force in 2004. By 2012, 145 countries and the EU were parties. The Rotterdam Convention is designed principally to assist developing countries in deciding whether to permit the import of a chemical by increasing their access to risk information and managing trade through the PIC procedure. The PIC procedure stipulates that a party can export chemicals listed in the treaty to another party only after prior consent by the national government of the importing country. Parties must notify the convention secretariat when they ban or severely restrict a chemical, so that information may be made available to other parties. By early 2012, the Rotterdam Convention covered 43 chemicals and the parties are working to expand the list of controlled chemicals.

The global Basel Convention controls the generation, transboundary movement, and the environmentally sound disposal of hazardous wastes, including discarded hazardous chemicals or used goods containing such substances. It was adopted in 1989 and entered into force in 1992. By 2012, 177 countries and the EU were parties. The Basel Convention prohibits export of hazardous wastes to Antarctica and to parties that have taken domestic measures to ban such imports. Permitted waste transfers from one party to another are subject to a PIC procedure; an importing party must give consent to a waste import before a shipment from an exporting party can take place. Exports of hazardous wastes to non-parties must be subject to an agreement at least as stringent as the Basel Convention requirements. Over time, parties have strengthened the legal structures for waste transports, and developed technical guidelines for the environmentally sound management of waste categories and streams.

In addition, there are many regional chemicals treaties. One of the most important ones is the 1998 POPs Protocol under the Convention on Long-Range Transboundary Air Pollution (CLRTAP), covering North America and Europe. This agreement, which addresses many of the same POPs as the Stockholm Convention, regulates the production, use, and environmentally sound transport and disposal of pesticides and industrial chemicals, as well as sets technical standards and guidelines for controlling emissions of by-products of production and combustion processes. Like with the Stockholm Convention, additional chemicals are on track to be regulated. Furthermore, countries all over the world have established a large number of agreements around shared seas, lakes, and rivers that contain provisions against chemical pollution and dumping. Some of these are part of the Regional Seas Programme set up by United Nations Environment Programme (UNEP) in 1974, involving over 140 countries collaborating around 13 action plans targeting a long list of pollutants.

The development of international institutions for chemicals management

Early national chemicals legislation was shaped by emerging studies that demonstrated that the use of many of the growing number of modern chemicals was not as harmless to the environment and human health as was initially believed. Famously, Rachel Carson, in her ground-breaking book *Silent Spring*, first published in the United States in 1962, warned that the growing use of DDT and other similar pesticides led to the extinction of local bird populations around fields where these chemicals were extensively sprayed, thus causing "silent springs". Writing in 1972 about Rachel Carson and her life's work, Paul Brooks observed that "Within a decade of its publication *Silent Spring* has been recognized throughout the world as one of those rare books that change the course of history – not through incitement to war or violent revolution, but by altering the direction of man's thinking" (1972, p. 227).

The UN Conference on the Human Environment in Stockholm in 1972 focused extensively on hazardous substances. In part building on the Stockholm Action Plan, countries and organizations began to develop regional and global standards. The Organisation for Economic Co-operation and Development (OECD) coordinated testing requirements and data generation among member states and promoted chemical safety measures. The World Health Organization (WHO) created its Environmental Health Criteria Programme in 1973 to assess environmental and human health data and provide guidelines for exposure limits. The WHO also worked with the Food and Agriculture

Organization (FAO) in the Codex Alimentarius Commission on recommendations for maximum pesticide residues in food. In 1976, UNEP created the International Register of Potentially Toxic Chemicals to collect and disseminate information about domestic regulations on chemicals (Lönngren 1992).

In the 1970s, a growing number of countries and organizations did not only want to expand scientific and technical collaboration, but also sought political actions on mitigating risks of hazardous substances (Selin 2010). In response to concerns about the dumping of hazardous chemicals in developing countries, UNEP and FAO-led activities resulted in the creation of two voluntary instruments aimed at generating information about the international trade in potentially dangerous chemicals – the 1985 International Code of Conduct for the Distribution and Use of Pesticides and the 1987 London Guidelines for the Exchange of Information on Chemicals in International Trade. Similarly, the UNEP Governing Council in 1987 adopted the voluntary Cairo Guidelines and Principles for the Environmentally Sound Management of Hazardous Wastes, which established a principle of notification and consent by states prior to the import of hazardous wastes.

By the late 1980s, a growing number of governments and environmental advocacy groups called for more controls on the hazardous waste trade to better protect humans and the environment. Reacting to these political pressures, the UNEP Governing Council authorized negotiations on a legally binding agreement that would strengthen the Cairo Guidelines in 1987. In particular African countries and Greenpeace called for a complete trade ban, which they argued was the only way to stop the global North's "toxic imperialism" of shipping their hazardous wastes to developing countries. In contrast, most industrialized countries and industry organizations preferred a prior informed consent procedure that would regulate but not outlaw trade. The Basel Convention, which was the outcome of these negotiations, did not introduce a total ban on waste transports, but merely made the voluntary PIC procedure mandatory.

The members of the pro-ban coalition, consisting of many African countries, the Nordic countries, and environmental advocacy groups, continued to advocate for stricter trade regulations. However, rather than promoting a complete trade ban, they shifted toward supporting to a more politically feasible ban on the North–South trade in hazardous wastes in the early 1990s (Kummer 1995; Brikell 2000). At the third Basel Convention conference of the parties in 1995, the ban-coalition gained enough political support to ensure that the parties adopted the so-called

Ban Amendment, which was incorporated into the Basel Convention. This Ban Amendment prohibits the export of hazardous wastes for final disposal and recycling from countries listed in Annex VII (parties that are members of the OECD and the EU as well as Liechtenstein) to all other parties (developing countries). However, ratification of the Ban Amendment has been slow and it has yet to enter into force.

Early Canadian, European, and Japanese support for the Basel Convention is reflected in their relatively quick ratifications. Canada and the EU signed the Basel Convention at the time of its adoption and became parties in 1992 and 1994, respectively. Japan did not originally sign the agreement in 1989, but became a party in 1993. In contrast, the United States signed but has never ratified the Basel Convention because of domestic opposition to international regulations on the waste trade and Congressional skepticism of international environmental agreements. However, concurrence between Canada, Europe, and Japan broke down over the Ban Amendment. Whereas the European Commission and many European countries actively supported the majority of developing countries in their quest for a North–South trade ban, and the EU became a party in 1997, both Canada and Japan have rejected the Ban Amendment on the grounds that it is too trade restrictive.

The international political chemicals agenda was further expanded during the early 1990s. In addition to the efforts on the intentional distribution of chemicals through trade and the voluntary harmonization of national assessments and regulations, issues relating to long-range transport of emissions of chemicals were added to the international agenda. This included a change in the perception of chemicals pollution from a local issue to a transboundary one. Earlier studies had confirmed that chemicals could cause severe local damage to the environment and human health, but now the long-range atmospheric transport of emissions was identified as a major concern. Many of these substances were part of the sub-category of substances now labeled as POPs. Canada and Europe in particular were critical in bringing the POPs issue to the attention of the international policy community.

In the 1980s, scientific data from the Arctic raised new concerns. The existence of hazardous chemicals in Arctic was known since the early 1970s, but the contamination levels discovered in the 1980s were much higher than expected. Scientific studies revealed three interrelated conditions: systematic long-range atmospheric transport of hazardous emissions to the Arctic, high environmental contamination levels throughout the Arctic region, and actual and potential environmental and human health implications. Studies in Canada in the late 1980s demonstrated alarmingly high levels of hazardous chemicals in breast milk and blood samples taken from the Arctic indigenous population, some levels among the highest measured in the world (Dewailly and Furgal 2003). Subsequent assessments have generated additional data on the extent of Arctic contamination (Arctic Monitoring and Assessment Programme 2009, 2010).

The United Nations Conference on Environment and Development (UNCED) in 1992 re-intensified global political attention to hazardous chemicals. Chapter 19 of Agenda 21 outlined priority areas for improved chemicals management. Agenda 21 also called for the establishment of an intergovernmental forum on chemical safety to aid the coordination of the many different organizations involved in international chemicals management. For that purpose, the international community established the Intergovernmental Forum on Chemical Safety (IFCS) in 1994. In addition, Agenda 21 called on states to create a new mandatory PIC procedure for traded chemicals. The FAO Council in 1994 and UNEP Governing Council in 1995 supported the development of a legally binding PIC instrument. Political negotiations began in 1996, and the Rotterdam Convention was adopted in 1998.

As international preparations for creating a mandatory PIC procedure started, the North–South dimension of the trade in chemicals loomed large, similar to North–South controversy on the trade in hazardous wastes. Many developing countries believed that a strong PIC mechanism could protect them against the dumping of hazardous chemicals in their countries, and called for an absolute ban on the export of domestically prohibited chemicals from OECD countries to other countries. Yet, the idea of banning trade in chemicals was opposed by many industrialized countries and the chemicals industry, and the Rotterdam Convention only transformed the existing voluntary procedure of sharing information and responsibility between exporting and importing states into a legally binding agreement without introducing any additional bans.

Canada, the EU, and Japan supported the political effort to make the voluntary PIC procedure legally binding through the development of the Rotterdam Convention, and they were all active during the negotiations. The EU signed the Rotterdam Convention at the time of its adoption in 1998 and became a party in 2002. Canada did not sign the Rotterdam Convention at the diplomatic conference, but became a party in 2002. Japan signed the Rotterdam Convention in 1999 and joined as a party in 2004. The United States signed the Rotterdam Convention in 1998, but the US Senate has yet to take all the necessary steps for ratification. Most major developing countries, including China, India, Brazil, and South Africa are parties to the Rotterdam Convention.

Parallel to the creation of the Rotterdam Convention, the international community began targeting POPs. The CLRTAP countries started their work on POPs in the late 1980s, due in large part to Canadian political action and leadership. POPs were discussed briefly during the UNCED preparations, but were not a major issue at the conference. Instead, it was first in 1995 when the UNEP Governing Council called for an international assessment of 12 POPs – "the dirty dozen" – that POPs became a major global issue. In 1996, the IFCS-led assessments concluded that a global POPs treaty was needed to address risks to human health and the environment. The global negotiations benefited greatly from the CLRTAP process where there are significant regulatory overlaps between the Stockholm Convention and the CLRTAP POPs Protocol. Both Canada and the EU are parties to the CLRTAP POPs Protocol (Japan is not a party because it is located outside the CLRTAP region).

As the Stockholm Convention was adopted in 2001, Canada, the EU, and Japan continued to show their support. Canada was the first country to ratify the Stockholm Convention, as it both signed and submitted its instrument of ratification during the diplomatic conference. The EU also signed the treaty in 2001 and became a party in 2004. Japan did not sign the Stockholm Convention during the diplomatic conference, but became a party in 2002. The United States signed the Stockholm Convention in 2001, but the US Senate has yet to accept it and pass necessary implementing legislation. Major developing countries such as China, India, Brazil, Mexico, and South Africa are all parties to the Stockholm Convention. The EU and Canada have also supported expanding the list of regulated POPs under the CLRTAP POPs Protocol and the Stockholm Convention.

The WSSD in 2002 reviewed the implementation of Agenda 21 and set priorities for continued efforts. Many stakeholders, including Canada, the EU, and Japan, believed that there was a need to better coordinate the growing number of chemicals agreements. In response, the UNEP Governing Council launched in 2003 a process to develop a Strategic Approach to International Chemicals Management (SAICM), which was adopted in 2006. SAICM is policy framework for improving and better coordinating chemicals governance toward the 2020 goal on the safe production and use of chemicals set at the WSSD, including, measures to support further risk reduction; improve knowledge and information sharing; strengthen institutions, law, and policy; enhance capacity building; and address illegal traffic. Alongside implementation of the main chemicals agreements, these are long-term issues for well beyond 2020.

The EU, Canada, and Japan as Minervian actors

Canada, the EU, and Japan have engaged in international politics and policy making on chemicals since the 1960s, but the EU and Canada have often played more active and critical roles than Japan. The three Minervian actors have supported extensive policy expansion under the global chemicals regime and participated in efforts by international organizations to improve international and local chemicals safety. As part of their support for expanded chemicals management, they have hosted, financed, and attended numerous international political and expert meetings, initiated and developed many new policy proposals, produced a large number of background and assessment reports, and supported a host of capacity-building programs in developing countries. Of course, the Minervian actors have done all this in collaboration with other countries and organizations, but their individual and collective contributions have often been considerable.

However, there have been important policy issues on which Canada, the EU, and Japan have diverged. For example, the EU has often supported the inclusion of more substances and/or stricter controls under the different international agreements and program than Canada and Japan. European countries and the European Commission have also been more ready to support developing countries in their demands for more extensive trade regulations and bans than Canada and Japan, including with respect to the Basel Ban Amendment. On some of these issues, Canada and Japan have been more closely aligned with the United States and other countries seeking to limit the regulatory scope of chemicals treaties. The EU has further more forcefully advocated for the high prominence of the precautionary principle in international declarations and agreements than Canada and Japan.

Of course, the actions of the EU, Canada, and Japan in global chemicals forums are shaped by a multitude of domestic and regional political and economic factors. Some of these are relatively similar across the three Minervian actors, while other factors are more distinctly unique for one or two of them. Looking more specifically at the EU, Canada, and Japan, which domestic and regional factors have driven their actions on international chemicals management?

The European Union

Already in the first Community Environment Action Programme in 1973, European leaders stated that active engagement in external multilateral forums is critical for achieving regional environmental interests (Weale et al. 2003). Thus, European policy makers have long viewed international policy and organizations such as the UNEP and the WHO necessary for meeting EU chemicals safety goals, including on issues relating to the long-range transport of emissions as well as international trade in chemicals and goods. The need for international cooperation was also recognized in the 2001 EU Sustainable Development Strategy. The WSSD 2020 goal adopted one year later is largely based on a similar objective in this strategy, which identifies better chemicals management as a critical sustainable development challenge for Europe and the world, and states the intention to, "by 2020, ensure that chemicals are only produced and used in ways that do not pose significant threats to human health and the environment" (European Commission 2002, p. 35).

As the EU has become a regional leader on chemicals management, much EU structural and intellectual leadership and support for international agreements has been motivated by a desire to upload its relatively strict standards and controls to the international level to reduce the long-range transport of emissions to Europe and other parts of the Northern hemisphere. The first EU directive on chemicals was adopted in 1967. This directive, however, primarily aimed to harmonize regulations across member states to facilitate the development of the common market, rather than regulating chemical hazards for environmental and health purposes (Lönngren 1992; McCormick 2001). Additional controls protecting handlers and users of hazardous substances were adopted in the 1970s. From the late 1980s and onwards, EU chemicals legislation has been expanded as part of a broader political initiative to improve European standards for environmental and human health protection.

The 2007 registration, evaluation, and authorization and restriction of chemicals (REACH) regulation is one of the largest pieces of EU environmental law ever to have been passed, and one that radically reformed its chemicals policy and regulation (Selin 2007). To fully operationalize REACH will take more than a decade, as it institutionalizes a more precautionary chemicals management system that puts increased responsibility on industry to generate data on chemicals. REACH aims to improve environmental and health protection through better risk assessment and earlier identification of hazardous chemicals based on their intrinsic properties, and through quicker and more comprehensive regulatory action. In addition, the EU passed directives on waste electrical and electronic equipment (WEEE) and the restriction of the use of certain hazardous substances in electrical and electronic equipment (RoHS) in 2002. The continuing implementation and updating of these three laws will shape much future European chemicals management.

The significant expansion of EU chemicals policy over the past three decades, including through REACH, has been driven by multiple factors. Much European chemicals policy has been pioneered by leading member states that were among the first in the world to develop comparatively precautionary chemicals policy domestically. As EU policy was developed, leader states acted to have their relatively stringent standards accepted at the EU level. For example, Germany exerted strong pressure to strengthen regional standards in the 1980s and 1990s through the expansion and harmonization of the EU internal market (Vogel 1997; Wurzel 2004). The accession of Austria, Finland, and Sweden in 1995 increased the number of green member states and helped move the Council of European Union toward a more pro-environment stance. Leader states also pioneered chemicals policy developments under regional seas agreements since the 1970s, including around the Baltic Sea and the Northeast Atlantic (Selin and VanDeveer 2004).

In addition, the gradual expansion of qualified majority voting on environmental issues in the Council of European Union facilitated the adoption of more progressive chemicals policy in the 1990s and 2000s, as leader states worked closely with EU organizations to raise standards. The European Commission, because of its significant role in setting political agendas, developing policy proposals, and supervising implementation, has been instrumental in strengthening EU's authority on chemicals policy. Expanded influence of the European Parliament and the creation of formal decision-making equality between the Council of European Union and the European Parliament on most environmental issues have also accelerated EU policy making on chemicals. In the European Parliament, the Environment Committee has been one of the most active committees and supported the development of many higher standards on chemicals management (Burns 2005; Selin 2007).

In addition to raising standards for environmental reasons, EU actions are also sometimes economically motivated (Vogel 1997; Selin and VanDeveer 2006; Kelemen 2010). Implementing REACH, WEEE, RoHS, and other laws, European firms have to invest in new technology as well as incur other kinds of compliance costs. This creates an economic interest for the EU to put a similar level of regulatory burden on foreign firms. At the same time, if non-EU firms want to sell their products in the EU they have to comply with EU standards. Firms operating in multiple markets often prefer to produce their products to as few different standards as possible. As a result, they often follow the highest regulatory standard, which is increasingly set in the EU. Furthermore, the EU promotes innovation by European firms, ideally enhancing their competitiveness and global market shares. In addition, the EU acts politically under international agreements to ensure that chemicals regulated in the EU are similarly controlled in other countries.

Canada

Like in the case of the EU, Canada has long viewed multilateralism critical to achieving national political and environmental goals. Many of Canada's early initiatives focused on North American transboundary pollution. For example, Canada and the United States signed the Great Lakes Water Quality Agreement in 1972 in response to early public and political concern about toxic chemicals and water pollution. In international chemicals politics, Canada demonstrated early structural and intellectual leadership in a host of forums, supporting efforts to push pollution issues higher on the global political agenda (Strong 2000). Canada was also an active participant in the early chemicals work under the OECD as well as in the work carried out by the UNEP, FAO, and the WHO. In addition, Canada promoted the goals outlined in the chemicals chapter of Agenda 21. Related to this, Canada was a critical force behind the development of the CLRTAP POPs Protocol and the Stockholm Convention, driven by a desire to address the long-range transport of emissions to northern latitudes.

The first Canadian Environmental Contamination Act was adopted in the mid 1970s, and was folded into the first Canadian Environmental Protection Act in 1988. Over the years, Canadian chemicals policy has been developed in collaboration between federal and provincial authorities. Sometimes, there has been a contentious relationship between national and local interests (Harrison 2002). Current Canadian chemicals law is outlined in the second Canadian Environmental Protection Act (1999). This act mandated a screening of commercial chemicals to identify those that exhibit potentially dangerous characteristics of toxicity, persistence, and bioaccumulation and to assess their environmental and human health impacts. Building on these assessments, Canada launched the Chemicals Management Plan in 2006 as a main tool for regulating hazardous chemicals. A second phase of the Chemicals Management Plan was initiated in 2011, running until 2016.

In Canada perhaps more than any other country, POPs became a major issue early on. The importance of the POPs issue in Canada was in large part related to scientific and political concerns about the Arctic environment and the risks posed by chemicals to indigenous peoples living there. By the late 1980s, a growing number of scientific studies demonstrated high levels of hazardous substances in remote areas of the Arctic environment and identified atmospheric transport as the main pathway (Dewailly and Furgal 2003). Around the same time, researchers began to worry about associated risks to humans, and in particular for Arctic indigenous communities (Kuhnlein et al. 2003). Indigenous peoples are exposed to POPs mainly through their dietary intake of traditional foods that are hunted and harvested locally. These traditional foods may contain high levels of POPs that are transferred to humans through consumption. These findings triggered a series of scientific responses that were often coordinated through Indian and Northern Affairs Canada (Shearer and Han 2003).

Indigenous peoples were often marginalized during much early Canadian environmental politics and policy making, but have since then become a great deal more active and effective in promoting their interests with provincial and federal authorities (Poelzer 2002). Indigenous peoples' rights became a hot political issue in Canada in the 1980s in addition to chemicals issues, and the inclusion of indigenous groups in scientific assessments, policy making, and political negotiations on chemicals increased the sensitivity and profile of the POPs issue in Canada (Downie 2003; Fenge 2003; Watt-Cloutier 2003). Indigenous groups were active participants in Canadian and circumpolar research programs that produced results that prompted Canada and other Arctic countries to push for international policy responses. Indigenous groups also aggressively lobbied the Canadian federal government to support strict POPs controls, and attended negotiation sessions for the CLRTAP POPs Protocol and the Stockholm Convention.

Canada, mainly through Indian and Northern Affairs Canada, also played an instrumental leadership role in bringing international attention to POPs. Canada, together with Sweden, pioneered many of the scientific assessments and early political efforts in the late 1980s and first half of the 1990s that resulted in negotiations of the CLRTAP POPs Protocol and its adoption in 1998 (Thrift et al. 2009; Selin 2010). This regional work on POPs also served as a critical stepping stone for the global actions launched by UNEP in 1995. For example, the identification of "the dirty dozen" chemicals for global assessments and controls was heavily influenced by the CLRTAP POPs assessments at the time

(Selin and Eckley 2003). Canada, under the watchful eyes of Arctic indigenous peoples groups, was highly active throughout the global negotiations and, as mentioned earlier, became the first country to ratify the Stockholm Convention. Canada has also remained an active participant in the continuous implementation of the main chemicals agreements.

Compared to the EU, Canada has had less of a market-based role in shaping international standards with respect to the economic interests of domestic firms and the kinds of chemicals that can be used in products. The EU, through its implementation of REACH, WEEE, RoHS, and other relatively recent laws on products and wastes, in many ways remains the global forerunner with respect to these policy issues. However, as Canada moves forward with assessments and regulations under the second phase of the Chemicals Management Plan, Canadian economic interests may change in the future. It is also clear that Canadian domestic efforts are influenced by what the EU seeks to do under REACH. However, it is too early to say exactly how much policy convergence there will be between Canada and the EU in the future, and how that will shape Canadian pursuit of multilateralism, its leadership efforts, and its political and economic interests with respect to international chemicals management.

Japan

Compared to the EU and Canada, Japan did not demonstrate much leadership in early international chemicals politics and management. In the 1970s and the 1980s, Japan regularly attended major conferences, including the United Nations Conference on the Human Environment, and participated in chemicals meetings organized by UNEP, OECD, and other international organizations. Yet Japan rarely initiated new international policy. Japan, however, has taken on a much larger role in international environmental politics since the late 1980s (Imura 2005). Japan became a major financial supporter of UNEP and other international organizations as well as a leader in foreign aid and loans in the environmental field to developing countries in the post-Cold War period. These developments reflected the growing importance of Japan's economy in the world, a heightened political and public sensitivity to environmental issues, and an increasing willingness to assist developing countries (Peng 1993).

Japanese domestic chemicals legislation developed around the same time as in Europe and North America. Early Japanese law and public views were influenced by major domestic contamination scandals

(Kuratsune et al. 1996; Zuber and Newman 2012). In Minamata in the 1950s and Niigata in the 1960s, methylmercury was emitted by factories into waters, contaminating fish that were later consumed by people living close by. Symptoms in affected people included neurological damage and disturbances of sensation and movement, in several cases ultimately resulting in fatalities. In 1968, many people were poisoned after consuming rice cooking oil contaminated with high levels of PCBs (polychlorinated biphenyls). Health effects included skin disfigurations and birth defects in babies given birth to by mothers exposed to the PCBs. The Chemical Substances Control Law enacted in 1973 was part of a national effort to tackle a series of pollution problems stemming from rapid industrial expansion and causing serious environmental and human health problems (Imura 2005; Hiraishi 1989; Darby 1997).

The Chemical Substances Control Law was amended in 1986, 2004, and 2009. In addition, Japan adopted the Law Concerning Reporting, etc. of Releases to the Environment of Specific Chemical Substances and Promoting Improvements in Their Management in 1999, which established a pollutants release and transfer register as a means for gathering and tracking data on sources and emissions of hazardous chemicals. Japan also adopted a specific Law Concerning Special Measures against Dioxins in 1999. The development of early modern Japanese chemicals policy was thus one piece of a broader political initiative during the 1970s and 1980s to address a looming environmental crisis and develop more comprehensive environmental legislation. As a part of this initative, expanding chemicals policy and regulations were characterized by a dominating technocratic approach to pollution control and were established with little involvement by domestic civil society.

Japan has made considerable progress in addressing domestic chemicals pollution and contamination problems since the 1960s (OECD 2002). Yet Japan largely continues to be less pro-active on national and international chemicals management than Canada and the EU, as this issue seems not to be given the same level of public and political priority in Japan as by the EU and in Canada. On the other hand, Japan can be important in global environmental politics and has often been a reliable partner for the EU and Canada as they have pushed for expansions on international chemicals policy and the development of the more recent agreements and programs. Also, Japan's ratification pattern of the three major treaties is closer to those of Canada and the EU than the United States. One area of chemical management where Japan has been fairly active is on the issue of regulating the use of endocrine disrupters (a category of chemicals that may act like hormone estrogen and cause reproductive and behavioral abnormalities) (Colborn et al. 1996; Krimsky 2000).

Because Japan has not been a frontrunner in domestic policy making on chemicals, Japanese governments and firms have had few economic interests in exporting national standards on substances and products or uploading them into international agreements. However, through recent legislative and regulatory developments associated with the 2009 amendment of the Chemical Substances Control Law, Japan is taking steps to develop a more pro-active and ambitious chemicals policy. Several of the most recent policy changes focusing on assessments and regulations have been shaped by REACH and the other EU laws on hazardous substances. In this respect, policy changes in Japan and other major producers of electrical and electronic products, including China and South Korea, are an indication of EU's standard-setting influence; measures are taken both on environmental grounds and to make domestic firms compliant with EU standards to ensure continued market access in Europe and elsewhere.

Minervian politics: past, present, and future

Global and regional cooperation and policy making over the past four decades has resulted in the creation of a multitude of agreements and programs on chemicals management. Many industrialized and developing countries have been part of these efforts to improve chemicals safety, but Canada and the EU have often demonstrated critical intellectual and structural leadership. Since the 1980s, they have consistently championed new policy ideas, supported international scientific assessments, and worked to build political coalitions to create new institutions. However, Canada and the EU have also disagreed over some policy issues, such as controls of specific chemicals and the need for particular policy instruments including the Ban Amendment to the Basel Convention. Japan has typically been less active on the international stage, but generally supportive of many policy ideas pioneered by Canada, the EU, and others.

Much structural and intellectual leadership by Canada and the EU on international chemicals management from the 1980s and onwards was assumed in response to domestic concerns about adverse human health and environmental effects from the worldwide use of chemicals. Chemicals issues are politically and publicly important in Canada and the EU, as they have passed comparatively stringent systems for assessing and controlling hazardous chemicals. Both Canada and the EU have actively pushed to develop more wide-ranging international responses to reduce atmospheric transport of emissions to the Arctic. In Canada, the chemicals issue became part of a broader set of issues relating to the rights of Arctic indigenous peoples, therefore intensifying attention to hazardous chemicals. The EU is a regional policy leader on banning hazardous substances in goods and is increasingly trying to raise global product and waste standards on hazardous substances.

Yet the political leadership mode of policy change cannot explain all international actions by Canada and the EU. At times, the behavior of the EU in particular has been more consistent with the Minervian framework's first mode of institution building. In such cases, economic interests motivate actors' initiatives in international forums as they advocate for stricter policies and regulatory standards. In these instances, uploading of national and regional regulations and requirements is, in part, intended to help domestic firms to compete in international markets by imposing similarly strict standards on competitors in other countries and regions that operated under less stringent obligations. Since the early 2000s, the EU has used its market-based influence to become one of the most important setter of international standards on chemicals and the use of hazardous substances in electrical and electronic products, shaping production decisions far beyond Europe.

Attempting to look into the future, the EU may be the one Minervian actor that is most likely to remain constant in its leadership ambitions in international chemicals politics, based on its recent internal policy developments. Consistent with its actions in other environmental issue-areas including climate change, the EU continues to be highly involved under the major chemicals agreements. For example, the EU is one of the most active parties when it comes to proposing controls on new chemicals under the Stockholm and Rotterdam Conventions and the CLRTAP POPs Protocol. Canada remains fairly consistent in its policy position even if it often is less aggressive than the EU – the kind of noteworthy Canadian policy reversal recently seen under the climate change regime, including withdrawing from the Kyoto Protocol, has not taken place in international chemicals politics. Furthermore, Canada is moving forward domestically with assessments and regulations under the Chemicals Management Plan.

There are recent signs that Japan is increasing some of its political activities on hazardous substances. Japan has gradually reduced its emphasis on official development assistance and increased other forms of international cooperation. Japan, like Canada, is hesitant to take on mandatory and stringent greenhouse gas reduction targets for 2020 and beyond. However, Japan, together with the EU, has demonstrated both structural and intellectual leadership in the negotiations on a global mercury convention. These started in 2010 and the convention is scheduled for adoption at a meeting in Japan in 2013. It will likely be named the Minamata Convention, as mercury and Minamata remain important in Japan. As Japan also moves forward reforming domestic chemicals laws and management practices, this may indicate that Japan is ready and willing to take on a larger international political role. In any case, national and regional political and economic factors will continue to shape international behavior and aspirations of Canada, the EU, and Japan.

12
Enough Rope: The Role of Minervian Actors in Establishing the International Criminal Court

Joanne Lee[1]

Introduction

The idea of an International Criminal Court has been on the international agenda for at least 100 years. In the mid-1990s, this idea suddenly gained momentum and became a reality much quicker than anyone had predicted, with the Court officially coming into existence on July 1, 2002.

In this chapter I focus on the crucial role of "Minervian" actors in the formation and strategizing of a large, diverse, transnational advocacy network that included the "Like-Minded Group" (LMG) of states supporting the ICC's establishment – led by Canada – plus the NGO "Coalition for the ICC" (CICC), and United Nations officials. With the Cold War behind them, domestic political leaders from Minervian states projected a liberal, legalistic interest in "international justice" onto the UN's agenda in the early 1990s, which resonated with many non-Western states that had been arguing in favor of such a focus for many years. As numerous commentators have now highlighted, within a few short years the combined efforts of these actors defied all predictions and led to the adoption of the treaty establishing the ICC in July 1998, by an unexpected majority of states participating in a diplomatic conference in Rome (Bassiouni 1998; Broomhall 2003; Glasius 2006; Leonard 2005; Schiff 2008; Wippman 2004).

In order to understand the creation of this institution more fully – especially the role of Minervian actors and global civil society in the "norm cascade" that followed the Rome Conference – this chapter will also look beyond the dynamics of the negotiations in Rome, which have already been the focus of previous analyses. Arguably, it could have taken many more years for the treaty (the "Rome Statute") to attract the necessary state commitment to bring a fully functioning Court into being. Yet only four years after its initial adoption in July 1998, more than 60 governments had ratified the treaty, thereby bringing the Rome Statute into force and allowing the ICC to begin its operations in July 2002.[2]

While most states supported the idea of an international criminal court, certain features of the Rome Statute were controversial. Some states were concerned that the ICC was too independent, by having a Prosecutor who could initiate investigations. Other states were concerned that the ICC was not independent enough, given that the Security Council could close down an investigation at any time. The transnational advocacy network that had successfully negotiated the adoption of these provisions had to conduct a much broader, global campaign in order to convince political leaders from a wide variety of states to accept the jurisdiction of the ICC over their territory, and over themselves and their nationals, and to commit credible resources to allow the ICC to operate as a legitimate criminal court. Many of the same domestic political leaders who initially projected their domestic concerns onto the international agenda in order to stimulate negotiations about an ICC then worked in concert with domestic and global civil society actors and media outlets to bring the new norm to the "tipping point" of July 2002 (Finnemore and Sikkink 1998, p. 901). The process was driven by several Minervian actors and supported by a number of non-Minervian actors from the Global South, providing the opportunity to test the resilience and universality of the new norm.

Of all the Minervian actors this socialization stage proved the greatest test for Japan, which only managed to overcome significant domestic political obstacles five years later, in July 2007, when it acceded to the Rome Statute. Therefore, the ICC presents a partial exception to the "Minervian process," in terms of all three Minervian actors actually *driving* the creation of the institution in concert.[3] However, Japanese representatives did help to place the ICC on the agenda of the General Assembly in the early 1990s, participated positively at the Rome Conference, subsequently made numerous supportive statements about the ICC during key stages of the Court's operationalization phase, and clearly indicated when the treaty entered into force in July 2002, that the Japanese government would "accelerate" the domestic processes required for joining the treaty (Kawaguchi 2002). The ICC and its Assembly of States Parties now benefit enormously from Japan's significant financial contribution and political commitment from 2007 onward.[4] Japan has also committed to taking a leadership role in promoting the institution in the Asian region – where support has been minimal to date. In its own way, then, Japan has quietly become a norm entrepreneur, and an important one because of its special relationship with the United States, which had steadfastly opposed the ICC under the Bush administration.

This refinement of the respective interests of Japan and the US over time further supports this book's hypothesis that *domestic political leadership* is emerging as a crucial variable in the establishment of new global institutions. In fact, in this chapter I argue that domestic political leadership was an *essential* factor in the successful establishment of the ICC, and has generally been overlooked in the literature on the ICC. Unlike other cases of institution building, the successful establishment of the ICC required a *personal* commitment from a number of politicians, predominantly from Minervian states, who were willing to make themselves individually accountable to their domestic constituents and to the international community for their future observance of the laws of war. International criminal law is one of the few issue-areas in international law where individuals – not just states – can be held *directly* responsible for violations, due to the precedent set by the Nuremberg Tribunal. As the experiences of Presidents Slobodan Milosevic (Serbia) and Charles Taylor (Liberia) demonstrate, even the most senior government officials may be arrested lawfully and tried by an international tribunal.

At the same time, I argue that one of the *main* driving forces in the establishment of the ICC was the projection of the domestic agendas of several Minervian states onto the global agenda, especially in the initial stages of negotiations in the 1990s. During that time, domestic political leaders in many Western states had become increasingly frustrated by their national courts' unsuccessful attempts to take responsibility for prosecuting international crimes at the domestic level – in the absence of an effective international mechanism – and by the growing list of atrocities being committed across the globe, without any institution on the horizon to deter them (Axworthy 2003, pp. 206–7). The final straw was the eruption of ethnic conflict in the Former Yugoslavia in 1991, right on the doorstep of Western Europe. Key individuals representing Minervian actors recognized that cooperation was necessary in order to address these types of situations, and took advantage of the post-Cold War landscape by attempting to shift responsibility for the problem back to the international level.

Causal modes used by Minervian actors

The intention of the Minervian actors in establishing the ICC was clearly not anti-hegemonic; therefore disqualifying *competitive global institution building* as the salient causal mode of explantion.[5] However, some US officials have interpreted the Rome Statute as an attempt to constrain their government's power, because the ICC does not require the consent of the Security Council to conduct a prosecution (Cerone 2007; Sewall and Kaysen 2000; Thakur 2006). The US delegation in Rome was particularly concerned with the tactics of Canadian Ambassador Philippe Kirsch and other Minervian actors, who had ensured the adoption of a compromise final text in Rome that did not accord with several key US preferences (Benedetti and Washburn 1999). Canadian and UK officials had, in fact, bent over backwards trying to encourage the US to join the general consensus in support of the Court at the Rome Conference (Axworthy 2003, pp. 203–4). But the US delegation was not prepared to compromise in any way that could potentially expose US nationals to prosecution, however unlikely that outcome would be. The US therefore found itself among a small minority of seven states voting against the Rome Statute in July 1998,[6] and Minervian actors were left carrying the enormous cost of a permanent Court without US assistance.[7]

The two relevant causal modes in the establishment of the ICC are the *normative mode* and the *domestic political leadership mode*. As Gary Bass has highlighted, public opinion has often motivated world leaders to create international criminal institutions since the First World War (Bass 2000). Undoubtedly, one of the major forces driving the ICC's establishment was a large, well-organized, international coalition of civil society actors – the NGO "Coalition for the ICC".[8] The ICC would not have come into being without the CICC (Benedetti and Washburn 1999; Glasius 2006; Struett 2008; Wippman 2004). Their powerful influence was especially remarkable given that many issues involved high security concerns, such as the Court's relationship with the Security Council (Barrow 2003).

However, the interests of states did not require as much shaping by civil society actors in the case of the ICC, or at least not to the same extent when compared to other cases that feature high levels of involvement or influence by civil society. Most states already accepted prohibitions against genocide, crimes against humanity, and war crimes, as well as the idea of an international criminal court. (Glasius 2006). CICC members acknowledge that they had little influence on capitals until after the treaty was adopted (Benedetti and Washburn 1999, p. 21). Given the different dynamics between state actors and civil society at various stages in institution building, and the enormous number of actors involved, it would be next to impossible to establish empirically whether the ICC institutionalization process was predominantly "bottom–up" or "top–down." In fact, the institution-building phase of the ICC was quite remarkable for the way that the lines between government and non-government actors were often blurred, with many NGO activists also taking roles within, or on behalf of, governments at certain times,[9] and government officials and intergovernmental organizations sometimes acting as NGOs.[10]

Much of the scholarship about the ICC negotiations has focused on the roles of individual leaders in the Rome negotiations (Bassiouni 1998; Benedetti and Washburn 1999; Leonard 2005). The leaders within the CICC and key UN officials, not just government actors, are frequently recognized as major contributors to the "ideational causation" that led to the "overwhelming success of the Rome Conference" (Leonard 2005, pp. 125–26; see also Deitelhoff 2009; Struett 2008).

Far less attention has been paid to the power of *domestic political leaders*; especially neglected is their role in advancing the norm of international criminal justice *after* the Rome Statute was adopted, when the domestic socialization process became a critical precondition for the successful establishment of the institution. The ICC provoked considerable debate within most states, either because it was perceived as too powerful, or not powerful enough, depending on one's expectations. Thus individual political leaders who were committed to the ICC were crucial players in socializing their peers, especially military leaders. In some instances they also had to sell the new institution to a skeptical, self-interested domestic civil society, as happened in Canada, where a number of other domestic agendas came to the fore (Franceschet and Knight 2001, p. 66). As Risse et al. have highlighted, government officials working for Western states are critical players within most "transnational advocacy networks" promoting human rights norms (1999, p. 17). Many commentators since have tended to ignore the possibility that states and state actors, not just NGOs and non-state actors, can also be human rights norm entrepreneurs (Franceschet and Knight 2001).

All things considered, I argue that because of the high stakes involved in establishing a permanent ICC – including *personal* transaction costs for individual leaders – this institution had to be shaped primarily by elite rather than grassroots actors, in order for it to come into being and to have enduring legitimacy. As Zoe Pearson observes, having interviewed a large number of civil society actors involved in the various stages of the ICC's creation:

> NGOs that I interviewed were on the whole realistic and cautious about the extent of NGO influence on the ICC negotiations, and anxious not to overestimate or overstate this. Most explicitly recognized the importance of these negotiations being primarily a state-based process for the ultimate success of the Court. (2006, p. 269)

As I discuss in the section 'The global ratification campaign', the evolving position of Japan also demonstrates some of the limits to global civil society influence in such a high politics area.

This chapter thus focuses on the political leadership of Canada and various EU members,[11] with a particular emphasis on the role of individual political actors, who were playing to both an international and a domestic audience. I first give a brief overview of the main steps in the establishment of the ICC, and then elaborate the key stages in the process of the institution's formation, demonstrating how political leadership in key countries can play a crucial stimulating role in generating an effective, multi-actor, transnational coalition, even when the institution in question challenges significant realist interests.

The story of the ICC

In the first half of the twentieth century, there were attempts to establish international criminal tribunals after both World Wars. The victors were mostly responsible for these efforts, especially states whose citizens were most directly affected by German occupation or u-boat warfare. The UK and the US played key roles after both wars, while Italy and Japan were prominent in the wake of the First World War, and the USSR after the Second World War.

The UN adopted a permanent international criminal court as one of its early agenda items. However, the Cold War stifled any meaningful progress toward the creation of such an institution. In the early 1990s a revitalized (and expanded) UN General Assembly revisited the idea of an ICC and the Security Council's successful establishment of the International Criminal Tribunal for the Former Yugoslavia (ICTY) in 1993 provided additional momentum. Most of the General Assembly members appeared to embrace the idea of a permanent tribunal along similar lines.

After several years of preparatory negotiations, a diplomatic conference of plenipotentiaries was held in Rome in 1998, where the treaty for the ICC was adopted by a majority of participants. The ICC is designed to enforce the laws of war and thus regulate the use of force to some extent. The treaty represents a delicate compromise between the interests of the permanent Security Council members in maintaining international peace and security, and the international community's interest in international justice through transparency and accountability. The Court remains external to the UN system, although it has a relationship with the Security Council, and the UN has entered an agreement to cooperate in certain respects with the Court.

The final vote on the treaty was not recorded, but all the Minervian actors appear to have voted in favor of the Rome Statute. Amongst those states voting against the Statute were the US, China, and Israel. Within four years, a successful advocacy campaign resulted in the ratification of the Statute by more than 60 states, thereby bringing the treaty into force, and the institution into being. At the time of writing this chapter, more than one hundred states are parties, and several others have signaled their intention to become a party before too long.

The ICC is a permanent judicial institution that has jurisdiction over individuals who commit genocide, crimes against humanity, and war crimes. For the first time ever, at the insistence of a permanent institution that is not completely controlled by the Security Council, government and non-government officials from any nation can potentially be held *individually* accountable for their role in ordering or implementing policies deemed criminal by the international community. Initially, the Court's primary focus was on the leaders of non-state armed groups who threaten civilian populations, predominantly in Africa. In response to Security Council referrals, the Court has now issued arrest warrants for several senior government officials, including President Al Bashir of Sudan and Saif Al-Ghadafi of Libya.

Narrative

Political leadership in finalizing the blueprint for an international criminal court

The successful establishment of the ICC is due, in part, to the historically entrenched norms that are the basis of the institution. As many commentators have noted, criminal trials and the laws of war were both well-established norms prior to the twentieth century (Broomhall 2003; Cryer 2005; Schiff 2008). European and other Western states were instrumental in codifying humanitarian law and human rights norms in the aftermath of the First World War. But the Cold War made both sides nervous about handing over authority to an international institution that may adjudicate their conduct during hostilities. In particular, neither side could agree on what constituted a "crime against peace," even though this was the main charge laid against those on trial in Nuremberg and Tokyo.

The key issues and the various negotiations leading to the Rome Conference in 1998 have been well-documented elsewhere (Schiff 2008; Struett 2008). Briefly, the ILC spent two years elaborating the Code of Crimes and another couple of years drafting a treaty for a permanent international criminal court.

In the meantime, Iraq invaded Kuwait and war broke out in the Federal Republic of Yugoslavia. These events marked a major turning point in post-Cold War relations, with the Security Council united on issues of international peace and security for the first time in a long while. In the wake of the first Gulf War, Japan decided to contribute military personnel to UN peacekeeping operations and other humanitarian missions for the first time, changing its post-Second World War policy of avoiding any type of military engagement (Mayama 2004).

In 1993 the Security Council took an unprecedented step in establishing an international criminal tribunal – the ICTY – to prosecute the worst offenders in the Balkans conflict, in an effort to deter further atrocities. Despite having significant problems in its early years, the creation of this tribunal inspired many of those who were working toward a permanent model of international justice.

The largest supporters of an international criminal court became known as the "Like-Minded Group". In 1995, a group of around 12 states – including some Minervian actors such as Canada and several EU members – first began to describe themselves as "like-minded" during the Ad Hoc Working Group negotiations.[12] These states shared an interest in setting a clear deadline for preparatory negotiations and establishing a UN-backed Preparatory Committee. In other words, the LMG members were serious about making sure that the ICC did not languish on the UN agenda for another 50 years, even if the establishment of the actual institution was still seen as a distant goal. Given Canada's reputation as the "honest broker," Canada was made the coordinator of the LMG, and establishing the court became its key foreign policy objective (Axworthy 2003, pp. 5–6). As Franceschet and Knight point out, such a policy was consistent with Canada's continuing identity as a "good international citizen," as well as with Canada's more "pragmatic idealism" under the Chrétien administration. A "permanent ICC would contribute to a more stable and just world order, the pursuit of which has been one of the main planks of Canada's 'internationalist' foreign policy." (Franceschet and Knight 2001, p. 66).

Both like-minded and non-like-minded governments were content to support the idea in principle at this point, since it was unlikely to affect their interests any time soon. At this stage of the negotiations, domestic political leadership was less of a driving force than entrepreneurial and intellectual leadership (Young 1991) by the "like-minded" individuals involved in the negotiations, mostly legal experts who had a general mandate from their governments to work toward a new institution of some kind.

The recently formed European Union also had a general commitment to multilateral institutions such as the ICC, although the two permanent members of the Security Council were initially wary of any institution that could potentially undermine the authority of the Security Council.

Another key group of actors in the lead-up to the Rome Conference, which has been the subject of extensive literature, was the NGO "Coalition for an ICC". A small group of international NGOs had been observing the ILC's work with keen interest, and in February 1995 they decided to join forces in order to jointly "advocate the establishment of an effective and just" ICC (Pace and Thieroff 1999, p. 391). The LMG and the CICC worked closely together through to the end of the Rome Conference, promoting a set of core negotiating principles to ensure the ICC would be as independent and effective as possible (Deitelhoff 2009; Struett 2008).

Membership of both the LMG and the CICC increased dramatically between 1995 and 1998, with most EU member states joining the LMG. By late 1996, most states were keen to see an international criminal court come into existence, even though they could not agree on the details.

This is when domestic political leadership emerged as a key ingredient, with the General Assembly (which decided to schedule a diplomatic conference in 1998) providing an international forum at which states and especially state leaders could project their identities and interests.

One of the most important domestic political leaders representing a Minervian actor was British Prime Minister Tony Blair, who assumed office in May 1997 with the promise of a new "ethical foreign policy" for

Britain. By the end of the year, the UK had joined the LMG; it had realized that overbearing Security Council scrutiny of the ICC would prove unpopular with too many states, thereby jeopardizing any consensus on establishing the ICC and possibly scuttling the idea altogether. The UK thus became a key conduit between the P5 and the court's supporters for the remaining negotiations.

With this shift in position by the UK, all of the Minervian actors except Japan and France were united in their common mission to finalize the ICC treaty at the diplomatic conference the following year, with the greatest possible support, even if it meant alienating the rest of the P5 members, who at this point were still adamant that the Security Council must authorize any ICC prosecutions.

The Government of Japan "fully supported the establishment of an international criminal court," but still had reservations about several LMG positions and was uncomfortable about the idea of creating an institution without the "universal participation" of all states, especially the other members of the Security Council.[13] However, if the Security Council was allowed to control the ICC, then the majority of states would never fully support it, and the treaty may not have been ratified by enough states to enter into force.

In early March 1998, Bill Pace – the Coordinator of the CICC – had approached another key domestic political leader, Canadian Foreign Minister Lloyd Axworthy (Axworthy 2003, p. 202). Axworthy was a highly visible supporter of the ICC, given that such an institution fell squarely within his "human security" agenda by providing justice for victims and deterrence against future atrocities (Franceschet and Knight 2001, p. 67). Pace and Axworthy – who had worked together on the Ottawa landmines process – were particularly concerned that the whole conference could fail to finalize a treaty unless it was extremely well planned and executed (Pace and Thieroff 1999, p. 201). They agreed that it was necessary to socialize as many domestic political leaders as possible beforehand, in order to impress upon them the urgency of finding consensus in Rome and to ensure that they sent sufficiently senior and proficient delegates to the conference. Norm internalization by as many actors as possible would also prevent negotiations from becoming "bog[ged] down over technicalities" as they progressed (Axworthy 2003, p. 202). To this end, Canadian and EU government officials and NGOs, working in tandem, promoted the ICC agenda at regional meetings in Africa, the Caribbean, and Latin America. Thus, a strong, transnational advocacy network with a clear strategy for the negotiations was already in place by the time the Rome Conference started.

Of the Minervian actors, Canada and most of the EU were active members of this network, while Japan and France remained independent players. The transnational advocacy network was the main driver of the negotiations at the Rome Conference, although the (Canadian) Chair of the Committee of the Whole, Philippe Kirsch, devised and carried out the most important strategic step of the negotiations, arguably compromising certain LMG positions in order to ensure that a final text would be achieved. He put together a "package deal" proposal, on the basis of what appeared to be the most widely accepted positions on key issues, but including some important concessions for powerful states such as France and the US. Much to the surprise of the US, and to the relief of the LMG, the Statute was adopted with a vote of 120 in favor, 7 against, and 21 abstentions.

Strategic analysis of the Rome Conference

By the start of the Rome Conference in June 1998, the LMG membership officially comprised 60 states. However, this number did not represent the large number of states that agreed on almost every position taken by the LMG, even if they had other affiliations.

Domestic political leaders had a key role to play as the negotiations progressed. Several Foreign Ministers from Minervian states gave speeches at the early plenary sessions in Rome, thereby signaling how important the issue of the ICC was to their government. Other LMG politicians also lobbied their counterparts in other capitals. Lloyd Axworthy was even called upon by Philippe Kirsch to "sell" Kirsch's final package to governments and to NGOs in the final few days of the Conference. For example, Axworthy recounts his conversation with Madeleine Albright just a few hours before the final vote was taken, in which he explained the reasoning behind the "package" approach:

> I stressed that it met many of the American concerns and that I detected a strong movement of support. She heard me out, but said her own reports were that the package would fail. Having already counted the votes,[14] I said that the U.S. could find itself in a very small bloc of opposition, which would be most regrettable considering how she and the president had played such an important role in giving momentum to the idea. (2003, p. 204)

In terms of the "Minervian process," Japan was never part of the LMG, although it supported the general principles behind the institution. Its representatives gradually entered into the spirit of cooperation that dominated in Rome, albeit with a tendency toward compromise rather than strict principle (Owada 2004, p. 108).

Other coalitions and their demise

The large Non-Aligned Movement (NAM) of states had actively supported developments in international criminal law for many years. When the Western states began to take the lead on the issue of an ICC in the 1990s, many NAM members were concerned that the Court would not serve their interests and initially proved obstructionist. The Security Council's treatment of its two tribunals gave them no cause for comfort, and cemented their perception that the ICC would become yet another tool for the Great Powers to control the rest of the world. But most NAM members eventually defected to the LMG, seeing a window of opportunity.

The permanent members of the Security Council were not completely united, although their major common interests are reflected to a large degree in the Rome Statute. The UK defected to the LMG prior to the Rome Conference, and during the subsequent negotiations it played a key role in the effort to find acceptable compromises for the P5 members on various issues. China, France, Russia, and the US used their material power to gain many concessions, but ultimately these appeals to power "failed to impact the final outcome of the negotiations" (Struett 2005, p. 200). All P5 members initially agreed that the Security Council should have ultimate control over the Court – arguably they achieved this with the inclusion of article 16, even though this was not sufficient for the US – and none of them wanted nuclear weapons listed as a prohibited weapon, which they also achieved (Glasius 2006, p. 26). Only China was opposed to the whole idea of an ICC from the outset.[15]

France also took an idiosyncratic approach on a range of issues, and found an ally in Japan. France's main objection was allowing the Court to have jurisdiction over all war crimes, arguing that the proposed provisions of the Rome Statute went beyond certain widely accepted international standards. During the Rome Conference, the Japanese Ambassador, Hisashi Owada, stepped in and attempted to negotiate an acceptable compromise between the LMG's insistence that the Court *must* have jurisdiction over all war crimes, and France's view (shared by China and the Arab states) that certain war crimes did not reflect customary international law and therefore should *not* be included within the jurisdiction of the ICC. Ambassador Owada proposed an acceptable compromise that would allow any State Party to opt-out of the ICC's jurisdiction over war crimes, but only for a period of seven years (Glasius 2006, p. 65).

Political leadership in moving from the blueprint to a functioning institution

The global ratification campaign

Once the Rome Statute was finalized and adopted, the next step was to find at least 60 governments willing to expose their national jurisdiction to the reach of the Court. Even though so many states had voted in favor of the Rome Statute at the final plenary meeting of the Conference, most delegates went home to face a mixed reception from politicians, senior military officials, and bureaucrats. It was one thing to support the idea of an ICC, and quite a different matter for a state to cede sovereignty to a permanent institution (Simmons and Danner 2010). Thus an even broader range of actors across the globe had to be socialized into accepting the new norms established by the Rome Statute before they could be institutionalized.

One of the LMG principles was to promote "universal participation" in the new regime, and the CICC was of a similar mind. Therefore, once again, the transnational advocacy network established in the build-up to Rome was activated, now on an ever-expanding scale. The combined forces of this transnational advocacy network motivated a large number of politicians from a diverse group of states to make their own personal commitment to uphold the principles of the ICC.

LMG members predominantly turned their attention to their own governments first. Most of the politicians who had become norm entrepreneurs for the ICC were initially Ministers for Foreign Affairs. As their portfolio does not usually extend to ordering or directly supervising military operations, they also had to convince their own defense chiefs, Presidents, Prime Ministers, and Justice Ministers to make themselves *personally* accountable for all future military action on behalf of the State. The adoption of the ICC treaty in Rome was therefore far less of a challenge than the global ratification campaign, which focused attention back onto the domestic stage, as each government official debated whether to allow an international institution to adjudicate his or her actions in such a sensitive issue-area.

Canada's Foreign Minister, Lloyd Axworthy, realized at a very early stage that LMG members would need to allocate substantial resources to assist smaller states in this process (Axworthy 2003, pp. 205–6). He made promotion of the ICC a "diplomatic priority" for the entire Canadian Government, and allocated substantial resources from his ministry to fund NGOs involved in ICC advocacy and legal analysis in other parts of the world (Axworthy 2003, pp. 202, 205–6). Also under Axworthy's guidance, Canada's *Crimes Against Humanity and War Crimes Act 2000* was the first comprehensive piece of ICC implementing legislation to be adopted, providing a model for the rest of the common law world. The EU took longer to prioritize ICC promotion, although several states followed Canada's lead in promoting the Statute more broadly from the outset, notably Sweden and Germany. The first EU Common Position on the ICC did not emerge until 2001, followed by a more expanded version in 2003, and an "Action Plan to follow-up on the Common Position" in 2004. The first Common Position provided that all members of the EU and all those wishing to accede to the EU must become Parties to the Rome Statute. The second Common Position and Action Plan addressed the need for EU members to promote the universality and integrity of the Rome Statute. These positions were reached only after intense lobbying by the CICC's European arm.[16]

This domestic internalization phase proved particularly difficult for Japan. The Foreign Ministry was consistently supportive of the ICC, while the Justice Ministry sometimes spoke out publicly against the ICC. It was only when domestic debates about Japan's military role for the twenty-first century had reached a certain point of consensus, and Prime Minister Abe took office in 2006, that Foreign Minister Taro Aso – appointed by Koizumi in October 2005 – was given enough support to drive the domestic ratification processes forward at a much faster pace. In fact, Prime Minister Abe formally announced Japan's intention to ratify the Rome Statute within his first month in office, as a new plank in his "value-oriented diplomacy."[17]

The Justice Ministry had long argued that it needed to implement the Geneva Conventions and Additional Protocols – in the form of Japan's "emergency laws" – before Japan could ratify the ICC Statute, in order to ensure that Japanese courts could prosecute war crimes (Mayama 2004). However, none of the Prime Ministers or the Justice Ministers since 1998 had been willing to allocate the same kind of resources for this purpose as Canada and some of the EU governments had done.

The 60th ratification of the Rome Statute was achieved in April 2002, during a special ceremony to mark the occasion. In the same month, the Netherlands Institute for War Documentation released its report condemning the Dutch government for its role in the 1995 tragedy at Srebrenica. Prime Minister Wim Kok and his entire cabinet immediately resigned in order to show their personal remorse and sense of responsibility for the failure of Dutch peacekeepers to intervene and save thousands of civilian lives. By 2002, it had become clear that the new ICC had provided "enough rope" for all political leaders who were in a position to prevent such atrocities, to "hang" themselves if the ICC did not. A few months later, the Rome Statute entered into force.

The global anti-ratification campaign by the US

In 2001, the newly elected Bush administration launched a systematic assault on the ICC, using intense diplomatic pressure and denial of foreign aid to dissuade smaller states from ratifying the Rome Statute. The US also requested that every government in the world sign an agreement granting immunity from ICC prosecution to US personnel. The latter campaign was quite successful, but for the most part it was all "too little too late." Even in December 2000, when President Clinton signed the Rome Statute, it was clear that the treaty was likely to enter into force much sooner than anyone had anticipated.

In terms of the "Minervian process," these tactics provided an extreme test for the resilience of the ICC norm, and for the resolve of its advocates. The EU and Canada both conducted international campaigns to limit the scope of any agreements granting ICC immunity to US forces. Twenty one states decided they would rather lose US military aid than compromise the integrity of the Rome Statute by signing such agreements (close US allies such as Japan, Canada, and EU member states were not subject to such penalties).[18] Still, the US State Department website claimed that 100 states eventually signed these immunity agreements; whether or not they ever entered into force is unknown (Kelley 2007).

With the election of President Obama in 2007, and his more conciliatory and pragmatic policy toward the ICC ("constructive engagement"), the Court and its supporters no longer have to devote resources to battling such a powerful detractor. In fact, the US has demonstrated increased symbolic support for the Court since 2005, when the Security Council agreed to refer Sudan to the ICC for investigation. In June 2012 the US also agreed to an ICC reference in a Human Rights Council resolution for the first time.[19]

Conclusion

Clearly the establishment of the ICC was a complex, dynamic process, involving many more actors and interests than outlined here. However, this chapter has demonstrated that *domestic political leadership* was a crucial variable in the process, which is generally overlooked in the literature to date. Political leaders projected onto the international arena their concerns about a lack of credible institutional mechanisms to deal with a growing tide of ethnic violence and other disruptive activities by non-state actors. This leadership was also present during all of the international agenda setting and negotiations, when delegations representing most of the Minervian actors took instructions from their Foreign Ministers to proceed with the establishment of a unique judicial institution. Undoubtedly, global civil society played an enormous role in building the institution and driving the normative process. But ultimately they required the additional material power of state actors, especially Canada and EU member states, in order to move the idea from paper to reality. With Japan's accession in 2007, the Asian region is now under increasing pressure to support the Court as well.

The establishment of *ad hoc* international criminal tribunals in the past has been shown to be consistent with both realist and institutionalist theories (Rudolph 2001; Mégret 2002). In terms of realism, from Nuremberg to Sierra Leone,[20] experience shows that militarily powerful states have little to lose by establishing *ad hoc* war crimes tribunals that can prosecute defeated aggressors and anti-government militia leaders. In fact, these tribunals can provide some strategic benefits, as in the case of the ICTY. The Security Council agreed to establish the ICTY while hostilities were continuing, at least partly in order to pressure hardliners like Milosevic into negotiating a peace deal, or to sideline them if they resisted (Hazan 2004, p. 52).

Arguably, the US and other members of the Security Council are now using the ICC for similar purposes – this is especially the case with the referral of the situation in Libya to the ICC in early February 2011, when the international community was trying to de-legitimize the Ghaddafi regime rather than undertake costly military intervention.[21] Some of the governments that referred "situations" on their territory to the ICC – such as the Democratic Republic of Congo and Uganda – were also hoping the ICC's investigation would diminish the capacity of non-state militia to continue threatening the stability of those states, and avoid subjecting government forces to similar scrutiny (Gaeta 2004).

However, realism has a much harder time explaining the *establishment* of the ICC. The Court was not created to address a particular conflict, but was established as a permanent mechanism to adjudicate potentially all military conflicts. Therefore, each state would be expected to have a realist interest in opposing the establishment of the ICC, in order to prevent permanent, independent scrutiny of all its military activities. Yet the entire European Union made support for the ICC its common policy in 2001.[22] Japan's 2007 accession also challenges the realist assumption that "states with the largest relative share of military power should be among the least likely to support a supranational international criminal court with substantial autonomous authority" (Struett and Weldon 2006, p. 14).

Institutionalist explanations of the ICC are also limited, especially rationalist analysis. Rudolph argues that such tribunals may serve an institutionalist agenda in the longer term, in particular "by containing the spread of conflict and by preventing conflict in the future" (Rudolph 2001, p. 658). But there is little evidence to suggest that the "public good" of ending impunity through deterrence will work, even in the long term, particularly when the ICC has the resources to prosecute only a small, representative handful of perpetrators in any given conflict (Wippman 2006, p. 108).

Therefore, the most plausible explanation for the establishment of the ICC must take into account the power of ideas and norms, not just material interests, and the way that state interests and identities can be shaped through a leadership-driven interactive process, such as the ICC negotiations and subsequent global ratification campaign.

Today the Court is facing a range of criticisms from various quarters. In ten years of operation, it has completed only one trial – against Congolese warlord Thomas Lubanga Dyilo (in March 2012). NGOs have also criticized the Court for charging Lubanga only with conscripting child soldiers, not for mass rape and other crimes against humanity committed by his forces against civilians.[23] The African Union has adopted annual resolutions since 2009, calling on all its members to refuse to cooperate with the Court in arresting Sudanese President Al Bashir, who has been charged with genocide in Darfur. The ICC's narrow focus on Africa generally is also challenging the Court's legitimacy.

Yet all Minervian actors continue to support the ICC to a considerable extent, both because of its utility as a tool for the Security Council and also because the institution they created allows the ICC Prosecutor to conduct his/her own investigations independently in places like Kenya and Guatemala. International justice has always been slow – the trial of former Liberian President Charles Taylor has concluded after five years. However, the reality of a permanent international criminal court now at least provides pause for thought for leaders of all persuasions.

Notes

1. The opinions expressed in this chapter solely reflect the personal views of the author, and are not intended in any way to represent the views of the Australian Government or of any organization or institution with which the author has been associated at any time.

2. The Rome Statute required 60 ratifications before the treaty entered into force (article 126). This number was deliberately set high in order to ensure the Court would have an adequate base of support for its activities. As at November 1, 2012, the ICC had in fact received the full commitment of 121 states.

3. Note that France, despite being an EU member and its strong leadership role in establishing all previous international criminal tribunals, was not a leader on the ICC either. Unlike every other EU member, France never joined the LMG supporting and driving the establishment of the ICC. France did ratify the Rome Statute (in June 2000) in accordance with EU policy, but was one of the few states to take advantage of a provision in the Statute whereby a state party could not be subject to the ICC's jurisdiction over war crimes committed in a non-international armed conflict until 2009.

4. In accordance with the Rome Statute, Japan is required to provide approximately 22% of the Court's budget.

5. However, the establishment of the ICC reflected a clear, anti-hegemonic agenda on the part of many "Non-Aligned" states, which had been advocating an international criminal court for many years – one that would be independent of the Security Council.

6. The vote was not recorded, but the most likely states voting alongside the US were China, India, Israel, and several Arab states.

7. Even when the Security Council has referred a "situation" to the ICC for investigation – as with Darfur and Libya – the US has ensured that the UN (and therefore its members) will not be liable to contribute funds to that investigation.

8. More information about the 1,500+ member coalition is available at: www.iccnow.org

9. For example, an Italian NGO called No Peace Without Justice – which was associated closely with the Italian Transnational Radical Party – paid a number of young Western lawyers to "represent" some of the poorer States not entitled to access the LDC Trust Fund, and to report back to that state and take instructions from the capital during diplomatic negotiations.

10. For example: Parliamentarians for Global Action ("PGA"), "a non-profit, non-partisan international network of elected legislators with over 1300 members in more than 100 countries and regional parliaments around the globe, [which] aims to promote peace, democracy, the rule of law, human rights, sustainable development and population issues by informing, convening, and mobilizing parliamentarians to realize these goals."

11. As I will discuss further below, the EU did not maintain a unified position on the ICC.

12. Due to the informal nature of this alliance at the time, reports vary as to the states involved. At least half were European, although neither France nor the UK were "like-minded" at this stage. Other likely members were Argentina, Australia, and South Africa.

13. See Ambassador Owada's statement at the second plenary session in Rome, June 15, 1998 – Official Records of the Rome Conference.

14. The CICC had established a practice of recording and publicizing "virtual" votes, by asking its members to follow the position of all delegations on the key issues and compiling these.

15. China has since softened its position somewhat, being particularly impressed by the sensibilities of the Prosecutor elected in 2003, and his clear decision to avoid blatantly political tactics (Pitty 2006, p. 362).
16. Today the EU continues to fund substantial ICC promotion in under-represented regions, such as Asia and the Middle East, while the conservative Canadian Government has gradually reduced its expenditure considerably on the global ICC ratification campaign since 2007.
17. Foreign Minister Aso's support for the ICC appears to derive from his close personal association with Ambassador Owada, who led Japan's delegation to the ICC negotiations (anecdotal information provided by Professor Kent Anderson, ANU).
18. Source: CICC website.
19. Resolution on the deteriorating situation of human rights in Syria.
20. A "Group of Interested States," including the UK and the US, supports the Special Court for Sierra Leone.
21. Russia's and China's refusal to support a similar referral for Syrian President Assad in early 2012 demonstrates the highly politicized nature of these referrals.
22. Council Common Position on the ICC, November 6, 2001.
23. Some of the ICC judges also made this point when delivering their verdict against Lubanga.

13
The Last Call for the Minerva's Owl: The Politics of the 11th Hour in Negotiating the Nagoya Protocol at the CBD COP 10 Meeting

Elena Feditchkina

> The owl of Minerva takes its flight only when the shades of night are gathering.
>
> Hegel, *Philosophy of Right*, preface

Introduction[1]

Rarely had international environmental fairness been given so much hope, and generated so much despair, as anxiety over the acceptance of a new multilateral agreement, the Nagoya Protocol on Access and Benefit Sharing (the ABS Protocol), reached the highest point in the final hours of negotiations at the tenth meeting of the Convention on Biological Diversity's (CBD) Conference of the Parties (COP 10) held in Japan's Nagoya, during October 18–29, 2010. Despite the preceding two weeks of intense negotiations between CBD parties, it remained uncertain until the very end of the overnight plenary session whether the new Protocol would pass the consensus-based approval of an UN meeting. Negotiations resembled an emotional roller-coaster, as positions between the biodiversity rich Global South and the financially rich Global North over the Protocol's scope, genetic derivatives, and compliance mechanisms remained wide apart. Besides the Protocol, the approval of the plenary session was needed for two other crucially important documents, each contingent upon one another for acceptance – a new Strategic Plan containing conservation targets for 2020 and a new Resource Mobilization Strategy for meeting these targets. It appeared that developing countries, collectively owning more than 80 percent of the world's biological diversity, had a bargaining leverage over the industrially developed world and therefore were unwilling to accept new conservation targets unless the ABS Protocol was also accepted and more finances were made available. Given that all three documents came as a package deal, *troika*, the prospects of failing the entire COP 10 loomed large. Therefore, it appeared as a political miracle when the new international agreement was finally born, at 1:30 in the morning in the plenary hall of Nagoya Congress Centre, packed with the delegations of 179 countries, causing "standing ovations, tears of joy and a great feeling of relief" (ENB 2010a, p. 26).

Why did Nagoya produce an impressive package of new documents, including a new multilateral agreement on environmental equity, the ABS Protocol, despite the current tendency of multilateral environmental negotiations to yield sub-optimal results, as exemplified by the recent COP meetings of the UN Framework Convention on Climate Change? And how did negotiating parties manage to bridge seemingly irreconcilable differences that persisted for a decade during preparatory negotiations prior to the meeting in Nagoya?

The classical Realist perspective – the strongest does what he wants – fails to explain the creation of this new international regime, whose main objective is to benefit the weak, including "the poorest of the poor" in the developing world, indigenous and local communities (ILCs) (World Bank 2010). Another variation of the Realist approach, that major powers participate in institution building to counter-balance the US as a hegemon, is also unconvincing: the Minervian players, in this case it was Japan, the EU, and Norway, went against their immediate self-interest in helping to create the new treaty, whereas the more conventional US rivals, China and Russia, remained disinterested in either helping or blocking this new regime. When a hegemon abandons its role – the US essentially stood alone vis-à-vis other nations in its choice to not ratify the CBD – the formation of a new international treaty follows a somewhat different pattern.

The Constructivist approach, with its focus on the impact of global civil society in shaping new environmental regimes (Wapner 1996; Liftin 1998; Haas 1990; Newell 2000), is not a very good fit for explaining this case either. Although environmental NGOs (ENGOs) and indigenous organizations played a significant role in popularizing and shaping the discourse on access and benefit sharing, their input during the crucial negotiations in Nagoya was rather limited and did not replicate the 1992 Earth Summit in Rio, where NGOs played a significant role in the process of negotiations by joining government delegations (Willetts 1996). Compared to that, the negotiations in Nagoya lacked transparency, with the most important final sessions happening behind closed doors. Another constructivist model based on the "boomerang" affect of ENGOs (Keck and Sikkink 1998) does not explain the outcome of Nagoya either, although the boomerang strategy was enacted and did have some impact. That said, the influence of NGOs was an important enabling condition, especially during the "pre-negotiation" phase (Arts and Mack 2003) and in their collaboration with small states' delegations, which were frequently short of staff and resources (Chasek 2001, p. 171).

This chapter advances another normative explanation that focuses on the behavior of Minervian actors willing to engage, sometimes reluctantly, in global institution building because of their ideational convictions and long-term vision of a global public good. How do Minervian players overcome the propensity to free-ride as clearly described by Garrett Hardin? Tiberghien defines Minervian actors as "states or organizations such as the European Union that choose to commit significant resources and power (that is, not just discourse) to the advancement of global institutions and global governance … [they] do not extract much tangible benefit from their involvement in global institution building" (see Introduction). Their behavior is neither entirely altruistic nor self-centered but is somewhere in between these two extremes. It instead combines the normative with the pragmatic: strategic in scope, transcending immediate tactical gains, and instead incorporates a wider perspective and an appreciation for the long-term benefits of having stable international governance over a certain policy domain.

Based on this, a variety of Minervian actors are observed in an analysis of ABS treaty making: "the ideal type" exemplified by Norway, as it advanced the ABS treaty by clearly siding with the position of the developing world,[2] the EU as the "reluctant Minervian": while acting with a degree of reservation on some specific ABS questions, on balance the EU served the Minervian role as a committed mediator between different interests (Bille et al. 2010), and in making important compromises and financial pledges. Strategically, the European Union was committed to strengthening the Convention, given the EU's critical role in pushing forward an earlier CBD treaty, the Cartagena Protocol on Biosafety. Finally, Japan played the role of "the entrepreneurial Minervian," taking the advantage of its COP 10 Presidency and acting as a decisive leader, especially in the last few days of the COP 10 meeting.

What motivates political entrepreneurs and why do they act? As observed by Tiberghien,

> political entrepreneurs act the way they do because they anticipate that taking on the case of reform will improve their political position in the long-term ... In a competitive political environment, emerging new political leaders seek novel issues to build a visible reputation on ... to spot an opportunity for arbitrage under the situation of uncertainty and offer a clear solution. (2007, p. 20)

However, the entrepreneurial behavior of Japan at the COP 10 was not a given, as it extended its efforts and resources way beyond the expected duty of the conference host in pushing for the acceptance of the ABS Protocol. The years 2009 and 2010 marked the high point of Japanese environmental politics, defined by the election of a new government, the Democratic Party of Japan (DPJ), with a new internationalist agenda and characterized by a strong multilateral undertone and commonality with the EU (Tiberghien 2010). Strong linkages between the PM, the Ministry of the Environment, and key environmental organizations such as Greenpeace and WWF brought the issues of climate change and biodiversity loss to the fore of the political agenda. Japan assumed its Minervian entrepreneurial role in regards to a new CBD treaty first under Prime Minister Hatoyama during the preparation phase (2009–10), and then under Prime Minister Kan (2010–11) during the Nagoya negotiations. Moreover, in addition to the desire to establish itself in a new role as the champion of an important and emerging international policy domain, Japan wanted to see yet another protocol carrying the name of its city.

This chapter also argues that it would be impossible to overcome the dilemma of collective action even if a few Minervian players were involved, without having three other important conditions in place, as follows: 1) *Set*: a strong normative pressure coming from the developing world and global civil society and imposed on the developed world for *not acting* on the Protocol. The ABS treaty serves as a proxy for international fairness in accessing and using the biological resources of the Global South; 2) *Setting*: even though parties assumed very different positions initially, the consensus-based decision-making process of a UN forum, accompanied by the strong expectations to produce concrete results at the end of the meeting, forced parties to look beyond extremes, for a middle ground. The CBD Secretariat played an important role by providing necessary expertise crucial in this very technical policy domain; 3) *Window of Opportunity*: when the level of uncertainty increases, conventional procedures are no longer effective and several pathways leading to different outcomes emerge, a unique window of opportunity opens for a political entrepreneur to present new creative solutions. In the COP 10 meeting, the window of opportunity briefly opened after the negotiations came to the final stretch – the proverbial 11th hour – when all other means were exhausted and parties were still stuck in impasse.

The chapter will proceed in four sections: it will first evaluate the significance of the ABS Protocol and will describe its most important elements. Then it will look at the timeline of the ABS regime since its inception at Rio, and will assess the regional blocks along with their negotiation postures. Subsequently it will turn its attention to the negotiation process during the COP 10 meeting and the roles played by Minervian actors. The final section will focus on the role of the Japanese Presidency, who performed unconventional, "risky but necessary" political maneuvers during the COP 10 meeting.

Evaluating the ABS Nagoya protocol: promises and shortcomings

Called "the most important meeting on biodiversity in UN history,"[3] the tenth Conference of the Parties meeting of the Convention on Biological Diversity in Nagoya marked an important tipping point for the Convention in terms of its capacity to finally address its third objective: the fair and equitable sharing of the benefits arising out of the utilization of genetic resources (CBD, Article 1).[4] Because the CBD affirms the sovereign rights of states over their biological and genetic resources, there exists *a quid-pro-quo* arrangement at the heart of the Convention: countries that provide access to their genetic resources (predominantly, biodiversity rich countries of the Global South) should receive a share of benefits from those that access and utilize these resources, in the form of funding or technology transfers (CBD, Article 15).

In a nutshell, as a consequence of accepting the Nagoya Protocol, users of genetic resources – a diverse group including the pharmaceutical, biotech, agriculture, and cosmetic industries, as well as collectors, botanical gardens, and research institutions, will be required to receive permission (prior informed consent) from the providers of biodiversity – governments that have sovereign rights over genetic resources as well as indigenous and local communities should they claim traditional knowledge (TK) over the resource in question, for example the practices surrounding a medicinal plant or plant's chemical compound valuable for pharmaceutical industry. In return for acquiring access to genetic resources and traditional knowledge, the users should share benefits, including financial, arising from the utilization of these resources. Overall, the ABS Protocol makes a great promise to the poorest of the poor and the indigenous communities of the Global South, and intends to contribute to two objectives simultaneously: poverty alleviation and sustainable use.

However, the compromise text of the Protocol accepted as the result of difficult negotiations in Nagoya may lack effectiveness in meeting these two objectives, as it lost its edge on definitions, scope, and implementation. The Protocol is criticized by some developing world parties for being too general, having many legal loopholes, and for being incapable of stopping biopiracy because of its weak compliance measures (Third World Network 2010b). Moreover, the "elephant in the room," the US, is not a CBD party, which significantly limits the scope of the ABS application, given the very strong position of American biotech and pharmaceutical industries. The new Protocol will enter into force on the ninetieth day after deposit of its 50th ratification, with the deadline of 2015. As of February 2012, it was signed by 92 parties and ratified by two.

The set: the long and winding road to Nagoya

Although the Convention on Biological Diversity was accepted as early as 1992, it was not until 1999 that its parties began to work on the equity objective of the Convention. Normative gravitas that surrounded an access and benefit-sharing regime was enormous from the very start of negotiations due to the intention of the new regime to tackle biodiversity loss and poverty alleviation simultaneously. By the time of the CBD COP 10 meeting in October 2010, the normative pressure to fulfill the promise given 18 years ago in Rio – to follow the equity objective of the Convention – reached a critical threshold. Delays were no longer morally justifiable vis-à-vis developing countries that became increasingly reluctant to accept new CBD conservation targets without seeing the developed world's commitment to address access and benefit sharing.

Despite this normative pressure, the acceptance of an ABS treaty was not immanent. The powerful players, the EU, Canada, Australia, and Japan, were not eager to go against their politically powerful domestic life science industries. The proposed Protocol would introduce new costs to biotech and pharmaceutical industries, by legally binding them to share financial benefits in exchange for accessing genetic resources – which were accessed for free for many decades. Moreover, parties that would benefit from an ABS regime, the poorest countries with large indigenous populations, lacked the resources necessary to create and sustain an effective mobilization campaign and to spur negotiations. Many of them did not have enough resources and technical expertise to continuously engage in preparatory meetings defined by increasingly technical language and occurring in different locales of the world. Not every country could afford to stay on top of MEAs' negotiations that increased in numbers dramatically in the past two decades, and was especially difficult for developing countries and small states (Chasek 2001, p. 168). Moreover, the indigenous peoples from the developed world – Australia, Canada, New Zealand – also lacked political resources; their voices were not formally incorporated in the negotiation process based on the UN, state-centered approach.

In addition, world public opinion, defined by short attention spans and issue attention cycles (Downs 1972), was captivated by the parallel high drama of negotiations over climate change. Consequently, the majority of ENGOs consolidated their limited resources on the UNFCCC's Kyoto Protocol instead of CBD. As a result, the ABS Protocol did not generate much media frenzy, as compared to the amount of media attention given to its cousin treaty, and therefore did not captivate the attention of the domestic constituencies of most CBD parties. The Alliance of CBD, an umbrella organization representing non-governmental organizations, was a drop in the bucket as compared to the engagement of ENGOs in UNFCCC COP meetings. Not surprisingly, the negotiations over the ABS Protocol were bogged down for many years and stayed off the radar of mainstream media coverage.

However, by the year 2000, the increased reluctance of the developing world to move on with conservation targets without addressing the objective of access and benefit sharing necessitated the CBD Secretariat to start the process of preparing for a new Protocol on equity. In 2002, the UN World Summit on Sustainable Development, acknowledging the failure to implement the third objective of the CBD, called to establish a new international regime "to promote and safeguard the fair and equitable benefits arising from genetic resources" (Chiarolla 2010; Third World Network 2010a). In 2006, CBD COP 8 meeting established the deadline: an ABS Protocol should be accepted prior to COP 10 meeting, scheduled for October 2010 (ENB 2010a, p. 2). The commitment was reaffirmed at the 9th COP meeting where the ABS Working Group was instructed "to finalize the international regime and to submit for consideration and adoption by the Conference of the Parties at its tenth meeting in 2010" (Third World Network 2010b).

As parties were approaching the deadline, the negotiations around the ABS treaty intensified and grew in complexity. Between the COP 9 and COP 10 meetings, the ABS Working Group met four times with the objective to prepare a viable draft by April 2010, as UN rules mandate that a treaty draft be circulated six months prior to its formal adoption. However, parties were unable to prepare a compromise text in advance due to the persisting wide divisions between developed and developing countries on the key questions related to the Protocol's scope and compliance (Third World Network 2010b). Only the fourth meeting, an interregional negotiation group held in July 2010 in Montreal, managed to reach a first draft of the Protocol, with a significant part of it still remaining in brackets. Only three out of the 32 articles of the draft were agreed upon by negotiating parties by the end of the meeting (Third World Network 2010b). In the last effort to prepare a more viable draft immediately before COP 10 Nagoya in October, negotiators met once again on September 18–21 in Montreal. However, deep divisions remained and a compromise text appeared beyond reach. With no clean text ready for the COP 10 meeting in Japan, parties were faced with a procedural challenge – to subject the text that was expected to emerge out of the COP 10 meeting to the rule of unanimous approval at the final plenary session.

Anticipating the possible failure to reach a compromise on ABS as the result of key players' entrenched positions, Brazil's Minister of the Environment, Izabella Teixeira, warned on the behalf of the Like Minded Mega Diverse Countries (LMMC) that failure to reach an ABS Protocol would undermine the legitimacy of the entire Convention. The Brazilian minister made it clear that two other important documents on the COP 10 agenda, the Strategic Plan for 2020 and the Strategy on Resource Mobilization, will be treated by the LMMC as "an indivisible package," together with the ABS Protocol (Third World Network 2010b). The message was clear: without having an ABS regime accepted, further cooperation by the developing countries, the custodians of the overwhelming bulk of planetary biodiversity, would be jeopardized. Thus, the ABS Treaty was framed immediately prior to the COP 10 meeting as "too big to fail," a grand bargaining strategy orchestrated by developing countries. The future of COP 10 negotiations promised to be either a complete failure of total success.[5]

The setting: parties, regional blocks, and their positions

Given the scope of the remaining text in brackets, a consensus over the ABS Protocol was unlikely, and arguably due to two main reasons: a very wide polarization of interests and its high technical complexity. The Informal Consultative Group (ICG) on ABS was established at the beginning of the COP 10 meeting, co-chaired by Fernando Casas (Colombia) and Timothy Hodges (Canada), to prepare a compromise text of the Protocol. Within this group, several smaller groups were established to work on more specific sections: utilization and derivatives, compliance mechanisms, the protocol's linkages with other international agreements, emergency situations and pathogens, TK-related questions, and other COP decisions (ENB 2010a, p. 3). But the progress on making a compromise text was too slow, despite the intensity of the meetings and the overall strong commitment of the parties to produce concrete results by the end of COP 10.

Negotiating parties were divided into two sides. The first side was represented by countries with significant indigenous populations and vast genetic resources, including the Like-Minded Mega Diverse Countries,[6] GRULAC (representing Latin American and Caribbean countries), the African Groups, and the Like-Minded Group of Asia-Pacific (excluding Korea, Japan, Australia, and New Zealand) – all collectively pushing for a comprehensive ABS regime with a strong compliance system. The Like-Minded Mega Diverse States, with Brazil as their leading voice, advocated a wider definition of genetic materials, a broad scope of application, and the legal recognition of indigenous knowledge. The African Group and the Like-Minded Asia-Pacific countries shared their position, and were opposed on many issues by most industrialized nations – the EU, Canada, Australia, New Zealand, Switzerland, and Japan, who rejected the broad definition of genetic materials. "Temporal scope," a key demand of the African group, referred to the continued use of genetic resources acquired prior to the Protocol's entry into force. This proposal was strongly opposed by the EU and other developed nations as "inconsistent with the principle of international law" and undesirable because of potential lawsuits of pharmaceutical and biotech industries by indigenous peoples for taking, without prior consent, medicinal plants and organisms from their land for commercial purposes (The Japan Times 2010b). The International Indigenous Forum on Biodiversity (IIFB), an NGO speaking on behalf of indigenous peoples across the borders, requested that the Protocol confirmed their right to Prior Informed Consent as "collective owners of Traditional Knowledge."[7]

The position of the developing world on most issues was shared by Norway and, to some degree, by Central and Eastern European countries. Norway acted by far as the strongest supporters of a comprehensive benefit-sharing regime among the industrially developed countries and was a key player in negotiating between the Global South and North (Chiarolla 2010; CBD Alliance 2010b). However, the negotiation postures of other developed nations were very different from that of the developing world. Most of them took a more cautious approach toward institutionalizing the benefit-sharing component and mandatory compliance measures, such as information disclosure related to utilization of genetic resources and mutually agreed terms – a proposal strongly opposed by the EU's biotech and pharmaceutical domestic industries (ENB 2010a, p. 26). The developed world also rejected its retroactive application and pushed for the exclusion of pathogens, non-commercial research, and situations of health emergencies. Traditional knowledge (TK) of indigenous peoples became one of the central issues of disagreement, with the developing world, Norway, and NGOs pushing for the inclusion of TK in the various sections of the Protocol, whereas the EU wanting to see TK in a separate section. Canada and New Zealand assumed the least cooperative approach on this issue, by advocating not accepting compliance measures to support TK and re-directing this issue under the auspices of World Intellectual Property Organization (WIPO), a position which would weaken the claims of Indigenous peoples.[8]

Yet both the developed and the developing world had a very important point of convergence: they believed the ABS treaty was necessary *in principle*, the developed nations for the reason of having a more stable and predictable international governance on access to genetic resources, and the developing world because of the economic gain resulting from the benefit-sharing component.

Although the EU, and especially Germany, was frowned upon by NGOs as an "ABS blocker" for its frequent bracketing during ABS working sessions (CBD Alliance 2010b), on balance the EU engagement in negotiations over the Protocol was constructive. The EU, the strong supporter of the CBD's first binding treaty, the Cartagena Protocol on Biosafety, was strategically committed to create the next important building block of the Convention, an ABS treaty. Even though individual EU member states had varying levels of commitment to the new ABS regime, ranging from more reluctant Germany to very supportive Nordic countries, as a whole the EU worked hard to overcome international political obstacles to accepting the Protocol. Environmental groups singled out the EU because they judge its performance by much higher standards, due to the EU's reputation as the international environmental leader.[9] Therefore, many NGOs were disappointed to see the reluctance of some EU members to compromise on a number of key issues. Yet the overall direction of the EU remained Minervian, steadily motivated by the intention to have an ABS regime accepted for keeping the Convention functional and growing. This intention was visible through the intensity of the EU voice and its commitment to negotiations, as well as in the signals sent from the very top prior to the during meeting in Nagoya. Janez Potocnik, the European Commissioner for the Environment, speaking at a three-day summit on the Millennium Development Goals just a few weeks before Nagoya, stated that "It will be essential that we conclude negotiations on the [ABS] Protocol. Now it is time to deliver" (Third World Network 2010b). Joke Schauvliege, Belgium's Minister for the Environment, also indicated a high level of commitment, as follows, "we are all committed to successful negotiations in Nagoya," and that biodiversity protection will play an essential role in poverty eradication. Finally, Denmark's Minister for the Environment, Karen Ellemann, called negotiators "to stand up to our responsibility as leaders...we must deliver the deal that will set the world back on track.... A legally binding Protocol on ABS must be part of the outcome from COP 10" (Third World Network 2010b.).

By contrast, the Canadian position on ABS was not constructive enough to consider it to be truly Minervian. Given the role played by Canada as an active supporter of the Convention during its initial stages, as well as the permanent host of the CBD Secretariat (located in Montreal), one should expect to see a strong commonality between Canada and the EU regarding a new CBD treaty. However, these two players, who initially pushed the CBD forward, have demonstrated very different levels of commitment in regards to the Convention's two legally binding instruments – the Cartagena Protocol on Biosafety (2000), and the Nagoya ABS Protocol (2010).[10] Unlike the EU, Canada did not sign the first CBD treaty, the Cartagena Protocol on Biosafety that brought together 163 parties in governing the transborder movement of living organisms modified by biotechnology (LMOs). On this, the position of Canada was much more similar to that of the US, which domestic and international policy postures were driven by its powerful biotech and agricultural lobbies unfavorable of government regulations. Perhaps it was not accidental that the very same industries resisted the new regime on access and benefit sharing. The lack of Canada's enthusiasm was apparent throughout the ABS negotiations in Nagoya and, according to one delegate, seemed to replicate the US position.[11]

Being accustomed to a different image of Canada in past multilateral meetings, some civil society representatives were taken by surprise, and consequently commented in a daily newsletter prepared by the CBD Alliance, the umbrella organization for civil society members working on CBD issues, "Remember the good old days when Canada could do the right thing and join hands with the civil society groups that founded the International Campaign to Ban Landmines, to launch the Ottawa Process that resulted in the historic Mine Ban Treaty?" Canada was particularly criticized by civil society groups for its strong opposition to the inclusion of Traditional Knowledge, as well as its opposition to the reference to the rights of indigenous peoples as follows: "taking into account the significance of the 2007 UN Declaration on the Rights of Indigenous Peoples." Canada insisted that this text should be blocked and deleted from the preamble.[12] Consequently, the CBD Alliance granted Canada with the status of "Life-time underachiever" and also awarded it, along with the EU, "the Dodo Award" (Dodo being the symbol of species extinction) for undermining the voices of the indigenous peoples and for being "the most visible obstacle in the ABS Protocol Negotiations."[13]

Canada's lack of enthusiasm for creating a new CBD protocol was consistent with its under-achieving behavior in other recent environmental treaty negotiations. Canada was an under-performer during most recent climate change meetings and even decided to withdraw from the Kyoto Protocol altogether during the meeting in Durban in December 2011. Canada's Environment Minister, Peter Kent, called signing this Protocol "an incompetence of the previous Liberal government."[14] This position over multilateral environmental treaties reflects the new course taken by the Conservative government of Stephen Harper who repeatedly sets the environment against economic development.[15] It is also worth noting that Canadian opposition to seeing the legal recognition of the rights of indigenous peoples in the ABS Protocol, which could potentially strengthen their claims over genetic resources, was shared by other industrialized countries with significant indigenous populations, Australia and New Zealand (Chiarolla 2010).

As the end of the COP 10 meeting approached, the parties' positions over the ABS protocol remained wide apart. The developing world decided to cast its bargaining chips by blocking progress on non-ABS items in response to the developed countries' lack of good will toward the ABS. Playing big, Brazil proposed to increase funding for the

Strategic Goals 2020 at least in the order of 100-fold, to reflect the CBD principle "common but differentiated responsibilities," which would bring funding levels to halt biodiversity loss to 200 billion dollars (ENB 2010a, p. 10). Some commentators took this request as the indicator of the amount the developing countries were ready to accept for their compromise over some key ABS issues (Chiarolla 2010, p. 9).

Two days before the end of the COP 10 meeting, Japanese Prime Minister Naoto Kan announced a very generous contribution, two billion dollars for biodiversity-related projects in developing countries, provided that the ABS Protocol and Strategic targets were adopted. The announcement was reported to strongly influence the spirit of negotiations. Thus a former Japanese official at the CBD Secretariat was quoted to say that Japan's investment became a driving force in the negotiations, and arrived at a very appropriate moment, when the negotiating parties were "under a lot of pressure" (The Japan Times, 2010c). The EU also made some important financial pledges: France promised do double its funding as part of the official development assistance by 2012 (200 million euros annually allocated for biodiversity). From 2014, this amount should increase up to 500 million euros per year. In addition, the EU pledged 120 million dollars for the CBD Life Web initiative, to strengthen Protected Areas (Bille et al. 2010, p. 3). However, the general amount of financial pledges did not come near to what the developing world expected as appropriate.

Japan's political entrepreneurship: masters of creative uncertainty

After most of the repertoire of a UN-based COP meeting was tried and failed to produce a compromise ABS text, many delegates and observers turned to the Japanese Presidency in the belief that "only strong political leadership at the top will yield results" (The Japan Times 2010a). Several important conditions were in place that enabled the Japanese Presidency to perform very risky political maneuvers that finally pushed negotiations out of an impasse in the final hours. These conditions were as follows:

1) The existence of Knightian uncertainty, defined by "a character of the situation in which agents cannot anticipate the outcome of a decision and cannot assign probabilities to the outcome" (Frank Knight, quoted in Blyth, 2002).

2) There was, however, no obvious opposition to the Protocol *in principle*. Despite wide disagreements, all parties would derive some important benefits from a new ABS regime.

3) Also, no one wanted to sink the entire Convention, considering the enormous gravitas of the ABS Protocol. The stakes around accepting the Protocol were extremely high, as two other crucial documents hinged upon its approval: the CBD Strategic Plan 2020, and the new financial mechanism – a great bargaining strategy, "all or nothing."

These conditions – especially the first, the condition of uncertainty when multiple pathways for actions were possible – enabled the Japanese Presidency to take on the role of a political entrepreneur. Willing and able to take political risk, bending some procedures, making deals, and being ready to accept responsibility in case of failure is arguably conducive with the Japan's ethos of samurai – exceptional commitment to high service accompanied by readiness for risk and sacrifice.

On Thursday, the last day of negotiations before the Friday's concluding plenary session, the co-chairs of ABS Working Group reported the persistence of fundamental differences on utilization and derivatives of genetic resources. It appeared unlikely that agreement would be reached on the ABS' most contentious issues (ENB 2010a, p. 26). Pressed for time, the President of COP 10, recently appointed Japanese Environmental Minister Ryu Matsumoto, decided to hold meetings behind closed doors with selected parties in attendance. The EU, Brazil (LMMC), the African group, and Norway were invited to participate in these "secret" meetings, in order to work out the final compromise draft. The negotiations continued over night and extended in the informal ministerial breakfast on Friday morning, when an agreement was rumored to have been reached, on the basis of the proposal made by the Japanese presidency (Bille et al. 2010). Some observers later commented that these diplomatic maneuvers performed by Japan were necessary but also very risky, as they could potentially alienate other parties who were not invited to the table but whose votes were necessary for the consensus-based approval at the plenary session (ENB 2010a, p. 26).

Extended well beyond its deadline hour, the overnight final plenary session, chaired by the Japan's Environment Minister, brought together the delegates of 179 countries to conclude the 15–day-long intense negotiations. "Balancing on the razor's edge between failure and success" (Earth Island Environmentalist 2010), parties continued to bargain until the very end, as the negotiation process spilled from the formal procedural exchange recorded in the minutes to the informal "parallel deliberations" during short breaks, unfolding right on the audience floor of the Plenary session hall.[16]

The most dramatic moment occurred after midnight, when the fate of the Protocol appeared to be on a brink of failure. Venezuela made a statement for the record that it did not support the compromise text proposed by the Japanese Presidency because it was "too weak to tackle biopiracy," thus jeopardizing final unanimous approval. The position of Venezuela was supported by Cuba, Bolivia, and Ecuador – the Bolivarian Alliance for the People of Our America (ALBA) all requesting to take the ABS Protocol out of the troika package and vote on the Strategic Plan and the Resource Mobilization separately, one by one. It appeared for a moment that the Protocol would not pass a consensus after all, partly because of the anger of the parties who were excluded from the final behind-the-scene negotiations. An open discussion followed, in which parties appeared divided over Venezuela's proposal. President Matsumoto asked delegates to confirm their approval of the ABS protocol first and then to vote on each document one by one (ENB 2010a, p. 25). Several important statements were made, with the African group and Brazil expressing their support for the proposed text. The ABS Protocol passed, with ALBA states expressing on record their deep disappointment with the ABS Protocol but not blocking its adoption. At 1:30 in the morning, the Nagoya Congress hall, packed with delegates and observers, burst into a standing ovation and released a genuine collective sigh of relief and joy. The President of the meeting, Japan's Environment Minister Ryu Matsumoto, raised the hammer to end the COP 10 meeting while appearing visibly relieved of his very demanding role.[17]

Conclusion

Japan's entrepreneurial leadership was praised by some delegates as "creative" and "effective," while criticized by others as "lacking trans-parency" and setting up a dangerous example for future negotiations in making behind-the-scene deals (ENB 2010a, p. 25). For example, some delegates from the Like-Minded Asia-Pacific states and the Latin American and Caribbean Group felt excluded from the last informal meetings, and felt betrayed by Japan; they perceived Japan as siding with the industrialized states and neglecting the interests of its Asian neighbors.[18] Similarly, the Japanese "host syndrome" was criticized by ENGOs for secrecy and exclusivity: "all happens between a small group of facilitating ministers. Even some parties are not sure what's going on. The critical voice of countries with rich biological diversity and strong presence of Indigenous peoples such as India, Malaysia, Nepal and the likes are missing."[19]

However, the overwhelming opinion expressed by COP 10 observers and delegates was supportive of Japan's creative and risky leadership, and believed it to be a necessary strategy. "In the end, it allowed cutting a deal that would have otherwise not have been reached in Nagoya as negotiations had ground to a halt" (ENB 2010a, p. 26). Many COP 10 delegates felt very satisfied with the results of compromise, praising the ABS protocol as the "best possible solution at this point in time" (ENB 2010a, p. 26). The EU Commission's Director General for the Environment, Karl Falkenberg, cheerfully commented immediately after the plenary session was over, "It is a great day for Japan, the environment and for the UN. Even in these enormous groups we can reach consensus" (Earth Island Environmentalist 2010). Another Environment Minister, Netumbo Nandi-Ndaitwah of Namibia, stated that "we are happy that consensus was reached. The ABS is a compromise document, none can say they are 100% happy, but if implemented it will be able to assist the poor in Africa who are the custodians of biodiversity" (Earth Island Environmentalist 2010.).

In conclusion, COP 10 illustrates a fascinating causal pattern of international treaty making in the absence of a hegemon and under the mounting normative pressure coming from the developing world, international environmental and human rights organizations, and indigenous groups. The contribution of Minervian actors was critical and was based on using their bargaining and financial leverage, negotiation skills and technical expertise, and also on acting as a political entrepreneur when a unique window of opportunity opened. The dramatic adoption of the Nagoya Protocol on Access and Benefit Sharing in the final hour of intense UN-based negotiations marks a positive milestone for environmental multilateralism in resolving a massive collective action dilemma and creating a global public good – a new governance regime over world's genetic resources. But of course, some serious obstacles remain on the road to its ratification and implementation. As of June 2012, the Protocol has been signed by 92 parties, including influential CBD actors such as the EU, Japan, Australia, Norway, and Brazil. Among the notable abstainers from the list of the Protocol's signatories so far remain Canada, China, New Zealand, Russia, and the US (not a CBD party). The Protocol will enter into force after it is ratified by 50 parties in their domestic legislature, which pushes the beginning of the Protocol's implementation even further away in time.

Notes

1. I very much thank my advisor Dr. Yves Tiberghien for encouragement, support, and for covering my travel expenses to Nagoya from his Canada's SSHRC research grant. Also, I express my sincere thanks to Francis Dijon from the Earth Negotiation Bulletin for initial and crucial introduction to CBD COP meetings, Drs Alex and Cornelia Paulsch for taking their time from observing the session to patiently explain the ground rules of COP working groups, PhD Candidate Linda Wallbott for her inspiring spirit in researching ABS Protocol negotiations, Dr Mari Momii for her kindness to strangers, Hiroki Kawakita for guiding me once through the streets of Nagoya, Dr Ken Macdonald and his research team, Deborah Scott and Ted Maclin for good company, and the people of Nagoya for their extraordinary generosity and helpfulness.
2. Norway had already internalized the elements of the ABS regime in its domestic legislation, and was first among the industrialized world to do so. The Norway's Nature Diversity Act 2009, Section 60, includes measures on the access and benefit sharing of genetic resources.
3. CBD Executive Secretary Ahmed Djoghlaf (ENB 2010a, p. 3).
4. Indigenous peoples and their organizations largely dispute the claim of sovereignty over genetic resources. See, for example, "Draft Protocol: Indigenous Peoples' Objections to the Current text – A Call for Justice and Solidarity." UNEP/CBD/WG-ABS/9/INF/22 September 2010.
5. Personal interview with a COP 10 delegate from the developing world, Nagoya Congress Centre, October 29, 2010.
6. The LMMC group includes 17 countries as follows: Bolivia, Brazil, China, Colombia, Costa Rica, Democratic Republic of Congo, Ecuador, India, Indonesia, Kenya, Madagascar, Malaysia, Mexico, Peru, Philippines, South Africa, and Venezuela.
7. See "Draft Protocol: Indigenous Peoples' Objections to the Current Text – A Call for Justice and Solidarity." Also in ENB, 2010b.
8. The International Indigenous Forum on Biodiversity repeatedly states that it did not trust WIPO to tackle their rights to Traditional Knowledge and would prefer instead to see the issue to be addressed by a strong ABS regime. See, for example, Third World Network, April 1, 2010a.
9. CBD Alliance meeting, the Nagoya Centre, October 25, 2010.
10. Here, it is important to make a distinction between signing the Convention, which can be seen as a general framework of principles and goals, and signing specific Protocols of the Convention, legally binding, and therefore more consequential in terms of domestic policies adjustments and costs.
11. Personal interview, Nagoya Congress Centre, October 28, 2010.
12. However, the final ABS Protocol text retained this reference in the preamble.
13. See, for example, Third World Network, "United Nations: Biodiversity Treaty Implementation at Stake," September 24, 2010; "Indigenous Representatives Denounce Canada's Obstructionist Position at COP 10," CBD Alliance, 2010a.
14. CBC News, "Canada Pulls Out of Kyoto Protocol," December 12, 2011, http://www.cbc.ca/news/politics/story/2011/12/12/pol-kent-kyoto-pullout.html

15. See, for example, Jeffrey Simpson, "Canada' s Message: The World and Its Climate Be Damned," *Globe and Mail*, December 17, 2011.
16. Personal observation of the COP 10 final Plenary session, Nagoya Congress Centre, October 29–30, 2010.
17. Based on personal observations and on the records of ENB 2010a:. 25–26.
18. Press conference with IIFB and JCN, Nagoya Congress Centre, October 28, 2010.
19. Press conference with ENGOs, Nagoya Congress Centre, October 28, 2010.

Part V
Conclusion

14
The End of the Minervian Moment

Zaki Laïdi

Introduction

The general thesis of this book is based on three powerful ideas. The first is that during a decade from 1995 to 2005 multilateralism grew into new areas such as the environment, human security, and cultural diversity. The second, which follows from the first, is that this multilateralization of international regulation occurred against the will and consent of certain major powers, including in particular the United States. Finally, the third is to attribute credit for this reinvigorated multilateralism to an informal coalition of states or groups of states such as Canada, Japan, and the European Union, which can be labeled Minervian actors.

These actors are characterized by their strong support for multilateralism, for the institutions that are supposed to implement it, and for its production of norms. Several authors of this book essentially share a constructivist vision of the world order, that is, the antithesis of a realist interpretation. Others take a perspective rooted in domestic political leadership, a perspective that also stands against realism. Indeed, both groups of authors consider cooperation among states within international organizations to effectively contribute to the regulation of the international system. Like all innovative constructs, this raises a number of methodological issues that need to be addressed. The purpose of this chapter is to discuss the Minervian concept and its causal modes, while raising larger questions about them. It also serves the purpose of a reality check on the Minervian concept in 2012, past the Minervian apex.

Specifically, for the sake of this broader discussion, my chapter raises three sets of questions. First, do Minervian actors share any political coherence beyond their apparent common behavior? Second, why has the behavior of these failed to hold up past 2006, at least in the case of

Canada and partly Japan, as acknowledged by the authors of the book? Finally, is this concept still relevant in 2012, at a time when multilateral trade regulation is blocked; progress in international financial regulation is relatively limited and pursued in a climate of strong distrust among states; the consensus on climate change is increasingly fragile; international security issues are re-emerging; regulatory bodies for collective security such as the Security Council are gridlocked due to veto politics; the greatest power in the world continues to be skeptical of multilateralism despite the break created by Barack Obama's presidency; and sovereign powers like India, Brazil, Russia, China, and India are seeking to revisit a number of commonly agreed principles within the international community, such as the responsibility to protect. The book undeniably raises more questions than it resolves on these three questions, although the authors' defense of their point of view is quite coherent and remarkable. This chapter seeks to complement the Minervian thesis with a healthy stress test and some larger points.

Typological questions

The starting point for this research was the authors' empirical observation that some states clearly shared positions on a certain number of key international regulatory issues unrelated to the use of force, and that this naturally made them normative powers, more commonly referred to as soft powers. This is where the difficulties begin. While the authors adopt an anti-realist perspective, they use the categorization of a neoconservative realist (Kagan), for whom the international system is divided between the powers from Venus and those from Mars. The former are disinclined to use force, while the latter do not have this inhibition. In a way, by using relatively simple categorizations that ultimately aim to discredit soft powers, the authors turn Kagan's proposed classification against him.

At the same time, by accepting this dichotomy between powers from Venus and powers from Mars they risk boxing themselves into a normative classification that is analytically unsatisfactory. It should be noted that the classification between powers from Venus and from Mars was widely exploited by the Bush Administration during the Iraq war to disparage all those who opposed the intervention: on the one hand were virile powers, so to speak, willing to take risks, and on the other were risk-averse powers lacking courage. Kagan's categorization is therefore not value-neutral.

Yet it is reasonable to assume that between the powers from Mars and Venus there is a range of intermediate situations with which most states can be identified. European states constitute the most flagrant case. For example, the Libyan crisis and resulting military intervention demonstrated that the rift was not between the Europeans and the Americans, but rather among the Europeans themselves. If the European Union might be labeled a Minervian power, the same cannot be said of European Union members France and Great Britain, the staunchest supporters of NATO's military intervention in Libya. Furthermore, an enormous gap appeared between perceptions of the Libyan crisis by the EU, which claimed to be neutral, and by deeply involved member states such as France and Great Britain, which on the contrary deemed it necessary for Europe to intervene as a political entity. Alain Juppé revealed the magnitude of this disagreement when he stated that the European Union is not a non-governmental organization. Finally, France and Great Britain have extremely strong positions on the Iranian nuclear issue that are very close to the US position. Where is Minerva in all this?

Difficulties with the EU as an actor

One consistent challenge with the EU relates to its ambivalent identity. In some empirical cases, it becomes very important to differentiate between the European Union's members and the European Union itself to understand the behavior of "Europe." What is the meaning of the EU's global agenda today if what Brussels does is largely contradicted by the actions of certain member states? While this has always been an issue, in many respects it has become a crucially important one today as Europe wavers in its political integration.

Indeed, one could essentially argue that European states sometimes choose to leave the Minervian agenda to the European Union while preserving, as member states, their freedom of action and judgment. This is especially true for France and Great Britain. Thus, in some issue-areas, it is difficult to consistently treat the EU as a unitary actor. It is crucial to consider not only the actions of the EU as an actor, but also the political interactions between the European Union and its member states.

Furthermore, one may argue that the European unity is increasingly problematic on the global scene, where its dynamic contributions have dramatically declined. As always, these processes are certainly not unequivocal. The European Union's desire to extend the ETS mechanism to airline companies operating within European airspace met with hostility from the rest of the world. Pointedly, key Minervian actors such as Japan and Canada are clearly not siding with Europe on this issue and seem to have lost their Minervian identity. Moreover, it must be noted that in response to very strong international pressure some European states with powerful commercial interests such as Germany are tempted to compromise rather than to support the European Union's position. This example is not the only one. Europe's political cohesion in the environmental area is not nearly as strong as it was during Kyoto, and adherence to the Kyoto commitments masks considerable differences in national behavior. In a context of crisis some European states want to delay Europe's decision to move forward in the fight against climate change.

With respect to the selection of Minervian actors, clearly, the EU, Japan, and Canada are not the only Minervian players. There is room to extend the questions raised in this book and the case analysis to other significant countries such as Brazil and South Africa that have played an important contribution to global institution building.

The decline of the Minervian Moment after the mid-2000s

How consistent has the actions of Minervian actors been in space and time? In order to attribute a distinctive characteristic to an international actor, it is reasonable to expect this characteristic will be apparent over the long term. With regard to biodiversity, the International Criminal Court, and the Kyoto Protocol, these actors do hold similar positions. However, does this collective affirmation still have any meaning today? Europe's failure in Copenhagen showed that while the European Union started with a common position it lacked a common bargaining power. If Europe did not succeed, in an area of shared competence between the states and the Commission, to muster a unified bargaining power it is because national positions were far from convergent.

While there was a burst in global EU activism in the 1990s, common EU foreign action has clearly receded after the mid-2000s. Key members like France, Germany, and the UK are clearly not committed to the pooling of sovereignty any longer in 2012.

The financial crisis has shown that the intergovernmental approach and Franco–German leadership clearly prevail in Europe. The counter argument is that the financial crisis is now forcing Europe to convert to monetary federalism. This is very likely, but it would be the result of an uneven process rather than any teleology of European integration.

Europe is unquestionably the only region in the world that has taken the sharing of sovereignty so far. However, this sharing comes painfully and involves great confusion. Today, the project's survival is at stake. The spillover effect that has often been identified with the construction of Europe no longer functions smoothly, and spheres of action remain extremely compartmentalized. France and Germany work very closely on economic and financial issues, while France and Great Britain work closely on military and strategic issues. Yet nobody currently foresees the economic cooperation leading to military cooperation, or inversely, military cooperation leading to political integration. Even the Lisbon Treaty, which gave the Union an international legal personality, did not really yield any new common dynamics. For instance, Britain makes a great difference between intergovernmental cooperation and political integration. The British have no problem militarily cooperating with France, but they remain adamantly against any military integration, as demonstrated by their categorical opposition to the creation of a European headquarters.

Thus, the cases and time period covered by the authors of the book may represent a specific moment, when the balance of forces indicated a strong degree of coordination with the EU. But that moment has clearly passed and Europe's current capacity for political integration should not be overestimated. In addition, it must be recognized that since the beginning of the 1990s Europe's influence in the world has weakened due to the emergence of new national actors. Europe played a decisive role in Kyoto. Since Copenhagen it no longer does, although objective factors account for the change. Twenty years ago Europe was key to reaching trade agreements. It no longer is. And on other fronts such as Genetically Modified Organisms (GMOs), it could end up on the losing side globally, for lack of unity and common will. This difficulty is compounded by the fact that the relevant international forums today, like the G20, operate on the basis of national representation, which does not inherently encourage Europeans to unite. Because it has large trade surpluses, for instance, Germany has aligned with China to block US proposals to limit current account balances, even though France was supportive in light of its huge trade deficit. On the other hand, capital taxation measures advocated by France face German skepticism, not to mention, of course, strong British opposition.

One further question relates to the lack of durability in the behavior and commitment of some Minervian actors. As an emblematic case, Canada supported the Kyoto Protocol and then became the first country to renege on its commitments in Copenhagen. Canada is increasingly becoming a revisionist state on climate change. One could certainly argue that a change in the country's political majority could reverse the situation. One may thus ask: how could a country like Canada have a Minervian identity and suddenly lose it after an election? Alberta's oil interests are clearly the main drivers of this environmental revisionism. Why and how could these interests suddenly override the Minervian identity? Does Canada embrace multilateralism in matters where the cost is low, and unilateralism when its core economic interests are at stake? Does it mean that Minervian states see multilateralism as only one option among others? When multilateralism clashes with their national interests they tend to renounce the practice. There are not many examples of countries that choose a multilateral approach when it undermines their interests or they have the means to choose a different option. Multilateralism often remains the method of choice for weak countries.

What model for world politics?

The authors of this book describe actors that are wedded to a growing institutionalization of the international system that is increasingly moving the world away from power politics. Here they follow a line of thought that Richard Haas developed in 2005. While Haas is a realist he had concluded that power politics were declining. The authors are pleased to have found a realist author from whom they can draw to buttress their arguments. But if this same author were asked to issue an opinion today, would he make the same analysis? How can one claim that power politics are declining when they are so forcefully re-emerging in all the international forums: climate change, financial regulation, responsibility to protect.

A political assumption that Europe has made for over 20 years now, and that is implicitly adopted by this book's authors, is to think that the development of global public goods and the decrease in interstate conflicts would attenuate the classical dynamics of power politics to the benefit of interdependence. This might have seemed true for a while: Minervian powers undoubtedly reached their peak during the 1990s and early 2000s.

Since then, global dynamics have profoundly changed. The rising power of emerging countries has subverted multilateral practices. At the same time the development of a very aggressive US policy beginning in 2003 considerably affected the international climate and hardened emerging country responses to American hegemony. The best illustration of this turning point is the 2003 WTO conference in Cancun. Under the leadership of Brazil and India emerging countries prevented the United States and Europe from setting the terms of the final agreement, whereas until then Euro–American agreements had generally paved the way for multilateral agreements. In Cancun emerging countries like Brazil specifically wanted to break with this approach. Accordingly, they decided to politicize international trade negotiations. Brazil can thus be credited with creating the first G20 that brought together the contesting states of Cancun. Since then, multilateral trade negotiations have stalled, albeit due to a different set of actors. In 2008 it is India and the United States that prevented a final agreement.

The situation has since continued to evolve. The United States is now one of the principal opponents of a multilateral agreement at the WTO. It much prefers to pursue bilateral agreements and the implementation of a trans-Pacific partnership, which in reality aims to isolate China. This example alone shows that Obama's coming to power has not brought the United States back into the folds of multilateralism. Again, there is a considerable range of options between unilateralism and multilateralism, including that of choosing one or several adequate partners to help resolve issues that the United States is not able to settle on its own. Europe has followed suit. While it continues to advocate for multilateral negotiations, like the United States it understands the need to prioritize reaching bilateral agreements with high-potential emerging countries such as Korea and India. In fact, the free trade agreement between the European Union and Korea pushed the United States to reach a similar agreement with Seoul to prevent the Europeans from gaining too much ground.

International reality is perpetually shifting and hard to typologize. This is a constant challenge that all international relations analysts face. The situation may be evolving, but the need to understand the underlying dynamics is also important. With hindsight, the idea of a Minervian moment is meaningful but cannot easily explain the post-2005 return to an international dynamic based on renewed competition among states. There is no question, however, that for an important political period of time these actors truly sought to imbue the international system with new dynamics. In this perspective, the book's key contribution lies in its ability to analyze the unusual dynamics that drove some outcomes in international politics during a decade, even it may have just been an interlude.

15
Successes and Limits of the Minervian Moment

Yves Tiberghien

An important transformation took place in international relations between the early-1990s and the mid-2000s. The international community took an important step forward in the creation of global institutions to address public good issues. A series of significant global institutions, international treaties, and international norms were created in the fields of global environment, human security and international law, and cultural diversity.

Interestingly, this process of global institution building departed from the hitherto dominant pattern of post-war international politics: while the first wave of institution building (1945–94) followed a hegemonic path on the basis of undisputed US leadership, the second wave (s1995–2010) followed a non-hegemonic pathway. Remarkably, these institutions came about despite US withdrawal from the process or outright opposition to it. Observing this non-hegemonic process, scholars and observers have heralded a new age marked by a growing global civil society, global norms and ideas, and the rise of non-state networks. In this book, we have argued that these observations were incomplete. Some states other than the US remained extremely active in the process of global institution building and played an indispensable role. In fact, this second ring of states carried the torch of Wilsonian and Rooseveltian multilateralism that the US chose to leave behind at that time.

The general pattern observed in this book is a remarkable concordance of actions between players that have not necessarily been accustomed to working together without US leadership. We call these players "Minervian" in that particular time period to refer to their commitment to multilateral institutions and rules and their readiness to commit resources and political capital to these goals. The key Minervian players in most of the cases covered in this book are the European Union (either the EU directly as an actor or a coalition of key European states often acting in coordination with the EU), Japan, and Canada. In some cases, other Minervian states played important roles, particularly Norway, South Africa, Brazil, or Australia. Although this book has focused more on the core three players, extending the Minervian agenda to all other states that endorsed the identity in key battles is a good avenue for future research.

Further, this book has argued that Minervian players pursued global institution building for different reasons. It has identified three general causal patterns behind the process. In the first competitive mode, Minervian players were actually realist actors in disguise, seeking to upload their own domestic constraints or to balance against the US hegemon. Examples of this pattern included the UNESCO cultural diversity convention (Chan), the accounting regulation effort (Véron), and the Cartagena Biosafety Protocol on the trade of genetically modified seeds and plants (not covered in this book). In the second normative mode, Minervian actors acted as partners with international networks and communities, such as the global civil society movement, epistemic communities of experts, or international organization staff members. These networks generated and transmitted norms that Minervian actors were particularly responsive to. Examples of this pattern include the landmine ban (Flowers), the CITES regime (Sakaguchi), the adoption of the R2P norm (Coleman), or the return to the peacebuilding norm in Irak (Higashi).

The book also identified a third causal mode that is less understood in the literature: the domestic leadership mode. In this case, we find that the political leaders in Minervian states or in the EU play a key role, as they choose to act as political entrepreneurs and to tilt the balance of power among their domestic interest coalitions toward the Minervian agenda. Political leaders take those bets in response to values expressed in their national public opinion or even in anticipation that public option will resonate to their international actions. They use the international arena to project global leadership and they calculate that this global projection will resonate with their domestic audiences. In this mode, the international and domestic arenas are clearly intertwined; domestic political leaders play the role of interface between them. In the case of the EU, the game even embeds three levels, as domestic state leaders compete with each other and with EU-level institutions in the elaboration of global agendas and the projection of global leadership. This causal mode is particularly visible in the cases of the Kyoto protocol on climate change (not included in this book), international chemical bans and regulations (Selin), the International Criminal Court (Lee), and the Nagoya Protocol on Biodiversity (Feditchkina).

In addition to these general patterns, the contributors of this book have highlighted some specific causal processes at play during the Minervian episode in international institution building.

Minervian patterns and identities

In Chapter 2, Tiberghien argued that the general Minervian pattern was quite robust and visible in the voting behaviors of Minervian actors at the UN General Assembly. Yet the empirical record presents three other sub-types. In some cases, only the EU and Japan acted as Minervians, while Canada sided with the US (Kyoto after 2006, Biosafety-Cartagena, Biodiversity-Nagoya). This sub-type highlights the disputed nature of Canadian identity, caught between its normative commitment to multi-lateralism rooted in its tradition of political leadership and high degree integration with the US in the North American sphere.

In other cases, Japan did not join the Minervian coalition (e.g., the long initial delay with the ICC, difficulties with CITES, Japan's position at the International Whaling Commission, or Japan's position on Kyoto in 2007 or 2011). These cases and the general ambivalence exhibited by Japan in many other cases before eventually joining other Minervian actors reveal the disputed nature of Japanese decision making on global institutional issues. Ministerial coalitions and interest groups are divided on many issues, creating stalemates between economic interest groups or groups linked with the US and groups pushing for the Minervian agenda; such stalemates can be broken only by strong political leaders who are not always present on the Japanese scene.

As for Europe, there are no cases where the EU did not back the multi-lateral agenda, but individual member states like France and the UK often took different individual positions from the EU's official position. The EU voice covers a broad spectrum.

Finally, the chapter recognized another pattern where Minervian players were successful in enlarging their sphere of influence to China (and often other emerging powers). It is striking that China has been on board with Minervian actors on most environmental issues and on the UNESCO issues, but not on human security issues.

Turning their attention to two particular Minervians, the EU and Canada, Manners (Chapter 3) and Nossal (Chapter 4) have taken very different views on the intrinsic Minervian identity of both players. While Manners takes a constructivist position and argues that the EU behavior follows a constitutive "'normative power' self image" and thus derives from the very nature of the EU, Nossal shows that the Canadian Minervian identity is more political and time-defined: Canada acted forcefully as a Minervian leader because of a particular window in international politics, in domestic party politics (the Liberal domination), and in the leadership of the Liberal Party (Jean Chretien). But once these factors changed, particularly with the end of Liberal Party dominance in 2006, Canada dropped its Minervian identity and tilted back toward an interest based foreign policy.

Not everyone agrees, however, that the Minervian identity of the EU is so constitutive to its project and institutions. In his incisive rejoinder and 2012 stress test, Laïdi argues that this EU normative identity is more tenuous than it seems (Chapter 14). Large states often act in more realist ways and may play a double game of good cop (the EU)–bad cop (big states). In addition, Laïdi doubts that the EU will be able to continue to act Minervian in the future, due its growing internal tensions in the wake of the 2008 financial crisis and intensifying power dynamics in the international system.

Regarding Japan, the analysis made by Flowers in the case of the landmine treaty (Chapter 8), Feditchkina on the Nagoya Biodiversity Protocol (Chapter 13), and the empirical record on climate change (Kyoto protocol implementation) point toward a more disputed and more political identity. Although quite similar to the Canadian case in its political foundation, the Japanese case is actually more fluid and exhibits multiple Minervian equilibria: as long as a political leader is willing to tilt coalition stalemates toward the Minervian agenda, it can happen as well under the conservative leadership of the Liberal Democratic Party (Hashimoto in 1996–97, Obuchi in 1999–2000) or under the ostensibly more social-democratic Democratic Party (Hatoyama in 2009 or Kan in 2010).

From general pattern to plastic realities: insights from the case studies

In Chapters 6 and 7, Chan and Véron highlight two cases of mostly competitive behavior by Minervian actors. Chan argues that Canada and the EU (led by the French position) primarily followed a counter-hegemonic motivation in leading the push for the 2005 UNESCO cultural diversity convention. Japan and others gave support to the push (but not the US). Interestingly, Chan also highlights how Minervian players engaged in a strategic alliance with NGO coalitions in reaching their goal and in implementing the convention. But while NGOs thus had significant influence, Minervian states played a key role in the pursuit of their national interests. The case of the adoption of IFRS accounting standards features a similar counter-hegemonic move spearheaded by the EU. The EU specifically pushed for the development of international standards as a way to counter the influence of US standards. The EU was successful in gaining Canadian support and later, grudgingly, Japanese support (as well as Australian, Brazilian, and Korean support). But the case also features the important role of non-state economic elites in steering the process and a gradual effort to involve the US.

Under this competitive mode, one should also include the crucial case of the Cartagena Biosafety Protocol signed in 2000, which featured a coalition between the EU and developing countries to upload the "precautionary principle" to the global level and develop rules for international labeling of genetically engineered crops as a clear strategy to counter US dominance in the field of agricultural biotechnology. Japan ratified the protocol in 2005, although it was more a mediator than a leader during the negotiations themselves.

Chapters 7, 8, 9, and 10 emphasize a more externally driven and normative process of institution building. In these cases, Minervian states feature as important players but rarely set the agenda. In her analysis of the landmine ban treaty, Flowers analyzes an interactive process of identity politics, where global civil society networks played a key role in shaping the identity of states such as Canada or Germany, as well as the more NGO-resistant states of France, the UK, and Japan (helped by the political leadership of prime minister Obuchi). Civil society networks helped nudge state identities and foreign policy processes. Flowers also admits that the landmine treaty benefitted from a special window and is harder to reproduce in a time where not only the US, but also a rising China, Russia, and India are clear obstacles to such normative politics.

In Chapter 8, Sakaguchi studied the more mature regime of wildlife conservation (CITES) and argued that its resilience and ability to overcome some tensions between opposing norms (that pitted the EU, Canada, and the US against Japan) derived from the presence of a "diffuse normative community" of experts acting through Minervian actors (except Japan). Thus, it is a story of successful norm socialization, rather than state leadership.

Coleman's chapter focused on the adoption of the Responsibility to Protect Norm at the 2005 UN World Summit. She has argued that the R2P process was driven by a coalition of states (primarily Canada, the UK, other European states, but also South Africa and Mexico) that shared an important normative commitment. Yet, it is a network of high-ranking diplomats, bureaucrats from international organizations and a few eminent individuals who played a key role in shaping the agenda and developing the norm. Thus, it is a partial story of socialization, but one of socialization driven by elite networks. Yet, while the R2P norm is getting gradually entrenched, its practice remains highly disputed, particularly with key players such as China and Russia.

Chapter 10 focused on a key battle over the peacebuilding norm in the wake of the Iraq war of 2003. Higashi argues that the US was forced to return to the practice of this norm developed by the UN staff in part because of a coalition between key Minervian states (especially Germany and France) and the UN secretariat. It is a fascinating case of interactive behavior between the staff of an international organization and states in the reestablishment of a norm that they see as important and useful.

In all these four cases, international networks of norm entrepreneurs or elite actors played a key role as agenda-setters; yet, they could not have impact without the relay of Minervian actors. They often acted through Minervian players in gaining the critical mass for action. Canada was particularly prone to such normative penetration, as well as European states and components of the EU institutions. Japan was a harder case, but often prone to surprising late bandwagoning under the impact of a coalition of NGOs, media impact, and political entrepreneurs. The nature of transnational coalitions was different in the four cases, ranging from classic grassroots NGOs (Flowers) to elite knowledge networks (Sakaguchi) or even elite supranational networks (Coleman and Higashi). In all four cases, however, the process is fragile and relies on windows of opportunity that can close in important states.

Finally, Part IV (Chapters 11, 12, 13) unpacked the third Minervian mode of action: political leadership mode. The case of the Kyoto Protocol on climate change (not included in this book) provides a good illustration of this mode: normative explanations, international realist explanations, or domestic coalitional explanations are insufficient in explaining why the EU, Japan, and Canada took strong positions in support of the Kyoto Protocol and its ratification. In the cases of Japan and Canada, political entrepreneurs broke deadlocks and pushed for ratification in the face of strong domestic opposition and in the name of identity projections and calculations regarding public opinion (Harrison and Sundstrom 2010; Tiberghien and Schreurs 2010). A similar, yet larger game has been at play in the EU with a competitive leadership cycle between different poles of the EU on the issue of climate change (Schreurs and Tiberghien 2007). Acting on climate change is a way to project value leadership on the domestic scene for many European actors. Yet, this model has shown great limits after 2007.

In Chapter 11, Selin argued that the EU, European States, and Canada have played a leading role in the adoption of tight regulations on hazardous chemicals and international chemical treaties, mainly as a response to domestic environmental, health, or indigenous concerns. Yet Selin also sees some elements of the first competitive mode, particularly in the EU's desire to upload its stringent domestic regulations to the global level. Japan ends up signing international treaties and supporting the emerging regime (unlike the US), but is more reactive than leading.

Turning to the genesis of the Rome treaty that created the International Criminal Court, Lee argues that it was mainly the result of leadership by Canada and European states (as well as the EU itself) in cooperation with NGO networks that made the difference. It was the personal commitment of key leaders from these Minervian states that pushed the ICC over the hump. Japan was hesitant, but eventually resisted US pressures and domestic opposition to join the ICC in 2007 and provide a major part of its funding.

Feditchkina's chapter turned its attention to one of the most recent cases of Minervian leadership: the Nagoya Protocol on Biodiversity from 2010. It is also a crucial case of individual political leadership, but one that features Japan as the critical player (as host and stalemate breaker), together with the EU and Norway (but not Canada). The Japanese creative leadership was clearly linked to the renewed Minervian commitment under the new DPJ leadership of Prime ministers Hatoyama and Kan. It was an exercise of global leadership right in front of a domestic audience.

These three chapters highlighted the importance of domestic politics in shaping the global behavior of Minervian actors. In these cases, Minervian actors act in such a way because political leaders have decided to use political credit to break domestic interest stalemates and tilt policy in favor of global governance and global public good. In human security arenas, Canadian leadership is particularly striking. In environmental issues, the EU is the leading actor, as the two-level interactions between state and EU institutions create a mutually reinforcing system. Japan rarely exhibits leadership, but always ends up supporting the global Minervian process, as one political leader eventually finds ways to nudge the process forward. As for the processes analyzed under the normative mode, such domestic political leadership requires auspicious windows of opportunities; it is hard to sustain over time.

The Minervian legacy

For all its limitations, the Minervian moment of institution building did generate significant institutions (such as the ICC, the landmine treaty, or the Cartagena protocol) that are still with us today.

Yet, it is also clear that some of the Minervian institutions are weaker and more disputed than institutions created in the first wave of global institution building (such as human rights treaties or the WTO). A case in point is the Kyoto protocol on climate change.

Further, Minerva's rule took place at a defined moment and is clearly on the wane today. This is the result of two parallel but related trends: the decrease in commitment to the Minervian agenda in Canada, Japan, and even some European countries; and the return of competitive power politics in international relations in the larger context of a gradual power transition from the US liberal order to China, India, Brazil, and other emerging powers (as argued by Laïdi in Chapter 14). So far, the EU and other remaining Minervian actors have had limited successes in building alliances with these critical rising nations, although the environmental arena is a potentially fruitful one.

With respect to the UN regime itself, Minervian actors exhibited both a clear readiness to work with UN institutions (R2P, peacebuilding norm, UNESCO), and a readiness to create new institutions outside the UN mold when they found it aging and dysfunctional (ICC, landmine treaty). On balance, the Minervian moment was broadly UN-conforming.[1]

An interesting implication relates to the power and reputation of the US. Remarkably, the US was mostly not successful in blocking the advance of these global institutions. Its very active campaign to cripple the ICC by convincing countries around the world not to join or to sign side-agreements with the US mostly failed. After 2008, the US decreased its opposition to the ICC and supported its role in the case of Ivory Coast (2010) and Libya (2011). One of the factors behind the lack of ability for the US to stop the Minervian moment in institution building was the fact that it actually represented a continuation of the Rooseveltian vision of international relations and had strong thinkers and allies within the US who played important roles in building these institutions. In addition, in the cases of environmental treaties, remaining out

Table 15.1   Typologies of Minervian outcomes

	Competitive	Normative	Political leadership
Binding the hegemon	Accounting	R2P Peacebuilding norm	ICC
Inverse U-curve and decline		Landmine ban?	Kyoto
Enlarged coalition	Biosafety-Cartagena UNESCO	CITES	Biodiversity-Nagoya Chemical Treaties

of these institutions provided short-term economic advantages to US firms. But it did carry a cost in terms of international influence and in terms of negative impact on the global institutions themselves.

Three types of outcomes

The Minervian moment has had three kinds of long-term outcomes: the creation of hegemonic constraints, an inverse U-curve, and successful coalition building.

In the first category, Minervian actors succeeded, and the US hegemon gradually rallied behind Minervian institutions. Cases in point are the ICC and the peacebuilding norm (Iraq case).

In the second category, Minervian actors won the battle of institution creation, but gradually lost the battle of institutional diffusion. The hegemon continued its opposition and found new partners or Minervian defectors. Gradually, the regime weakened. A case in point is the Kyoto protocol, which, by 2012, has essentially been abandoned by both Canada and Japan. The cost for the institution is high.

Finally, there is a third category of cases where Minervian actors did not manage to bind the hegemon, but managed to find new emerging partners, particularly China and Brazil. Cases in point include the Cartagena Biosafety protocol or the Nagoya Biodiversity convention. Such a situation of enlarged coalition guarantees the long-term durability of the institution. Table 15.1 summarizes these outcomes.

The bigger picture

If both the first phase of global governance under hegemonic leadership and the second phase of global institution building under Minervian leadership are coming to an end, what model can we envision for the advancement of global governance?[2] What can a third phase of global institution building look like, especially at a time where the functional need for global governance and coordination is greater than ever (cf. Introduction)?

Clearly, the hegemonic mode of global governance has run its course and is not able to solve public good problems at the level of the planet or even to stabilize the global economic system. The fallback Minervian mode that took over for a decade reached its apex around 2005 and is unable to generate enough global leadership on its own to tackle the problems that we face today.

Two possibilities emerge from the analysis of this book. The first one would be an enlarged Minervian coalition, where China, India, and Brazil could become key players, and gradually a re-embedded US. Such a process would be flexible, ad hoc, and facilitated by catalyzing networks or smaller players.

A second solution lies in the creation of a new structure that can embed key players and nudge them toward cooperation, taking its cues from the more successful results of the EU process. A possible embryo for such a structure is found in the current G20, although its institutional system remains weak and uncertain.

What is certain, however, is that global governance may be one of the most important questions in international relations today. The Minervian moment showed that diverse nations could find incentives to cooperate toward global institutions and norms out of a variety of motivations under creative leadership. The challenge today is to take that model to a large scale and to find ways to involve both the US and powerful emerging nations such as China, India, and Brazil.

Parting words

Global governance has reached a crossroads; the obsolescence of past modes of global institution building can lead us either to despair or to a search for innovation. Innovation is better than despair.

Notes

1. I would like to thank Brian Job for an insightful exchange on this question.
2. I am indebted to Arjun Chowdhury for raising this fascinating question.

Works Cited

Alexandroff, A. S. and A. F. Cooper (eds) (2010) *Rising States, Rising Institutions: Challenges for Global Governance* (Washington, D.C.: Brookings Institution Press).

Anderson, K. (2000) "The Ottawa Convention Banning Landmines, the Role of International Non-governmental Organizations and the Idea of International Civil Society," *European Journal of International Law*, 11 (1), 91–120.

Annan, K. (1999) "Two Concepts of Sovereignty," *The Economist*, September 18.

Arctic Monitoring and Assessment Programme (2009) *AMAP Assessment 2009: Human Health in the Arctic* (Oslo: AMAP).

Arctic Monitoring and Assessment Programme (2010) "AMAP Assessment 2009: Persistent Organic Pollutants in the Arctic," *Science of the Total Environment*, 408, 2851–3051.

Arts, B. and S. Mack (2003) "Environmental NGOs and Biosafety Protocol: A Case Study on Political Influence," *Environmental Policy and Governance*, 13 (1), 19–33.

Attali, J. (2011) *Demain, Qui Gouvernera Le Monde?* (Paris: Fayard).

Avant, D. D., M. Finnemore, and S. K. Sell (2010) *Who Governs the Globe?* (Cambridge, UK; New York: Cambridge University Press).

Axworthy, L. (1997) "Canada and Human Security: The Need for Leadership," *International Journal*, 52 (2), 183–96.

Axworthy, L. (2003) *Navigating a New World: Canada's Global Future* (Toronto: Alfred A. Knopf Canada).

Bail, C., R. Falkner, and H. Marquard (eds) (2002) *The Cartegena Protocol on Biosafety: Reconciling Trade in Biotechnology with Environment and Development?* (London: The Royal Institute of International Affairs).

Baker, S. (2006) "Environmental Values and Climate Change Policy: Contrasting the European Union and the United States." In *Values and Principles in European Union Foreign Policy* edited by Sonia Lucarelli and Ian Manners, 77–96. London: Routledge.

Balfour, R. (2006) "Principles of Democracy and Human Rights: A Review of the European Union's Strategies towards its Neighbours." In *Values and Principles in European Union Foreign Policy* edited by Sonia Lucarelli and Ian Manners, 114–29. London: Routledge.

Barcelona Study Group (2004) "A Human Security Doctrine for Europe: The Barcelona Report of the Study Group on Europe's Security Capabilities." Presented to EU High Representative for Common Foreign and Security Policy Javier Solana. Barcelona, September 15.

Barnett, M. N. and M. Finnemore (2004) *Rules for the World: International Organizations in Global Politics* (Ithaca, NY: Cornell University Press).

Barrow, K. (2003) "NGOs in Security Politics: The International Criminal Court," Paper read at Australasian Political Studies Association Conference, at University of Tasmania, Hobart, Australia, September 29 – October 1.

Barry, D. (2005) "Chrétien, Bush and the War in Iraq," *American Review of Canadian Studies*, 35 (2), 215–45.

Bass, G. J. (2000) *Stay the Hand of Vengeance: The Politics of War Crimes Tribunals* (Princeton, NJ: Princeton University Press).

Bassiouni, M. C. (1998) "Historical Survey: 1919–1998." In M. C. Bassiouni (ed.) *The Statute of the International Criminal Court: A Documentary History* (Ardsley, NY: Transnational Publishers Inc).

Bassiouni, M. C. (1999) "Negotiating the Treaty of Rome on the Establishment of an International Criminal Court," *Cornell International Law Journal*, 32 (3), p. 443.

Beck, U. (2003) "Understanding the Real Europe." *Dizsent*, Summer: 32–38.

Bellamy, A. (2006) "Wither the Responsibility to protect? Humanitarian Intervention and the 2005 World Summit," *Ethics and International Affairs*, 20 (2), 143–69.

Benedetti, F. and J. L. Washburn (1999) "Drafting the International Criminal Court Treaty: Two Years to Rome and an Afterword on the Rome Diplomatic Conference," *Global Governance*, 5 (1), 1–37.

Bengtsson, R., I. Manners, H. Persson, O. Zetterquizt, and L. Gröning (2012) *Det Europeizka Projektet: Juridik och Politik, Historia och Framtid* (Stockholm: Liber).

Benson, H. (1989) *Accounting for Life* (London: Kogan Page).

Benston, G., M. Bromwich, R. Litan, and A. Wagenhofer (2003) *Following the Money: The Enron Failure and the State of Corporate Disclosure* (Washington, DC: AEI Press).

Bercuson, D. J. and D. Stairs (eds) (2005) *In the National Interest? Assessing Canada's International Policy Statement* (Calgary: Canadian Foreign Affairs and Defence Institute).

Berlin, I. (1972) "The Bent Twig: A Note on Nationalism," *Foreign Affairs* 51 (1), 11–30.

Bernier, I. and H. Ruiz Fabri for Quebec's Ministère de la Culture et des Communincations (2006) "Implementing the UNESCO Convention on the Protection and Promotion of the Diversity of Cultural Expressions," http://www.cptech.org/unesco/

Bernstein, S. (2002) "International Institutions and the Framing of Domestic Policies: The Kyoto Protocol and Canada's Response to Climate Change," *Policy Sciences*, 35 (2), 203–36.

Bille, R., C. Chiarolla, and L. Chabason (2010) "COP10 in Nagoya: A Success for Global Biodiversity Governance?" *Institut Du Developpement Durable Et Des Relations Internationales*, No 6, December 10.

Birchfield, V. (2011) "The EU's Development Policy: Empirical Evidence of 'Normative Power Europe'?" In *Normative Power Europe: Empirical and Theoretical Perspective*, edited by Richard Whitman, 140–59 (Basingstoke: Palgrave Macmillan).

Björkdahl, A. (2011). "Building Peace: Normative and Military Power in EU Peace Operations." In *Normative Power Europe: Empirical and Theoretical Perspective*, edited by Richard Whitman, 103–25 (Basingstoke: Palgrave Macmillan).

Blair, T. (1999) "Speech on the Doctrine of the International Community at the Economic Club, Chicago." April 24. Transcript at www.number10.gov.uk/output/Page1297.asp, accessed January 25, 2007.

Blanchfield, M. (2011a) "Nobel Laureate Accuses Tories of Delaying Clusterbomb Treaty." *Star,* 8 March.

Blanchfield, M. (2011b) "Canadian Ex-Arms Negotiator Breaks Silence on Cluster Bombs." *Star,* 1 April.

Blyth, M. (2002) *Great Transformations. Economic Ideas and Institutional Change* (New York: Cambridge University Press).

Bolton, J. (2005) Representative of the USA to the UN, Letter to UN Colleagues of 30 August. Accessed at http://r2pcoalition.org/content/view/21/47/ on January 22, 2007.

Bonaglia, F., A. Goldstein, and F. Petito (2006) "Values in European Union Development Cooperation Policy." In *Values and Principles in European Union Foreign Policy,* edited by Sonia Lucarelli and Ian Manners, 164–84. London: Routledge.

Bosold, D. and W. von Bredow (2006) "Human Security: A Radical or Rhetorical Shift in Canada's Foreign Policy?" *International Journal,* 61 (4), 829–44.

Boutros-Ghali, B. (1992) "An Agenda For Peace: Preventive Diplomacy, Peacemaking, and Peace-keeping," A/47/277-S/24111.

Bowman, R. S. (2003) *Bosnia: U.S. Military Operations* (SRS Issue Brief For Congress).

Bremer, P. (2006) *My Year in Iraq* (New York: Simon & Schuster, Inc).

Bretherton, C. and J. Vogler (2006) *The European Union as a Global Actor* (London; New York: Routledge).

Brikell, B. H. (2000) *Negotiating the International Waste Trade: A Discourse Analysis* (Örebro Studies in Political Science 2. Doctoral Dissertation. Örebro University).

Brooks, P. (1972) *The House of Life: Rachel Carson at Work* (Boston: Houghton Mifflin Company).

Broomhall, B. (2003) *International Justice and the International Criminal Court: Between Sovereignty and the Rule of Law* (New York: Oxford University Press).

Brzezinski, Z. (2012) *Strategic Vision: America and the Crisis of Global Power* (New York: Basic Books).

Bull, H. (1977) *The Anarchical Society: A Study of Order in World* Politics (London: Macmillan).

Burney, D. (2005) "Foreign Policy: More Coherence, Less Pretence," *Simon Reisman Lecture in International Trade Policy,* March 14, (Ottawa), available online at www.carleton.ca/ctpl/pdf/conferences/2005reismanlectureburney.pdf

Burnham, P., K. Gilland, W. Grant, and Z. Layton-Henry (2004) *Research Methods in Politics* (Basingstoke: Palgrave Macmillan).

Burns, C. (2005) "The European Parliament: The European Union's Environmental Champion?" in A. Jordan (ed.) *Environmental Policy in the European Union: Actors, Institutions and Processes,* 2nd edn (London: Earthscan).

Byers, M. (2007) *Intent for a Nation: What Is Canada For? A Relentlessly Optimistic Manifesto for Canada's Role in the World* (Vancouver: Douglas & McIntyre).

Cameron, M. A., R. J. Lawson, and B. W. Tomlin (eds) (1998) *To Walk Without Fear: The Global Movement to Ban Landmines* (Toronto: Oxford University Press).

Cameron, M. A., R. J. Lawson, and B. W. Tomlin (1998) "To Walk Without Fear." In *To Walk Without Fear: The Global Campaign to Ban Landmines,* edited by M. A. Cameron, R. J. Lawson, and B. W. Tomlin (New York: Oxford University Press).

Camfferman, K. and S. Zeff (2007) *Financial Reporting and Global Capital Markets: A History of the International Accounting Standards Committee, 1973–2000* (Oxford: Oxford University Press).

Camps, M. (1964) *Britain and the European Community, 1955–63* (London: Oxford University Press).

Camps, M. (1966) *European Unification in the Sixties: From the Veto to the Crisis.* London: McGraw-Hill.

Canada (2005) *Canada's International Policy Statement: A Role of Pride and Influence in the World.*

Canada, Department of Foreign Affairs and International Trade (1999) *Human Security: Safety for People in a Changing World.* Ottawa, April, www.summit-americas.org/Canada/HumanSecurity-english.htm

Caplan, R. (2005) *International Governance of War-torn Territories: Rule and Reconstruction* (New York: Oxford University Press).

Carson, R. (1962) *Silent Spring* (Cambridge: The Riverside Press).

Caves, R. (2000) *Creative Industries: Contracts Between Art and Commerce* (Cambridge, MA: Harvard University Press).

CBD Alliance (2010a) "Indigenous Representatives Denounce Canada's Obstructionist Position at COP 10," *Eco*, 35 (5), October 22.

CBD Alliance (2010b) "Welcome Ministers! An Assessment of Progress from Civil Society," *Eco*, 35 (8), October 27.

CBD Secretariat (2002) *Bonne Guidelines on Access to Genetic Resources and Fair and Equitable Sharing of the Benefits Arising Out of Their Utilization*, http://www.cbd.int/doc/publications/cbd-bonn-gdls-en.pdf, date accessed February 20, 2012.

CBD Secretariat (2010) *The Nagoya Protocol.* Text available at http://www.cbd.int/abs/text/, date accessed February 20, 2012.

CCFR and GMF (2002b) *Worldviews 2002 – European Public Opinion and Foreign Policy.* Survey accessed at www.worldviews.org/detailreports/europeanreport/index.htm on January 21, 2007.

CCFR and GMF (Chicago Council on Foreign Relations and the German Marshall Fund of the United States). (2002a) *Worldviews 2002 – American and European Public Opinion and Foreign Policy.* Surveys accessed at www.worldviews.org/detailreports/compreport/index.htm on January 21, 2007.

Cerone, J. P. (2007) "Dynamic Equilibrium: The Evolution of US Attitudes toward International Criminal Courts and Tribunals," *European Journal of International Law*, 18 (2), 277–315.

Chabasse, P. (1998) "The French Campaign." In *To Walk Without Fear: The Global Campaign to Ban Landmines*, edited by M. A. Cameron, R. J. Lawson, and B. W. Tomlin (New York: Oxford University Press).

Chan-Tiberghien, J. (2004) *Gender and Human Rights Politics in Japan: Global Norms and Domestic Networks* (Palo Alto, CA: Stanford University Press).

Chan-Tiberghien, J. (2006) "Cultural Diversity as Resistance to Neoliberal Globalization: The Emergence of a Global Movement and Convention," *International Review of Education*, 52 (1–2), 93–110.

Chapnick, A. (2005) *The Middle Power Project: Canada and the Founding of the United Nations* (Vancouver: UBC Press).

Chasek, P. (2001) "NGOs and State Capacity in International Environmental Negotiations: The Experience of the Earth Negotiation Bulletin," *Review of European Community & International Environmental Law*, 10 (2), 168–76.

Chiarolla, C. (2010) "Making Sense of the Draft Protocol on Access and Benefit Sharing for COP 10," *IDDRI SciencesPo*, 07, October.

CITES (1994) "Summary Report: Thirty-third Meeting of the Standing Committee," Fort Lauderdale, United States of America. November 17.

Cloutier, G., Y. Théoret, and R. Laplante (2005) "Diversite culturelle, une convention bien fragile," *Forces*, October, http://www.magazineforces.com/news.html?L=0&nid=107

Cohen, A. (2003) *While Canada Slept: How We Lost Our Place in the World* (Toronto: McClelland and Stewart).

Colborn, T., D. Dumanoski, and J. P Myers (1996) *Our Stolen Future* (New York: Dutton).

Coleman, K. (Forthcoming) "Locating Norm Diplomacy: Venue Change in International Norm Negotiations," *European Journal of International Relations*.

Commission of the European Communities (2003) The European Union and the United Nations: The Choice of Multilateralism, Communication from the Commission to the Council and the European Parliament. COM(2003) 526 final. Brussels, October 9.

Commission of the European Communities. 2004. European Neighbourhood Policy Strategy Paper, Communication from the Commission. COM(2004) 373 final. Brussels, December 5.

Cooper, A. F. (1997) *Niche Diplomacy: Middle Powers after the Cold War* (New York: St. Martin's Press).

Cooper, A.F., R.A. Higgott, and K.R. Nossal (1993) *Relocating Middle Powers: Australia and Canada in a Changing World Order* (Vancouver: UBC Press).

Cooper, B. and D. Bercuson (1999) "Canada's 'Soft Power' Stance Won't Get the Job Done," *Calgary Herald*, January 27.

Copeland, D. (2001) "The Axworthy Years: Canadian Foreign Policy in the Era of Diminished Capacity." In *Canada Among Nations 2001: The Axworthy Legacy*, edited by F. O. Hampson, N. Hillmer, and M. Appel Molot (Toronto: Oxford University Press).

Cortell, A. P. and J. W. Davis, Jr. (2000) "Understanding the Domestic Impact of International Norms: A Research Agenda," *International Studies Review*, 2 (1), 65–87.

Council of the European Union (2005) Council Regulation (EC) No. 980/2005 of 27 June 2005 Applying a Scheme of Generalised Tariff Preferences. *Official Journal of the European Union*, 30.6.2005, L 169/1–43.

Crawford, N. (1993) "Decolonization as an International Norm: The Evolution of Practices, Arguments, and Beliefs." In *Emerging Norms of Justified Intervention: a Collection of Essays from a Project of the American Academy of Arts and Sciences*, edited by L. W. Reed (American Academy of Arts and Sciences).

Cryer, R. (2005) *Prosecuting International Crimes: Selectivity and the International Criminal Law Regime* (New York: Cambridge University Press)

Curtis, G. (2004) "For the United States and Japan Multilateralism Is the Key." *Foreign Affairs*, March/April.

Daalder, I. H. and M. E. O ' Hanlon (2000) *Winning Ugly: NATO's War to Save Kosovo* (Washington, DC: The Brookings Institution).

Darby, J. (1997) "The Environmental Crisis in Japan and the Origins of Japanese Manufacturing in Europe," *Business History*, 39 (2), 94–114.

Davis, C. (1993) "Japanese Diplomacy in the United Nations: Assuming a More Active Role? Deal to Fight Biopiracy," *Earth island Journal*, October 29. Date accessed February 20, 2010. Available online at http://www.earth-island.org/journal/index.php/elist/eListRead/world_governments_reach_biodiversity_agreement/

Deitelhoff, N. (2009) "The Discursive Process of Legalization: Charting Islands of Persuasion in the ICC Case" *International Organization* 63 (1), 33–65.

Della Porta, D. and S. G. Tarrow (2004) *Transnational Protest and Global Activism* (Lanham, MD: Rowman & Littlefield).

Dew-Becker, Ian and Robert Gordon (2005) "Where Did the Productivity Growth Go? Inflation Dynamics and the Distribution of Income," *Bookings Papers on Economic Activity*.

Dewailly, E. and C. Furgal (2003) "POPs, the Environment, and Public Health." In *Northern Lights against POPs: Combating Toxic Threats in the Arctic*, edited by D. L. Downie and T. Fenge (Montreal: McGill-Queens University Press).

Diamond, L. (2004) "What Went Wrong in Iraq," *Foreign Affairs*, 83 (5), 34–57.

Diez, T. and R. Whitman (2002) "Analysing European Integration, Reflecting on the English School: Scenarios for an Encounter." *Journal of Common Market Studies* 40 (1): 43–67.

Diez, T., I. Manners, and R. Whitman (2011) "The Changing Nature of International Institutions in Europe: the Challenge of the European Union." *Journal of European Integration*, 33(2): 117–138.

Diez, T. and M. Pace. 2011. "Normative Power Europe and Conflict Transformation." In *Normative Power Europe: Empirical and Theoretical Perspectives*, edited by Richard Whitman, 210–55 (Basingstoke: Palgrave Macmillan).

Dover, R. (2006) "The EU's Joint Actions on Anti-personnel Mines and Unexploded Ordnance: Finding a Security Policy Identity." *European Foreign Affairs Review*, 11 (3): 401–16.

Downie, D. L. (2003) "Global POPs Policy: The 2001 Stockholm Convention on Persistent Organic Pollutants." In *Northern Lights against POPs: Combatting Toxic Threats in the Arctic*, edited by D. L. Downie and T. Fenge (Montreal: McGill-Queens University Press).

Downs, A. (1972) "Up and Down with Ecology: 'The Issue-Attention Cycle,'" *Public Interest*, 28, 38–50.

Doyle, M. and N. Sambanis (2006) *Making War and Building Peace: United Nations Peace Operations* (Princeton: Princeton University Press, 2006).

Duchêne, F. (1972) "Europe's Role in World Peace." In *Europe Tomorrow: Sixteen Europeans Look Ahead*, edited by Richard Mayne, 32–47 (London: Fontana).

Earth Negotiation Bulletin (ENB) (2010a) *A Reporting Service for Environment and Development Negotiations*, 9 (544), 18–29.

Earth Negotiation Bulletin (ENB) (2010b) *A Reporting Service for Environment and Development Negotiations*, 9 (500), March 26.

Eichengreen, B. J. (2011) *Exorbitant Privilege: The Rise and Fall of the Dollar and the Future of the International Monetary System* (New York: Oxford University Press).

Ellickson, R. C. (2001) "The Market for Social Norms," *American Law and Economics Review* 3 (1), 1–49.

European Commission (2002) *A European Union Strategy for Sustainable Development* (Luxembourg: European Communities).

European Community (1992) "CITES: The African Elephant," Report of the EC Mission to Africa. November 26 to December 7, 1992.

European Parliament, Council and Commission (2006) The European Consensus on Development. Joint statement by the Council and the representatives of the governments of the Member States meeting within the Council, the European European Parliament and the Commission (2006/C 46/01) *Official Journal of the European Union*, February 24.

European Union @ United Nations (EU@UN) (2005) EU Presidency Statement – GA consultations on Cluster III – Freedom to live in dignity. April 19. Accessed at www.europa-eu-un.org/articles/es/article_4591_es.htm on January 25, 2007.

Evans, G. (2005a) "Genocide or Crime? Actions Speak Louder than Words in Darfur," *European Voice*, 18 February, www.crisisgroup.org/home/index.cfm?id=3278&1=1

Evans, G. (2005b) *Making a Difference*. Convocation Address at Carleton University. Ottawa, 13 November.

Evans, G. (2006) *The Responsibility to Protect: From an Idea to an International Norm*. Keynote Address to the Chicago Council on Global Affairs Conference on *The Responsibility to Protect: Engaging America*. Chicago, November 15.

Evans, G. and M. Sahnoun (2002) "The Responsibility to Protect," *Foreign Affairs*, 81 (6), 99–110.

Everts, P. and P. Isernia (eds) (2001) *Public Opinion and the International Use of Force* (London: Routledge).

Falkner, R. (2000) "Regulating Biotech Trade: The Cartagena Protocol on Biosafety," *International Affairs* 76 (2), 299–313.

Falkner, R. (ed.) (2007) *The International Politics of Genetically Modified Food: Diplomacy, Trade and Law* (Basingstoke, England; New York: Palgrave Macmillan).

Fenge, T. (2003) "POPs and Inuit: Influencing the Global Agenda." In *Northern Lights against POPs: Combatting Toxic Threats in the Arctic*, edited by D. L. Downie and T. Fenge (Montreal: McGill-Queens University Press).

Ferri, D. (2005) "EU Participation in the UNESCO Convention on the Protection of the Diversity of Cultural Expressions: Some Constitutional Remarks," *European Diversity and Autonomy Papers* 3: 1–34.

Finlayson, J. A. (1988) *Limits on Middle Power Diplomacy: The Case of Commodities* (Ottawa: North-South Institute).

Finnemore, M. (1996) *Defining National Interests in International Society* (Ithaca, NY: Cornell University Press).

Finnemore, M. (2003) *The Purpose of Intervention: Changing Beliefs About the Use of Force* (Ithaca, NY: Cornell University Press).

Finnemore, M. and K. Sikkink (1998) "International Norm Dynamics and Political Change," *International Organization*, 52 (4), 887–917.

Flahault, F. (2011) *Où Est Passé Le Bien Commun?* (Paris: Mille et une nuits).

Fossum, J. E. (2006) "Gidsland and Human Security: Cosmopolitan Vehicles?" *International Journal*, 61 (4), 813–28.

Franceschet, A. and W A. Knight (2001) "International(ist) Citizenship: Canada and the International Criminal Court," *Canadian Foreign Policy*, 8 (2), 51–74.

Frank, T. (1990) *The Power of Legitimacy Among Nations* (New York: Oxford University Press).

Friedman, T. L. and M. Mandelbaum (2011) *That Used to Be Us: How America Fell Behind in the World It Invented and How We Can Come Back* (New York: Farrar, Straus and Giroux).

Frost, M. (1996) *Ethics in International Relations: A Constitutive Theory* (Cambridge: Cambridge University Press).

Fukushima, A. (1999) *Japanese Foreign Policy: The Emerging Logic of Multilateralism* (New York: St. Martin's Press).

Gaeta, P. (2004) "Is the Practice of 'Self-Referrals' a Sound Start for the ICC?" *Journal of International Criminal Justice*, 2 (4), 949–52.

Gélard, G. (2006) "Démarche normative et cadre conceptuel," *Revue Française de Comptabilité*, 393, 35–39.

Gilpin, R. (1981) *War and Change in World Politics* (Cambridge; New York: Cambridge University Press).

Glasius, M. (2006) *The International Criminal Court: A Global Civil Society Achievement* (Abingdon, Great Britain and New York: Routledge).

Gotlieb, A. (2004) "Romanticism and Realism in Canada's Foreign Policy," *Benefactors' Lecture, 2004* (Toronto: C.D. Howe Institute), available on-line at www.cdhowe.org/pdf/benefactors_lecture_2004.pdf

Gotlieb, A. (2005) "Romanticism and Realism in Canada's Foreign Policy," *Policy Options*, 26 (February).

Government of Norway (2009) *Nature Diversity Act*. Act of 19 June 2009 No. 100 Relating to the Management of Biological, Geological and Landscape Diversity.

Granatstein, J.L. (2003) "The Importance of Being Less Earnest: Promoting Canada's National Interests through Tighter Ties with the U.S.," *Benefactors' Lecture, 2003* (Toronto: C.D. Howe Institute), available on-line at www.cdhowe.org/pdf/benefactors_lecture_2003.pdf

Granatstein, J.L. (2007) *Whose War Is It? How Canada Can Survive in the Post-9/11 World* (Toronto: HarperCollins).

Grant, P. and C. Wood (2004) *Blockbusters and Trade Wars: Popular Culture in a Globalized World* (Vancouver and Toronto: Douglas and McIntyre).

Green, M. J. (2001) *Japan's Reluctant Realism: Foreign Policy Challenges in an Era of Uncertain Power* (New York: Palgrave Macmillan).

Gwodzdecky, M. and J. Sinclair (2001) "Landmines and Human Security." In *Human Security and the New Diplomacy*, edited by R. McRae and D. Hubert (Montreal and Kingston: McGill-Queen's University Press).

Haas, P. M. (1990) *Saving the Mediterranean: The Politics of International Environmental Cooperation* (New York: Columbia University Press).

Haas, P. (1992) "Introduction: Epistemic Communities and International Policy Coordination," *International Organization* 46 (1), 1–35.

Haass, R. (2005) *The Opportunity: America's Moment to Alter History's Course* (New York: PublicAffairs).

Habermas, J. (2003) "Toward a Cosmopolitan Europe." *Journal of Democracy*, 14 (4), 86–100.

Haglund, D. G. (2006) "Québec's 'America Problem': Differential Threat Perception in the North American Security Community," *American Review of Canadian Studies*, 36 (4), 552–67.

Hampson, F. O. and D. F. Oliver (1998) "Pulpit Diplomacy: A Critical Assessment of the Axworthy Doctrine," *International Journal*, 53 (Summer), 379–406.

Hampson, F. O., N. Hillmer, and M. Appel Molot (eds) (2001) *Canada Among Nations 2001: The Axworthy Legacy* (Toronto: Oxford University Press).

Hardin, G. (1968) "The Tragedy of the Commons," *Science*, 162, 1243–48.

Harrison, K. (2002) "Federal-Provincial Relations and the Environment: Unilateralism, Collaboration, and Rationalization." In *Canadian Environmental Policy: Context and Cases*, edited by D. L. VanNijnatten and R. Boardman (Oxford: Oxford University Press).

Harrison, K. and L. Sundstrom (eds) (2010) *Global Commons, Domestic Decisions: The Comparative Politics of Climate Change* ed (Boston: MIT Press).

Hart, M. (2002–03) "Lessons from Canada's History as a Trading Nation," *International Journal*, 58 (1), 25–42.

Hataley, T.S. and K. R. Nossal (2004) "The Limits of the Human Security Agenda: The Case of Canada's Response to the Timor Crisis," *Global Change, Peace and Security*, 16 (February), 5–17.

Hay, C. (2002) *Political Analysis: A Critical Introduction* (Basingstoke: Palgrave Macmillan).

Hay, R. J. (2000) "Present at the Creation? Human Security and Canadian Foreign Policy in the Twenty-first Century." In *Canada Among Nations 1999: A Big League Player?* Edited by F. O. Hampson, M. Hart, and M. Rudner (Toronto: Oxford University Press).

Hayner, P. (2007) *Negotiating Peace in Sierra Leone: Confronting the Justice Challenge, December 2007 Report.* International Center for Transitional Justice. Geneva: Switzerland.

Hazan, P. (2004). *Justice in a Time of War: The True Story behind the International Criminal Tribunal for the Former Yugoslavia*, translated by J. T. Snyder (College Station: Texas A & M University Press).

Heinbecker, P. (2004a) "The UN in the Twenty-first Century: Canada Needs This Old Dog to Learn New Tricks." In *Canada Among Nations 2004: Setting Priorities Straight*, edited by D. Carment, F. O. Hampson and N. Hillmer (Montreal and Kingston: McGill-Queen's University Press).

Heinbecker, P. (2004b) "Re-Engineering Global Linkages," Presentation to Atlantic Brücke Conference, Banff, Alberta, October 15–17, available online at www.heinbecker.ca/Speeches/AtlantikBruckeoctober2004.pdf

Heinbecker, P. (2007) "Canada and Multilateralism in a New Era," Presentation at 2007 MPA Policy Forum, Queen's University, Kingston, April 27, available online at http://www.heinbecker.ca/Speeches/Queens2007MPApolicyForum.pdf

Heinbecker, P. (2010) *Getting Back in the Game: A Foreign Policy Playbook for Canada* (Toronto: Key Porter Books).

Herman, J. (2005) "The Dutch Drive for Humanitarianism: Inner Origins and Development of the *Gidsland* Tradition and its External Effects," *International Journal International Journal*, 61 (4), 859–74.

Higashi, D. (2008) "The Challenge of Constructing Legitimacy in Peacebuilding: Case of Afghanistan," Report to the UN Department of Peacekeeping Operation. Accessed by from http://www.peacekeepingbestpractices.unlb.org/PBPS/Pages/Public/library.aspx?ot=2&cat=34&menukey=_4_3

Higashi, D. (2009) "The Challenge of Constructing Legitimacy in Peacebuilding: Case of Timor-Leste," Accessed from http://www.peacekeepingbestpractices.unlb.org/PBPS/Pages/Public/library.aspx?ot=2&cat=34&menukey=_4_3

Hillmer, N. and A. Chapnick (2001) "The Axworthy Revolution." In *Canada Among Nations 2001: The Axworthy Legacy*, edited by F. O. Hampson, N. Hillmer and M. Appel Molot (Toronto: Oxford University Press).

Hiraishi, T. (1989) "Control of Chemicals." In *Environmental Policy in Japan*, edited by S. Tsuru and H. Weidner (Berlin: Edition Sigma).

HLP (High-level Panel on Threats, Challenges and Change) (2004) *A More Secure World: Our Shared Responsibility* (New York: UN Department of Public Information).

Holdgate, M. (1999) *The Green Web: A Union for World Conservation* (London: Earthscan). http://www.peacekeepingbestpractices.unlb.org/PBPS/Pages/Public/library.aspx?ot=2&cat=34&menukey=_4_3

Hubert, D. (2000) "The Landmine Ban: A Case Study in Humanitarian Advocacy," Occasional Paper #42, The Thomas J. Watson Jr. Institute for International Studies, Brown University.

Hughes, C. W. (2004) *Japan's Re-Emergence as a "Normal" Military Power* (Oxford; New York: Oxford University Press).

Hurd, I. (2002) "Legitimacy, Power, and the Symbolic Life of the UN Security Council," *Global Governance*, 8, 35–51.

ICISS (International Commission on Intervention and State Sovereignty) (2001a) *The Responsibility to Protect: Report of the International Commission on Intervention and State Sovereignty* (Ottawa: International Development Research Centre).

ICISS (2001b) *The Responsibility to Protect: Research, Bibliography, Background – Supplementary Volume to the Report of the International Commission on Intervention and State Sovereignty* (Ottawa: International Development Research Centre).

Ikenberry, G. J. (2002) *America Unrivaled: The Future of the Balance of Power* (Ithaca, NY: Cornell University Press).

Ikenberry, J. G. (2010) "The Three Faces of Liberal Institutionalism." In *Rising States, Rising Institutions: Challenges for Global Governance*, edited by A. S. Alexandroff and A. F. Cooper, 17–47 (Washington, DC: Brookings Institution Press).

Imura, H. (2005) "Japan's Environmental Policy: Past and Future." In *Environmental Policy in Japan*, edited by H. Imura and M. A. Schreurs (Cheltenham: The World Bank and Edward Elgar).

Inoguchi, T. (2001) *Global Change: A Japanese Perspective* (Houndmills, Basingstoke, Hampshire; New York: Palgrave Macmillan).

International Centre for Trade and Sustainable Development (2005) "Unesco Overwhelmingly Approves Cultural Diversity Treaty." http://ictsd.org/i/news/bridgesweekly/6211/

International Commission on Intervention and State Sovereignty (2001) *The Responsibility to Protect: Report of the International Commission on Intervention and State Sovereignty* (Ottawa: International Development Research Council).

Ishii, A. (2011) "Seibutsu Tayosei ni okeru Kagaku to Seiji." In *Seibutsu Tayosei wo meguru Kokusai Kankei*, edited by K. Mori (Tokyo: Daigaku Kyoiku Shuppan) (in Japanese)

Japan House of Representatives (1998) Foreign Affairs Committee Meeting, September 18.

Japan House of Representatives (1998) Peace and Security Committee Meeting, March 12.

Japan Times (2010a) *COP 10 End Near: Unified Political Will for Biodiversity Eludes*, by E. Johnston, October 27.

Japan Times (2010b) *COP 10 Goes Extra Mile for a Deal*, by E. Johnston and S. Kamiya, October 30.

Japan Times (2010c) *COP 10 Signs Off On Protocol*, by E. Johnston and S.Kamiya, October 31.

Johnston, A. I. (2001) "Treating International Institutions as Social Environments." *International Studies Quarterly*, 45 (4), 487–515.

Johnston, A. I. (2008) *Social States: China in International Institutions, 1980–2000* (Princeton, NJ: Princeton University Press).

Jurado, Elena. 2006. "Signing Duties in the Global System of Human Rights: The Role of the European Union." In *A Responsible Europe? Ethical Foundations of EU External Affairs*, edited by H. Mayer and H. Vogt, 119–39 (Basingstoke: Palgrave Macmillan).

Kagan, R. (2003) *Of Paradise and Power: America and Europe in the New World Order* (New York: Alfred A. Knopf; Distributed by Random House).

Kawaguchi, Y. (2002) Statement by Minister for Foreign Affairs Yoriko Kawaguchi concerning the Entry into Force of the Rome Statute of the International Criminal Court (Japan: Ministry of Foreign Affairs).

Kawashima, Y. (2003) *Japanese Foreign Policy at the Crossroads Challenges and Options for the Twenty-First Century* (Washington, DC: Brookings Institution Press).

Keating, T. (2002) *Canada and World Order: The Multilateralist Tradition in Canadian Foreign Policy*, 2nd edn (Toronto: Oxford University Press).

Keating, T. and P. Gecelovsky (2001) "Liberal Internationalism for Conservatives: The Good Governance Initiative." In *Diplomatic Departures: The Conservative Era in Canadian Foreign Policy, 1984–1993*, edited by N. Michaud and K. R. Nossal (Vancouver: University of British Columbia Press).

Keck, M. E. and K. Sikkink (1998) *Activists Beyond Borders: Advocacy Networks in International Politics* (Ithaca, NY: Cornell University Press).

Kelemen, R. D. (2010) "Globalizing European Union Environmental Policy," *Journal of European Public Policy*, 17 (3), 335–49.

Kelemen, R. D. and D. Vogel (2010) "Trading Places: The Role of the United States and the European Union in International Environmental Politics," *Comparative Political Studies*, 43 (4), 427–56.

Kelley, J. (2007) "Who Keeps International Commitments and Why? The International Criminal Court and Bilateral Nonsurrender Agreements," *American Political Science Review*, 101 (3), 573–89.

Kenzo, O. (Representative of Japan to the UN) (2005) Statement on the Informal Thematic Consultation of Cluster III, 19 April. Accessed at www.mofa.go.jp/announce/speech/un2005/un0504-3.html on February 16, 2007.

Keohane, R. (1984) *After Hegemony: Cooperation and Discord in the World Political Economy* (Princeton: Princeton University Press).

Kinnvall, C. and P. Nesbitt-Larking (2011) *The Political Psychology of Globalization: Muslims in the West* (Oxford: Oxford University Press).

Kioko, B. (2003) "The Right of Intervention under the African Union's Constitutive Act: From Non-Interference to Non-Intervention," *International Review of the Red Cross*, 85 (852), 807–25.

Kitagawa, Y. (2005) "Mine Ban Policy of the Japanese Government 1994–2004," unpublished paper presented at a workshop, "Caught between Realism and Institutionalism," University of British Columbia, Vancouver, Canada.

Klotz, A. (1995) *Norms in International Relations: The Struggle Against Apartheid* (Ithaca, NY: Cornell University Press).

Knight, W. A. (2005) "Plurilateral Multilateralism: Canada's Emerging International Policy?" In *Canada Among Nations 2005: Split Images*, edited by A. F. Cooper and D. Rowlands (Montreal and Kingston: McGill-Queen's University Press).

Krasner, S. D. (1982) "Structural Causes and Regime Consequences: Regime as Intervening Variables," *International Organization*, 36 (2), 185–205.

Krieger, H. (ed.) (2001) *The Kosovo Conflict and International Law* (Cambridge: Cambridge University Press).

Krimsky, S. (2000) *Hormonal Chaos: The Scientific and Social Origins of the Environmental Endocrine Hypothesis* (Baltimore: Johns Hopkins University Press).

Kuhnlein, H. V., L. H. M. Chan, G. Egeland, and O. Receveur (2003) "Canadian Arctic Indigenous Peoples, Traditional Food Systems, and POPs." In *Northern Lights against POPs: Combatting Toxic Threats in the Arctic*, edited by D. L. Downie and T. Fenge (Montreal: McGill-Queens University Press).

Kummer, K. (1995) *International Management of Hazardous Wastes: The Basel Convention and Related Legal Rules* (Oxford: Clarendon Press).

Kuratsune, M., H. Yoshimura, Y. Hori, M. Okumura, and Y. Masuda (eds) (1996) *Yusho: A Human Disaster Caused by PCBs and Related Compounds* (Fukuoka: Kyushu University Press).

Laïdi, Z. (2005) *La Norme Sans La Force: L'énigme De La Puissance Européenne* (Paris: Presses de la fondation nationale de science politique).

Laïdi, Z. (2010) *Le Monde Selon Obama* (Paris: Stock).

Landmine Monitor, online at www.hrw.org/hrw/reports/1999/landmine.

Laux, C. and C. Leuz (2010) "Did Fair-Value Accounting Contribute to the Financial Crisis?" *Journal of Economic Perspectives*, 24 (1), 93–118.

Lenarcic, D. A. (1998) *Knight-Errant: Canada and the Crusade to Ban Anti-Personnel Land Mines* (Toronto: Irwin).

Leonard, E. K. (2005) *The Onset of Global Governance: International Relations Theory and the International Criminal Court* (Aldershot, England: Ashgate Publishing Limited).

Levy, F. and P. Temin (2007) "Inequality and Institutions in 20th Century America," *Massachusetts Institute of Technology Department of Economics Working Paper Series*, Working Paper 07–17, May 1, 2007.

Li, S. (2010) "Does Mandatory Adoption of International Financial Reporting Standards in the European Union Reduce the Cost of Equity Capital?" *Accounting Review*, 85 (2), 607–36.

Liftin, K. (1998) *The Greening of Sovereignty in World Politics* (Cambridge, MA: MIT Press).

Lightfoot, S. and J. Burchell (2004) "Green Hope or Greenwash? The Actions of the European Union at the World Summit on Sustainable Development." *Global Environmental Change* 14 (4), 337–44.

Lightfoot, S. and J. Burchell (2005) "The European Union and the World Summit on Sustainable Development: Normative Power Europe in Action?" *Journal of Common Market Studies* 43 (1), 75–95.

Long, D. (2002) "The European Union and the Ottawa Process to Ban Landmines," *Journal of European Public Policy*, 9(3), 429–46.

Lönngren, R. (1992) *International Approaches to Chemicals Control: A Historical Overview* (Sweden: The National Chemicals Inspectorate).

Lucarelli, S., and R. Menotti (2006) "The Use of Force as Coercive Intervention: The Conflicting Values of the European Union's External Action." In *Values and Principles in European Union Foreign Policy*, edited by S. Lucarelli and I. Manners, 147–63 (London: Routledge).

Mackenzie, L. (2003) "Making Foreign Policy on the Fly," *National Post*, February 17, A14.

Malloch-Brown, M. (2011) *The Unfinished Global Revolution: The Limits of Nations and the Pursuit of a New Politics* (London: Allen Lane).

Malone, D. and Y. F. Khong (2003) *Unilateralism and U.S. Foreign Policy: International Perspectives* (Boulder, CO: Lynne Rienner Publishers).

Mandelbaum, M. (2010) *The Frugal Superpower: America's Global Leadership in a Cash-Strapped Era* (New York: PublicAffairs).

Manners, I. (2002) "Normative Power Europe: A Contradiction in Terms?" *Journal of Common Market Studies*, 40 (2), 235–58.

Manners, I. (2010) "Global Europa: Mythology of the European Union in World Politics," *Journal of Common Market Studies* 48 (1), 67–87.

Manners, I. and R. Whitman (2003) "The 'Difference Engine': Constructing and Representing the International Identity of the European Union." *Journal of European Public Policy* 10 (3), 380–404.

Manners, I. (2000a) *Normative Power Europe: A Contradiction in Terms?* Copenhagen Peace Research Institute, Working Paper 38/2000.

Manners, I. (2000b) *Substance and Symbolism: An Anatomy of Cooperation in the New Europe* (Aldershot: Ashgate).

Manners, I. (2006a) "The Constitutive Nature of Values, Images and Principles in the European Union." In *Values and Principles in European Union Foreign Policy*, edited by Sonia Lucarelli and Ian Manners, 19–41 (London: Routledge).

Manners, I. (2006b) "European Union 'Normative Power' and the Security Challenge." *European Security* 15 (4), 405–21.

Manners, I. (2007) "The Normative Power of the European Union in a Globalised World." In *European Union Foreign Policy in a Globalised World: Normative Power and Social Preferences*, edited by Z. Laïdi (London: Routledge).

Manners, I. (2008) "The Normative Ethics of the European Union." *International Affairs* 84 (1), 65–80.

Manners, I. (2009a) "The EU's International Promotion of the Rights of the Child," *The European Union and the Social Dimension of Globalization: How the EU influences the World*, edited by J. Orbie and L. Tortell, 228–41 (London: Routledge).

Manners, I. (2009b)"The Social Dimension of EU Trade Policies: Reflections from a Normative Power Perspective." In *The Social Dimension of European Union External Trade Relations*, edited by J. Orbie and L. Tortell. Special Issue of *European Foreign Affairs Review* 14 (5), 785–803.

Manners, I. (2010) "Global Europa: the Mythology of the European Union in World Politics." In *Mythologizing the European Union*, edited by Vincent Della Sala, Special Issue of *Journal of Common Market Studies*, 48 (1), 67–87.

Manners, I. (2011) "The European Union's Normative Power: Critical Perspectives and Perspectives on the Critical." *Normative Power Europe: Empirical and Theoretical Perspectives*, edited by Richard Whitman, 226–47 (Basingstoke: Palgrave Macmillan).

Manners, I. (forthcoming) "European Communion: Political Theory of European Union." *Journal of European Public Policy* 20 .

Martin, Mary (2011) "Human Security and the Search for a Normative Narrative." *Normative Power Europe: Empirical and Theoretical Perspectives*, edited by Richard Whitman, 187–209 (Basingstoke: Palgrave Macmillan).

Mattleart, A. (2005) "Cultural Diversity Belongs to Us All," *Le Monde diplomatique*, November, http://mondediplo.com/2005/11/15unesco

Mayama, A. (2004) "Japan's New Emergency Legislation and International Humanitarian Law," *Japanese Annual of International Law*, 47, 69–95.

McAdam, D., S. G. Tarrow, and C. Tilly (2001) *Dynamics of Contention* (New York: Cambridge University Press).

McChesney, R. (2000) *Rich Media, Poor Democracy: Communication Politics in Dubious Times* (New York: The New Press).

McCormick, J. (2001) *Environmental Policy in the European Union* (New York: Palgrave Macmillan).

McCormick, J. (2007) *The European Superpower* (Houndmills, Basingstoke, Hampshire; New York, NY: Palgrave Macmillan).

McRae, R. and D. Hubert (eds) (2001) *Human Security and the New Diplomacy* (Montreal and Kingston: McGill-Queen's University Press).

Mégret, F. (2002) "The Politics of International Justice," *European Journal of International Law*, 13 (5), 1261–84.

Meyer, J. W., J. Boli, J. Boli, G. M. Thomas, and F. O. Ramirez (1997) "World Society and the Nation State," *American Journal of Sociology* 103 (1), 144–81.

Michalski, K. (ed.) (2006) *What Holds Europe Together?* (Budapest: Central European University Press).

Michaud, N. and K. R. Nossal (2001) "The Conservative Era in Canadian Foreign Policy, 1984–93." In *Diplomatic Departures: The Conservative Era in Canadian Foreign Policy, 1984–1993*, edited by N. Michaud and K. R. Nossal (Vancouver: University of British Columbia Press).

Miyaoka, I. (2004) "Japan's Conciliation with the United States on Climate Change Negotiations," *International Relations of the Asia-Pacific*, 4 (1), 73–96.

Mofson, P. (1996) *The Behavior of States in an International Wildlife Conservation Regime: Japan, Zimbabwe and CITES*. Ph.D. Dissertation Submitted to the Faculty of the Graduate School of the University of Maryland.

Munton, D. (2002–03) "Whither Internationalism?" *International Journal*, 58 (1), 155–80.

Munton, D. and T. Keating (2001) "Internationalism and the Canadian Public," *Canadian Journal of Political Science*, 34 (September), 517–49.

Murata, K. (2003) "Japan." In *Humanitarian Intervention: the Evolving Asian Debate*, edited by K. Watanabe (Tokyo: Japan Center for International Exchange).

Musitelli, J. (2006) "The Convention on Cultural Diversity: Anatomy of a Diplomatic Success Story," http://www.diplomatie.gouv.fr/fr/IMG/pdf/0701-MUSITELLI-EN.pdf

Neil, G. (2003) "Arts and Culture in World Trade: Promoting Cultural Diversity." In *Civilizing Globalization: A Survival Guide*, edited by R. Sanbrook (Albany, NY: State University of New York Press).

Newell, P. (2000) *Climate for Change: Non-State Actors and the Global Politics of the Greenhouse* (Cambirdge: Cambridge University Press).

Newell, P. and R. MacKenzie (2000) "The Cartagena Protocol on Biosafety: Legal and Political Dimensions," *Global Environmental Change*, 10, 313–17.

NHK Documentary (2004) "Rebuilding Iraq: Challenge of the UN." Aired on April 18, in Japan. Directed by Daisaku Higashi.

Nicolaisen, D. (2005) "A Securities Regulator Looks at Convergence," *Northwestern Journal of International Law and Business*, 25 (3), 661–86.

Noble, J. (2003) "Canada-US Relations in the Post-Iraq-War Era: Stop the Drift towards Irrelevance," *Policy Options*, May, 19–24.

North, D. C. (1990) *Institutions, Institutional Change and Economic Performance* (Cambridge; New York: Cambridge University Press).

Nossal, K. R. (1998–99) "Pinchpenny Diplomacy: The Decline of 'Good International Citizenship' in Canadian Foreign Policy," *International Journal*, 54 (1), 88–105.

Nossal, K. R. (1998) "Foreign Policy for Wimps," *Ottawa Citizen*, April 23, A19.

Nossal, K. R. (2000) "Mission Diplomacy and the 'Cult of the Initiative' in Canadian Foreign Policy," *Worthwhile Initiatives? Canadian Mission-Oriented Diplomacy*, edited by A. F. Cooper and G. Hayes (Toronto: Irwin Publishing).

Nossal, K. R. (2005a) "The Responsibility to be Honest." In *In the National Interest? Assessing Canada's International Policy Statement*, edited by D. J. Bercuson and D. Stairs (Calgary: Canadian Foreign Affairs and Defence Institute).

Nossal, K. R. (2005b) "Ear Candy: Canadian Policy toward Humanitarian Intervention and Atrocity Crimes in Darfur," *International Journal*, 60 (4), 1017–32.

Nossal, K. R. (2007a) "Defense Policy and the Atmospherics of Canada-U.S. Relations: The Case of the Harper Conservatives," *American Review of Canadian Studies*, 37 (1), 23–34.

Nossal, K. R. (2007b) "Canada: An On-Going Act of Anti-Americanism" in B. O'Connor (ed.) *Anti-Americanism: History, Causes, and Themes*, vol. 3: *Comparative Perspectives* (Oxford: Greenwood World Publishing).

Nossal, K. R. (2013) "The Liberal Past in the Conservative Present: Internationalism in the Harper Era," in Heather A. Smith and Claire Turenne Sjolander (eds) *Canada in the World: Internationalism in Contemporary Canadian Foreign Policy* (Toronto: Oxford University Press).

Nossal, K.R. and S. Roussel (2000) "Canada and the Kosovo War: The Happy Follower" in P. Martin and M. R. Brawley (eds), *Alliance Politics, Kosovo, and NATO's War: Allied Force or Forced Allies?* (New York: Palgrave Macmillan).

NUPI (Norwegian Institute of International Affairs) (2006) *A Fork in the Road or a Roundabout? A Narrative of the UN Reform Process 2003–2005* (Oslo: NUPI).

Nye, Jr, J. S. (1990) *Bound to Lead: The Changing Nature of American Power* (New York: Basic Books).

Oberthur, S. and T. Gehring (2004) "Reforming International Environmental Governance: An Institutionalist Critique of the Proposal for a World Environment Organisation," *International Environmental Agreements*, 4 (4), 359–81.

(OECD) Organisation for Economic Co-operation and Development (2002) *Environmental Performance Reviews Japan* (Paris: OECD).

Ortega, M. (ed.) (2005) *The European Union and the United Nations: Partners in Effective Multilateralism*. Chaillot Paper 78 (Brussels: EU Security Studies).

Osa, Y. (1998) "Keynote Report: NGO Tokyo Conference '98 on Anti-Personnel Landmines," on file with author.

Owada, H. (2004) "The Creation of the International Criminal Court: A Critical Analysis." In *Dynamics of International Law in the New millennium*, edited by R. K. Dixit and C. Jayaraj (Delhi: Manak).

Owens, H. and B. Arneil (1999) "The Human Security Paradigm Shift: A New Lens on Canadian Foreign Policy," *Canadian Foreign Policy*, 7 (1), 1–12.

Pace, W. R. and M. Thieroff (1999) "Participation of Non-Governmental Organizations." In *The International Criminal Court: The Making of the Rome Statute – Issues, Negotiations, Results*, edited by R. S. Lee (The Hague: Kluwer Law International).

Paris, R. (2001) "Human Security: Paradigm Shift or Hot Air?" *International Security*, 26 (2), 87–102.

Paris, R. (2004) *At War's End: Building Peace after Civil Conflict* (Cambridge: Cambridge University Press).

Parliament and the Commission (2006/C 46/01) *Official Journal of the European Union*, February 24.

Pearson, Z. (2006) "Non-Governmental Organizations and the International Criminal Court: Changing Landscapes of International Law," *Cornell International Law Journal*, 39 (2), 243–84.

Peck, C. (1998) *Sustainable Peace: The Role of the UN and Regional Organizations in Preventing Conflict* (Lanham, MD: Rowman & Littlefield).

Pei, M. and S. Kasper (2003) "Lessons from the Past: The American Record on Nation Building." *Policy Brief for Carnegie Endowment for International Peace.* Issued on May 24.

Pempel, T. J. (1998) *Regime Shift: Comparative Dynamics of the Japanese Political Economy* (Ithaca, NY: Cornell University Press).

Peng, Y. (1993) "The Earth Summit and Japan's Initiative in Environmental Diplomacy," *Futures*, 25 (4), 379–91.

Perle, R. (2003) "Thank God for the Death of the UN," *Guardian*, March 21.

Pető, A. and I. Manners (2006) "The European Union and the Value of Gender Equality." In *Values and Principles in European Union Foreign Policy*, edited by Sonia Lucarelli and Ian Manners, 97–113 (London: Routledge).

Piketty, T. and E. Saez (2006) "The Evolution of Top Incomes: A Historical and International Perspective," *National Bureau of Economic Research Working Paper*, No. 11955.

Pitty, R. (2006) "Political Constraints upon the International Criminal Court." In *The Challenge of Conflict: International Law Responds*, edited by U. Dolgopol and J. Gardam (Leiden: Martinus Nijhoff Publishers).

Poelzer, G. (2002) "Aboriginal Peoples and Environmental Policy in Canada: No Longer at the Margins." In *Canadian Environmental Policy: Context and Cases*, edited by D. L. VanNijnatten and R. Boardman (Oxford: Oxford University Press).

Politis, Y. (1999) "The Regulation of the Invisible Enemy: The International Community's Response to Land Mine Proliferation," *Boston College International & Comparative Law Review*, 22 (2), 465–93.

Posner, E. (2006) "The New Transatlantic Regulatory Relations in Financial Services," *First Annual GARNET Conference: Global Financial and Monetary Governance, the EU and Emerging Market Economies*, September, Amsterdam.

Posner, E. and N. Véron (2010) "The EU and Financial Regulation: Power without Purpose?" *Journal of European Public Policy*, 17 (3), 400–15.

Pratt, C. (1990) *Middle Power Internationalism: The North-South Dimension* (Kingston [Ont.]; Buffalo: McGill-Queen's University Press).

Price, R. (1998) "Reversing the Gun Sights: Transnational Civil Society Targets Land Mines," *International Organization*, 52 (3), 613–44.

Price, R. (2003) "Transnational Civil Society and Advocacy in World Politics," *World Politics*, 55, 579–606.

Price, R. (2004) "Emerging Customary Norms and Antipersonnel Landmines." In *The Politics of International Law*, edited by C. Reus-Smit (Cambridge: Cambridge University Press).

Rahman, R. (Malaysian Representative to the UN and Chairman of the Coordinating Bureau of the Non-Aligned Movement) (2005) Statement on the Draft Outcome Document of the High-Level Plenary Meeting of the General Assembly, June 21. Accessed at www.un.int/malaysia/NAM/nam210605.html on January 22, 2007.

Remacle, E. (2005) "The European Security Strategy and Its Impact on Europe-Japan Relations." In *Japan and Enlarged Europe: Partners in Global Governance*, edited by Takako Ueta and Eric Remacle, 35–46 (Brussels: P.I.E.-Peter Lang).

Rempel, R. (2006) *Dreamland: How Canada's Pretend Foreign Policy Has Undermined Sovereignty* (Montreal and Kingston: McGill-Queen's University Press for Breakout Educational Network).

Reus-Smit, C. (2004) *The Politics of International Law* (Cambridge; New York: Cambridge University Press).

Richmond, O., A. Björkdahl, and S. Kappler. 2011. "The Emerging EU Peacebuilding Framework: Confirming Or Transcending Liberal Peacebuilding?" *Cambridge Review of International Studies* 24 (3), 449–69.

Risse, T., S. C. Ropp, and K. Sikkink (eds) (1999) *The Power of Human Rights: International Norms and Domestic Change*. In Vol. 66, *Cambridge Studies in International Relations*, edited by S. Smith (Cambridge: Cambridge University Press).

Roberts, S. (1998) "No Exception, No Reservations, No Loopholes: The Campaign for the 1997 Convention on the Prohibition of the Development, Production, Stockpiling, Transfer and Use of Anti-Personnel Mines and on Their Destruction," *Colorado Journal of International Law and Policy*, 9.

Robinson, D. (2001) "The International Criminal Court." In *Human Security and the New Diplomacy*, edited by R. McRae and D. Hubert (eds) (Montreal and Kingston: McGill-Queen's University Press).

Rodrik, D. (2011) *The Globalization Paradox: Democracy and the Future of the World Economy* (New York: W. W. Norton & Co.).

Roper, M. (1996) "Seduction and Succession: Circuits of Homosocial Desire in Management." In *Men as Managers, Managers as Men*, edited by D. Collinson and J. Hearn, 210–26 (London: Sage).

Ross, J. (2001) "Is Canada's Human Security Policy Really the 'Axworthy' Doctrine?" *Canadian Foreign Policy*, 8 (2), 75–93.

Ruby, M. (ed.) (2010) *Le Pari D'un Gouvernement Mondial Géopolitique Du Monde Contemporaine* (Paris: A2C médias).

Rudolf, P. (2000) "Germany and the Kosovo Conflict." In *Alliance Politics, Kosovo, and NATO's War: Allied Force or Forced Allies?* Edited by P. Martin and M. R. Brawley (New York: Palgrave Macmillan).

Rudolph, C. (2001) "Constructing an Atrocities Regime: The Politics of War Crimes Tribunals," *International Organization*, 55 (3), 655–91.

Rutherford, K. (2001) "The Evolving Arms Control Agenda: Implications of the Role of NGOs in Banning Antipersonnel Landmines," *World Politics*, 53, 74–114.

Sakaguchi, I. (2006) *Global Environmental Governance and the Process of Regime Development: CITES, NGOs and States* (Tokyo: Kokusai Shoin) (in Japanese).

Sakaguchi, I. (2008a) "The Transformation of IWC Regime: Strategies of Activist NGOs and the Process of Norm Acceptance." *Kokusai Seiji*, 153, 42–57 (in Japanese).

Sakaguchi, I. (2008b) "Yasei Seibutsu no Hozen to Kokusai Seido Keisei." In *Yasei to Kankyo*, edited by K. Iketani and Y. Hayashi (Tokyo: Iwanami Shoten) (in Japanese).

Sakaguchi, I. (2011) "Nihon No Kankyo Gaiko (Environmental Diplomacy of Japan: Middle Power, NGOs, and Local Governments)," *Kokusai Seiji* 166, 26–41.

Sands, C. (2001) "A Chance to End Culture Trade Conflict between Canada and the United States," *American Review of Canadian Studies*, 31 (3), 483–99.

Sands, P. (2003) *From Nuremberg to the Hague: The Future of International Criminal Justice* (Cambridge; New York: Cambridge University Press).

Sawhill, Isabel and John Morton (2007) Economic Mobility: Is the American Dream Alive and Well? *Economic Mobility Project Report*, The Brookings Institution and the Pew Charitable Trusts.

Scheipers, S. and D. Sicurelli (2007) "Normative Power Europe: A Credible Utopia?" *Journal of Common Market Studies*, 45 (2): 435–57.

Schiff, B. (2008) *Building the International Criminal Court* (Cambridge: Cambridge University Press).

Schreurs, M. A. and Y. Tiberghien (2007) "Multi-Level Reinforcement: Explaining European Union Leadership in Climate Change Mitigation," *Global Environmental Politics*, 7 (4), 19–46.

Schreurs, M. A., H. Selin, and S. D. VanDeveer (eds) (2009) *Transatlantic Environment and Energy Politics: Comparative and International Perspectives* (Aldershot: Ashgate).

Schwanen, D. (2006) "Canada and the Kyoto Protocol: When Reality Sets In." In *Canada Among Nations 2006: Minorities and Priorities*, edited by A. F. Cooper and D. Rowlands (Montreal and Kingston: McGill Queen's University Press).

Schwartz, S. (2003) "U.N. Go Home," *Weekly Standard*, April 14.

Schwartz, F. J. and Susan J. P. (2003) *The State of Civil Society in Japan* (Cambridge; New York: Cambridge University Press).

(SEC) Securities and Exchange Commission (2003). *Study pursuant to section 108(d) of the Sarbanes-Oxley Act of 2002 on the adoption by the United States Financial Reporting System of a principles-based accounting system*, report dated 25 July.

Selin, H. (2003) "Regional POPs Policy: The UNECE/CLRTAP POPs Agreement." In *Northern Lights against POPs: Combatting Toxic Threats in the Arctic*, edited by D. L. Downie and T. Fenge (Montreal: McGill-Queens University Press).

Selin, H. (2007) "Coalition Politics and Chemicals Management in a Regulatory Ambitious Europe," *Global Environmental Politics*, 7 (3), 63–93.

Selin, H. (2010) *Global Governance of Hazardous Chemicals: Challenges of Multilevel Management* (Cambridge: MIT Press).

Selin, H. and N. Eckley (2003) "Science, Politics, and Persistent Organic Pollutants: Scientific Assessments and Their Role in International Environmental Negotiations," *International Environmental Agreements: Politics, Law and Economics*, 3 (1), 17–42.

Selin, H. and N. Selin (2008) "Indigenous Peoples in International Environmental Cooperation: Arctic Management of Hazardous Substances," *Review of European Community & International Environmental Law*, 17 (1), 72–83.

Selin, H. and S. D. VanDeveer (2004) "Baltic Sea Hazardous Substances Management: Results and Challenges," *Ambio*, 33 (3), 153–60.

Selin, H. and S. D. VanDeveer (2006) "Raising Global Standards: Hazardous Substances and E-waste Management in the European Union," *Environment*, 48 (10), 6–18.

Sens, A. (2004) "From Peace-keeping to Peace-building: The UN and the Challenge of Intrastate War." In *The UN and Global Security*, edited by R. Price and M. Zacher (New York: Palgrave Macmillan).

Sewall, S. B. and C. Kaysen (eds) (2000) *The United States and the International Criminal Court: National Security and International Law* (Lanham, MD: Rowman & Littlefield Publishers, Inc).

Sharp, R. (1997) "The African Elephant: Conservation and CITES." *Oryx*, 31 (2), 111–19.

Shearer, R. and S.-L. Han (2003) "Canadian Research and POPs: The Northern Contaminants Program." In *Northern Lights against POPs: Combatting Toxic Threats in the Arctic*, edited by D. L. Downie and T. Fenge (Montreal: McGill-Queens University Press).

Shinoda, H. (2000) "The Politics of Legitimacy in International Relations: A Critical Examination of NATO's Intervention in Kosovo," *Alternatives*, 25 (4), 515–36.

Siebert, H. (2009) *Rules for the Global Economy* (Princeton, NJ: Princeton University Press).

Simmons, B. A. and A. Danner (2010) "Credible Commitments and the International Criminal Court," *International Organization*, 64, 225–56.

Slaughter, A. (2004) *A New World Order* (Princeton: Princeton University Press).

Soeya, Y. (2005) *Japan's "Middle Power" Diplomacy: Decisions and Initiatives of Postwar Japan (Nihon No "Midoru Pawa" Gaiko: Sengo Nihon No Sentaku to Kousou)* (Tokyo: Chikuma Shinsho).

Solana, J. (2003) A Secure Europe in a Better World: The European Security Strategy. Approved by the European Council held in Brussels on December 12, 2003 and drafted under the responsibilities of the EU High Representative Javier Solana.

Stairs, D. (2001) "Canada in the 1990s: Speak Loudly and Carry a Bent Twig," *Policy Options*, January/February, 43–49.

Stairs, D. (2003a) "Myths, Morals, and Reality in Canadian Foreign Policy," *International Journal*, 58 (2), 239–56.

Stairs, D. (2003b) "Challenges and Opportunities for Canadian Foreign Policy in the Paul Martin Era," *International Journal*, 58 (4), 481–506.

Stairs, D., D. J. Bercuson, M. Entwistle, J.L. Granatstein, K. R. Nossal, and G. S. Smith (2003) *In the National Interest: Canadian Foreign Policy in an Insecure World* (Calgary: Canadian Foreign Affairs and Defence Institute).

Steinar, A. and L. H. Gulbrandsen (2003) "The Role of Green NGOs in Promoting Climate Compliance," FNI Report, 4 (Lysaker: Fridtjof Nansen Institute).

Stjernø, S. (2005) *Solidarity in Europe: The History of an Idea* (Cambridge: Cambridge University Press).

Stoett, P. (1999) *Human and Global Security: An Exploration of Terms* (Toronto: University of Toronto Press).

Strange, S. (1971) "International Economic and International Relations: A Case of Mutual Neglect." *International Affairs*, 46 (2): 304–15.

Strong, M. (2000) *Where on Earth are We Going?* (New York: Texere).

Struett, M. J. (2005) *The Politics of Constructing the International Criminal Court.* PhD thesis, International Relations, University of California, Irvine, CA.

Struett, M. J. (2008) *The Politics of Constructing the International Criminal Court: NGOs, Discourse, and Agency* (London: Palgrave Macmillan).

Struett, M. J. and S. A. Weldon (2006) "Explaining State Decisions to Ratify the International Criminal Court Treaty," Paper presented at American Political Science Association Annual Meeting, at Philadelphia PA.

Tardy, T. (2005) "EU-UN Cooperation in Peacekeeping: A Promising Relationship in a Constrained Environment." In *The European Union and the United Nations*, edited by M. Ortega (Institute for Security Studies: Chaillot Paper). Available online at: www.iss-eu.org

Tarrow, S. G. (1998) *Power in Movement: Social Movements and Contentious Politics* (Cambridge, UK; New York: Cambridge University Press).

Tarrow, S. G. (2005) *The New Transnational Activism* (Cambridge, UK; New York: Cambridge University Press).

Taylor, P. M. (Undated) "British Public Opinion, the Media, and International Crises," Unpublished paper available at ics.leeds.ac.uk/papers/vp01.cfm?outfi t=pmt&folder=4&paper=229. Accessed January 24, 2007.

Telo, M. (2005) "The Concept of 'Civilian Power' in the Light of the Constitutional Evolution of the European Union." In *Japan and Enlarged Europe: Partners in Global Governance*, edited by T. Ueta and E. Remacle, 47–56 (Brussels: P.I.E.-Peter Lang).

Thakur, R. (2006) *The United Nations, Peace and Security: From Collective Security to Responsibility to Protect* (New York: Cambridge University Press).

Third World Network (2010a) "Rocky Road Still Ahead for ABS Protocol," http://www.twnside.org.sg/title2/intellectual_property/info.service/2010/ipr. info.100401.htm, date accessed February 20, 2012.

Third World Network (2010b) "Biodiversity Convention Adopts Landmark Decisions," http://www.twnside.org.sg/title2/intellectual_property/info. service/2010/ipr.info.101103.htm, date accessed February 20, 2012.

Thrift, C., K. Wilkening, H. Myers, and R. Raina (2009) "The Influence of Science on Canada's Foreign Policy on Persistent Organic Pollutants (1985–2001)," *Environmental Science & Policy*, 12 (7), 981–93.

Tiberghien, Y. (2007) *Entrepreneurial States. Reforming Corporate Governance in France, Japan, and Korea* (Ithaca, NY: Cornell University Press).

Tiberghien, Y. (2010) "Regime Change and Green Shift in Kyoto." In *Green Tigers. The Politics and Policy of Climate Change in Northeast Asian Democracies*, edited by B. Wakefield (Washington, DC: Woodrow Wilson International Centre Scholars).

Tiberghien, Y. (2012) *L'asie Et Le Futur Du Monde* (Paris: Presses de Sciences Po).

Tiberghien, Y. and M. A. Schreurs (2007) "High Noon in Japan: Embedded Symbolism and Post-2001 Kyoto Protocol Politics," *Global Environmental Politics* 7 (4), 70–91.

Tiberghien, Y. and M. A. Schreurs (2010) "High Noon in Japan: Embedded Symbolism and Post-2001 Kyoto Protocol Politics." In *Global Commons, Domestic Decisions: The Comparative Politics of Climate Change*, edited by K. Harrison and L. Sundstrom, 139–68 (Boston: MIT Press).

Tomlin, B. W. (1998) "On a Fast-Track to a Ban: The Canadian Policy Process," *Canadian Foreign Policy*, 5 (3), 3–24.

UNEP/CBD/WG-ABS/9/INF/22 (2010) *Draft Protocol: Indigenous Peoples' Objections to the Current text – A Call for Justice and Solidarity*, a document distributed during COP10 meeting in Nagoya.

UNGA (United Nations General Assembly) (1999a) Verbatim record of the 4th Plenary Meeting of the Fifty-fourth Session of the General Assembly. New York, September 20. United Nations document A/54/PV.4.

UNGA (1999b) Verbatim record of the 5th Plenary Meeting of the Fifty-fourth Session of the General Assembly. New York, September 20.

UNGA (1999c) Verbatim record of the 6th Plenary Meeting of the Fifty-fourth Session of the General Assembly. New York, September 21.

UNGA (1999d) Verbatim record of the 7th Plenary Meeting of the Fifty-fourth Session of the General Assembly. New York, September 21.

UNGA (1999e) Verbatim record of the 8th Plenary Meeting of the Fifty-fourth Session of the General Assembly. New York, September 22.

UNGA (1999f) Verbatim record of the 10th Plenary Meeting of the Fifty-fourth Session of the General Assembly. New York, September 23.

UNGA (1999g) Verbatim record of the 35th Plenary Meeting of the Fifty-fourth Session of the General Assembly. New York, October 20.

UNGA (2005) *Resolution 60/1 2005 World Summit Outcome*. October 24.

UNGA (2009) *Implementing the Responsibility to Protect – Report of the Secretary-General*. January 12.

Union for Ethical Biotrade (2010) *Nagoya Protocol on Access and Benefit Sharing. Technical Brief*, document distributed via email to subscribers of IISD mail list on biodiversity, www ethicalbiotrade.org.

United Nations (2002) *Report of the World Summit on Sustainable Development*. (Johannesburg, South Africa, August 26–September 4).

UNSC (United Nations Security Council) (2006) *Resolution 1674*, April 28.

UNSC (2011a) *Resolution 1970*. February 26.

UNSC (2011b) *Resolution 1973*. March 17.

UNSC (2011c) *Resolution 1975*. March 30.

van den Hoven, A. (2006) "European Union Regulatory Capitalism and Multilateral Trade Negotiations." In *Values and Principles in European Union Foreign Policy*, edited by S. Lucarelli and I. Manners, 185–200. London: Routledge.

Véron, N. (2007) *The Global Accounting Experiment* (Brussels: Bruegel Blueprint Series).

Véron, N. (2011) "Keeping the Promise of Global Accounting Standards," *Bruegel Policy Brief 2011/05*.

Véron, N., M. Autret, and A. Galichon (2006) *Smoke & Mirrors, Inc.: Accounting for Capitalism* (Ithaca, NY: Cornell University Press).

Vogel, D. (1997) *Trading Up: Consumer and Environmental Regulation in a Global Economy* (Cambridge: Harvard University Press).

Vogel, D. (2003) "The Hare and the Tortoise Revisited: The New Politics of Consumer and Environmental Regulation in Europe," *British Journal of Political Science* 33 (4), 557–580.

Vogler, J. (2005) "The European Contribution to Global Environmental Governance." *International Affairs* 81 (4): 835–50.

Wallace, H. (1971) "The Impact of the European Communities on National Policy-making." *Government and Opposition*, 6, 520–38.

Wallace, H. (1973) *National Governments and the European Communities* (London: Chatham House/PEP).

Walt, S. M. (2005) *Taming American Power: The Global Response to U.S. Primacy* (New York: W. W. Norton).

Wapner, P. (1996) *Politics Beyond the State: Environmental Activism and World Civic Politics* (Albany, NY: State University of New York Press).

Warmington, V. and C. Tuttle (1998) "The Canadian Ban." In *To Walk Without Fear: The Global Campaign to Ban Landmines*, edited by M. A. Cameron, R. J. Lawson, and B. W. Tomlin (New York: Oxford University Press).

Watt-Cloutier, S. (2003) "The Inuit Journey Towards a POPs-Free World." In *Northern Lights against POPs: Combatting Toxic Threats in the Arctic*, edited by D. L. Downie and T. Fenge (Montreal: McGill-Queens University Press).

Weale, A., G. Pridham, M. Cini, D. Konstadakopulos, M. Porter, and B. Flynn (2003) *Environmental Governance in Europe: An Ever Closer Ecological Union?* 2nd edn (Oxford: Oxford University Press).

Webb, Carole (1977) "Introduction: Variations on a Theoretical Theme." In *Policy-making in the European Communities*, edited by H. Wallace, W. Wallace, and C. Webb, 1–31 (Chichester: John Wiley).

Weiss, T. G. and L. Gordenker (1996) *NGOs, the UN, and Global Governance* (Boulder, CO: Lynne Rienner).

Weiss, T. G. and R. C. Thakur (2010) *Global Governance and the Un: An Unfinished Journey* (Bloomington, IN: Indiana University Press).

Weller, M. (ed.) (1999) *The Crisis in Kosovo 1989–1999: From the Dissolution of Yugoslavia to Rambouillet and the Outbreak of Hostilities* (Cambridge: Documents and Analysis Publishing Ltd).

Welsh, J. (2004) *At Home In the World: Canada's Global Vision for the 21st Century* (Toronto: HarperCollins).

Wendt, A. (1994) "Collective Identity Formation and the International State," *American Political Science Review*, 88 (2), 384–96.

Wendt, A. (1999) *Social Theory of International Politics*. Cambridge: Cambridge University Press.

Wheeler, N. J. (2001) "Legitimating Humanitarian Intervention: Principles and Procedures," *Melbourne Journal of International Law*, 2 (2), 550–67.

Wheeler, N. J. (2005) "A Common Victory for Humanity? The Responsibility to protect after the 2005 World Summit," Paper presented at a conference on *The UN at Sixty: Celebration or Wake?* at the Faculty of Law, University of Toronto, October 6–7.

Whitman, R. (2006) "Road Map for a Route March? (De-)civilianizing through the EU's Security Strategy." *European Foreign Affairs Review*, 11(1): 1–15.

Whitman, R. (2010) "The EU: Standing Aside from the Changing Global Balance of Power?" *Politics*, 30 (S1), 24–32.

Wijnstekers, W. (2001) *The Evolution of CITES: A Reference to the Convention on International Trade in Endangered Species of Wild Fauna and Flora*, 6th edn (Geneva: CITES Secretariat).

Willetts, P. (1996) "From Stockholm to Rio and Beyond: The Impact of the Environmental Movement on the United Nations Consultative Arrangements for NGOs," *Review of International Studies*, 22 (1), 57–80.

Williams, J. and S. Goose (1998) "The International Campaign to Ban Landmines." In *To Walk Without Fear: The Global Campaign to Ban Landmines*, edited by M. A. Cameron, R. J. Lawson, and B. W. Tomlin (New York: Oxford University Press).

Williams, P. D. and A. J. Bellamy (2005) "The Responsibility to Protect and the Crisis in Darfur," *Security Dialogue*, 36 (1), 27–47.

Williamson, O. E. (1985) *The Economic Institutions of Capitalism: Firms, Markets, Relational Contracting* (New York: Free Press).

Wippman, D. (2004) "The International Criminal Court." In *The Politics of International Law*, edited by C. Reus-Smit (Cambridge: Cambridge University Press).

Wippman, D. (2006) "Exaggerating the ICC." In *Bringing Power to Justice? The Prospects of the International Criminal Court*, edited by J. Harrington, M. Milde and R. Vernon (Canada: McGill-Queen's University Press).

Wood, B. (1988) *The Middle Powers and the General Interest* (Ottawa: North-South Institute).

World Bank (2010) "Indigenous Peoples Are Still Among the Poorest of the Poor," http://web.worldbank.org/WBSITE/EXTERNAL/TOPICS/EXTSDNET/, date accessed February 20, 2012.

Wurzel, R. K. W. (2004) "Germany: From Environmental Leadership to Partial Mismatch." In *Environmental Policy in Europe: The Europeanization of National Environmental Policy*, edited by A. Jordan and D. Liefferink (New York: Routledge).

Young, L. (2007) "Electoral Instability in Canada: Implications for the Canada-U.S. Relationship," *American Review of Canadian Studies*, 37 (1), 7–21.

Young, O. R. (1991) "Political Leadership and Regime Formation: On the Development of Institutions in International Society," *International Organization*, 45 (3), 281–308.

Zuber, S. L. and M. C. Newman (eds) (2012) *Mercury Pollution: A Transdisciplinary Treatment* (Boca Raton, FL: CRC Press).

Index

CPSIA information can be obtained
at www.ICGtesting.com
Printed in the USA
LVOW13*1615130417
530742LV00008B/166/P